HUMAN RIGHTS, HUMAN PLIGHTS IN A GLOBAL VILLAGE

HUMAN RIGHTS, HUMAN PLIGHTS IN A GLOBAL VILLAGE

ROB BUITENWEG

CLARITY PRESS, INC.

© 2007 Rob Buitenweg

ISBN: 0-932863-55-8
  978-0932863-55-3

In-house editor: Diana G. Collier

**Published in co-operation with
Kosmopolis
(Humanist Institute for Global Ethics and World Citizenship)
Utrecht, the Netherlands**

and

**HIVOS
(Humanist Institute for Development Cooperation)
The Hague, the Netherlands
www.hivos.nl**

ALL RIGHTS RESERVED: Except for purposes of review, this book may not be copied, or stored in any information retrieval system, in whole or in part, without permission in writing from the publishers.

Library of Congress Cataloging-in-Publication Data

Buitenweg, Rob, 1938-
  Human rights, human plights in a global village / Rob Buitenweg.
    p. cm.
  Includes bibliographical references.
  ISBN-13: 978-0-932863-55-3
  ISBN-10: 0-932863-55-8
  1. Human rights. I. Title.

K3240.B849 2007
341.4'8—dc22
\2007031191

Clarity Press, Inc.
Ste. 469, 3277 Roswell Rd. NE
Atlanta, GA. 30305
USA
http://www.claritypress.com

TABLE OF CONTENTS

INTRODUCTION
Bibliography 15
Endnotes 16

CHAPTER 1:
A SHORT HISTORY OF HUMAN RIGHTS
1. Rights of a special kind 17
2. Natural law 20
3. The social contract 23
4. The Right of Nature 26
5. Natural rights 28
6. Constitutionalization 30
7. Differentiation 32
8. Internationalization 36
9. The Universal Declaration of Human Rights 38
10. The International Covenants 40
Bibliography 44

CHAPTER 2:
THE STATE OF AFFAIRS OF INTERNATIONAL SOCIAL RIGHTS
1. Fighting poverty 49
2. Social rights 51
3. Economic rights 58
4. Cultural rights 61
5. Differences between CP-rights, and ESC-rights 63
6. Bridging the gap 64
7. Regional ESC-rights 67
8. The treatment of ESC-rights in constitutions 69
9. Neglect of ESC-rights 71
10. Why are ESC-rights neglected? 73
11. The argument against ESC rights as real,
    universal human rights 75
Bibliography 77

CHAPTER 3:
A DIGNIFIED LIFE
1. Introduction 82
2. Human dignity 83
3. Existing as a person 85
4. A life worthy of a human being: Generic rights to
   freedom, participation and well-being 86

5. The primary values underlying human rights 89
6. Freedom or autonomy? 92
7. Freedom, first among equals 95
8. Well-being 98
9. Participation 100
10. Individuality 102
11. Equality 107
12. Neutrality 111
13. Concluding comments 113
Bibliography 113

CHAPTER 4:
POVERTY: IS ANYONE TO BLAME?
1. Introduction 118
2. Skeptics on social justice 119
3. Libertarian skepticism 122
4. Poverty is human-made 130
5. A duty to refrain and a duty to protect 134
6. A duty to help 136
7. Who is the duty-bearer? 138
Bibliography 140

CHAPTER 5:
THE ILLUSIONS OF LIBERTARIANISM
1. Introduction 144
2. The illusion of the legitimacy of the current distribution 146
3. Negative and positive freedom 149
4. Poverty is a violation of negative freedom 152
Bibliography 153

CHAPTER 6:
THE SURPLUS VALUE OF A RIGHTS-BASED APPROACH
1. Introduction 156
2. Interests 160
3. Normative guideline or duty? 161
4. Duties, disabilities, liabilities, no-rights 164
5. Rights as immunities and ESC-rights 166
6. Rights meaning powers 170
7. Rights/liberties 173
8. Claim-rights 178
Bibliography 179

CHAPTER 7:
THE VAGUENESS OF ECONOMIC, SOCIAL AND CULTURAL RIGHTS
1. Introduction 183
2. The dynamics of human rights 186

3. Obligations flowing from ESC-rights 188
4. What do various authors say? 191
5. Some more categories 193
6. The result of the search: a scheme of obligations 196
7. Justiciable duties? 203
Bibliography 205

CHAPTER 8:
A RIGHT IS A PRECIOUS THING
1. Introduction 210
2. Duty + interest = right: a minimalist view 213
3. Intentionality 216
4. Personhood 219
5. Discretion 221
6. Discretion and human rights 222
7. Societal recognition of rights 225
8. Effective societal support: justiciability, enforceability,
   social control 228
9. Elements of a right: the notion of a right versus a concrete right 230
10. Justiciability again 233
11. Aspects and elements 235
12. Genuine, justiciable rights 236
Bibliography 238

CHAPTER 9:
GLOBAL NORMS FOR A GLOBAL VILLAGE
1. Introduction 242
2. Historical relativity vs. historical universality 244
3. Contemporary relativity or universality 246
4. Normative relativity or universality 249
5. Unacceptability and inconsistency of cultural relativism 253
6. Normative universalism and justificatory universalism 255
7. A dialogue 257
Bibliography 260

CHAPTER 10:
IN DEFENSE OF UNIVERSALISM: WORLD CITIZENSHIP
1. Cultural relativism vs. universalism 263
2. The universality of the right-holder 264
3. The universality of the object of the right 267
4. The universality of the addressees of human rights 268
5. Global citizenship 271
Bibliography 274
Endnotes 275

ACKNOWLEDGEMENTS

I want to acknowledge the support of many people who have accompanied me in the writing of this book.

In particular I would like to thank the board of HIVOS, the Dutch Humanist Institute for Development Co-operation, that enabled me to write this book.

I also thank the staff of Kosmopolis Institute and Nick Garlic for their valuable advice. I thank Diana Collier, my editor, who skillfully helped me to prepare this book.

And I would like to thank Marianne, Joost, Kathalijne, Anouk, Maarten, Olivier, Stijn, Marit and Jelle for their love and affection which are a source of inspiration.

INTRODUCTION

Imagine a little village, somewhere in the world. Two villagers meet.
"Good morning".
"Good morning to you. Did you hear about Mrs. Johnson being killed last night?".
"No. What happened?"
"Well, I don't know Mrs. Johnson. But my wife has a sister who has a son who's a football player at a club where John Johnson is a trainer. Well, Johnson's wife went to the post office last night . . ."

The person who relates what happened to Mrs. Johnson does not know her personally, but knows her indirectly, via his wife, her sister, the son, and the trainer. In such a way, everyone knows one another in a village. Well, our world is a village too. In fact, it is said that we are only a few steps away from one another; experiments conducted in the 1960s suggest that every person is connected to every other person in the world through an average of about six personal acquaintances. Which means that if you could find the right string of friends, relatives, colleagues and lovers, you could move in about six steps to anyone else in the world.

I 'know' a little girl, Li Mei Wang, in a little village in China, because I know the president of the International Jurists Organization in New Delhi, who knows a Chinese member of that organization, who has a sister in that little village where Li Mei Wang lives. And, I 'know' John Doe, a farmer in Texas, because I know a member of the American Humanist Association, who knows his car-dealer, who is married to a woman who comes from Texas and was a friend of his. This is the world we live in today. We are at best six steps away from the child in India who is the victim of child labor, from the woman in Nigeria who is beaten to death, from the youngster who is executed in the American gas chamber, from the HIV-infected man in South Africa with no access to the proper medicines, from the street child in Bolivia, from the woman in the refugee camp in Darfur, from the child that was killed by a suicide car bomb in Baghdad, and from the woman in Haiti who is starving from hunger.

We used to live in separate worlds, cut off from one another by rivers, seas, deserts, oceans. But these former barriers no longer hinder us: in both real and virtual terms, we can travel almost anywhere in the world we want to. The world today is open to tourists as well as terrorists, to coffee-traders as well as women-traffickers, to employers as well as employees and the actions and policies of one country can now affect situations in other parts of the world. Greenhouse gas emissions in the USA affect the climate in Siberia. The waste from Britain's Sellafield nuclear power plant affects the fish population in Norway.[1] This is the 'one' world in which we live our lives today, in which we hope and try to lead a human life.

Many, many people hope, and try, to lead a human life. But also many don't succeed. They live in abject socio-economic misery, are exploited, slave in horrible working conditions, do not have enough food, are struck by illness and disease and have no access to education. More than 1 billion people live below the World Bank's $1 per day (extreme) poverty line. About 2.8 billion people, which is 46 % of all the people in the world, live below the $2/day poverty line.

But poverty is not just a lack of material resources; it does not just imply that people have only one or two dollars a day. It affects the very quality of their lives. The Human Development Report 2005 issued by the United Nations Development Program (UNDP) documents the growing inequality and absolute decline in living standards and social conditions in large areas of the world. Kevin Watkins, one of the officers of the United Nations Development Program and chief author of the United Nations Development Report 2005, has pointed out that the latest survey of 177 countries (175 UN members, plus Hong Kong and occupied Palestine *"shows in clear, cold numbers that many countries are not only failing to progress, but are actually slipping backwards, and they will continue on that downhill path unless the international community steps in to help with more resources and new policies."*[2]

The report refers to the devastating tsunami of 2004 that killed some 300,000 people to underscore the human cost of poverty. *"The tsunami was a highly visible, unpredictable and largely unpreventable tragedy. Other tragedies are less visible, monotonously predictable and readily preventable. Every hour more than 1,200 children die away from the glare of media attention. This is equivalent to three tsunamis a month, every month, hitting the world's most vulnerable citizens—its children. The causes of death will vary, but the overwhelming majority can be traced to a single pathology: poverty."*[3]

How is it possible that this occurs to people who are only 'six steps' away from us? How can human misery continue despite the economic, technological and moral progress mankind has made?[4]) In particular, how can this misery continue despite the economic, social and cultural human rights that are recognized by many legal, international and national, documents? These rights, like the right to adequate housing, to food, to health(care) and to social security are intended to alleviate human misery and, in so doing, contribute to a dignified life. Knowing that these rights exist might lead one to think: is not such widespread, socio-economic human misery a violation of people's human rights, more especially of their economic, social and cultural rights?

An oft-quoted, longstanding answer contends that socio-economic misery cannot be seen as a violation of rights. Rather, it should be seen, so it is said, as the result of spontaneous socio-economic developments, as the lot that falls upon some people, just as a tsunami overwhelms hundreds of thousands of innocent victims. Socio-economic misery, so it is said, is like illness, death, bad luck and other existential occurrences: regrettable but nothing that anybody can be blamed for. Socio-economic misery cannot be called a violation of rights because the idea of violation presupposes that human actors are involved, that human beings have caused it. You cannot say that someone's right to life has been violated when that person has been fatally struck by lightning, nor can you speak of a violation of the right to housing when a tsunami has swept away thousands of houses. Equally, so the traditional view argues, you cannot speak of a violation of human rights when people have fallen victim to socio-economic misery. You cannot speak of a violation inflicted upon the poor and the weak by their fellow nationals, and you certainly cannot speak of a violation by other human beings. You cannot say that the well-off in India—or even myself, living in the Netherlands—have violated the human rights of the poor in that country. So it is often thought.

Of course, traditionalists agree, people who have met with socio-economic misery should be helped, as much as possible. It is virtuous and praiseworthy to help the poor and the weak. They should be helped in the first place by their fellow nationals. Besides, people in other countries should do their utmost to help the weak and poor. But, helping the poor and the weak is not strictly a matter of justice. It is not a question of a duty that can or should be enforced. And, if this help does not result in an alleviation of poverty, it is certainly to be regretted. Maybe it can even be said that the rich have omitted to do enough, but it cannot be said that they have committed a crime.

Underlying such ideas is a particular view of economic, social and cultural rights, often referred to as esocul-rights or ESC-rights. These rights are seen as fundamentally different from the 'real' human rights, i.e. the civil and political rights (CP-rights), such as the right to freedom of belief, the right to freedom of expression, the right to a fair trial or the right to be free from torture. The latter are seen as genuine, universal, human rights; the former however, the economic, social and cultural rights, are not thought to qualify for the status of human rights.

This view assumes a dichotomy between civil and political rights on the one hand and economic, social and cultural rights on the other. And such a dichotomy still exists today despite many formal expressions of devotion to economic, social and cultural rights. Almost all human rights documents of United Nations organizations mention the interdependency, the interrelatedness and indivisibility of the CP-rights and the ESC-rights. In practice, however, much more attention is paid to civil and political rights than to the economic, social and cultural rights. Even non-governmental organizations (NGOs) rank CP-rights higher than ESC-rights: Amnesty International, for instance, has always been focused on civil and political rights. Yet recently, it has acknowledged that it should also be concerned with ESC-rights. *"To that end, AI has initiated a set of pilot projects in countries where AI's existing work on civil and political rights can be strengthened by integrating work on economic, social, and cultural rights."*[5] While this change should, of course, be applauded, it should be noted that it also reveals that concern for ESC-rights is subordinate and complementary to CP-rights.

Even in the circles of the United Nations concerned with fighting poverty, very little has been said about the connection between development and ESC-rights. The Human Development Report 2000 broke the silence that prevailed about this connection by stating that the basic idea of human development has much in common with the concerns expressed by declarations of human rights. It called for a human rights-based approach to human development. In its foreword it says that the report *"... is intended primarily to help promote practical action that puts a human rights–based approach to human development and poverty eradication firmly on the global agenda"*[6]. It went on to acknowledge that human rights literature has often focused primarily, or exclusively, on CP-rights. And while it admits that an adequate conception of human development cannot ignore the importance of CP-rights, it also emphasizes the importance of ESC-rights. Later reports have been less explicit about the relationship between human development and human rights, in particular ESC-rights. However, the reports appear to be aware of that relationship, which for instance is shown by the Human Development Report 2005. It starts its considerations by referring to the UN Charter that 60 years ago pledged to free future generations from the scourge of war, to protect fundamental human rights and to promote social progress and better standards of life in larger freedom. The HDR 2005 continues by saying that the world's governments renewed that pledge at the start of the new millennium by adopting the Millennium Declaration in 2000, which contains the Millennium Development Goals (MDGs) that can be seen as a set of time-bound and quantified targets for reducing extreme poverty and extending universal rights by 2015.[7]

The relationship between human development and human life is undeniable. Human life is not like the existence of a rock that, though it is susceptible to all the influences of the weather, just lies where it is and remains practically unchanged for centuries. Human beings grow. But they do not just want to accept the fact of their growth; they do not want to sit and

Introduction

passively watch their lives passing by. They want to play an active role. They want to develop their capabilities, to enhance the range of what they can do, and not in any random fashion: they have specific yearnings, aspirations and ideals. That is what makes them human. They want to develop the capabilities that will enable them to realize those yearnings, aspirations and ideals, and in so doing, truly flourish as human beings.

The UN Development Reports describe human development as *"enhancing human capabilities"* and as *"building human capabilities—the range of things that people can do, and what they can be"*[8]. It seems to be an adequate description of human development. But human capabilities have an internal and an external aspect. The former concerns *capacities*: the personal qualities, talents and skills that are inborn or that people have acquired during their lives. The latter, the external aspect, refers to *possibilities*, circumstances that do not prevent the development of personal qualities and capacities.

Capabilities consist of capacities and possibilities. Developing capabilities implies developing capacities and possibilities. You may try to develop your capacities, but when others or circumstances block your efforts, it will be difficult to reach an adequate level of development. You may try to receive an adequate education, but if others prevent you from gaining access to that education, your efforts will run aground. You may take care of your health, but if—when you become ill—you are prevented from getting necessary medicines by governmental policies, or by a lack of proper health-care arrangements, your capability for leading a healthy life will be undermined.

This is where human rights come in. Human rights claim to protect and foster the external aspects of basic capabilities, and to create an environment that makes a dignified human life possible. ESC-rights want to emphasize that human beings have a right to socio-economic goods that are necessary if they are to lead a dignified life. They are an important and powerful tool for poverty eradication.[9]

Yet ESC-rights cannot fulfill their job adequately because they are not taken seriously by the prevailing dichotomist view mentioned above. It is this view that contributes to the continuation of socio-economic misery, and in the following chapters I hope to expose the illusions behind it and to develop a coherent view on ESC-rights that will, hopefully, be of help in fighting socio-economic misery. And by doing that, I also hope to clarify the added benefits of a human rights-based approach to development.

Chapters 1 and 2 are introductory chapters offering a thin sketch of human rights, and in particular economic, social and cultural rights. Chapter 1 describes the development of human rights. Given that ESC-rights are a species of the genus human rights, I thought it appropriate to take a brief look at the history of human rights. I will distinguish five phases in the their development, which I will call the phases of natural law, natural rights, constitutionalization, differentiation, and internationalization.

Chapter 2 offers an overall picture of international ESC-rights, in particular as far as they are embedded in the Universal Declaration of Human Rights and in the International Covenant on Economic, Social and Cultural Rights. (I will throw a brief glance at the European Social Charter). References to Human Development Reports will show that these rights are far from being fulfilled. The chapter will reveal that economic, social and cultural rights still are neglected and treated as second-hand rights when compared to civil and political rights.

Chapters 3, 4 and 5 offer ethical considerations on ESC-rights. Chapter 3 raises the question of the extent to which socio-economic rights contribute to a dignified life and can accordingly be regarded as *human* rights. Chapters 4 and 5 form the heart of my refutation of the view that socio-economic misery is regrettable but not a question of justice and rights. Many people will agree with Nelson Mandela's statement that *"Massive poverty and obscene inequality are such terrible scourges of our times—times in which the world boasts breathtaking advances in science, technology, industry and wealth accumulation—that they have to rank alongside slavery and apartheid as social evils."*[10] Many will admit that poverty and socio-economic misery is regrettable and deplorable, but, so is asked in chapter 4, "Is poverty a question of injustice?" Is someone to blame for it and is requiring us to relieve it in other people a question of justice?

Chapter 5 continues the argument by focusing on objections to ESC-rights. Many people, for instance strict libertarians, stress freedom-rights as paramount and are averse to a politics of social justice, to a politics of implementing ESC-rights.[11] Such an implementation, so it is argued, boils down to a violation of freedom, and in particular to an infringement of the right of the well-off to property. Libertarians attach much value to freedom and advocate non-intervention by states and individuals. Libertarians expect the free-market to do the job of alleviating poverty. The spirit of this libertarianism is also noticeable in the policies of the World Bank, the International Monetary Fund and the World Trade Organization. These proponents of the free-market ideology hold the view that a global free market will enhance overall welfare and that its beneficial effects will, eventually, serve as a remedy against the socio-economic misery. But, if libertarianism is interpreted as strict libertarianism, not accepting a politics of social justice at all, it does not take its own presumptions seriously. In this chapter, I intend to demonstrate that such a strict libertarianism is based on misleading illusions.[12]

Chapters 6, 7 and 8 offer conceptual considerations on ESC-rights. Chapter 6 pays attention to the correlative of a right and asks whether ESC-rights, like CP-rights, imply real and genuine obligations for governments and individuals. Chapter 7, starting from an affirmative answer to this question, attempts to formulate what kind of duties flow from ESC-rights and, correspondingly, what the holders of such rights can expect individuals and

Introduction

governments to do. In general these rights are supposed to be vague and ambiguous, which means that it is difficult to assert what can be expected of duty-holders. I try to deal with this supposed vagueness of ESC-rights and this chapter tries to examine whether these rights really are vague. I finish this chapter by raising the question whether ESC-rights are justiciable i.e. whether independent bodies are capable and allowed to issue judgments about the realization of these rights. Chapter 8 continues with the search for the surplus value of a rights-based approach by looking for the particular properties of rights. What is special and particular to rights? What does it mean to say that someone has a right, for example, to housing, to food, to health care, to education?

Chapters 9 and 10 deal with the question of the universality of ESC-rights. The universality of human rights in general is questioned by cultural relativists and it is this debate that is the subject of chapter 9. The universality of human rights is heavily under fire in this era of so-called clashes of civilizations. The debate covers three questions: Do all subscribe to human rights? Can we expect others to subscribe to human rights? Can we justify such an expectation? I will pay attention to these questions in chapter 9. Chapter 10 deals with the attacks on the universality of economic, social and cultural rights in particular. A famous critic of ESC-rights, who regards civil and political rights as universal but who does not accept the universality of ESC-rights, poses the following question: can we expect the government of India to provide all its inhabitants with the goods that are required for a dignified life? His answer is: we cannot, which means, according to the critic, that economic, social and cultural rights are not universal. Such a criticism brings me, in response, to three other questions with regard to the issue of universality that I will try to answer in chapter 10: Does everyone have economic, social and cultural rights? Is everyone entitled to the same quantity or quality of the goods mentioned in the economic, social and cultural rights (for instance, food or housing)? Is everyone the addressee of economic, social and cultural rights?

Or, to put it differently, what do we have to do with one another's misery?

BIBLIOGRAPHY

Thomas Pogge, *World Poverty and Human Rights* (Cambridge: Polity Press, 2003)
Peter Singer, *One World* (New Have & London: Yale University Press, 2002)
Hans Otto Sano, "Development and Human Rights: The Necessary, but Partial Integration of Human Rights and Development", in: *Human Rights Quarterly 22* (The Johns Hopkins University Press, 2000)
Human Development Report 2000, United Nations Development Programme
Human Development Report 2005, United Nations Development Programme

ENDNOTES

1. Singer, 2002, p.20
2. http://hdr.undp.org/docs/news/hdr2005/BBC_Sept_7_2005.pdf
3. Human Development Report 2005, p.1
4. Thomas Pogge, 2003, p.3
5. (http://www.amnestyusa.org/activist_toolkit/amnestyinaction/esc_rights.html).
6. Human Development Report 2000, p.IV
7. Human Development Report 2005, p.17
8. Ibidem, p.2, Human Development Report 2005,p.18
9. Human Development Report 2000, p.77
10. http://weekly.ahram.org.eg/2005/760/in2.htm, retrieved 02-02-2006
11. Nigel Dower, 2003, p.39
12. I am not referring to "strict liberalism" as mentioned by Anthony de Jasay. This rightly opposes "Rightsism". From the idea that people have "rights" to do certain specific things and that certain other things ought not to be done to them, rightsism takes "rights" to be the exceptions to a tacitly understood general rule that everything else is forbidden. (http://www.dejasay.org/bib_journals_detail.asp?id=33, retrieved 17 Jan. 2007)

CHAPTER 1

A SHORT HISTORY OF HUMAN RIGHTS

FIVE PHASES

> *"The test of our progress is not whether we add more to the abundance of those who have much; it is whether we provide enough for those who have too little."*
>
> **President Franklin D. Roosevelt**
> **second inaugural address, 1937**

1. Rights of a special kind

What can be meant by a rights based-approach to development? According to the United Nations High Commissioner on Human Rights, "*A rights-based approach to development is a conceptual framework for the process of human development that is normatively based on international human rights standards and operationally directed to promoting and protecting human rights. Essentially, a rights-based approach integrates the norms, standards and principles of the international human rights system into the plans, policies and processes of development.*"[1] This probably will mean that the protection and promotion of CP-rights will be part of development policies. And, as ESC-rights form an integral part of the international human rights system, it will also mean that ESC-rights should be involved in development policies.

Do the 1 billion people who live below the World Bank's $1/day (extreme) poverty line have a human right to food? Do they have a human right to health care, to education, to adequate housing? And, if they have, what do we mean or imply by saying that they have these as human *rights* instead of saying that they *want* the goods involved or that it is in their *interest* to have these goods? What is so specific about human rights? To find answers to these questions I will first, in this chapter, take a brief look at the history of human rights and of the emergence of ESC-rights.

Currently, we are very familiar with the idea of human rights. Almost every day the subject appears in papers or other media. But human rights have not always existed in the way they do nowadays. They were born long ago and have grown up during many centuries.

Human rights are rights, but rights of a special kind. They are not ordinary legal rights, rights that are based on the law of a country and that are accorded to people by its national law. Human rights are considered to be of a higher order, superior to ordinary rights. But to what extent are human rights superior?

It is often said that human rights are moral rights that people possess by virtue of their humanity, which are held equally by all people and which are superior to ordinary law.[2] The idea of moral rights requires explanation. Many automatically associate rights with law. For them rights have a juridical sound. It must be stressed, however, that the term 'right' is not reserved for the juridical domain: the notion of a right is used also in the field of morality or ethics. When the term 'moral right' is used it means that the source of a right need not be the law of a country, or international law. People can and do have rights, whether or not those rights are accorded to them by national or international law.

For example, let us assume that B has promised to A to do a job: to tidy up A's garden. I think that most people will accept that B is morally obliged to tidy up A's garden and that A has a right to have his garden tidied up by B. The source of the right is the promise that B has made. Of course, the right may be backed by the national law if, for instance, the law says that promises should be kept. The point here is whether a right based on a promise only exists when backed by law, or whether it also exists even if the law does not support it. Defenders of moral rights will argue that their existence is independent of legal recognition.

In the previous example, the moral right is special, to that extent that it flows from a special relationship, the relationship between a promisor and a promisee. But moral rights can also be general, rights that people are supposed to possess not on the basis of a special relationship or anyone's voluntary acts (e.g. a promise) but on the basis of their humanity. Human rights are such general, moral rights—although sometimes the term 'natural rights' is also used, suggesting that people have rights by nature.[3] Human rights *"are contrasted to legal or conventional rights, which exists in virtue of the laws and conventions of a given society: people have such rights as members of a legal community or whatever, not as human beings"*.[4] "Human Rights are not legal fictions conferred by governments but are inherent features of our nature as human beings," argues Robert Grant in his article, "The Social Contract and Human Rights," in the January-February issue of *The Humanist*. Nowadays human rights are incorporated in international documents, in the Universal Declaration of Human Rights and in various other declarations and conventions. In that sense, human rights have acquired a legal or quasi-legal status. But the point here is also: do these rights exist because—and from the time that—they were incorporated in these documents, or did they already exist prior to the adoption of the Universal Declaration of Human Rights and the subsequent documents? The drafters of the UDHR obviously were of the latter view. They did not think they were framing new rights; they believed that they were just formulating ones that already existed.

It should be noted, however, that the idea of moral, natural rights is not undisputed. Jeremy Bentham, for instance, regarded talk of natural rights as rhetorical nonsense.[5] He argued that speaking of rights only has sense within a legal framework. Rights are derived from legal rules and cannot exist independently of these rules, or of the government and state that go with these rules. Edmund Burke expressed similar views when he said that human rights do not exist. Only the rights of an Englishman or a Frenchman exist. Our contemporary, Adisdair MacIntyre, sees the belief in human rights as a belief in 'unicorns' or 'witches'.[6]

Yet despite such opposition to the idea of moral human rights, it is an idea that has gained widespread recognition and approval. According to Jack Donnelly, people appeal to human rights in particular when legal rights are not available. And by appealing to such moral rights, a desire is being expressed for such rights to be transformed into legal rights. People who are in favor of particular moral rights want them to be supported and strengthened by legal recognition. They believe that moral human rights constitute standards for the legal arrangements of society.[7]

The appeal to moral human rights during the last centuries has led to their 'juridification'. They are now included in *national* documents, in particular in constitutions, which in turn form the basis of ordinary legislation. When included in constitutions, such rights generally are no longer referred to as 'human' rights but as 'constitutional' rights.

As said above, moral human rights are also incorporated in *international* documents, many of which have appeared in the form of declarations and treaties since the end of the Second World War. It is worth noting here that there is a distinction to be drawn between declarations and treaties. Declarations do not have legally binding force. (This also holds for the Universal Declaration of Human Rights, a declaration that has, however, gained such authority and holds such moral force that it has become almost legally binding, even though the procedure by which it came into existence deviated from the procedure required for legally binding international documents.) Treaties, on the other hand, are formally binding for those parties that have signed and ratified them. Despite this distinction, today the term 'human rights' is generally used for the rights granted by both these international declarations and treaties and this in turn has given new meaning to the idea of a higher order of rights.[8] It does not—or not mainly—refer to moral rights superior to ordinary legislation, but to rights that extend national borders, to rights that are agreed upon by representatives of all countries and which have global validity.

In this chapter, I would like to explore more in detail the development of human rights. And in so doing, I will distinguish five phases in that development.

2. Natural law

Although we are familiar with human rights today, it has taken a long time for the concept to arrive at its current position. It could be said to have begun with the recognition of natural law by the Greeks. They believed that such a law existed, just as the law of gravitation existed, and that it offered guidelines for people to live in accordance with human nature. It was an important moment in human history, observed Otfried Höffe and Paul Cliteur, when the idea arose that a distinction could be drawn between the law of a secular power and a higher law, and that natural law could be taken to be superior to the law of the secular legislator.[9] It was an idea that was then transmitted to the Romans—Cicero says, *"There is a true law, right reason, in accordance with nature; it is unalterable and eternal"*[10]

Later, during the Middle Ages, Western Europe adopted the idea of a higher law, but also supplied it with a religious dimension.[11] Higher law became not just natural law, but the law of God with which the law of the secular legislator had to comply. Then, during the Renaissance, the religious dimension in some writers—Thomas Hobbes, for instance—disappeared, ushering in a period of secular natural law: the idea of a higher law was maintained, but was now detached from God.

The recognition of natural law need not imply the recognition of natural rights, rights that are seen as inherent in the nature of people. Using the term natural rights may give the impression that universal rights have existed since the existence of humankind. We should be aware that the idea of universal rights, even the idea of rights in general, has not always existed and that it is a rather modern notion. According to Peter Jones, worlds without rights did and do exist. *"Rights are so common in our world that we might suppose that they are woven into the very fabric of human existence. But there have been worlds without rights. The conventional wisdom is that neither the ancient Greeks nor the ancient Romans possessed the concept of a right. They did, of course, possess ideas of right conduct, but it seems that our notion of a right did not figure in their moral thinking or in their systems of law."*[12] He further says that the idea of rights was introduced in Europe somewhere between the twelfth and fourteenth century. If we leave undecided the question of whether or not the Greeks and Romans possessed the concept of a right, Jones' remarks make us see that law need not necessarily be connected with rights. For someone like me, living in the West, in the 21st century, and familiar with rights, this sounds odd, but it is good to be aware that the concept of a right is essentially a modern one. And it may be that cultures still exist where rights have played a less important role than they play in most modern Western cultures, even though such cultures cannot be said to lack law and morality. Law and morality, after all, can contain guidelines for people's behavior without appealing to the idea of rights. Such guidelines can be expressed in rules, duties and obligations without needing to be accompanied by individual rights.

For instance, the law or morality of a culture might have rules prohibiting theft. And in such a culture, people might possibly know that they have a duty not to steal even though the idea that other people have a *right* not to be robbed might simply not cross their minds. To take another example, the law and morality of a community might imply rules that call for helping people in need and the members of such a community might know that they have a duty to do so, without once speaking in terms of the right of people to be helped.

Most of us are familiar with the Ten Commandments. It is a list of religious and moral imperatives, according to the bible written by God and given to Moses in the form of two stone tablets. Although interpretations of the Ten Commandments vary, it is generally accepted that the Ten Commandments do not speak in terms of rights. They are what they are called: commandments. "Thou shall....", or "Thou shall not…" You may call them duties but you cannot call them rights.

We who are used to the idea of rights might be inclined to say that when rules and duties exist, rights also exist; but if we do so then we are interpreting the moral or legal code of a different culture in our terms. We should also realize that even the laws of modern, Western cultures still often possess rules, obligations and duties that could hardly be transferable into rights. We have traffic rules, and obligations flowing from these rules, but where are the rights? What is the right corresponding to rules limiting the speed we can drive at? When someone driving faster than the speed limit is arrested by a police officer, does the officer say that the driver is violating a right (leaving aside entirely the question of whose right that might be), or that he is breaking a rule?

I will not deal here with the question of when the idea of rights took a place in the law or morality in other parts of the world. Although it is a question that is certainly very important, I will restrict myself to the West. This will result in views that are somewhat one-sided, but such on-sidedness does not mean that the views themselves are wrong. It only means that they should be complemented by scholarly investigations in other parts of the world. And to a certain extent I feel justified in restricting myself to the West, in that developments in the West have been of significant importance for the history of international human rights, as will be shown later.

In the West, the idea of rights emerged during the Renaissance. The previously mentioned recognition of a higher *law* with which ordinary law has to comply can be seen as the first phase in the development of human rights. The emergence of the notion of individual *rights* during the Renaissance can be seen as the second phase. Guidelines for human behavior were no longer worded in terms of duties and obligations, or in terms of obedience to rules of law, but in terms of the rights of individuals. This not only led to rights becoming important in the sphere of the national laws of individual countries, but also to their becoming crucial within the sphere of morality.

However, while people were thought to have individual natural rights, such rights were still often considered to be linked to natural law, which in turn was equated, according to some, with the law of God. The law of God, of Reason or of Nature was still the source of the natural, individual rights, as was argued by John Locke.[13] Increasingly, though, natural law lost its religious dimension, but in the views of many this (now secular) natural law still remained the source of natural rights. Later, the idea of natural law began to lose its attractiveness, and the notion of natural rights and that of natural law loosened. It then became common to speak of 'human' rights instead of 'natural' rights.

Three developments during the Renaissance heavily influenced human rights. The first concerned the dominant position of Roman Catholicism. The self-evident truth of Roman Catholic views began to waver as other religious convictions fought for the possession of truth. This heralded the plurality of beliefs in modern Western Europe and, as a consequence, the conviction arose that ideas about the arrangement of society could no longer be derived from one particular religion. The idea that Roman Catholicism could rule politics was no longer undisputed, but rather was increasingly replaced by the view that society should no longer be based on one particular belief or conception of the good life, but on ideas that have to be acceptable to people of varying beliefs. (I follow the view of the Human Rights Committee, the committee that monitors the implementation of the International Covenant on Civil and Political Rights, that says that the term belief is to be broadly construed. "*Article 18 protects theistic, non-theistic and atheistic beliefs, as well as the right not to profess any religion or belief..... Article 18 is not limited in its application to traditional religions or to religions and beliefs with institutional characteristics or practices analogous to those of traditional religions...*", General Comment nr.22).

The second significant development was a shift in the relationship between the community and the individual. In the Middle Ages, people were regarded as rooted in their community and identified in terms of the role they played within it. In the Renaissance, on the other hand, people were increasingly seen as bearing an identity as individuals, more or less irrespective of their role in the community, and as themselves setting their course in life.[14]

The third development was the emergence of the idea of human equality. Traces of a recognition of human equality can also be found in the Middle Ages and earlier, for example in the Stoa of the ancient Graeco-Roman world. For the Stoics all human beings were members of the community of mankind, which was more fundamental than the community of a city or country and all human beings were bound by a universal ethic.[15] Also Christianity knew the doctrine of fundamental human equality by regarding all human beings as equal creatures of God. But, human equality then was less a legal reality than a philosophical or religious idea.[16] In the Renaissance, the idea of human equality entered the political domain and pushed aside the obstinate idea that some people are by nature superior to others. Human equality became a yardstick of political measures and arrangements: these measures and arrangements would take into consideration and respect human equality.

The first development—the disappearance of the old self-evident truths of the Roman Catholic Church—generated the search for new, and generally acceptable, views of life, man and society, often stimulated by local rulers seeking an ideology that facilitates their acquisition of power. The second development led to these views taking the individual as their starting point. And the third development resulted in the assumption that everyone should play a role in, and be the beneficiary of, politics. The model then appropriate for designing new conceptions of the social order was the model of the social contract. As Charles Leben points out, referring to N. Bobbio, society from the eighteenth century onwards was no longer interpreted in organic terms, but in contractual terms. It was no longer a natural entity independent of the ideas and desires of its members, but an artificial entity constructed by, and designed for, the well-being of its members. This was a Copernican revolution in political thinking.[17]

3. The social contract

Characteristic of social contract theories is that society, especially its political structure, is explained or justified by starting from an initial situation in which no society exists and individuals live without political authority or political bonds. A social contract theory can have a historical signature ("In the long ago past, people lived as solitary beings.") or it can be of a more hypothetical nature ("Imagine that we had neither a political society, nor a political authority"). The question then becomes how these individuals would have acted and behaved towards one another in this pre-societal or pre-political situation. The answer is that this situation appears to be so problematic—dangerous, chaotic, threatening, inconvenient—that people, out of purely self-serving motives, will conclude a treaty by which a state is established and the problems of the initial situation are relieved.[18]

It must be admitted that such an approach seems attractive: a complex phenomenon is reduced to its elementary parts. Society is explained or justified by its smallest element, the individual.[19] It also fits in perfectly with common sense. Suppose that someone complains about being fined for speeding and grumbles about the police. The reply could be, "Yes, but suppose we didn't have police. What would that be like?" There the existence of the police is explained or justified by first supposing that they do not exist, and by then concluding that a situation without police is undesirable.

Despite its attractiveness the social contract theory also presents some flaws. Although it takes as its starting-point the pre-social individual, such an individual did and does not exist and is, actually, unimaginable.[20] Can we imagine how an individual who has not had a mother, who has not grown up among others, who has not experienced feelings of love, anger, hatred, compassion, mercy towards others, will be, act or behave? The theory even implicitly recognizes the "socialness" of individuals, because its assumes that individuals will conclude a treaty and that they will abide by it. But, why should self-serving individuals who want to have nothing to do with others abide by a treaty when it is in their best interests *not* to do so? In assuming that individuals are both self-serving and that they will perform the contract, the theory reveals its inconsistency.[21]

Many critics of the social contract theories point out that it is unlikely that people ever concluded such an agreement. But defenders of the theory might well respond that the contract is not to be seen as a real event that occurred in the past but rather as a symbolic treaty concluded time and again. By participating in society, people consent to the course of events that unfold within it and can, to that extent, be said to have concluded a treaty. By adhering to traffic rules, by posting mail, by buying food, or by going to the office, people express their agreement with the organizational structure of society: in that sense it can be said that they continually conclude and confirm a treaty.[22] To which critics of the theory would reply that it is too big a step to assume that by participating in particular social activities, people give their consent to the organization of society in general. The buying of stamps does not imply agreement with a society's constitution.

The defender of the contract theory could then respond that the idea of a contract is not to explain society by describing what actually happened in the past—or what is happening now—but to use a hypothetical contract to justify a particular arrangement of society, as has been shown in the aforementioned conversation concerning the need for police.

Of course, it must be admitted that a hypothetical contract is not a real contract and that it does not generate obligations in the way that a real contract does, as is also stated by Ronald Dworkin.[23] Why should I be bound by a contract that I might conclude in a hypothetical situation? However, this objection need not undo the usability of the idea of a hypothetical contract. The contract could be used as one element in a more comprehensive argument on the question of how to arrange a just society. One could for instance argue as follows. "We have to find out what is just. Our starting-point is that people, despite their numerous differences, are equal in a moral sense. They have a duty to respect one another and to treat others as they themselves want to be treated. To find out what arrangement is just, let us then rule out the possibility of people proposing an arrangement that mainly benefits themselves, and instead pretend that we do not know in what particular circumstances we live, that we do not know our place in society, our class position or social status, that we do not know whether we are well-off or less privileged, whether we live in the developed or the developing world, whether we are male or female, whether we are intelligent or less intelligent—and let us suppose that we then have to agree on principles to arrange and regulate society. What would we consider just if no one is able to design principles to favor his or her particular condition?[24] The hypothetical contract then becomes a method to implement our principle that people are equal and have a duty to treat one another as equals. (This is how the idea of a contract is used by the contemporary social contract theorist John Rawls. I will speak about Rawls' ideas later, but let us first go back to the seventeenth century, in search of the emergence of the idea of human rights and hope that knowing more about that will help us to understand ESC-rights and their contribution to human development.)

The seventeenth century philosophers Thomas Hobbes and John Locke are social contract theorists who have much influenced the development of human rights. Locke is often called the 'father of human rights' owing to the fact that his theory of natural rights is closely related to what are currently called human rights.[25]

Both philosophers undertook to draw up a theory of political order. In conformity with the spirit of the times, they took as their starting points the individual human being, the idea of human equality and the plurality of the beliefs, which entails that their theory had to be acceptable to people with varied and different conceptions of a 'good life'. Despite the similarities, their theories also show some important differences, differences that justify calling Locke the father of human rights and withholding the title from Hobbes.

Hobbes and Locke were revolutionary in that they wanted to explain or justify political order with an appeal to the agreement of all individual citizens.[26] The idea that political authority has to be based on the agreement of citizens is not in itself revolutionary. It also can be found in ancient times, for instance in the writings of Aristotle, although many would be reluctant to connect Aristotle's views with such an idea. For Aristotle believed in the subordination of some individuals to others. In his view, slaves were subordinate to their masters and women were subordinate to men. Slaves and women lacked the capacity to reason effectively and had, therefore, to be guided by the reason of (free) men. This would benefit all. Clearly, Aristotle apparently did not believe in equality for all. Yet with regard to free men he did recognize equality. He felt that for a society to be just, it had to be founded on the agreement of free men and that authority had to be based on the consent of the subjects of that authority.[27]

This idea lived on during the Middle Ages, although it was then taken as a complementary element in justifying political authority since, in the main, authority was or had to be legitimized by God. Such an idea of authority by consent manifested itself, for example, in England's Magna Charta in 1215, the document which often is seen as the harbinger of later human rights documents. The Magna Charta was an agreement between the English King John and his baronets and intended to end a conflict between the two. King John had, according to the baronets, violated old laws and customs. To avoid misunderstandings in the future, these laws and customs needed to be set down in a legally binding document. The Magna Charta formally defined the relationship between the king and nobility and contained, among others, rules about the levying of taxes, corruption, free trade, property, inheritance, and fair trial. It gave birth to the idea of political authority by agreement of the subjects of that authority—and also to the idea of the conditionality of such authority—an authority that could be withdrawn if the sovereign abused his power. Although the only subjects who were entitled to have a say in such matters were the nobility, the Magna Charta can be seen as a harbinger of later human rights documents, even if it can not itself be regarded as such a document, because it is not a catalogue of individual rights to which everyone is entitled.

The idea of authority by agreement was extended to all subjects in the theories of Hobbes and Locke. Individual human equality means that we are born free and equal and that no one is by nature subject to the power of others.[28] This was the revolutionary element of their theories, a departure from the classical and mediaeval view that some people are by nature superior to others and therefore entitled to power and authority.

4. The Right of Nature

Thomas Hobbes (1588 - 1679) offers a social contract theory, trying to give an explanation and/or justification of political authority based on individuality, equality and plurality of beliefs. He starts from an initial situation in which no political authority exists and where people are individual, solitary human beings without societal bonds. He calls this pre-societal situation the 'natural condition', an indication that he is not writing about a historical situation that has occurred, but about the human condition in general and the properties and characteristics of human nature. What can be said about the 'natural condition' of people? What would human beings be like if not restrained by society? Hobbes' answer is that in such a condition, people are individuals characterized by an instinct for self-preservation and a restless lust for power. Towards others they display competitiveness, distrust and pride, which are the main reasons for conflicts between them. Hobbes emphasizes self-preservation as the strongest of human strivings. This does not mean that he does not have an eye for other strivings; rather, that self-preservation is basic. To quote Larry Arnhart, *"self-preservation is not so much the end as it is the necessary means to all of men's ends."* [29]

In the 'natural condition', the individual has a natural right, the 'Right of Nature'. This holds that everyone has the freedom *"to use his own power, as he will himself, for the preservation of his own Nature..."* [30] This marks a break with traditional political thinking. Hobbes recognized individual rights, or to put it more correctly, *one* particular individual right, the 'right of nature'. This is a right people have by virtue of their being human and it could be said that it is therefore a human right. But I doubt whether it really merits the title of a human right, a point I will return to when comparing Hobbes' view with that of Locke.

Hobbes' individuals in their natural condition are fundamentally equal as regards their human capacities. Of course, some people are stronger than others, just as some are more clever or more intelligent or bigger. But no one is so clever, intelligent, talented, strong or big that he can claim to be entitled to natural authority over the others. The weakest or most simple person is capable of killing the smartest or strongest person, even if only by trick, device or design. And the strongest is always vulnerable when asleep. This fundamental equality means that, in principle, people are relatively equal when it comes to acquiring valued goods. They do not have to abandon their hope to acquire these goods in advance. They can try to find ways to compete with others. Of course, such human equality turns out to have bad consequences when combined with another important human characteristic: the imitation of desires. By this I mean that people want to have what others *have* but, more importantly, they also want to have what others *want*. Certain desires are generated by perceiving other people desiring certain goods: seeing that others desire something makes that thing desirable. For example, my desire to have a new car is prompted by my neighbor having a new car but, more importantly, also by realizing that having a new car is something obviously desired by others and therefore desirable. Other people form a model of people's desires and the combination of human equality and the imitation of desires leads to a war of all against all. [31]

But, happily human beings have other traits. They also have a fear of death, a longing for pleasure, and they are gifted with reason. These traits induce them to search for peace because they realize that, as long as political authority is absent, they will permanently face the possibility of war. Eventually they will be prepared to restrain themselves and to conclude a treaty, by which they will establish political authority and by which they will also subject themselves to an authoritative sovereign. They will do so, according to Hobbes, on the basis of the laws of nature. It is a law of nature that people will search for peace as long as they hope to acquire peace; should, however, peace be unattainable, people will abandon their hope and resort to war. But it is also a law of nature that war should be avoided at all costs and that people will therefore be prepared to do whatever it takes to achieve peace.[32]

This is how Hobbes explains and justifies political authority. Hobbes' ideal sovereign is necessarily strong and powerful in order to prevent individuals from waging war against one another, but this may have some unwelcome side-effects. While Hobbes' solution restrains violence between subjects and prevents people from treating one another violently by the establishment of a powerful sovereign, it raises the question of how to restrain the powerful sovereign who might use violence against his subjects. This question was very much a point of concern for Locke.[33]

5. Natural rights

Locke (1632 - 1704), like Hobbes, took as his starting-points human individuality, human equality and the plurality of beliefs. Locke too wanted to draft a theory that was acceptable to people with various beliefs or conceptions of the good. And Locke, too, started from an initial situation in which no political authority existed. He calls this situation the 'state of nature'. Sometimes his wording and formulations give the impression that this state of nature really existed in the distant past. He gives examples of native peoples who gathered in the past to make arrangements about their society, even though he realizes that it can be objected that in history no such examples can be found. He has an answer to that objection, though. According to Locke, all these events took place before history was written down, and they have slipped out of our memory, in the way that children forget all about their birth. Yet despite these wordings and formulations, in my view Locke does not want to give an historical description of what happened. He is describing what *could* have happened, intending this to be a supportive argument for his theory about the justification of a particular political order and he advances fictitious examples to support his views on the justification of that order. He wants to demonstrate that his views are correct by using examples that are, in view of human nature and condition, both imaginable and probable. For him it is of little importance whether the events described in the examples did, in fact, occur.[34]

Whether or not the state of nature is to be seen as a reality explaining society or a hypothetical device for the justification of society, let us ask what is going on in Locke's state of nature in which political order is absent.

Locke depicts human beings in the state of nature as free and equal.[35] But this freedom does not imply that people may do whatever they want to do: the state of nature is not lawless. This state is ruled by the law of nature, which is a law of reason and a law of God. This law commands people to preserve themselves and the rest of humanity and, in order to be able to obey these commands, people have natural rights towards one another: rights to life, liberty and estate. (Life, liberty and estate all were considered people's property in Locke's view.) These rights are accompanied by corresponding duties that people have towards one another. Without these rights people cannot obey the commands of the law of nature to preserve themselves and the rest of humanity.[36]

These natural rights differ from the right of nature in Hobbes. In Hobbes' 'natural condition', everyone has a right of nature, implying the liberty to use their own power, as he will himself, for the preservation of their own nature. But no one has a duty to respect or support that right. My question then would be: what kind of a right is it that does not impose a duty on others, a right nobody needs to mind? No moral considerations that rights of other people should be respected are involved in Hobbes' natural condition. That his individuals eventually restrain themselves to prevent a war of all against all is a matter of reasonable self-interest, not of morality. It is only the insight that the unrestricted pursuit of desires will lead to misery, and even self-destruction, that motivates people to conclude an agreement.

But in Locke's state of nature a morality already exists. That morality is provided by the law of nature or, you may call it, the law of reason and the law of God. It is independent of the law of a national state. Locke's idea is that even if no state and political authority existed, a (moral) law would still exist, on the basis of which individuals would have natural rights to life, liberty and estate and all other people would have a corresponding duty to respect those rights. Admittedly, problems will also appear in Locke's state of nature. For while people may be morally required to respect the rights of others, this does not imply that such rights are always respected. People are humans, not angels, by which I mean that they also have bad inclinations, that they are limited, that they make mistakes, that it is difficult for them to foresee all the consequences of their actions and that, even doing what they see as just, they may hurt other people. However well-intended their acts may be, they cannot always prevent other people being hurt or harmed.

Despite the existence of natural rights, the state of nature can degenerate into a state of war. In this state, people still have their rights but these rights are not—either partially or totally—respected. What is needed to stop this unwelcome degeneration is political authority, an authority that should take on itself the task of protecting the natural rights of people. And if such an authority does not exist people would agree by contract to establish it. He adds that such authority must itself respect the natural rights, because otherwise it would not accomplish what it was established to accomplish: the preservation of the natural rights that, unfortunately, were threatened in the authority-less situation.

Here, in Locke, we find natural rights, rights that people have by nature and which are derived from the Law of Nature. In assuming such a law of nature, Locke finds himself in the tradition of natural law. But he differs from that tradition, as developed up to the seventeenth century, in that he no longer interprets natural law in terms of rules or duties, but explicitly in terms of individual rights. This marks the beginning of an era in which natural rights play an important role in political thinking and practice, in which people are seen as autonomous beings who have rights that are not dependent on the arbitrariness of a sovereign.[37] Thus the phase of natural law passes into the phase of natural rights.

6. Constitutionalization

The emergence of the idea of natural law and the following emergence of the idea of natural rights constitute the first and second phases in the development of human rights. The idea of natural rights did not remain within the world of philosophers, but pervaded daily politics. In seventeenth century political Europe, the desire arose to curb the authority of the sovereign. The views of Locke were exactly what were needed. For, as I mentioned, Locke expected the sovereign not only to protect the natural rights of his citizens against violation by others, but also to respect these rights himself: the sovereign should always refrain from interfering in the life, liberty and property of his citizens. His ideas suited the times perfectly.

Locke even was physically in the neighborhood when, in England, the power of the sovereign was limited. There the King and Parliament were in conflict, which in turn mingled with a conflict that had arisen between the Catholics and the Protestants. King James II favored the Catholics, used autocratic methods and disbanded a hostile Parliament. The result was a civil war that was ended by the 'Glorious Revolution' of 1688 and James' forced departure. The Dutch William III, who was married to the daughter of James II, Mary, was then asked to become king of England. William, however, had to promise to respect certain rights of his subjects. This led to the drafting of the Bill of Rights in 1689. It's interesting to note that Locke, who had previously fled to Holland, accompanied William to England.

It could be said that, to a certain extent, Locke also influenced the famous documents which appeared a century later as the building blocks of the American and French revolutions. His views made their way to France where, in the middle of the eighteenth century, Montesquieu wrote his *De l'Esprit des Lois* in which he elaborated on Locke's views on the separation of powers and Rousseau developed the idea of the sovereignty of the people, which was also present in Locke's writing. The views of these two authors affected the famous French Declaration des Droits de l'Homme et du Citoyen of 1789, which spoke of the natural, unalienable and holy rights of man.

Locke's ideas also crossed the Atlantic. The American revolution was a fight for independence from England, started in reaction to tax laws imposed by the English. In 1776 the Declaration of Independence was announced. (The war itself continued for some years after.) The Declaration of Independence contains sentences that make one think immediately of the writings of John Locke, for instance, in its statement that people are born free and equal and endowed with unalienable rights. The American constitution of the 17th of September, 1787, also borrowed ideas from Locke via French thinkers; for example, Rousseau's idea of the sovereignty of the people and Montesquieu's idea of the balance of powers, ideas that were also very much present in Locke's writings. It also borrowed directly from Locke the idea of 'government by law'. When the American Bill of Rights appeared in 1791, listing the first ten of the so-called amendments attached to the American Constitution, it was pervaded by the idea of natural rights. It includes, among others, the right to freedom of religion, the right to freedom of the press, the right to a fair trial and the prohibition of cruel penalties.

Other countries soon followed suit. At the end of the 18th, and throughout the 19th century, many European countries embraced the idea that people have rights by virtue of their being human and that these rights should take precedence over national law. Accordingly, those countries adopted documents that included human rights. Many other countries in the world were not yet independent, and accordingly did not have constitutions of their own. Instead they were covered by the constitutions of the colonial powers. But then, as is well-known, the end of the Second World War saw the process of de-colonization take hold, and the states that acquired independence during this time were quick to draft their own constitutions, many of which also encompassed a bill of rights.[38]

But, back to Europe. Although it can be said, as I have done in the foregoing text, that Locke influenced the political arrangements in England, France and the United States, his influence should not be overestimated. It is more than probable that the philosophical and political climate in those countries rendered them ripe for a change, a change that implied the acknowledgement of the individuality of people, the recognition of human equality and the awareness of the plurality of conceptions of the good life. And it could well have been such a climate itself that generated the ideas worded and formulated by the aforementioned thinkers. Though Locke may well have suggested certain ideas to others, he himself would not have hit upon such ideas without the appropriate intellectual climate, just as that climate made others susceptible to the ideas that he produced.

This philosophical and political climate was in turn affected by economic developments. Mediaeval feudalism had disappeared and was making room for capitalism. Trade and urbanization had caused a break with traditional society. This was strengthened by the emerging industrialization. The capitalist system of free enterprise expanded and individual initiative and competition became characteristic of the new society, which manifested itself most clearly in the 'new land', the United States.[39] Within this changed climate, human beings were regarded as autonomous persons endowed with natural, individual rights. But how was the relationship between these individuals and the state to be seen? In Locke's theory, this relationship had two aspects. One: the state was established to protect citizens from violations of their rights by others. But, two: the state also itself had to refrain from violating the rights of its individuals. Increasingly, it was this latter aspect that became dominant in daily politics, while the idea of the state as the protector of individual interests faded away. The individual and the state came to be seen as the opposites of one another. This promoted a tendency to curb the power of the state and to fence in the private sphere of the individual by claiming their natural rights against the state.[40] Human rights came to be seen as the rights of individuals, while states came to be seen as the main addressees or duty-bearers.

7. Differentiation

Although the development of human rights did not stop after the issuing of the famous declarations at the end of the 18th century, it was definitely less spectacular. Charles Leben even speaks of a 'winter-sleep', one that lasted until 1945.[41] After the enthusiasm with which the declarations were welcomed, some criticisms of natural rights emerged. Conservative criticisms, formulated among others by Edmund Burke, observed that the French Revolution had thrown away the important attainments of tradition and replaced them with political whims and fancies, among which were natural rights. Utilitarian criticism was brought forward by Jeremy Bentham. He regarded the idea of natural rights as 'nonsense upon stilts'. Rights always had been and were accorded by rules of national law. Marx stressed another of the defects of human rights: he argued that the rights that were presented as universal and natural were, in fact, the rights of the bourgeoisie and served only the interests of the bourgeois.

These and other criticisms did not sweep away the idea of natural rights. It turned out to be too well established in political thought and practice. But some important changes showed up, that had already been set in motion before the issuing of the famous declarations of the 18th century.

The number of rights spoken about had actually increased. While Locke had limited himself to the rights to life, liberty and estate, the declarations also mentioned others: rights to freedom of religion, to freedom of the press, to a fair trial, the right to be prevented from torture. And at the same time, the term 'natural rights' began to fade into the background, its place taken by the term 'human rights', or 'citizens' rights'. The term 'human rights" was preferred to the term natural rights: like the term natural rights, it emphasizes that people have rights as human beings and by virtue of their being human, but, unlike the term natural rights, it does not suggest a belief in a fixed, immutable human nature. The term 'citizens' rights' shows some modesty compared to the term human rights and certainly to the term natural rights. 'Citizens' rights' does not refer to rights people have as human beings, but it emphasizes that certain rights are necessary for people to become full members of society and that citizens, therefore, are entitled to them. The contents of these rights, however, turned out to be very similar to rights that by others were called 'human rights'.

T.H. Marshall describes the development of citizens' rights. He observes that more and more rights, and more and more kinds of rights, were granted to citizens. He distinguishes three layers of citizens' rights with their corresponding embeddedment, i.e. civil rights, political rights and social rights, embedded respectively in the constitutional state with its rule of law, in the system of democracy and in the arrangements of the welfare state.[42]

According to Marshall, civil rights emerged during the eighteenth century, the period of the free-contracting citizen in the new economic order. The key notion of these rights is freedom, which is why they are also known as 'freedom rights'. These rights, including for instance that of the right to freedom of expression and freedom of religion, were seen mainly as a means of protecting the citizens from state interference in their private domain.[43] The institution that goes with the idea of civil rights is that of the constitutional state, a state with a constitution—including an allocation of competences, a division of powers and a list of citizens' rights—that also the state must observe.

Political rights take participation as their central value and their emergence, according to Marshall, can be located in the nineteenth century. Their underlying idea is not that citizens should be protected from state interference, but that citizens should be allowed to participate in the building and arranging of society. And the institutional system in which these rights— for example, the right to vote or the right to political association—are embedded, is democracy. The aim of these rights, together with democracy, is to guarantee that government is exercised not merely for the people, but *by* the people. Rousseau argued already in the eighteenth century that people should be both subjects and citizens, i.e. subject to the law and makers of the law.[44]

Social rights represent Marshall's third category. The emergence of civil rights in the 18th century and of political rights in the 19th had paved the way for social rights to appear in the 20th.[45] And their key value is well-being. Examples include the right to adequate housing, the right to work and the right to health care.

The rise of social rights cannot be detached from the social movements of the 19th and 20th centuries. Karl Marx was one of the critics of the American and French human rights declarations and he, like his predecessor Jean Jacques Rousseau, rejected the idea of natural individual rights—rights that people have by nature and that are inherent in human nature.[46] He argued that people are social beings who live in a community with others, are formed by society and need a society to flourish and to develop their individuality. For Marx, the so-called 'human rights' of the 18th century declarations were rights that originated from a capitalist, bourgeois society which reflected the views and needs of the members of the bourgeois class, and in which both the social nature of humanity and the needs of the masses of people were ignored. Such a society provided an unjust advantage to the members of the bourgeois class, the group that possessed and controlled the means of production, and 'human rights' only served the interest of this class. They guaranteed freedom and equality in a formal-legal sense—in law but not in fact—which implies that they were, in reality, only of benefit to the ruling class and worked to the detriment of the least-advantaged.[47]

Marx's criticism eventually resulted in a political system based on collective property instead of individual property, and on the moral priority of the collective. Collective well-being was to be achieved, individual well-being would follow in its wake. It can be doubted today whether Marx himself would have supported the suppression of individuals in favor of the well-being of the collective. I think he certainly had an eye for the well-being of individuals. He was very keen to stress that, although the human rights of the declarations pretended to contribute to a dignified life for all, they did not in fact guarantee a dignified life for very many. He believed that if certain socio-economic conditions were not met, a dignified life would turn out to be an illusion for many people. What is the worth of freedom for people who are starving?

This concern for social justice and the insight that much injustice is concealed behind formal-legal freedom and equality, have been an impetus for the development of social rights. Many people became their staunch proponents and they could be found not only in communist, but also in Western, countries. Franklin Delano Roosevelt, who was president of the United States from 1933 until 1945, stressed for instance the need to relieve socio-economic misery, and argued that "*true individual freedom cannot exist without economic security and independence.*" In his famous 'four freedoms speech', delivered on the 6th of January, 1941, he made a firm stand for the following freedoms: the freedom of speech and expression; the freedom of every person to worship God in his own way, the "*freedom from want, which, translated into world terms, means economic understandings which will secure to every nation a healthy peacetime life for its inhabitants..."* and the *"freedom from fear, which, translated into world terms, means a world-wide reduction of armaments to such a point and in such a thorough fashion that no nation will be in a position to commit an act of physical aggression against any neighbor..."*

Today the distinction drawn by Marshall between civil, political and social rights has become common in human rights discourse, although with a slight difference. Civil and political rights are now often taken together and considered one category (CP-rights), while social rights are regarded as also covering economic and cultural rights and forming a second category. Officially, that is, in various legal documents, this second category is referred to as 'economic, social and cultural' rights (ESC-rights, or Esocul-rights), although in practice the term 'social rights' is still often used.

Today some propose a third category of human rights, in addition to CP-rights and ESC-rights. This category however is slightly dubious and unclear, calling as it does for the right to peace, the right to a clean environment, the right to development and the rights of minority cultures and of indigenous peoples.

It must at this point be noted that the history of human rights, and in particular the history of the various categories, has been less straightforward than the sketch by Marshall supposes. In particular, the debate on economic, social and cultural rights started much earlier than the 20th century. At the end of the 18th century, Thomas Paine, a well-known proponent of human rights, had already revealed himself as an advocate of social rights and spoke about the need to support the poor and to provide pensions for the elderly. He added that this was not a favor granted to them but a right that they already had.[48] However, Paine's views were not accepted in England. He was banned from the country and fled to France.

There the climate was more favorable to social rights, which appeared in official documents, although they were not often worded as rights. The various constitutions of the end of the 18th century offered provisions that make one think of social rights, although they not always were formulated in terms of rights. For example, the French Constitution of 1791 stated that a system of public support had to be established with the aim of bringing up orphans, of helping those who were poor and ill, and of creating jobs for the handicapped. The constitution also demanded that a system of basic public education should be set up and that it should be freely accessible to all. The Montagnard Constitution of 1793 adopted these social rights and included them in a new Declaration of the Rights of Man and the Citizen. Article 21 stated that public support was a holy virtue and that society was obliged to provide its citizens with means of subsistence if they themselves could not succeed in doing so. Article 22 stated that everyone was entitled to education and that society had to guarantee it.[49]

At the same time, social rights were also being recognized in Germany, during the Bismarck period. The model developed there had a social-insurance character and demanded that people had to pay premiums to be entitled to receive support (i.e. payments). It also had a definite corporatist flavor, with different systems developed for the various classes. Therefore, this model could not completely be regarded as a system of human rights but, nevertheless, Eide dares to state that in Germany, social rights definitely appeared before political rights.[50]

International recognition of social rights took place at the end of the nineteenth century. In 1890, an international conference was held with the aim of achieving co-operation in the field of social rights of laborers; for example, the right to humane working conditions. Then, at the beginning of the twentieth century, efforts to come to agreements in the field of working conditions were carried on by the International Association for the Legal Protection of Workers. This organization, located in Basle, stimulated the Swiss government to organize conferences in 1905 and 1906. As a result, the first international labor treaties were concluded that, among other achievements, forbade women having to work at night. After the First World War, activities aimed at reaching international agreements on labor rights were taken up by the International Labor Organization (ILO), set up in 1919. This organization was motivated by the idea that political peace, guarded by the League of Nations, needed to be supplemented by a social peace guarded by the ILO. Thanks to the ILO's drafting of various conventions, an international system of labor law has come about with detailed monitoring procedures.[51]

The field of healthcare also witnessed the deployment of international activities at the beginning of the 20th century when, within the context of the League of Nations, the Health Organization of the League of Nations was set up. In 1946, when the League of Nations was replaced by the United Nations, the World Health Organization was established.

8. Internationalization

The period of the 17th to the 20th century can be seen as the period in which human rights emerged and gained a firm footing in the national systems of law. The 20th century is also the era in which human rights were institutionalized internationally.[52] The internationalization of human rights is the fifth phase in the development of human rights, coming after the phases of natural law, natural rights, constitutionalization and differentiation.

Previously, I mentioned international activities in the field of labor rights. Although these rights can be considered akin to social rights, an important difference must be noted. Labor rights are the rights of laborers, whereas human rights are the rights of every human being. The difference can be made less strong: it could be said that labor rights are the rights of every human being when found in a particular situation. This point will be taken up in Chapter 10, which deals with the universality of ESC-rights, so I will let the matter rest for the moment. Suffice it to say for now that, in addition to labor rights activities, other efforts were made to arrive at international standards.

After the First World War, the League of Nations set up a protection scheme for minorities. The First World War had ended in the dissolution of the Austro-Hungarian Empire, the creation of successor states and a redrawing of boundaries between states in Central and Eastern Europe. But it was impossible to draw the boundaries in a manner that avoided national minorities being created within the new states. Therefore, special arrangements were made to protect the various minorities. In the peace treaties with the former enemy-states (Austria, Bulgaria, Hungary, Turkey) chapters on the rights of minorities were included. With allied or newly created states (Poland, Czechoslovakia, and Yugoslavia, Romania and Greece) treaties on minority rights were agreed.[53] This scheme, among other things, gave international recognition to the German-speaking minorities in Czechoslovakia and Poland. Unfortunately, it was manipulated by the Germans (in the 1930s), who gave an irredentist flavor to the arrangements and incited the German minorities in those countries to vindicate the rights they had been granted by the peace treaties. Eventually, the Germans regarded an invasion as justified when these countries failed to, or did not sufficiently, comply with the escalating demands of the German minorities and within a few years, the Second World War broke out. It was the memories of these events that led to special minority rights being left off the human rights agenda after the Second World War finished.[54]

The Second World War witnessed an unbelievable violation of human dignity, so much so that its end was accompanied by the feeling that such a violation should never happen again and that an outbreak of such inhuman behavior should be prevented at all costs. So, in an echo of what had happened after the First World War, a structural form of interstate co-operation was sought in the years after 1945. An Atlantic Charter had already been drafted in 1941 by the leaders of the United States and England, Roosevelt and Churchill. This included the intention to promote co-operation in the socio-economic field with a view to improving working conditions and to guarantee an adequate standard of living. It was signed, in January 1942, by 26 countries at war with Germany and Japan and it cited the United Nations as the intended successor of the League of Nations.

The Charter of the United Nations was drafted by the United States, Great Britain, the Soviet Union and China in Moscow and Dumbarton Oaks (Washington, DC) in 1944. It was then submitted to, and accepted by, the representatives of fifty states who gathered in San Francisco in 1945. The charter not only gave guidelines for its organization, but also stated—among other items—that an Economic and Social Council should be set up

(ECOSOC) and that such a council should occupy itself with human rights. The Council delegated its task to the Commission on Human Rights, which was to draft an international Bill of Rights. The activities of the Commission, chaired by Eleanor Roosevelt, the widow of Franklin Delano Roosevelt, president of the United States from 1933 until 1945, soon resulted in a draft Universal Declaration of Human Rights. The Commission made grateful use of the Declaration of Essential Human Rights, drafted in 1944 by the American Law Institute, which in addition to civil and political rights, also contained economic, social and cultural rights. (The Commission on Human rights was replaced by the Human Rights Council in 2006. The High Commissioner for Human Rights, Ms. Arbour, saluted the creation of the Human Rights Council, calling its establishment "a historic opportunity to improve the protection and promotion of fundamental freedoms of people around the world.")

The Universal Declaration of Human Rights was adopted by the General Assembly of the United Nations in 1948, with 48 votes in favor and eight abstentions. The adoption of the Declaration was a landmark on the road to the internationalization of human rights.

9. The Universal Declaration of Human Rights

An often disputed point is whether the Universal Declaration of Human Rights (UDHR) is Western. Michael Ignatieff, in particular, queries its supposed Western signature. He points out that various traditions participated in the process of drafting and adopting the Declaration: China and the Middle East, but also Marxist, South American, Muslim and Hindu traditions. In addition, he puts forward the view that the Commission on Human Rights, which was charged with the task of drafting the declaration, did not intend to simply ratify Western convictions on human rights; it instead explicitly wanted to lay down universal standards rooted in varied and different backgrounds. This view of the Commission explains why no reference is made to God.[55] Also Cassese says that the Declaration is the fruit of many traditions. It transcends the ideologies of particular societies.[56] These remarks by Ignatieff and Cassese are important and should be taken into consideration, but they do not undermine the view that the UDHR has a Western signature. Its genesis and its contents show that it has a Western flavor and its roots lie definitely in the political and philosophical developments of modern Western Europe, a point which is not denied by Ignatieff.[57]

The number of states that participated in the debates leading to the adoption of the UDHR was about a third of the present number of member states of the UN. Most current states did not exist in the 1940s and many Third World countries were not yet independent. Besides, the states that were independent followed the views of the West or the Soviet Union.[58] The debates that took place in 1946-1948 were dominated by the opposition between the West and the Communist countries, an opposition that, until 1990, dominated the global human rights discourse.

This opposition presents some striking features, which I will sketch out roughly below.[59]

a. The Western views on human rights have originated from a tradition of natural law and natural rights. This tradition also had an often a-historical character, to the extent that natural law and natural rights were seen as criteria for human behavior with a validity independent of the particular historical situation in which people happen to live. The most prominent Western participants in the debates leading to the adoption of the UDHR were England, the United States and France: the very countries that formed the cradle of the famous human rights declarations at the end of the eighteenth century.

The Communist countries, though, have always emphasized the historical character of human rights. These rights are not given for once and for all, and are not independent of a historical context. They are dependent on the structure of a society in which the rights are granted. In this view, individual human beings and society do not stand opposite one another, with individuals trying to keep the state from encroaching on their territory, but rather individuals and the state are united in achieving a general well-being for all.

b. The West has always given first rank to civil and political rights, whereas the Communist countries have stressed the importance of social rights.[60] It must be added that these preferences were accentuated by the Cold War. The Cold War generated a tendency for the parties involved to take opposite positions, more or less independent of the contents of the views expressed. It should be noted that, initially, Western countries also had an eye for social rights. I have mentioned the draft declaration of the American Law Institute, 1944, that paid attention to social rights. And in the 1940s, the American president Franklin D. Roosevelt pointed out the importance of social rights, stressing in his 'four freedoms' speech, not only freedom of expression and religion, but also freedom from want and from fear. He was of the opinion that individual freedom cannot exist without socio-economic security. "*Necessitous men are not free men*". And of course, necessitous men can be rebellious: Governments may be inclined to embrace socio-economic rights from fear of revolt. They then tolerate these rights rather than see them as a source of genuine moral and legal duties. Perhaps Roosevelt acted primarily to preserve the capitalist system from challenge when it had broken down, by preempting revolution.

Many others in the West realized that what they designated as totalitarian regimes could only grow because of the widespread poverty and unemployment that preceded the Second World War. That was why Western countries were willing to include ESC-rights in the UDHR—to counter the appeal of totalitarian ideologies. And, indeed, the Declaration mentions civil and political rights as well as economic, social and cultural rights. But the

Cold War changed attitudes. The sympathy for ESC-rights disappeared in the West as the Communist countries embraced them. And conversely: the emphasis on civil and political rights by the West led to the communists paying them less attention.

      c. As a third point of difference, it should be mentioned that the West took a more positive approach towards international supervision and monitoring than the Communist countries. Although many Westerners argued that a state should be prepared to allow international supervisors to examine its human rights record, not all Western countries shared this view. The United States, for example, was reluctant to accept international supervision. The communists generally took the stand that while the international community had to set up international standards, it was up to the individual states to give effect and form to such standards: the state was responsible for providing its citizens with a dignified life.

      Even though this opposition between West and the Communist countries influenced the debates leading to the adoption of the UDHR, the eventual result was that the Declaration breathes a spirit of Western liberalism, as noted by writers such as Adamantia Pollis and Peter Schwab.[61] However, the assumption that human rights are originally a product of Western modernity need not imply that they are purely Western. Abu Zayd has argued that Western modernity is built upon 'modernities' that existed earlier and elsewhere. Western modernity and its human rights are the heritage, he says, of *"the history of human struggle, since Spartacus in Rome until Nelson Mandela in South Africa, against all kinds of human injustice"*, a statement that should be borne in mind when it is said that human rights are the product of Western modernity.[62] It could also be added that the fact that the rights of the UDHR were drafted and adopted in the 1940s by mainly Northern/Western states does not mean that they could not have become universally accepted since. There have been world conferences on human rights (in Teheran 1968; in Vienna 1993; the Women's Conference in Beijing, 1995) where newly emerged states have also endorsed the human rights of the UDHR and subsequent documents. Besides, most countries have formally signed and ratified most human rights documents. Consequently, the final declaration of the World Conference on Human Rights in Vienna says that the universality of human rights is beyond question. So, it may be concluded: all is well that ends well. Indeed, the *UDHR* is a standard of achievement for all. It has global significance and cannot be underestimated. Unavoidably, it is a compromise, but it has the potential to be valid for six billion people and to unite them on the point of the conditions for a dignified life.[63]

10. The International Covenants

      The Universal Declaration of Human Rights is not a legally binding document. It is a declaration with much moral force—that must be admitted—but without juridical effect. Richard Falk even thinks that the UDHR would never have been accepted if it had pretended to be a framework of enforceable rights. "*What made it politically acceptable was precisely its unenforceability, which was consistent with the Westphalian ideology of world order*", that put much emphasis of the sovereignty of states.[64] But, increasingly it was felt necessary to draft a treaty on the basis on the UDHR, since a treaty is legally binding upon the states that have ratified it. The Commission on Human Rights accordingly undertook to draft such a treaty. Then, however, a difference of opinion surfaced. The Cold War was raging even more than in the 1940s, fomenting the cultural differences between the West and the Communist countries in relation to human rights. The West embraced civil and political rights, whereas the Communist countries set themselves up as fierce proponents of ESC-rights.

Many Western countries argued for the composition of two treaties rather than trying to include all rights in one treaty. They were of the opinion that civil and political rights differ substantially from economic, social and cultural rights, with the former felt to fit more into the individualist human rights tradition rather than the latter. They felt that civil and political rights were real rights, rights that were justiciable: these rights could be invoked before a court or other judicial body. After all, they pointed out, it could be easily demonstrated whether and by whom someone's right to freedom of religion, or to freedom of expression, or freedom from torture, has been violated. Such rights require others to refrain from interfering, and when others do interfere, the rights are violated. But, how could it be proved that a right to healthcare or a right to housing has been violated? Such rights, it was argued, did not require abstinence; instead they required an active attitude on the part of the government. It is difficult though to determine exactly what a state (or someone else) has to do in order to comply with ESC-rights, and consequently it can hardly be determined when a social right has been violated.

Because of this fundamental difference between the two categories of rights, they were to be treated differently and two separate treaties were considered appropriate to do justice to the difference in nature. This was also the opinion of the Commission on Human Rights in charge of the drafting of a treaty in elaboration of the UDHR.

The representatives of the Communist countries were, in general, proponents of the idea of one treaty. They were of the view that ESC-rights were as important and as real as CP-rights are, with some ESC-rights regarded as being even more important and more real than CP-rights. The inclusion of all rights in one treaty would underline the unity and indivisibility of all human rights.

Initially this was the view of the General Assembly, too: it ordered the Commission to draft one treaty containing both categories of rights. The

Commission obeyed and came up with one draft treaty. However, within that draft, the two categories of rights were treated differently. For example, different monitoring procedures were proposed, the Commission arguing that the different character of both categories required a different treatment. What this amounted to, in fact, was two treaties gummed together. Therefore, in 1952, the General Assembly eventually acquiesced to the wishes of the Commission and decided in favor of two treaties.

The Western view, which was also the view of the Commission on Human Rights, had prevailed. The eventual result was that, in 1966, two covenants were concluded: the International Covenant on Civil and Political Rights (ICCPR) and the International Covenant on Economic, Social and Cultural Rights (ICESCR). These documents, which do not have the status of declarations, but of treaties, are both legally binding, but only with respect to states that have signed and ratified them, and taking into account the possible reservations they have made.

While the foregoing events show that the Cold War influenced the development of human rights, it is difficult to assess its real impact. It is especially difficult to determine what the position of ESC-rights would have been without it. The Communist countries were proponents of these rights and that may have strengthened their position. But, it also may have negatively affected the position of ESC-rights. The discord between the West and the Communists may well have resulted in one-sided stands, with the Western countries focusing on civil and political rights more than they would have done without the Cold War. After all, as shown above, social rights can be found in the writings of such Western writers as Thomas Paine, in such Western political documents as the French Constitutions of 1791 and 1793, and in the ideas of Western politicians such as President Roosevelt. All three show an awareness of the importance of social rights, even though such sympathy for social rights disappeared during the Cold War. On the other hand, the Communists may have been reluctant to see the value of civil and political rights thinking that they might impede the effort of the state to implement social planning or protect the fruits thereof, even though Marx himself had an eye for freedom of individuals.

The Cold War could have had an impact at the national level too. Proposals in Western countries to promote or strengthen ESC-rights might well have been rejected because they were seen as inspired by communism and, therefore, suspect. Proposals in Communist countries to promote civil and political rights could have been regarded as products of Western capitalism and thus suspect. It is, perhaps, no coincidence that a "revival" of ESC-rights can be noticed since the end of the Cold War.[65] Of course, the end of the Cold War is not the only, and not even the main reason for this revival. The socio-economic situation of many people is so rude and harsh that the need for ESC-rights has become evident.

The development of human rights did not end with the UDHR and the two subsequent treaties. Many other declarations and treaties have since appeared on the human rights scene: for example, the International Covenant on the Elimination of All Forms of Racial Discrimination (1965), the Convention on the Elimination of All Forms of Discrimination against Women (1979), the Convention against Torture and Other Cruel, Inhuman or Degrading Treatment or Punishment (1984), and the Convention on the Rights of the Child (1989).

Human rights documents have also been drafted within the European context. An important and effective instrument is the European Convention for the Protection of Human Rights and Fundamental Freedoms (1950). Less famous is the European Social Charter (1961). The former contains civil and political rights, whereas the latter holds social rights. These documents are products of the Council of Europe, an organization of 47 European countries that aims to defend and promote a common European heritage of democracy and human rights.

This organization should be distinguished from the European Union. This is an originally economic organization (previously named the European Economic Community) which has, since the Treaty of Maastricht in 1992, also become a political union. The EU currently has 27 members and has brought forth its own human rights document, the Charter of Fundamental Rights of the European Union (Nice, 2000).[66] While not a legally binding document, this charter was included in the draft European Constitution and if the constitution had entered into force, the human rights included within it would also have been legally binding. The Constitution has, however, been rejected by the French and the Dutch. It will be replaced by a Reform Treaty.

The European Union—as well as its predecessor, the European Economic Community—has already in its early stage of development recognized civil and political rights, even though such recognition was indirect: both the treaties and the jurisdiction of the European Court of Justice stated that the organization (EU/EEC) was committed to the above-mentioned European Convention for the Protection of Human Rights and Fundamental Freedoms. It has, however, always been reluctant to recognize socio-economic rights. And while it is interesting that the Charter mentions both civil, political *and* socio-economic rights, in my view it is, as far as socio-economic rights are concerned, less generous than the International Covenant on Economic, Social and Cultural Rights.

Also other regions have developed their human rights documents. With respect to America the *American Declaration of the Rights and Duties of Man* (1948), and the *American Convention on Human Rights* (1969) should be mentioned. Africa knows the *African Charter on Human and Peoples' Rights* (1981). There is also an *Arab Charter on Human Rights*, adopted by the League of Arab States (1997), and a *Universal Islamic Declaration of Human Rights* (1981) followed by the Cairo Declaration on Human Rights in

Islam (1990). All these documents pay attention to CP-rights and ESC-rights, although they seem to be more enthusiastic about CP-rights than about ESC-rights. I will clarify that statement in the next chapter.

BIBLIOGRAPHY

Abu Zayd, N. (1998b), 'The Concept of Human Rights, the Process of Modernization and the Politics of Western Domination', in: (1998) Politik und Gesellschaft online. International Politics and Society 4. Retrieved October 2001, from: http://www.fes.de/ipg/ipg4 _98/debabuzayd.html

Alston, P, >Economic and Social Rights=, in: L. Henkin en J.L. Hargrove (red.), *Human Rights: an Agenda for the Next Century* (Washington D. C.: American society of international law, 1994) p.137.

Arnhart, Larry, *Political Questions* (New York: Macmillan Publishing Company, 1987).

Bentham, J., H.L.A. Hart (ed.), *Of Laws in General: The limits of jurisprudence defined* (Londen: University of London, Athlone Press, 1970) p.220.

Burke, Edmund, *Reflections on the Revolution in France* (New York: Doubleday, 1961).

Cliteur, Paul, *De filosofie van mensenrechten* (Nijmegen: Ars Aequi Libri, 1997).

Cranston, Maurice, *What are Human Rights?* (Londen, Sydney and Toronto: The Bodley Head, 1973).

Dijk, P. Van, 'Het internationale recht inzake de rechten van de mens', in: P. van Dijk (red.), *Rechten van de Mens in Mondiaal en Europees perspectief* (Nijmegen: Ars Aequi Libri, 1991).

Donnelly, J., 'Human Rights, Individual Rights, and Collective Rights', in: J. Berting (ed.), *Human rights in a pluralist world: individuals and collectivities* (Westport, London: Meckler, 1990).

Donnelly, Jack, *International Human Rights* (Boulder, San Francisco and Oxford: Westview Press, 1993).

Dower, Nigel, *World Ethics, The New Agenda* (Edinburgh: Edinburgh University Press, 1998).

Dower, Nigel, *An Introduction to Global Citizenship*, (Edinburgh University Press, 2003).

Eide, Asbjørn, 'Economic, Social and Cultural Rights as Human Rights', in: Asbjorn Eide, Catarina Krause en Allan Rosas (ed.), *Economic, Social and Cultural Rights* (Dordrecht, Boston, London: Martinus Nijhoff Publishers,1995).

Eide, Asbjørn, 'Economic and Social Rights', in: Janusz Symonides (ed.), *Human Rights: Concept and Standards* (Aldershot, Burlinton, Singapore, Sydney: Ashgate, Dartmouth, Unesco Publishing, 2000).

Falk, Richard, 'Human rights and global civil society', in: Paul Gready (ed.), *Fighting for Human Rights* (London: Routledge 2004)

Feinberg, J., *Social Philosophy* (Englewood Hills, NJ: Pentice Hall, 1973).

W.J.M. van Genugten, >Oost en West, van Kemphaan naar partner=, in: *Ars Aequi* 41, nr.6 (Nijmegen, 1992)

Grant, Robert, *American Ethics and the Virtuous Citizen* (Washington: Humanist Press, 2003)

Haersolte, R.A.V. van, *Hi Lili, of het spel van kiezen en delen*, in: *Rechtsfilosofie en Rechtstheorie* 15, nr.1 (1986).

Hampton, Jean, *Political Philosophy* (Oxford UK and Boulder USA: Westview Press, 1997).

Hartogh, G.A. den, 'Inleiding', in: John Locke (G.A. den Hartogh, ed.), *Over het staatsbestuur* (Amsterdam: Boom, 1988).

Hobbes, Thomas, (Richard Tuck, red.), *Leviathan* (Cambridge: Cambridge University

Press, 1991)

Höffe, Otfried, *Political Justice* (Cambridge: Polity Press, 1995).

Paul Hunt, *Reclaiming Social Rights: International and Comparative Perspectives* (Aldershot: Dartmouth 1996)

Jones, P., *Rights* (London: Macmillan Press, 1994)

Kymlicka, W., *Contemporary Political Philosophy, an introduction* (Oxford: Clarendon Press, 1990)

Kymlicka, W., *Multicultural Citizenship: a liberal theory of minority rights* (Oxford: Clarendon Press, 1995)

Leben, Charles, 'A European Approach to Human Rights?', in: Philip Alston (ed.), *The EU and Human Rights* (Oxford: Oxford University Press, 1999)

Locke, John, *The Second Treatise on Civil Government* (New York: Prometheus Books, 1986)

Locke, John, (G.A. den Hartogh, ed.), *Over het staatsbestuur* (Amsterdam: Boom, 1988).

Lukes, Steven, *Individualism* (Oxford: Basil Blackwell, 1973)

MacIntyre, Alisdair, *After Virtue* (London: Duckworth, 1990).

Macpherson, C.B., *The political theory of possesive individualism* (Oxford: Oxford University Press, 1962)

Marshall, T.H., *Citizenship and Social Development* (London & Chicago: University of Chicago Press, 1977)

Martin, Rex, *A system of rights* (Oxford: Clarendon Press, 1997)

Marx, Karl, *Early Writings*, T.B. Bottomore (ed.), (New York: McGraw-Hill Book Company, 1963)

Paine, Thomas, *Rechten van de Mens, Bloemlezing, samengesteld door G.A. van der List*, (Kampen: Kok, Agora, 1992)

Pierson, Christopher, *Beyond the Welfare State?: the new political economy of welfare* (Cambridge: Polity Press, 1991)

Pollis, Adamanthia and Peter Schwab, 'Human rights: a Western Construct with Limited Applicability', in: Adamanthia Pollis and Peter Schwab, *Human Rights: Cultural and ideological perspectives* (New York: Praeger, 1979).

Shestack, Jerome J., 'The Philosophical Foundations of Human Rights', in: Janusz Symonides (ed.), *Human Rights: Concept and Standards* (Aldershot, Burlington, Singapore etc.: Dartmouth Publishing, Ashgate Publishing & Unesco Publishing, 2000)

Jeremy Waldron, *Cultural Identity and Civic Responsibility*, in: Will Kymlicka and Wayne Norman, *Citizenship in Diverse Societies* (Oxford University Press, 2000)

Wright, John T., 'Human Rights in The West: Political Liberties and the Rule of Law', in: Adamantia Pollis & Peter Schwab, *Human Rights: Cultural and Ideological Perspectives* (New York: Praeger, 1979).

Wal, G.A. van der, 'The individualism of Human Rights', in: *Rechtsfilosofie en Rechtstheorie* 18:3. (Zwolle: Tjeenk Willink, 1989)

ENDNOTES

[1] http://www.unhchr.ch/development/approaches-04.html, retrieved 3-02-2006.
[2] Feinberg 1973, p.85; Donnelly 1993, p.18.
[3] Dower 1998, p.79.
[4] Dower 2003, p.56.
[5] Bentham & Hart (ed.) 1970, p.220.
[6] Martin 1997, p.74; Burke 1961; Lukes 1973; MacIntyre 1990, p.70.
[7] Donnelly 1990, p.41.
[8] Cliteur 1997, p.13.
[9] Höffe 1995, p.3; Cliteur 1997, p.91.
[10] Cranston 1973, p.11.
[11] Cicero had been imported into Christian theology. St. Charles Borromeo Catholic

Church presents its Catechism of the Catholic Church of a few decades ago, that quoted Cicero saying, "For there is a true law: right reason. It is in conformity with nature, is diffused among all men, and is immutable and eternal; its orders summon to duty; its prohibitions turn away from offense .... To replace it with a contrary law is a sacrilege; failure to apply even one of its provisions is forbidden; no one can abrogate it entirely." (http://www.scborromeo.org/ccc/p3s1c3a1.htm, retrieved 17 January 2007)

[12] Jones 1994, p.1.
[13] Locke 1986, p.75.
[14] Leben 1999, p.73.
[15] Dower, 2003, p.6.
[16] Van Dijk 1991, p.7.
[17] Leben 1999, p.73.
[18] Locke 1986, pp.9,10,75.
[19] Van Haersolte 1986, p.64.
[20] Van Haersolte 1986, pp.65,66.
[21] Arnhart 1987, p.193.
[22] Robert Grant describes the social contract as "that fundamental agreement which human beings are *assumed* (my italics, RB) to have negotiated, that enables them to live together in social groups without killing each other". Grant 2003, p.3
[23] Kymlicka 1990, p.59.
[24] Rawls 1971/1976, p.12
[25] Shestack 2000, p.37.
[26] Hobbes & Tuck (ed.) 1991, p.120,153; Locke 1986, p.50.
[27] Hampton 1997, p.30.
[28] Locke 1986, p.8; Hobbes 1991, p.86; Kymlicka 1990, p.60; Jeremy Waldron 2000, p.157.
[29] Arnhart 1987, p.193; Dower 2003, p.70.
[30] Hobbes 1991, p.91.
[31] Hobbes 1991, p.88.
[32] Hobbes 1991, p.92; Dower 2003, pp.71,72.
[33] Grant 2003, p.141.
[34] Den Hartogh 1988, p.34.
[35] Locke 1986, p.8,9; Locke 1988, p.65.
[36] Locke 1988, pp.65,66,67.
[37] Pollis & Schwab 1979, p.2.
[38] To name a few: the constitution of India, originally composed in 1950 but amended several times in the years since, contains a section on rights: Part III, 'Fundamental Rights'. This does not, however, encompass ESC-rights. As far as they can be found in the Indian constitution, it is in Part IV 'Directive Principle of State Policy'. The constitution of Algeria, written in 1976 and amended in 1996, contains a chapter (4) on rights and liberties that also encompasses articles on duties. It also mentions both CP-rights and ESC-rights. The constitution of South-Africa of 1996 is one of the most progressive in the world, with a chapter 2, Bill of Rights, that includes both CP-rights and ESC-rights.
[39] Pollis & Schwab 1979, p.3.
[40] Wright 1979, p.20.
[41] Leben 1999, p.85.
[42] Marshall 1977, p.78; Dower 2003, p.37.
[43] As mentioned above, this was only one aspect of Locke's theory. This aspect, that the state must refrain from interference in the private realm of its citizens had pushed away the other aspect, i.e. the idea that also other citizens must refrain from interfering in the private domain of their fellow citizens and that if such interference took place, the state should protect people from it. But, today, this latter aspect is coming back again. It is increasingly assumed that civil rights also have a so-called horizontal effect: these rights not only concern the (vertical) relationship between the state and its citizens, but also the (horizontal) relationship between citizens among themselves. And the state not only has to refrain

from interference in the private domain of its citizens but also has to protect citizens from interference of their domain by fellow citizens.

[44] Dower 2003, p.40.
[45] Marshall 1977, p.78; Pierson 1991.
[46] Dower 2003, p.40.
[47] Marx 1963, p.22.
[48] Paine 1992, p.128.
[49] This constitution was then supplanted by the French Constitution of 1795 (the year III), which in turn was succeeded by the Constitution of the Year VIII.
[50] Eide 1995, p.27; Eide 2000, p.114.
[51] Van Dijk 1991, p.10.
[52] Pollis & Schwab 1979, p.3.
[53] Robertson & Merills 1992, p.19.
[54] Kymlicka 1995, pp.57, 58.
[55] Ignatieff 1999, p.34.
[56] Cassese 1990, p.9.
[57] Ignatieff 1999, pp.53,54.
[58] Cassese 1990, p.33.
[59] These features are also mentioned by W.J.M. van Genugten, Paul Hunt and Philip Alston (Van Genugten 1992, p.335; Hunt 1996, p.8; Alston 1994, p.137).
[60] Charlesworth 1994, p.59.
[61] Pollis en Schwab 1979, p.5.
[62] Zayd 1998, p.5.
[63] Cassese 1990, p.9.
[64] Richard Falk, 2004, p.37.
[65] Cassese 1990, p.55.
[66] Bulgaria and Romania have entered January 2007.

MILLENNIUM DEVELOPMENT GOALS

Goal 1. Eradicate extreme hunger and poverty, thus: halving the proportion of people living on less than $ 1 a day and suffering from malnutrition.

Goal 2. Achieve universal primary education, thus: ensuring that all children are able to complete primary education.

Goal 3. Promote gender equality and empower women, thus: eliminating gender disparity in primary and secondary schooling, preferably by 2005 and by no later than 2015.

Goal 4. Reduce child mortality, thus: cutting the under-five death rate by two thirds.

Goal 5. Improve maternal health, thus: reducing the maternal mortality rate by three quarters.

Goal 6. Combat HIV/AIDS, malaria and other diseases, thus: halting and beginning to reverse HIV/AIDS and other diseases.

Goal 7. Ensure environmental stability, thus cutting by half the proportion of people without sustainable access to safe drinking water and sanitation.

Goal 8. Develop a global partnership for development, thus reforming aid and trade with special treatment for the poorest countries.

CHAPTER 2

THE STATE OF AFFAIRS OF INTERNATIONAL SOCIAL RIGHTS

OR:
WHAT DO WE HAVE TO DO WITH ONE ANOTHER'S MISERY?

1. Fighting poverty

In 2000, at the start of the new millennium, the world adopted the Millennium Declaration. It sets out a promise of greater equity, social justice and respect for human rights. The Millennium Development Goals (MDGs)—a set of time-bound and quantified targets for reducing extreme poverty and extending universal rights by 2015—provide the benchmarks for measuring progress. [1]

In the first chapter, I sketched the development of human rights, ending with the adoption of the Universal Declaration of Human rights, which heralded a period in which many other international documents on human rights were framed. My special interest is in economic, social and cultural rights. For me, these rights can be a great contribution to the achievement of the Millennium Development Goals. They are important means to fight poverty and socio-economic misery and to promote people's well-being. The various Human Development Reports say that human development is about much more than the rise or fall of national incomes. *"It is about creating an environment in which people can develop their full potential and lead productive, creative lives in accord with their needs and interests. People are the real wealth of nations. Development is thus about expanding the choices people have to lead lives that they value. And it is thus about much more than economic growth, which is only a means—if a very important one—of enlarging people's choices. Fundamental to enlarging these choices is building human capabilities..."*.[2]

Human capabilities have an internal and an external aspect: capabilities include both capacities (the personal qualities, talents and skills that are inborn or that people have acquired during their lives) and possibilities (circumstances that enable the development of personal qualities and capacities). Developing capabilities implies developing capacities and possibilities. Human rights claim to protect and foster the external aspects of basic capabilities, and *to create the conditions that make a dignified human life possible*. ESC-rights, in particular, aim to create socio-economic and cultural conditions that enable people to lead a dignified life.

I will now focus on ESC-rights. (I will though not pay much attention to cultural rights. They would deserve more attention, but, although they have much in common with socio-economic rights, they also have characteristics that distinguish them from socio-economic rights). In this chapter I will briefly outline the position of ESC-rights, and mention the articles in human rights documents which deal with them. I also will give some examples chosen at random from various document showing that these rights are seriously violated.

This undertaking may not sound a very exciting story, and some readers may be inclined to jump to the next chapter. I cannot blame them for so doing, but nevertheless I do think that this chapter is important as we should need to know what we are talking about when speaking of economic, social and cultural rights. It is also important as it will show that ESC-rights are treated differently from civil and political rights. It is this treatment which prevents ESC-rights from playing the role they could play in human development. The difference in treatment seeks its justification in the traditional view that says that ESC-rights are by their very nature substantially different from civil and political rights. It is even argued that ESC-rights are not real human rights at all. At the end of this chapter I will have a look at this traditional view and the criticisms that are leveled against ESC-rights as human rights. And that is, in my opinion, the start of a much more exciting story that can contribute to answering the question why there is so little protest worldwide, while we are witnessing massive violations of ESC-rights day in and day out.[3]

Economic, social and cultural rights are mentioned in articles 22 to 28 of the Universal Declaration of Human Rights (UDHR). Article 22 is an introductory, general article, preceding the more specific articles regarding economic, social and cultural rights. It starts by saying that *"everyone, as a member of society, has the right to social security..."*. The term social security could refer to financial contribution or support in kind in cases of illness or unemployment but this is, however, explicitly dealt with in article 25. In view of the general character of article 22, I would suggest that the right to social security in this article should be interpreted more generally as meaning that everyone has to be socially secure and entitled to a solid social basis for his or her existence. Article 22 continues by saying that everyone is *"entitled to realization, through national effort and international co-operation and in* accordance with the organization and resources of each State, of the economic, social and cultural rights indispensable for his dignity and the free development of his personality."*

I will now briefly describe the more specific economic, social and cultural rights. In doing so, I will use the adverb 'social' in a narrow sense, not referring to the ESC-rights in general, but rather to the subcategory of 'social rights' within the category of economic, social and cultural rights.

2. Social rights

a. *The right to an adequate standard of living.*

The most general social right is the right to an adequate standard of living, laid down in article 25 of the UDHR and articles 9, 10, 11 and 12 of the International Covenant on Economic, Social and Cultural Rights (ICESCR). Article 25 of the UDHR states that *"everyone has the right to a standard of living adequate for the health and well-being of himself and his family, including food, clothing, housing and medical care and necessary social services, and the right to security in the event of unemployment, sickness, disability, widowhood, old age or other lack of livelihood in circumstances beyond his control."* This general right implies the more specific rights to *"food, clothing, housing and medical care and necessary social services ..."*

Article 11 of the ICESCR is partly a recapitulation of article 25 of the UDHR. It reads: *"1. The States Parties to the present Covenant recognize the right of everyone to an adequate standard of living for himself and his family, including adequate food, clothing and housing, and to the continuous improvement of living conditions.... 2. The States Parties to the present Covenant, recognizing the fundamental right of everyone to be free from hunger..."* What is striking is that article 11 of the ICESCR, unlike the UDHR, speaks about a right to be free from hunger. It is an interesting formulation because it demonstrates that social rights can be formulated both positively and negatively. It can be said that people have a right to food and it can be said that people have a right to be free from hunger. We should also remember that Franklin Delano Roosevelt used a negative formulation in his famous 'four freedoms' speech, when he made a firm stand for the freedom from want.

Finally, what is also striking is that article 11 of the ICESCR does not completely follow article 25 of the UDHR; unlike article 25 it does not say anything about social services and the right to medical care. The right to social services is mentioned in article 9 of the ICESCR while the right to healthcare is dealt with in article 12 of the ICESCR.

b. *The right to food*

The right to food is far from being fulfilled. According to the Food and Agricultural Organization of the United Nations (FAO) millions of people, including 6 million children under the age of five, die each year as a result of hunger. The FAO estimates that around 840 million people suffer from malnutrition: 800 million in the developing countries, 30 million in the countries in transition and 11 million in the industrialized countries. The largest number of victims live in Africa, where a staggering 34 percent of the population is severely malnourished. According to the FAO, the World Food Summit's 1996 goal to reduce the number of hungry by half by 2015 will not be reached unless trends are sharply reversed.[4] In its "State of Food Insecurity in the World 2006" the FAO says that despite the pledge by heads of State and Government of more than 180 nations attending the World Food Summit 1996 to eradicate hunger, the reality of 2006 shows that *virtually no progress* has been made towards that objective.[5]

It must be noted that hunger is not the result of absolute food shortages, as may be thought. Absolute food shortages are rare. Rich people never starve, whereas poor people do. Starvation is not the result of food shortages but of an unequal distribution of food, due to unequal power in the market. It can of course be made worse by natural disasters such as hurricanes and drought, and by war, but these are not the causes of structural hunger. The FAO clearly states that *"widespread hunger in a world of abundance is essentially the result of poverty".* [6] An example is offered by the situation in Somalia. Although the Horn of Africa contains some of the most productive food-growing regions in Africa (the Nile provinces in Sudan and Gojam in Ethiopia) nevertheless hunger is widespread. Sometimes people even starve in the relief camps on the outskirts of towns while the markets in those towns are full of food.[7]

c. The right to adequate housing

The right to adequate housing is also far from being fulfilled. This right concerns much more than simply having a roof over one's head. According to the Committee on Economic, Social and Cultural Rights, adequate housing means having shelter and adequate room but also adequate privacy, lighting, ventilation, and sewerage: people must have equal access to a safe, habitable, and affordable home. It also means that people must be protected against forced evictions. But, as UN Habitat, the UN Human Settlements Program, points out, more than a billion people live in inadequate housing conditions in urban areas alone, mostly in slums or in squatter settlements, or even on pavements. An estimated 100 million people are homeless around the world, with increasing proportions of women and children.[8] Millions live in shantytowns in cities such as Calcutta, Lagos, Mexico City. But also in the 'rich' world, many are homeless. In Dublin, roughly 7,000 people become homeless each year. And in the United States, about 750,000 people are homeless on any given night.[9] This is a great contrast to the luxury housing that many rich people enjoy and the situation is hardly improving. As Miloon Kothari, independent UN special rapporteur on adequate housing, puts it, *"the deepening inequalities of income and opportunities between and within nations has led to an increase in the number of people without adequate and secure housing. The human rights of people and communities to housing, water and sanitation (...) continue to erode as the process of privatization deepens and accelerates."*[10]

d. *The right to health*

The right to health is also a specific right under the heading of the right to an adequate standard of living. Article 25 of the UDHR speaks of medical care. Article 12 of the ICESCR uses a broader formulation. It speaks of the right of everyone to the enjoyment of the highest attainable standard of physical and mental health, a formulation that justifies using the phrase the right to *health*, instead of just the right to health care. This does not mean that an individual has the right to be healthy. Nobody, no state or other organization, can be expected to provide people with protection against every possible cause of ill health or disability. What can be expected, however, is that people are provided with a variety of facilities and conditions necessary for the attainment and maintenance of good health. Thus the right to health includes access to adequate healthcare (medical, preventative, and mental), and also to nutrition and sanitation. This implies that public healthcare facilities in sufficient quantity should be accessible and affordable, and of good quality. It also includes the right to be protected from a polluted and health-threatening environment and from unhealthy and hazardous working conditions.

The Committee on ESC-rights, in its session of 25th of April-12th of May 2000, says that it is aware that, for millions of people throughout the world, the full enjoyment of the right to health still remains a distant goal and is particularly remote for those living in poverty, who often suffer from diseases the rich have the resources to overcome. Take, for instance, AIDS, probably the most devastating crisis in the history of human health. Human Rights Watch states that more than 40 million people are living with HIV, that 25 million men, women and children have died from it, and that 15,000 people are infected every day—mainly the poorest, the weakest and the least educated.[11] However, HIV/AIDS is a preventable and manageable disease. Highly effective treatment and prevention regimes exist to contain it. Most people living in rich countries have access to these treatments. The majority of HIV/AIDS patients living in poor countries do not. Because of ignorance and neglect, because of lack of resources on the side of the poor, and their being denied access to provisions, HIV/AIDS has been turned into a pandemic that is destroying the lives of the most vulnerable.

Women and girls especially suffer from inadequate healthcare and denial of access to healthcare. In many societies, women and girls are discriminated against, which results in them having less access to food, healthcare and education, and makes them more vulnerable to diseases. In India, for instance, the number of girls that die between the ages of 1 and 5 exceeds the number of boys dying at that age by more than 300,000. In Latin America, the main causes of death of women are complications arising from pregnancy and unsafe abortions. If these women could have had better and earlier access to treatment, the majority of these deaths could have been prevented.[12]

e. The right to clothing

The right to clothing is also an aspect of the right to an adequate standard of living. It does not appear to be a very important right as most people will have some clothes in normal times. But, in times of disaster, the victims of those disasters often find themselves in a situation in which they are deprived of everything, even of their clothing. For instance, in October 2005 many people in Pakistan, Northern India and parts of Afghanistan were suffering—and even dying—from cold and did not have enough clothing. A powerful earthquake had hit this region, flattening villages, shaking houses. Roads had been wiped out by landslides. Thousands and thousands had been killed. Many were homeless and did not have enough clothing to protect themselves from the heavy rains or from the winter that was setting in. About three million people were without adequate protection from cold and rain.

Clothing not only protects people from hard weather conditions, it also contributes to a feeling of pride and self-awareness. Lack of decent clothing makes people find themselves inferior and poor indeed. It hinders children's attendance at schools and it keeps them away from educational meetings. A regional report of the United Nations Development Program, 2003, speaking about the Roma of Eastern Europe, mentions that one Roma out of five won't send kids to school for lack of decent clothing.[13] The loss of human dignity as a result of a lack of decent clothing appears from the words of a low-caste Indian woman, quoted by the Human Development Report 2006. She says *"We feel so dirty and unclean in the summer. We do not wash our clothes for weeks. People say, these Dalits are dirty and they smell. But how can we be clean without water?"*[14] Her words stress the importance of the right to clothing, but also that of the right to water.

f. The right to necessary social services and the right to social security

Article 25 UDHR also mentions *"necessary social services, and the right to security in the event of unemployment, sickness, disability, widowhood, old age or other lack of livelihood in circumstances beyond his control."* Art. 9 of the ICESCR says: *"The States Parties to the present Covenant recognize the right of everyone to social security, including social insurance."* In art. 10 the Covenant demands that special measures of protection and assistance should be taken on behalf of the family, children and pregnant women.

These articles are more specific than art. 22 of the UDHR. That also speaks of social security and says that *"Everyone, as a member of society, has the right to social security and is entitled to realization, through national effort and international co-operation and in accordance with the organization and resources of each State, of the economic, social and cultural rights indispensable for his dignity and the free development of his personality."* Article 22 of the UDHR is of a general character, introducing the section on ESC-rights and should be interpreted as meaning that everyone has to be socially secure and is entitled to a solid social basis for his or her existence. It covers all the articles of the section on ESC-rights. I take the articles 25 UDHR and 9, 10 ICESCR, to refer to the right to social security in a more specific sense.

The idea behind the right to social security (in this specific sense) is that nobody has to suffer want in the situations mentioned in article 25; a minimum level of livelihood is to be guaranteed. It seeks to ensure that even in situations of social distress—such as old age, disability, unemployment, illness, widowhood—people have the resources needed to live a life in human dignity. This may consist of financial support, or of provisions in kind in situations in which people do not have adequate financial resources, or cannot earn enough money to lead a dignified life or even, at the very least, to stay alive. This financial support can take the form of social insurance, where people receive benefits or services in recognition of contributions to an insurance scheme (retirement pensions, disability insurance, unemployment insurance). It can also take the form of income maintenance, where people receive cash without having contributed to an insurance scheme, in the event of unemployment, illness, disability and retirement[15]. (I will come back to the right to social security in the section about economic rights.)

The right to necessary social services, which is also mentioned by article 25 UDHR, implies more than financial support in the event of the lack of a livelihood. Many people do not have the capacities to develop and to adequately take care of themselves. They may even be deaf, blind, disabled, mentally retarded or handicapped, which is why all kinds of programs and services are needed to support their development, independence and empowerment. Generally, social services are delivered as part of the social and political system of a country. Therefore the type of services made available to citizens is dependant on the type of social and political system that the country has adopted.

The Committee on ESC-rights is preparing a General Comment on the right to social security. Towards that end it held a Day of General Discussion, where it stressed the importance of the right to social security. On behalf of the United Nations High Commissioner for Human Rights, Mr. Alessio Bruni said that the recognition of social security as a human right represented an essential bridge from needs-based charity to rights-based social justice.[16]

g. The right to water

The Human Development Report 2006 speaks of the right to water. Titled "Beyond Scarcity: Power, Poverty and the Global Water Crisis", the report says that clean water and sanitation can make or break human development, because they are fundamental to what people can do or what they can become. It obviously recognizes a right to water, when it says: *"Water, the stuff of life and a basic human right, is at the heart of a daily crisis faced by countless millions of the world's most vulnerable people—a crisis that threatens life and destroys livelihoods on a devastating scale".*[17]

However, the right to water is not mentioned in the UDHR or the ICESCR, perhaps because at their drafting, the issue had not yet seemed problematic. Nevertheless it is generally recognized by human rights experts and academics, sometimes as a right by itself, sometimes under the heading of the right to food, or the right to health and the right to housing.

The Committee on Economic, Social and Cultural Rights has dealt with the right to water in its General Comment No.15. It states that *"Water is a limited natural resource and a public good fundamental for life and health. The human right to water is indispensable for leading a life in human dignity. It is a prerequisite for the realization of other human rights."*[8] The Committee is of the view that a legal basis for the right to water can be found in the ICESCR, although 'water' is not explicitly mentioned by the Covenant. According to the Committee this right is covered by articles 11 and 12 of the covenant. Article 11, paragraph 1, of the Covenant provides for guarantees essential for securing an adequate standard of living, *"including adequate food, clothing and housing".* As the Covenant uses the word "including" this catalogue of rights is not to be seen as being exhaustive. The right to water clearly falls within the category of these guarantees. The Committee adds that the right to water is also inextricably related to the right to the highest attainable standard of health, the right to adequate housing and the right to food.

This is also the view of many others. At the Third World Water Forum, Kyoto, 16-23 March 2003, the Special Rapporteurs on adequate housing, the right to food, and the right to the highest attainable standard of physical and mental health jointly issued a statement, in which they emphasized the importance of the right to water. They confirmed that it is an essential resource for life and inextricably linked to the rights to adequate housing, food and the highest attainable standard of physical and mental health.[19]

As regards the linkage of the right to water with the right to housing, it should be borne in mind that, as has been said in the foregoing, the right to adequate housing is not merely about having a roof over one's head. Rather, it is the right of everyone to access to a safe, habitable, and affordable home, in which a dignified live can be lived. This includes access to properly maintained water facilities.

Water is also essential for the right to food to be realized. As drinking water, it can be regarded as included within the notion of food itself. If all other kinds of food are available but people do not have access to clean and sufficient drinking water, starvation and diseases will befall to them. Water is not only important as drinking water, it is also necessary to produce food.[20]

The right to water is also linked with the right to health. On the occasion of World Health day 2003, Paul Hunt, Special Rapporteur on the right to the enjoyment of the highest attainable standard of physical and mental health, stated that the human right to health is not simply the right to health care. It is also a right to the underlying determinants of health, including food and nutrition, housing, *access to safe drinking water and adequate sanitation*, and a healthy environment.[21] At the above mentioned Third World Water Forum in Kyoto, Sergio Vieira De Mello, High Commissioner for Human Rights, stated that water is essential to life itself as well as to good health. It can therefore be concluded that the right to water has been recognized as a human right and that it is protected by international law including through the International Covenant on Economic, Social and Cultural Rights.

However, many people, in particular the poor and other marginalized groups, have the greatest difficulty in getting access to sufficient and safe drinking water and to adequate sanitation. Insufficient or contaminated drinking water and unsanitary living conditions often result in diseases and are the main causes of infant and child mortality in developing countries. *"Yet, despite the centrality of the right to water to human dignity, one billion people still lack access to safe drinking water, more than 2 billion to proper sanitation and more than 3 million people die each year from water-borne diseases"*, so is said by Sergio Vieira De Mello.[22] This is in line with the findings of the Human Development Report 2006. The HDR 2006 says that one in five people living in the developing world do not have access to sufficient clean water, a suggested minimum of 20 liters per day, while average water use in Europe ranges between 200-300 liters per day and 575 liters in the United States. It estimates that 1.1 billion people lack access to clean water and 2.6 billion people lack access to decent sanitation. Almost 2 million children die each year for want of a glass of clean water and adequate sanitation. The report also mentions that the opportunities and choices of millions of women and young girls are restricted because they are forced to spend hours collecting and carrying water.

The lack of access to water cannot be attributed, or not mainly, to a general shortage of water. It is the different opportunities to get access to water that is the problem. Many people, in particular the poor, lack access to these basic needs for drinking water and decent sanitation, whereas many others have the disposal of an almost unlimited amount of water. Disparities in access within countries are widespread: 85% of the richest 20% of the population in developing countries have access to piped water, as opposed to 25% in the poorest 20%.

The Report argues that people in the rich countries, in particular in Europe and the US, tend to have short memories. They have sufficient access to water and hardly are aware of the problems that people face that do not have adequate access to water. But, in the past the situation was quite different. Life expectancy in the Europe of the beginning of the 19th century was only 40 years. From the late 19th century this picture started to change, due to increased income, better housing, improved nutrition and new medicine. But the most important factor was the improved sanitation, the separation of water from human excrement.

I will conclude this brief survey of social rights by mentioning that article 25 of the UVRM has a second paragraph that adds that mothers and children are entitled to special care and assistance. To some extent this is taken up in article 10 of the ICESCR, since this article requires protection and assistance to be given to the family, which is called the natural and fundamental group unit of society.

3. Economic rights

a. The right to property

Economic rights aim to provide people with an economic basis for a dignified life. The oldest economic right is the right to property. It is mentioned in the UDHR, although its position in the UDHR, in article 17, is somewhat remote from the place of the other economic, social and cultural rights. In fact most people do not regard it as belonging to this category: it is interpreted as a negative right, a right that requires others not to interfere in the property of the right-holder. It is not seen as a positive right, like the other economic, social and cultural rights, rights that—according to the traditional view—require others, in particular governments, to actively take steps to provide the right-holder with the object of the right.

The right to property was one of the natural rights described by Locke and functioned as the spearhead in the fight for individual freedom against feudalism.[23] It still is a very important right but curiously, after being mentioned in the UDHR, it no longer plays an important role in human rights documents. It is not mentioned in the International Covenant on Civil and Political Rights (ICCPR), nor in the ICESCR. The European Convention of Human Rights is silent on it. It does, however, pop up in 'Protocol No.1 to the European Convention for the Protection of Human Rights and Fundamental Freedoms, securing certain rights and freedoms other than those already included in the Convention.' Article 1 of this protocol states that everyone is entitled to the peaceful enjoyment of his possessions. Today, most national constitutions include the right to property but, like the UDHR, they generally place it under the category of CP-rights and not under that of ESC-rights.

The right to property often is seen as a cornerstone of capitalism. It offers the well off a means to protect their possessions. But we should be aware that the right to property is of vital importance to the poor too. Some poor people have a little piece of land and it can mean the difference between staying alive and starving from hunger. Having a piece of land provides people who do not have a job with the possibility of growing some food for themselves. Land may also be a symbol of their freedom, for if they do not own land anymore, they are at the mercy of other people giving, or not giving, them a job. In parts of India, many poor people belonging to the Dalits, the lowest rung of India's caste system, are denied access to landownership due to that very categorization, and because of that are forced to work in conditions determined by the upper class. Often, they are even expected to provide free labor.

One of the reasons that poor people remain poor is the absence of the possibility to borrow money. Property—in particular, land—would enable them to borrow against future earnings and to invest in production, the education of their children and other assets to reduce their vulnerability. In some countries, for instance, West Bengal, agricultural output and incomes rose following tenancy reform and recognition of the land rights of the poor.[24]

The Committee on Economic, Social and Cultural Rights, dealing with the situation in Paraguay, said in 1996 that the main reason for hunger and malnutrition of the indigenous population in Paraguay and the deprivation of their rights is linked to the severe problem of obtaining access to traditional and ancestral lands. It mentioned that all indigenous groups in the Chaco were expelled from their traditional land by cattle ranchers or industrial enterprises, with the result that *"in Paraguay today, 5 per cent of the population owns between 60 and 80 per cent of the national territory, a situation fraught with danger for Paraguayan peace and stability."*[25] The situation in Paraguay is far from unique.

When speaking about property one may, as I have done in the previous pages, refer to land as property. But the word is also often used to refer to intellectual property. There exists some tension between the right to (intellectual) property and human development. Protecting intellectual property may turn out to be to the detriment of poor people and countries because rules on intellectual property influence the terms on which poor countries can acquire and adapt the new technologies that they need to raise living standards and to fight socio-economic misery. These rules should take into consideration two objectives: on the one hand protecting ideas, methods and procedures from being copied without the permission of the inventors, thereby creating incentives for innovation, and on the other hand the need to spread the benefits of innovation and make the products available to as many people as possible.

The Human Development Report 2005 argues that the *"WTO's Trade-Related Intellectual Property Rights (TRIPS) agreement, along with "TRIPS plus" variants in regional and bilateral agreements, strikes the wrong balance* between the interests of technology holders and the wider public interest." The TRIPS agreement establishes a global regime for intellectual property rights that poses a threat to the development of poor countries, which must pay high prices to use patented technologies. It prioritizes the earnings of the patent holders over the needs of the poor. The TRIPS agreement threatens to widen the technological divide between developed and developing countries because it seeks to restrict or prevent the ability to copy technologies developed in economically advanced countries that has historically provided an important impetus and means for other countries to catch up. The Human Development Report 2005 mentions that in the 19th century, the United States copied British patents and that in the 20th century, Japan, the Republic of Korea, Taiwan and China have all upgraded technologies through reverse engineering and copying. "The space for such strategies has now been closed by the countries at the top of the technology ladder. With technology increasingly important to international trade competitiveness, the rising cost of technology imports could further marginalize many developing countries." [26]

In particular, in the field of health, the protection of intellectual property can have detrimental effects for the poor. Strengthened intellectual property rules will prevent cheap imitation drugs from entering the market, even though in many poor countries people cannot afford to buy expensive medicines, with the eventual result that they will suffer and die from a disease which is preventable or treatable.

b. *The right to work*

Besides the right to property, the right to work can also be considered an economic right. Today, the economic basis for a dignified life is not only, or mainly, achieved by having property, but by having work. The right is formulated in article 23 and 24 of the UDHR, and in articles 6, 7 and 8 of the ICESCR.

But, as mentioned above, having work does not guarantee a dignified life. Working conditions are often inhumane. Consider the labor of children in producing carpets and soccer balls and the poor working conditions in some factories of multinational firms. These multinational firms can improve overall welfare but, as is pointed out by the HDR 2000, they also can act to disempower poor people and to rob them of their dignity through hazardous and inhumane working conditions.[27] The UDHR and the ICESCR, therefore, do not restrict themselves to the right to work itself but also speak about work-*related* rights, such as the right to just and favorable remuneration, the right to just and favorable conditions of work, and the right to form and join trade unions. The right to strike does not occur in the UDHR, but it *is* included in article 8 of the ICESCR. The work-related rights are linked with an economic right (the right to work), but are themselves rather to be seen as social rights.

Although these rights are widely recognized by international documents, they are not widely respected. In particular women suffer disproportionately from a lack of respect for the right to work and work-related rights. They often do not have a contract, which exposes them to excessive levels of risk and insecurity. For example, according to the Human Development Report 2005, less than one-quarter of the women in Chile's fruit industry have a contract. *"Weak labor rights and discrimination against female workers, especially in core areas such as freedom of association and collective bargaining, limit the capacity of workers to negotiate reasonable wages and conditions."*[28]

Article 24 of the UDHR and article 7 of the ICESCR contain another work-related right, a very famous or—in the view of some—notorious right: the right to rest and leisure and to periodic holidays with pay. This is often quoted by the critics of economic, social and cultural rights to demonstrate the triviality of this entire category of rights. I will return to this alleged triviality in the next chapters.

c. *The right to (socio-economic) security*

Finally, again a few words on the right to social security, as described in article 25 of the UDHR. (It is also mentioned in article 9 of the ICESCR.) I have treated it as a social right in the foregoing section but here it must be said that it can also be regarded as an economic right, in addition to the right to property and the right to work. It is a right that guarantees a minimum economic level of existence, by providing financial support or support in kind in situations in which people do not have—or cannot earn—enough money to lead a dignified life, or at the very least, to stay alive. When people do not possess property and if they do not have work that supplies them with money, then the right to socio-economic assistance will at least provide them with an economic basis for a dignified life.

Again, this is a right that is widely recognized by UN documents but not widely respected. In Latin America, for instance, only 40% of employed workers are protected and have access to social security benefits. In East Asia the social security provisions are inadequate.[29]

But also in the United States and in various countries of Europe, many people live without an adequate economic basis for a decent life.

4. Cultural rights

a. *The right to education*

Article 26 speaks of the right to education. The UDHR says that elementary education shall be free and compulsory. It goes on to say, in its second paragraph, that education shall be directed to the full development of the human person and to the strengthening of respect for human rights and fundamental freedoms. It shall promote understanding and tolerance between nations and cultural groups. The right to education can, at least to an important degree, be seen as a *cultural* right. It is also, of course, of importance for people's economic positions and prospects: it will improve their chances of getting work, earning a living and making a career. The Human Development Report 2004 points out that investing resources in education is the first step out of the poverty trap.[30]

However, in many countries, opportunities for education are few. In Sub-Saharan Africa and South Asia, only a very few children attend school compared to in developed countries. The HDR 2005 says that, on average, a child born in Mozambique today can anticipate four years of formal education, whereas a child born in France will receive fifteen years at vastly higher levels of provision. Access to higher education remains a privilege available mainly to citizens of high-income countries. "*These education inequalities of today are the global social and economic inequalities of tomorrow.*"[31] In particular, the education of girls is limited due to gender inequalities. "*These deep gender disparities represent not just a violation of the universal right to education but also a threat to future human development prospects: girls' education is one of the most powerful catalysts for social progress across a wide range of indicators.*"[32]

b. *The right to participate in cultural life*

Article 27 of the UDHR, the final article of the paragraph on economic, social and cultural rights, contains other cultural rights. It speaks of the right "*freely to participate in the cultural life of the community, to enjoy the arts and to share in scientific advancement and its benefits.*" It also mentions the right "*to the protection of the moral and material interests resulting from any scientific, literary or artistic production of which he is the author.*" These rights are reiterated in article 15 of the ICESCR

c. *The right to enjoy one's culture*

It is striking that article 27, UDHR, does not speak of the right to preserve a cultural identity, or the right of cultural minorities. The right freely to participate in the cultural life of the community can hardly be interpreted as such a right. Article 27, UDHR, differs fundamentally from article 27 of the ICCPR which states, "*In those States in which ethnic, religious or linguistic minorities exist, persons belonging to such minorities shall not be denied the right, in community with the other members of their group, to enjoy their own culture, to profess and practice their own religion, or to use their own language.*" This formulation gives the opportunity, unlike article 27 of the UDHR, to interpret it as referring to a right to preserve a cultural identity, or the right of cultural minorities. Article 27 of the UDHR—and the UDHR in general—is silent on rights of cultural minorities, even though one would expect such a right to be included in a section on cultural rights. Why is it absent?

I have already suggested that the dominant ideology after the Second World War emphasized equal individual rights and non-discrimination.[33] Those who drafted the Universal Declaration of Human Rights of 1948 were reluctant to make any references to group-specific rights, rights that are related to membership of a cultural group. It was argued that the principle of equality, if adhered to strictly, would guarantee that every cultural group could preserve its identity. One of the reasons underlying the rejection of the idea of group-specific rights was the painful memories of the League of Nations' protection scheme of minorities.[34]

In the 1960s, however, a more sympathetic approach towards the rights of minorities emerged and accordingly, article 27 was included in the International Covenant on Civil and Political Rights, which can be seen as a right of cultural minorities. It must be stressed though, that the article does not allocate rights to groups but only to *persons* belonging to particular groups. Although it is difficult to see how such rights could be exercised other than in concert, they still are to be seen as rights of individuals rather than rights of groups.

5. Differences between CP-rights, and ESC-rights[35]

As mentioned before, the UDHR of 1948 was followed by many treaties, among which were the ICCPR and the ICESCR. The formulation of the socio-economic rights in the ICESCR and the monitoring procedures of these rights differ from the formulation and monitoring mechanisms of civil and political rights in the ICCPR. The formulations of the various rights were not yet different in the UDHR. The wording of the UDHR is, in general, very consistent and uniform. Both as regards civil and political rights and ESC-rights, the UDHR uses the formulation *"everyone has the right to ..."* It states that everyone has the right to life, liberty and security of the person (article 3), that everyone has the right to freedom of movement (article 14), that everyone has the right to freedom of thought, conscience and religion (article 18), that everyone has the right to freedom of opinion and expression (article 19), but also that everyone has the right to work, to free choice of employment and to just and favorable conditions of work (article 23), that everyone has the right to a standard of living adequate for the health and well-being of himself and his family (article 25), and that everyone has the right to education (article 26).

This wording was also adopted by the ICCPR, but not followed by the ICESCR. The ICCPR still states that everyone has the right to life (article 6), that everyone has the right to liberty and security of the person (article 9), that everyone shall have the right to freedom of thought, conscience and religion (article 18) and that everyone shall have the right to hold opinions without interference and the right to freedom of expression (article 19).

The wording of the rights in the ICESCR is more indirect. For example, it says that states parties recognize the right of everyone to the enjoyment of just and favorable conditions of work (article 7), that states parties undertake to ensure the right of everyone to form trade unions (article 8), that states parties recognize the right of everyone to social security (article 9), and that states parties recognize the right of everyone to an adequate standard of living (article 11).

These are not the only differences. The monitoring procedures of the two categories of rights also differ.

The ICCPR has three elements: a reporting procedure, a state complaint procedure and an individual complaint procedure. In the first procedure, the treaty demands that states parties periodically report on the measures they have taken to improve the effectuation of civil and political rights in their country. The reports are submitted to the Secretary General, who in turn submits them to the Human Rights Committee, established by the covenant (article 28) and consisting of independent experts of *"high moral character"*, who serve in their personal capacity. The Committee then eventually reports to the Economic and Social Council.

If a state has given prior consent to a state complaint procedure, the Committee can consider complaints against it lodged by another state. The Committee will then hear both the complaining state and the accused one.

In addition, an individual complaint procedure exists, regulated by the Optional Protocol to the International Covenant on Civil and Political Rights. If states have ratified this protocol, individual citizens can lodge a complaint against their state about a violation of their rights under the ICCPR.

The ICESCR, however, only has a reporting procedure. States parties are required to submit reports on the effectuation of economic, social and cultural rights to the Secretary-General, who in turn submits them to the Economic and Social Council. In comparison with the procedures of the ICCPR, it is rather weak.

If we look at the wording and monitoring procedures of both categories of rights, it cannot but be stated that ESC-rights are neglected in comparison with civil and political rights. However, it must immediately be added that the position of ESC-rights has become stronger in the course of time. In particular, the monitoring procedure of these rights has gained more force and impact, to some extent beyond the formal rules of the covenant.

6. Bridging the gap

The activities of the Committee on Economic, Social and Cultural Rights (CESCR) have contributed greatly to the reduction of the neglect of ESC-rights. This committee is the successor to a working group established by the Economic and Social Council (ECOSOC) and charged with the task of supervising the implementation of the provisions of the ICESCR. It consisted of representatives of governments but it did not function very well. So it was replaced by the formally-titled Committee on Economic, Social and Cultural Rights, a committee consisting of 18 independent experts, all acting in their personal capacity.[36] The Committee is not mentioned in the covenant itself, but it was established by a resolution of ECOSOC.[37] It started its activities in 1987 and has since then developed into an authoritative body.

The Committee plays an important role in the reporting procedure. The covenant prescribes, as mentioned, that states parties must submit reports to the Secretary General, who then transfers them to the Economic and Social Council. The Committee is authorized by the Council to deal with these reports. This reporting procedure aims at involving the state concerned in both a process of self-examination and a dialogue with the Committee on the implementation of ESC-rights in that state. As a start, a working group of the Committee drafts questions relevant to the special situation of the state concerned based on the data submitted by states and "all concerned individuals, bodies and non-governmental organizations". Then, at a session of the Committee, representatives of the state can amplify its report, which results in a constructive dialogue between the Committee and representatives of the state. In addition, NGOs are given the opportunity to present relevant information, although it should be noted, however, that regrettably few have taken advantage of this opportunity to date for providing the Committee with additional or even contradictory information which it might not otherwise have had access to. At the end of the procedure, the Committee presents its concluding observations.

Another important activity of the Committee is the drafting of General Comments, general considerations on specific subjects.[38] General Comment, No. 1 details the reporting procedure by states parties, as described above. General Comment No. 2 deals with international technical assistance measures, mentioned in article 22 of the Covenant. General Comment No. 3, which is very famous, deals with the nature of the obligations of states parties and is an interpretation of article 2.1 of the ICESCR.

As an example of a general comment that deals with a particular right, General Comment No. 4 (1991) discusses the right to adequate housing. General Comment No. 5 covers persons with disabilities. General Comment No. 6 is about older persons. General Comment No. 7 is, again, about the right to adequate housing and in particular, about forced evictions. General Comment No. 8 deals with a difficult issue, the relationship between economic sanctions and respect for economic, social and cultural rights. General Comment No. 9 discusses the domestic application of the covenant and General Comment. No. 10 the role of national human rights institutions in the protection of economic, social and cultural rights. General Comment No. 11

talks about the right to education, especially plans of action for primary education. General Comment No. 12 pays attention to the right to adequate food. General Comment No. 13 is, again, about the right to education. General Comment No. 14 deals with the right to the highest attainable standard of health. General Comment No. 15 discusses the right to water. General Comment No.16 deals with the equal rights of men and women to the enjoyment of all economic, social and cultural rights (art.3). General Comment No. 17 is on the right of everyone to benefit from the protection of the moral and material interests resulting from any scientific, literary or artistic production of which he is the author (art.15). Finally General Comment No. 18 discusses the right to work (art.6). As can be seen, the General Comments deal with various aspects of ESC-rights, with procedures as well as with the contents of particular rights.

There is also a third activity of the Committee that should be mentioned. Periodically, it organizes discussion meetings on a particular aspect of the ICESCR. Such meetings were held for example, on the right to food, the right to healthcare and the right to social security, which contributed to a better understanding of the contents of the ICESCR and to a clarification as to what aspects of the various rights are justiciable.

All in all, the position of the Committee on Economic, Social and Cultural Rights has become rather influential. It now shows similarities in stature to the Human Rights Committee, the supervising body of the International Covenant on Civil and Political Rights. But while in this context, I would like to mention another UN body that has strengthened the position of ESC-rights: the UN-Sub Commission on the Prevention of Discrimination and the Protection of Minorities, since 1999 titled the Sub-Commission on the Promotion and Protection of Human Rights, with protection of "racial, national, religious and linguistic minorities" against discrimination now forming only part (a) of its purview. This sub-commission has been very active in the field of ESC-rights, which have become one of the fixed issues on its agenda[39].

It cannot be denied that because of these developments, the position of ESC-rights has been strengthened. Neither can it be denied that ESC-rights still are neglected when compared to civil and political rights. An example of the less prominent position of ESC-rights today is the lack of an optional protocol, which would offer a provision to individual citizens to lodge a complaint against their state, provided that the state has recognized the protocol. The ICCPR recognizes such a protocol, whereas the ICESCR does not. The Optional Protocol to the ICCPR has strengthened the position of civil and political rights and it probably would contribute to the realization of ESC-rights. A protocol to the ICESCR is being proposed by many. The CESCR submitted the idea to the World Conference on Human Rights in Vienna in 1993. When the conference hesitated over adopting the idea, the CESCR then submitted a draft of an optional protocol to the UN Commission on Human Rights, which has not yet taken a decision.

7. Regional ESC-rights

ESC-rights are not only neglected in UN circles. In Europe, their position lags behind that of civil and political rights, although also there it is improving. Within the context of the Council of Europe, several treaties have been adopted. The best known is the already mentioned European Convention for the Protection of Human Rights and Fundamental Freedoms, often called the European Convention of Human Rights, (ECHR, Rome, 1950) which contains civil and political rights. The European Social Charter (ESC) appeared in Turin in 1961. This, the social counterpart of the ECHR, contains ESC-rights, although it does not use this term.

The monitoring procedures for civil and political rights of these European treaties are also more advanced, strict and precise than those for the ESC-rights. The procedure of the ECHR is exemplary. Its monitoring body, the European Court of Human Rights, settled in Strasbourg, has acquired an impressive reputation. Citizens of European countries that are party to the treaty can lodge a complaint against their government if their rights under the convention are violated and if national juridical remedies are exhausted. The counterpart of the ECHR, i.e. the European Social Charter, still does not have the same standing as the ECHR, notwithstanding some improvements. The Additional Protocol to the European Social Charter of 1988 and a Protocol amending the European Social Charter of 1991, as well as the Second Additional Protocol of 1995 have definitely improved the status of the rights of the Social Charter. The Charter has a reporting procedure and states parties have an obligation to report on the social rights situation in their country. Three committees are involved in this reporting procedure. The first committee, called the European Committee of Social Rights (of thirteen independent experts elected by the Committee of Ministers) examines the reports from a juridical and legal perspective, and assesses whether states have complied with their obligations under the ESC. The Committee has been willing to receive "shadow-reports" from various national bodies which could be considered alongside the formal report of the state. Its decisions, known as "conclusions", are published every year. If a state takes no action on a Committee decision to the effect that it does not comply with the Charter, the second committee, the Governmental Committee (composed of representatives of the Contracting Parties to the Charter and assisted by observers from European trade unions and employer organisations) prepares a proposal for the third committee, the Committee of Ministers, which then addresses a recommendation to the state involved, asking it to change the situation in law and/or in practice.

Since the adoption of the Second Additional Protocol, certain organizations (such as organizations of employers and employees, as well as international non-governmental organizations with consultative status that are recognized by the Governmental Committee) are allowed to lodge complaints of violations of the European Social Charter.[40] This certainly is a considerable improvement, although individual citizens are still not entitled to lodge complaints.

As for ESC rights in the Americas the American States adopted the American Declaration of the Rights and Duties of Man, in Bogotá, Colombia, in 1948. It was followed by the American Convention on Human Rights (also known as the Pact of San José, adopted Costa Rica, 1969).[41] The American Declaration contains both CP-rights and ESC-rights. For example article XI states that *"Every person has the right to the preservation of his health through sanitary and social measures relating to food, clothing, housing and medical care, to the extent permitted by public and community resources"*. The American *Convention* is more reserved with respect to ESC-rights. It has a chapter called "Chapter III: Economic, Social and Cultural Rights", but this has only one article, article 26, 'Progressive Development', that states *"The States Parties undertake to adopt measures, both internally and through international cooperation, especially those of an economic and technical nature, with a view to achieving progressively, by legislation or other appropriate means, the full realization of the rights implicit in the economic, social, educational, scientific, and cultural standards set forth in the Charter of the Organization of American States as amended by the Protocol of Buenos Aires."*

However, in 1988, an additional protocol to the Inter-American Convention on Human Rights was adopted: the Protocol of San Salvador. It includes various ESC-rights, and with respect to two rights—the right to freedom of trade unions and the right to education—also created the chance to lodge complaints, both for individuals and certain groups. As in Europe the American situation shows that ESC-rights are neglected compared to CP-rights but also hat the gap is being bridged.

Also other regions have human rights documents. The Council of the League of Arab States adopted the Arab Charter on Human Rights (1994), which contains mainly CP-rights. It does include also the right to work and the right to education, but it is rather silent on other ESC-rights. Article 38 states, *"The family is the basic unit of society, whose protection it shall enjoy."* and *"The State undertakes to provide outstanding care and special protection for the family, mothers, children and the aged"*. Article 39 continues with *"Young persons have the right to be afforded the most ample opportunities for physical and mental development"*. I doubt, however, whether these formulations can be interpreted as ESC-rights, for instance the right to health.

There is also a Universal Islamic Declaration of Human Rights, 1981, which has one article that refers to ESC-rights. Its article XVIII, 'Right to Social Security', states, *"Every person has the right to food, shelter, clothing, education and medical care consistent with the resources of the community.*

This obligation of the community extends in particular to all individuals who cannot take care of themselves due to some temporary or permanent disability".

The African Charter on Human and Peoples' Rights (1981) also looks very promising: it offers individuals the chance to lodge complaints if their ESC-rights have been violated. However, the procedures for filing communications to the monitoring commission (the African Commission on Human and Peoples' Rights) still show some shortcomings, and it remains to be seen whether the charter will be very effective. The commission's jurisdiction turns out to be far from compulsory and NGOs are hesitant in filing communications. Consequently, ESC rights have been deferred on the Commission's agenda.

8. The treatment of ESC-rights in constitutions

Domestic constitutions also treat both categories of rights differently. Take, for example, the Constitution of the Netherlands. It wholeheartedly speaks of rights when it comes to CP-rights, stating, for instance, that *"Everyone shall have the right to manifest freely his religion or belief,"* and that *"The right of association shall be recognized."* But it is less willing to use the notion of a right in the case of ESC-rights. It then states, for instance, that *"It shall be the concern of the authorities to promote the provision of sufficient employment,"* and *"It shall be the concern of the authorities to secure the means of subsistence of the population and to achieve the distribution of wealth."* It also states that *"The authorities shall take steps to promote the health of the population,"* and that *"Education shall be the constant concern of the Government."* Obviously, CP-rights and ESC-rights are treated differently.

To take another example: in the Constitution of India, part III, 'Fundamental Rights', contains mostly CP-rights. These rights can be invoked before a court. The constitution also contains a Part IV, 'Directive Principle of State Policy' which, although the Constitution does not use the formulations of the UDHR or of the ICESCR, can be said to contain ESC-rights. However, they do not receive the same treatment as the CP-rights of Part III. The Constitution itself explicitly states of Part IV that, *"The provisions contained in this Part shall not be enforced by any court..."*

The Constitution of Nigeria also treats CP-rights differently from ESC-rights. In its Chapter IV, headed 'Fundamental Rights', it mentions the right to life, the right to fair hearing, the right to freedom of expression and the right to freedom of choice. It uses formulations such as *"everyone has a right to life,"* or *"Every person shall be entitled to freedom of thought, conscience and religion..."* Provisions that seem to cover ESC-rights can be found in Chapter II, 'Fundamental Objectives and directive Principles of State Policy'.

There, different wordings appear. For instance, article 17 states that, "*....in furtherance of the social order....governmental actions shall be humane; .....The State shall direct its policy towards ensuring that: a) all citizens, without discrimination on any group whatsoever, have the opportunity for securing adequate means of livelihood as well as adequate opportunity to secure suitable employment; b) conditions of work are just and humane, and that there are adequate facilities for leisure and for social, religious and cultural life; c) the health, safety and welfare of all persons in employment are safeguarded and not endangered or abused; d) there are adequate medical and health facilities for all persons.....*"

The situation in the United States of America for ESC-rights is even worse as it relates to ESC-rights. The USA has a Bill of Rights (which refers to the Amendments—in fact the first ten amendments—to the Constitution. In none of these amendments can ESC-rights be found, except for Amendment XIII. This reads: "*Neither slavery nor involuntary servitude, except as a punishment for crime whereof the party shall have been duly convicted, shall exist within the United States, or any place subject to their jurisdiction*" While this certainly contains aspects of the right to work, other ESC-rights are completely absent.

Many other examples can be advanced that illustrate that national constitutions treat ESC-rights differently from CP-rights. It must also, however, be added that many constitutions can be found that seemingly treat both categories of rights on the same footing. Perhaps not surprisingly, given the primary role of the former USSR in promoting ESC-rights, while Chapter 2 of the Russian Constitution, 'Rights and Liberties of Man and Citizen' states that "*Everyone is guaranteed the right to freedom of conscience, to freedom of religious worship....*" and that "*Everyone has the right to freedom of thought and speech*", it also states, in the same vein and without equivocation, that, "*Everyone has the right to a home...*", that "*Everyone has the right to healthcare and medical assistance*" and that "*Everyone has the right to education.*"

The South-African Constitution is exemplary. Chapter 2 of its Bill of Rights mentions CP-rights and ESC-rights using similar wordings. For instance, it states that "*Everyone has the right to privacy...*", that "*Everyone has the right to freedom of conscience, religion, thought, belief and opinion...*" and that "*Everyone has the right to freedom of expression...*" But is also states that "*Everyone has the right to have access to adequate housing...*" and that "*Everyone has the right to have access to a) healthcare services, including reproductive healthcare...; b) sufficient food and water...; and c) social security, including, if they are unable to support themselves and their dependants, appropriate social assistance.*"

It will be obvious that an exemplary formulation of ESC-rights does not guarantee the disappearance of socio-economic misery, although it is true that the democratic governments elected in South Africa since 1994 have placed poverty and inequality at the center of their development agendas. It is also true that public expenditures on such items as housing, electricity, water, education and health have been increased. And indeed, as reported by the UNDP, four and a half million people have gained access to potable water, and 600,000 inexpensive houses are under construction. South Africa now also has free and compulsory 10 year education, as well as free medical care for pregnant women and for children under six years of age[42]. Nevertheless socio-economic misery still is widespread within the country. Pediatrician Hoosen Coovadia, Professor of HIV/AIDS Research at the Nelson Mandela Medical School of the University of KwaZulu-Natal (KZN), has said that high unemployment rates, poverty and lack of access to basic services, such as electricity, running water and housing, had thrown South Africa into a *"huge crisis"*, causing *"serious unhappiness"* among its population. *"As long as we cannot control poverty, we won't be able to control the HIV/AIDS pandemic,"* a pandemic that, with a quarter of all deaths in South Africa reported to be Aids-related is one of the greatest challenges the country has faced [43]

9. Neglect of ESC-rights

To summarize: Despite formal recognition of ESC-rights in international treaties and declarations, and in many national constitutions, further investigation reveals that the wording of these rights and the procedures for maintaining and upholding these rights are weaker than those of CP-rights, leading to the overall conclusion that ESC-rights are treated as second-rate rights. The position of international ESC-rights has been improved recently, but these improvements do not undo the factual neglect of ESC-rights in comparison with civil and political rights.

A similar statement can be made about domestic ESC-rights. In addition, examples chosen at random from various documents, e.g. reports of the UNDP, show that these rights are seriously violated. Why so much neglect and why so many violations that hardly cause protest and indignation?

ESC-rights do not live in the imagination and awareness of politicians, citizens and non-governmental organizations—is it that their recognition, assertion and provision might threaten powerful domestic interests and ideologies? ESC-rights rank well below civil and political rights and many people, including academics who should know better, think only of CP-rights when speaking of human rights. For instance, Kymlicka, speaking of human rights, refers to civil and political rights.[44] He consistently regards the human rights idea as providing *"a tool for protecting vulnerable individuals from abuse by their political leaders"*, and *"a shield for the weak against the abuse of political power."*[45] He seems to restrict the human rights idea to the political area, whereas ESC-rights really seek to extend the protection of the vulnerable and the weak to the economic, social and cultural domain. ESC-rights do not take part in Kymlicka's conception of human rights. Nor is he the only one who neglects them.

Philip Alston asserts that *"whether one takes the number of resolutions adopted, the length and incisiveness of the relevant debates, the emphasis adopted in fact-finding, the focus of the studies undertaken, economic, social and cultural rights continue to be very highly neglected or ignored."*[46] Many authors state that ESC-rights are not really acknowledged in many parts of the world and that states and individuals can be found that are of the view that ESC-rights are not really human rights.[47] Matthew Craven points out that there is an almost universal acceptance of the indivisibility and interdependency of human rights, but that in practice ESC-rights are not treated on the same footing as civil and political rights. He adds that the international community allows ESC-rights to be violated, whereas violations of civil and political rights raise enormous indignation and abhorrence: the massive violations of ESC-rights appear to be less unbearable than violations of civil and political rights.[48] Michael Windfuhr, of World Hunger Notes, says that both at the national and international level, ESC rights have been discriminated against, relative to political and social rights.[49] The draft Charter of Fundamental Rights of the European Union, 2000, is of the same view as it states that *"in the international human rights system, esc-rights are provided for with weaker instruments and have been largely neglected by international law. This discrimination against esc-rights should however not be used as an argument for continuing discrimination in the future."*[50]

Nor is it only authors or politicians who rank ESC-rights below civil and political rights: NGOs definitely have a keener eye for the latter, as pointed out by Paul Hunt when he observes that, *"Social and economic rights continued to be the step-children or illegitimate offspring of the human rights movement, especially on the part of NGOs based in the West."*[51] The interest of NGOs in participating in the monitoring procedures of ESC-rights is half-hearted. Human rights NGOs are very active in the field of civil and political rights, but play a less prominent role in the field of ESC-rights. Of course, there exist many NGOs fighting for a world without poverty, like Oxfam-Novib and HIVOS, and they certainly contribute to the reduction of socio-economic misery, but they are not *human rights* NGOs. The latter often restrict themselves to promoting CP-rights. Within Amnesty International (AI) a debate has started on whether the organization should become more active with regard to ESC-rights. The preliminary result is that AI has widened its scope to include ESC-rights, but that scope is focused on *discrimination* in the field of ESC-rights. The question AI is concerned with seems less to be whether ESC-rights are violated, than whether the enjoyment of these rights are withheld from some people without any acceptable reason while granted to others. In the document "Human Rights and Privatisation", 2005, AI also said that states should promote and protect services which are essential for the enjoyment of human rights. When people have a right to particular services the state has to ensure that there is no discrimination in access to specific services, and, so AI continues, no denial thereby of the service itself.[52]

10. Why are ESC-rights neglected?

The underlying reason for the neglect of ESC-rights when compared to civil and political rights, it is generally argued, is that these categories of rights are seen as different by nature. This essential difference justifies treating them differently, i.e. embodying the rights in different treaties and using different monitoring procedures. These differences in treatment in turn strengthen the idea that the rights of the two categories are different by nature. It's a tautological argument. The alleged essential difference between the two categories of rights has much to do with the duties upon states that exist as the corollary of the rights to be enjoyed by individuals.[53]

Rights for one imply duties for others. The idea of a right is that a certain interest or need of someone is protected by placing others under a duty—if not to fulfill it, at least not to abrogate or prevent it. For example, a right to healthcare entails that my interest in being healthy is protected by assuming that others have a duty not to damage my health and even to look after me when I am ill. Of course, it should be more clearly defined who the others involved are, but for a right to exist somebody must have a duty. If no one has a duty, if no one has to mind about the alleged right of an individual, then that individual does not have a right. And what is a right to food, with which no one has to comply?

It is generally assumed that governments are the main 'norm-receivers' of human rights, to use an expression of Galtung.[54] Or, to put it another way, governments are taken to be the main duty-bearers of human rights. They are responsible for ensuring the protection and enjoyment of rights.

Duties can be either negative or positive. A negative duty is a duty to refrain from doing something, whereas positive duties are duties to actively take action. Traditionally, civil and political rights have been considered as negative rights and that ESC-rights have been seen as positive rights. The right to freedom of belief implies a duty for others not to interfere with the belief of the right-holder.[55] The right to physical integrity means that others should abstain from doing anything that could do physical harm to the right-holder. On the other hand, the right to adequate housing is regarded as a right that requires others, in particular, a government, to provide the right-holder with adequate housing. The right to food implies a duty for the government to provide right-holders with the means that ensure they do not starve.

This difference between positive and negative rights has many consequences, according to the traditional view. Because ESC-rights are positive rights, they are less clear than the negative civil and political rights. The contents of ESC-rights become difficult to define in advance as no moral consensus on their contents exists. People will have different opinions on the contents of socio-economic rights: it cannot be determined in general terms what action, and by what duty-bearer, is to be taken. Even when it is assumed that the government is the duty-bearer concerned, it is still unclear what specific action should be taken by the government. What actions does a government have to take in the field of healthcare as a consequence of the right to healthcare? What measures are required by the right to adequate housing? On the other hand, the contents of civil and political rights are clear from the outset. They require abstinence. That is clear and transparent. Duty-bearers know exactly what has to be done: they should refrain from doing anything that could violate the freedom of a right-holder in a particular field.[56]

Another consequence of the different nature of the two categories of rights regards the costs of implementation. Since—still according to the traditionalist view—the correlative duty of civil and political rights consists of abstinence, the financial costs of implementation are minimal to zero. Accordingly, negative civil and political rights can be realized immediately, totally and with regard to everyone.[57] For example, it is argued, everyone's right to freedom of religion can be immediately and totally realized because it only requires that others refrain from interfering.

The implementation of ESC-rights, however, requires financial efforts and investments plus program planning and implementation by the state, and is dependent on the financial resources of the state concerned. That means that the implementation of ESC-rights only can be realized partially, gradually and selectively: governments will have to weigh their various duties flowing from the rights of various people and the costs they imply. Eventually, it would be determined whose rights should be implemented, to what extent, in which order and when.[58]

The different nature of both categories of rights also has consequences for the possibility of determining whether someone is accountable for the violation of a right. The violation of a negative right implies that harm has been done. The violator has done something that he or she should not have done. Therefore the violator can be held accountable for the injustice that is committed. Traditionalists doubt, however, whether the notions of violation and accountability can be used with respect to ESC-rights. Poverty, famine, unemployment, illiteracy, homelessness, and other socio-economic misery are not the result of intentional acts by people. They are regrettable and deplorable, it is traditionally argued, but not to be seen as the accountable acts of responsible actors.[59] And if it can be accepted that some people, or some agencies, could have done something to prevent the deplorable socio-economic misery, and therefore to some extent can be reproached for something, they are not to be reproached for having committed an injustice, but for having omitted to do well.[60]

11. The argument against ESC rights as real, universal human rights

The alleged differences between the two categories of rights raise doubts regarding their status as human rights.

Many query whether ESC-rights really can be called *human* rights, rights that people have as human beings and that enable them to lead a dignified life. Cranston is of the view that human rights should be able to pass the test of 'paramount importance', that is, that the protection of some interests are of paramount importance for a dignified life. Civil and political rights protect such interests, thus they can pass the test of paramount importance. But ESC-rights can not, for while, of course, people prefer to have the objects of these rights rather than be in want of them, the benefits they provide are not actually of paramount importance: people can have a dignified life without them. For instance, argues Cranston, social or economic security and holidays with pay (article 22 and 24 UDHR respectively) are important, but not of paramount importance.[61]

A second criticism concludes from the vagueness of ESC-rights that they are not genuine *rights*. Some go so far as to qualify ESC-rights as "manifesto rights", or even as Letters to Santa Claus. For the notion of a right to be used meaningfully, they aver, it should be possible to determine what duties are implied and what duty-bearers should do or not do. If not, the notion of a right is meaningless.[62] Civil and political rights can be seen as real rights because they have as their correlatives identifiable duties. ESC-rights, however, are different because it is difficult to determine what specific duties and duty-bearers are involved. It is for this reason that many people avoid using the term 'duty' and prefer terms such as 'political goals' or 'aspirations'.

Robertson and Merrills regard the International Covenant on Economic, Social and Cultural Rights (ICESCR) as a 'promotional convention'. This implies that it does not contain duties that *"the parties are required to implement immediately, but rather lists standards which they undertake to promote and which they pledge themselves to secure progressively, to the greatest extent possible, having regard to their resources."*[63] The covenant itself appears to be aware of the particular nature of ESC-rights because it does not expect states to realize the rights immediately, totally and with regard to everyone. Article 2 states that each state party *"undertakes to take steps ..., to the maximum of its available resources, with a view to achieving progressively the full realization of the rights recognized in the present Covenant by all appropriate means including particularly the adoption of legislative measures ..."*

The wording of this article differs from a similar article in the International Covenant on Civil and Political Rights (ICCPR). Article 2.1 of the ICCPR covenant states that each state party *"undertakes to respect and to ensure ... the rights recognized in the present Covenant ..."* Article 2.2. goes on to state that *"where not already provided for by existing legislative or other measures, each state party ... undertakes to take the necessary steps, ... to adopt such legislative or other measures as may be necessary to give effect to the rights recognized in the present Covenant."* The ICCPR also speaks of taking steps, but there is a slight, but important difference. The first paragraph of article 2 of the ICCPR says that states undertake to respect and ensure the rights. This indicates the existence of a direct obligation, notwithstanding the next obligation, that is, the obligation to take steps to adjust their national law to the requirements of the ICCPR. The latter obligation does not, however, remove the former, the direct obligation to respect and ensure the rights. That direct obligation to respect and ensure the rights includes, according to the third paragraph of the article, the provision of effective remedies when rights have been violated.[64].

A third criticism is targeted at the claim that ESC-rights are *universal* rights. Within this argument, two main lines can be distinguished. One line disputes the universality of norms in general, and therefore also the universality of human rights, both CP and ESC-rights. This is the line of cultural relativism that has accompanied the history of the Universal Declaration of Human Rights. During its drafting process, many argued that the idea of universal rights was an illusion, and also today many say that moral norms vary from culture to culture and that, accordingly, human rights are culturally defined. The second line opens fire on ESC-rights in particular. Civil and political rights, it says, are taken to be universal because they are rights of everyone against all others. But, so this arguments goes, ESC-rights are not universal, as they are not the rights of everyone against all others but, at best, the rights of citizens against their governments.[65] This clearly demonstrates that the word 'universality' has different meanings, a point I will clarify in chapters 9 and 10.

Finally, libertarians raise a fourth objection to ESC-rights.[66] They point out that social rights are *morally disputable* because their implementation is financed by taxes and citizens are compelled to contribute financially to their implementation by governments. This enforced contribution amounts to a violation of the property of others and to a limitation of their freedom. It is the opposition to ESC-rights by libertarians such as Hayek, Nozick and Narveson that has had a definite impact on political thinking, supporting as it does the liberal, capitalist market economy. The Swedish historian, Johan Norberg, together with many others are proponents of this libertarian freedom in the economic field.[67] They argue that people have a right to use their property as they think fit, that relationships between people should be based on free contracts and that saving and investing should be promoted and rewarded. They see taxes as a kind of penalty for good behavior: as if people who have worked hard and saved more than their neighbors are liable to a fine. President George W. Bush appears to be an adherent of a trickle-down economics. He has introduced tax-cuts, benefiting mainly the rich, who have as a result profited financially. Many others appear to be adherents of this libertarianism. President Bush of the USA showed his libertarian presidential agenda by these remarks about what is nonetheless a heavily state-subsidized American farm economy: *"The best way to make sure we've got a strong farm economy and to make sure our economy recovers from the recession is to let people keep their own money. I believe that when you let a person keep his own—his or her own money, they're going to spend it. And when they spend it, it increases demands for goods and services. And with an increase of demand for goods and services, somebody has got to produce that good and service. And when they produce it, it means somebody's going to find work."*[68]

It is these four criticisms that will be the object of study in the following chapters, in which I hope to refute these criticisms and to demonstrate that ESC-rights are genuine, universal human rights.

BIBLIOGRAPHY

Alston, Ph., 'The United nations and the Elliptical Notion of the Universality of Human Rights', in: *Is Universality in Jeopardy: report of a symposium organised by the United Nations in connection with the commemoration of the fortieth anniversary of the Organisation, Geneva, 16-17 December 1985* (New York: United Nations, 1987).

Alston, Ph., 'Denial and neglect', in: Richard Reoch (ed.), *Human Rights, the new consensus* (London: Regency Press, 1994).

Betten, L., 'De internationale bescherming van economische en sociale rechten', in: Petrus van Dijk (ed.), *Rechten van de Mens in Mundiaal en Europees perspectief* (Nijmegen: Ars Aequi Libri, 1991).

Bloch, Anne-Christine, 'Minorities and Indigenous Peoples', in: Asbjorn Eide, Catarina Krause and Alan Rosas, *Economic, Social and Cultural Rights* (Dordrecht, Boston, London: Martinus Nijhoff Publishers, 1995).

Cassese, A., *Human Rights in a Changing World* (Cambridge: Polity Press, 1990).

Cliteur, Paul, 'Neo-Liberal Globalism and Philosophical Presuppositions', in: Nieuwenhuys, Eva (ed.) *Neo-Liberal Globalism and Social Sustainable Globalisation* (Leiden,Boston: Brill 2006)

Coomans, A.P.M., *De werkzaamheden van het VN-Comité inzake economische, sociale en culturele rechten*, in: *NJCM Bulletin* 17, nr.8 (1992.).

Cranston, M., *What are Human Rights?* (London, Sydney and Toronto:The Bodley Head, 1973).

Craven, Matthew, *The International Covenant on Economic, Social and Cultural Rights* (Oxford: Clarendon Press, 1998).

Dower, Nigel, *An Introduction to Global Citizenship* (Edinburgh: University Press, 2003)

Eide, Asbjorn, and Rosas, Alan, 'Economic, Social and Cultural Rights: A Universal Challenge', in: Asbjorn Eide, Catarina Krause and Allan Rosas, *Economic, Social and Cultural Rights* (Dordrecht/Boston/London: Martinus Nijhoff Publishers, 1995).

Flinterman, Cees, 'De ondeelbaarheid van de rechten van de mens', in: A.P.M. Coomans, A.W. Heringa en I. Westendorp (ed.), *De toenemende betekenis van economische, sociale en culturele rechten* (Leiden: Stichting NJCM-boekerij, 1994).

Forsythe, David P., *Human Rights in International Relations* (Cambridge: Cambridge University Press, 2000).

Fried, C., *Right and Wrong* (Cambridge Massachussettes: Harvard University Press, 1978).

Galenkamp, M., *Individualism versus Collectivism* (Rotterdam, Rotterdamse filosofische studies, 1993).

Galtung, J., 'The Universality of Human Rights Revisited: Some Less Applaudable Consequences of the Human Rights Tradition', in: Asbjörn Eide en Bernt Hagtvet (ed.), *Human rights in perspective: A global assessment* (Oxford: Blackwell 1992).

Gewirth, A., 'Are There Any Absolute Rights', in: J. Waldron, *Theories of rights* (Oxford: Oxford University Press, 1984).

Gray, J., 'Classical Liberalism, Positional Goods and the Politicization of Poverty', in: A. Ellis en K. Kumar (ed.), *Dilemmas of Liberal Democracies* (London: Tavistock publications, 1983).

Hoof, G.J.H. van, 'The Legal Nature of Economic, Social and Cultural Rights: a Rebuttal of Some Traditional Views', in: *The Right to Food: From Soft to Hard Law* (Utrecht: Netherlands Institute of Human Rights, 1984).

Hunt, Paul, *Reclaiming Social Rights: International and Comparative Perspectives* (Aldershot: Dartmouth, 1996)

Ignatieff, Michael, *Whose Universal Values?* (Amsterdam, The Hague: Praemium Erasmianum Essay, 1999).

Kreide, Regina, 'Poverty, Human Rights and Responsibility', *Unesco Poverty Project*, 2002,http://portal.unesco.org/shs/fr/file_download.php/f801211fd968ea18aac401d5da3f7a79Kreide.pdf, retrieved February 2007

Kymlicka, W., *Multicultural Citizenship: a liberal theory of minority rights* (Oxford: Clarendon Press, 1995).

Kymlicka, W., *Politics in the Vernacular: Nationalism, Multiculturalism and Citizenship* (Oxford University Press, 2001)

Martin, Rex, *A System of Rights* (Oxford: Clarendon Press, 1997).

Nowak, Manfred, 'The right to Education', in: Asbjørn Eide, Catarina Krause en Allan Rosas (ed.), *Economic, Social and Cultural Rights* (Dordrecht, Boston and London: Martinus Nijhoff Publishers, 1995).

Office of the High Commissioner for Human Rights, *Human Rights and Poverty Reduction* (New York, Geneva: United Nations, 2004)

Orwin, Clifford, and Thomas Pangle, 'The Philosophical Foundation of Human Rights', in: Marc F. Plattner (ed.), *Human Rights in Our Time* (Boulder and London: Westview Press, 1984).

Plant, R. 'Needs, agency and welfare rights', in: J.D. Moon, *Responsibility, rights and Welfare, The Theory of the Welfare State* (Boulder: Westview Press, 1988).

Plant, Raymond, *Modern Political Thought* (Oxford etc.: Basil Blackwell, 1991).

Pogge, Thomas, *World Poverty and Human Rights, Cosmopolitan Responsibilities and Reforms* (Cambridge: Polity Press, 2002/2003)

Raz, J. *The Morality of Freedom* (Oxford: Clarendon Press, 1986).

Robertson, A.H., J.G. Merills, *Human Rights in the World* (Manchester, New York: Manchester University Press, 1992).

Staal, C.J. 'Het Herziene Europees Sociaal Handvest', in: *NCJM-Bulletin* 22, nr.3 (1997).

Tomasevski, Katarina, 'The Right to Development: Perspectives from Human Rights Law', in: Lars Adam Rehof en Claus Gulmann (red.), *Human Rights in Domestic Law and Development Assistance Policies of the Nordic Countries* (Kopenhagen and Dordrecht: Nijhoff, 1989).

Williams, Maurice, 'Human centred development', in: Richard Reoch (ed.), *Human Rights, the new consensus* (New York, London: Regency Press, 1994).

ENDNOTES

1. HDR 2005, p.17.
2. http://hdr.undp.org/hd, retrieved September 2006.
3. Kreide 2002/2007, p.1.
4. http://www.fao.org/english/newsroom/news/2002/9620-en.html, retrieved August 2006.
5. http://www.fao.org/docrep/009/a0750e/a0750e00.htm, retrieved February 2007
6. Alternatives, Action and Communication Network for International Development, http://www.alternatives.ca/article511.html, retrieved August 2006
7. http://www.unhchr.ch/huricane/huricane.nsf/0/271A763E727C481FC1256C7E002B1201?opendocument.
8. http://www.unhabitat.org/content.asp?typeid=19&catid=282&cid=789, retrieved February 2007.
9. HDR 2000, p.33.
10. See Choike, a portal dedicated to improving the visibility of the work done by NGOs and social movements from the South., http://www.choike.org/nuevo_eng/informes/1162.html, retrieved January 2007.
11. http://www.hrw.org/doc/?t=hivaids&document_limit=0,5#program, retrieved January 2007.
12. http://focus.hms.harvard.edu/1994/Oct7_1994/Community.html
13. http://roma.undp.sk, retrieved February 2007.
14. HDR 2006, p.48.
15. http://en.wikipedia.org/wiki/Social_security, retrieved Februari 2007.
16. http://www.ohchr.org/english/bodies/cescr/discussion.htm, retrieved Februari 2007.
17. HDR 2006, p.1.
18. Economic and Social Council, E/C.12/2002/11, 20 January 2003.
19. http://www.unhchr.ch/huricane/huricane.nsf/(Symbol)/HR.03.22.En?OpenDocument, retrieved 20 February, 2007.
20. Report submitted by the Special Rapporteur on the right to food, Jean Ziegler, E/CN. 4/2003/5410, January 2003.
21. http://www.unhchr.ch/huricane/huricane.nsf/view01/CADD06F385E4474AC1256D01004AD53A opendocument, retrieved January 2007.
22. Sergio Vieira De Mello http://www.unhchr.ch/huricane/huricane.nsf/(Symbol)/OHCHR.STM.03.14.En?OpenDocument, retrieved January 2007.
23. Hunt 1996, p.9.
24. Human Development Report 2005, p.71.
25. http://www.unhchr.ch/tbs/doc.nsf/(Symbol)/2748ffff2b0ce5e2c12563610046adbd?Opendocument, retrieved 12-08-2006.
26. Human Development Report 2005, p.135.
27. HDR 2000, p.79.
28. HDR 2005 p.124.
29. HDR 2000 p.22.
30. HDR 2004, p.39. See also Nowak 1995: 189, Human Development Report 2005 p.54.
31. HDR 2005, p.24.
32. HDR 2005, p.24.
33. Bloch 1995, p.312.
34. Robertson & Merills 1992, p.19, Kymlicka 1995, pp.57,58.
35. André Frankovits, at a Human Rights Conference of the Human Rights Council of Australia, said that the division between the two categories of rights persists today. He further mentioned that many governments in industrialized countries still maintain that economic, social and cultural rights are not real rights but rather statements of aspiration for a better life, whereas many governments in the southern region argue "in a similar vein that they are addressing these rights as a priority over civil and political rights. The arguments of the Cold War persist in the

	politics of the New World order." http://www.hrca.org.au/Trick_or_Treat.htm, retrieved Februari 2007.
36	Coomans 1992, p.862.
37	ECOSOC Rresolution 1985/17 of 28 May 1985.
38	To review the Committee's General Comments, see Committee on Economic, Social and Cultural Rights: General Comments, at http://www.ohchr.org/english/bodies/cescr/comments.htm.
39	The sub-commission also (in 1988) proposed appointing a Special Rapporteur on economic, social and cultural rights and later, in addition to this post, appointed a special rapporteur on extreme poverty and adequate housing.
40	http://www.coe.int/T/E/Human_Rights/Esc/4_Collective_complaints, retrieved Febrauri 2007; see also Staal 1997, p.349.
41	At present, 24 of the 35 OAS's member states are parties to the Convention: Argentina, Barbados, Brazil, Bolivia, Chile, Colombia, Costa Rica, Dominica, Dominican Republic, Ecuador, El Salvador, Grenada, Guatemala, Haiti, Honduras, Jamaica, Mexico, Nicaragua, Panama, Paraguay, Perru, Suriname, Uraguay, and Venezuela.
42	http://www.undp.org/povertyreport/countryprofiles/safrica1.html, October 2005.
43	http://www.afroaidsinfo.org/public/Home/news153.htm, October 2005.
44	Kymlicka 2001, p.73.
45	Kymlicka 2001, pp.82, 88, 89.
46	Alston 1994: 111.
47	Flinterman 1994, p.5, Eide 1995, p.17.
48	Craven 1998, p.9.
49	http://www.worldhunger.org/articles/global/foodashumrgt/windfuhr.htm
50	http://www.europarl.europa.eu/charter/civil/pdf/con156_en.pdf, retrieved February 2007.
51	Hunt 1996: 174, See also Forsythe 2000: 172, who makes the same observation.
52	Amnesty International, *Human Rights and Privatisation*, 17-03-2005, http://web.amnesty.org/library/ index/engpol340032005, retrieved February 2007.
53	Betten 1991: 134; Robertson en Merrills 1992: 230; Williams 1994: 122; Craven 1998: 9; Pogge 2002/2003, p.64.
54	Plant 1988: 35; Raz 1986: 167; Galenkamp 1993: 63; Galtung 1992: 153; Gewirth 1984: 92; Regina Kreide, 2002, p.1.
55	According to the Human Rights Committee, the committee that monitors the implementation of the International Covenant on Civil and Political Rights, "Article 18 protects theistic, non-theistic and atheistic beliefs, as well as the right not to profess any religion or belief. The terms 'belief' and 'religion' are to be broadly construed. Article 18 is not limited in its application to traditional religions or to religions and beliefs with institutional characteristics or practices analogous to those of traditional religions..." (General Comment nr.22)
56	Fried 1978, p.120; Grant 1999, p.104; Dower 2003, p.57, Cliteur 2006, pp.33,34,35
57	Williams 1994, p.122, Cliteur 2006, pp.34,35.
58	Plant 1991: 270; Van Hoof 1984, p.23; Williams 1994, p.122
59	Tomasevski 1989, p.117.
60	Plant 1991, p.279.
61	Cranston 1973, p.68, Grant 1999, p.88; Cliteur 2006, pp.37,38.
62	Martin 1997, p.25; Gray 1983, p.182; Orwin and Pangle, 1984, p.15; Cliteur 2006, p.37, Pogge 2002/2003, p.67.
63	Cranston 1973, p.68; Robertson and Merrills 1992, p.230.
64	ICESCR, Article 2 1. Each State Party to the present Covenant undertakes to take steps, individually and through international assistance and co-operation, especially economic and technical, to the maximum of its available resources, with a view to achieving progressively the full realization of the rights recognized in the present Covenant by all appropriate means, including particularly the adoption of legislative measures. 2. The States Parties to the present Covenant undertake to guarantee that the rights enunciated in the present Covenant will be exercised without discrimination of any kind as to race, colour, sex, language, religion,

political or other opinion, national or social origin, property, birth or other status. 3. Developing countries, with due regard to human rights and their national economy, may determine to what extent they would guarantee the economic rights recognized in the present Covenant to non-nationals. ICCPR Article 2 1. Each State Party to the present Covenant undertakes to respect and to ensure to all individuals within its territory and subject to its jurisdiction the rights recognized in the present Covenant, without distinction of any kind, such as race, colour, sex, language, religion, political or other opinion, national or social origin, property, birth or other status. 2. Where not already provided for by existing legislative or other measures, each State Party to the present Covenant undertakes to take the necessary steps, in accordance with its constitutional processes and with the provisions of the present Covenant, to adopt such laws or other measures as may be necessary to give effect to the rights recognized in the present Covenant. 3. Each State Party to the present Covenant undertakes: (a) To ensure that any person whose rights or freedoms as herein recognized are violated shall have an effective remedy, notwithstanding that the violation has been committed by persons acting in an official capacity; (b) To ensure that any person claiming such a remedy shall have his right thereto determined by competent judicial, administrative or legislative authorities, or by any other competent authority provided for by the legal system of the State, and to develop the possibilities of judicial remedy; (c) To ensure that the competent authorities shall enforce such remedies when granted.

[65] Cranston 1973: 70; Alston 1987: 54, see also Kreide 2002/2007, p.1.
[66] See: Pogge, 2002/2003, p.64.
[67] http://www.liberales.be/cgi-bin/showframe.pl?boek&norbergglobalisering, retrieved February 2006.
[68] http://www.ftlcomm.com:16080/ensign/desantisArticles/2002_600/desantis658/agenda.html.

CHAPTER 3

A DIGNIFIED LIFE

"What begins with the failure to uphold the dignity of one life, all too often ends with a calamity for entire nations".
UN Secretary-General Kofi Annan[1]

1. Introduction

"*Human rights are those moral rights which are owed to each man or woman by every man or woman solely by reason of being human*", according to Macfarlane. Donnelly says that "*...human rights are rights one has because one is a human being (person)*", and "*... human rights are ... the rights one holds by virtue of being a person.*" Gewirth joins these authors by saying that, within a secular defense of human rights, depending on the idea of moral reciprocity, human rights are rights "*that are had by every human being simply insofar as he or she is human.*"[2]

In other words, human beings have these rights whether or not they are allocated by a state or other political organization. In the course of time, though, these rights have been incorporated into official documents, even though such documents acknowledge that the rights are grounded in human beings themselves and connected with human dignity. The preamble to the Universal Declaration of Human Rights (UDHR) speaks about the *"recognition of the inherent dignity and of the equal and inalienable rights of all members of the human family ..."* and, somewhat further about *"the dignity and worth of the human person."* Similar formulations can be found in such other human rights documents as the International Covenant on Civil and Political Rights and the International Covenant on Economic, Social and Cultural Rights. In their preambles they say that "*... these rights derive from the inherent dignity of the human person.*"

From these documents it can be concluded that the connection between human rights and human dignity not only apply to CP-rights, but also to ESC-rights. However, sometimes the idea arises that the connection between ESC-rights and human dignity is not a matter of course. For instance, Michael Ignatieff says that, within a secular defense of human rights, depending on the idea of moral reciprocity, human rights are a limited category of special rights.[3] Maurice Cranston argues that ESC-rights, unlike CP-rights, are not of paramount importance.[4] Therefore, it is intriguing to explore the relationship between human dignity and human rights, in the hope that it will provide an answer to the question of whether ESC-rights are indeed connected with human dignity.

2. Human dignity

The Office of the High Commissioner on Human Rights states that "*it is commonly recognized that human rights derive from the dignity and worth of the human person*".[5] Also the UDHR in its preamble speaks of "*the worth of the human person*". The ICCPR and the ICESCR say in their preamble "*Recognizing that these rights derive from the inherent dignity of the human person...*"

The relationship between human rights and human dignity obviously is incontestable, but it is not incontestably obvious. Although the notion of human dignity is generally used in human rights circles, it is seldom clarified. That is understandable, for on the one hand, it appears to be self-evident that people are endowed with human dignity, while on the other hand it is very difficult to reach agreement on what is meant by such a statement.

It is certainly a notion with a lofty sound. It looks like it wants to emphasize the speciality, the superiority, the eminence of humankind. But that would be an illusion, for while it is attractive to think of human beings as something special, many would argue that we, humankind, form just a minute element in the cosmos, having entered it only a short while ago and doomed to be buried in oblivion in a 'few' years time. Taking the notion of human dignity to refer to the eminence of humankind is also an illusion in another sense. Considering the cruelties people are capable of committing against each other, one can hardly use a phrase like 'human dignity'. It can hardly be applied to the human species whose members permanently wage wars, kill, torture and humiliate one another, plunge others into poverty and discriminate against them.

Be that as it may, it does not imply that the notion of human dignity has no meaning whatsoever. In my view, such a notion does not want to say that humankind is a dignified species but that every individual human being is endowed with dignity and of equal value. In attaching equal value to all human beings the notion of human dignity has an egalitarian trait. Article 1 of the UDHR proclaims that "*All human beings are born free and equal in dignity and rights...*" Here also the idea that the notion comes down to an illusion may loom up again, because attaching value to every human being runs counter to our experiences and intuitions: we tend to attach more value to the lives of our friends, partners and our children than to that of foreigners, and more value to the life of Gandhi and Martin Luther King than to that of warlords and criminals.[6] But, although referring to individual human beings, the notion of human dignity does not refer to the value of the concrete lives that people live and the concrete persons they have become. It does not refer to their behavior, to their character, or to their contributions to the general welfare or to the well-being of fellow human beings; instead it wants to say that a human being, whatever their concrete lives, is of intrinsic value.

Human beings experience themselves as having value and want to be protected. Their lives may be miserable, marked by poverty and breakdown; they may have limited capacities and talents, but their existence is of value, for it is an existence that occurs only once, and which is unique and irreplaceable. It cannot be expressed in money or substituted for by somebody else's being. Each individual affirms their value in whatever they do: in their efforts to stay alive and to attach quality to their lives, to acquire particular things, to become a particular person, in their pursuit of ideals. Their strivings are not the determinable results of mechanical processes, but the manifestations of unique beings who, with the help of their mental and moral capabilities, have laid out their course. By valuing their strivings, people value themselves as persons, as beings that are the source of those valuable efforts and who are, hopefully, going to realize them.

This worth of the human person is inherent and intrinsic. It is inherent because indissolubly linked with the existence of each person. It is also intrinsic because it cannot be substituted by something considered to be of equal value. Gewirth takes these features of the worth of the human to be interwoven. Following Kant, he contrasts dignity with price. "*If a thing has a price, then it can be substituted for or replaced by something else of equivalent value, where value signifies ... a worth that is relative to a person's desires or opinions. ... In contrast, inherent dignity cannot be replaced by anything else, and it is not relative to anyone's desires or opinions.*"[7]

I take human dignity to refer to this worth of a human person that is experienced by everyone and that calls upon people to treat the human person as something precious, to treat everyone with equal respect and concern and to show an attitude of respect towards the humanity in each person.[8] "*Each and every human being—each and every member of the species Homo sapiens—has inherent dignity; therefore, no one should deny that any human being has, or treat any human being as if she lacks, inherent dignity. To say that all human beings have inherent dignity is to say that one's dignity inheres in nothing more particular than one's being human; it does not inhere, for example, in one's 'race, colour, sex, language, religion, political or other opinion, national or social origin, property, birth or other status '....*"[9]

We may now have some idea of the notion of human dignity, but it is far from clear why people endowed with human dignity have rights and why they have the rights we think they have (the rights as mentioned in the human rights documents). To explain that, we have to say more about human beings. But in doing that, we touch upon a controversial subject: human nature. Arguments about human nature attract skepticism because they are thought to lapse into metaphysical and disputable speculations. I think though, that the topic cannot be avoided, even though presenting a view on human nature is risky. Therefore I will try to sketch just a 'thin' anthropology: a view of human beings that, hopefully, does not lapse into speculations but remains close to the daily experiences of human beings and is capable of being accepted as a theory underlying universal human rights.

3. Existing as a person

The most important element of this anthropology is that human beings are regarded as 'persons'. This element appears in many human rights documents, as for instance when it is said that *"human rights are the rights possessed by all persons, by virtue of their common humanity, to live a life of freedom and dignity"*.[10] The true identity of human beings lies in their being a person. Animals are beings and can be individuals, but only human beings are persons, beings with self-awareness and feelings of joy, sorrow, distress, pride, beings with goals and beings that, endowed with moral and mental capacities, intentionally strive to realize their goals.[11] Michaël Novak puts it this way: *"What makes a person a person, rather more than merely an individual, is a spiritual capacity: the capacity to reflect and choose, to be imaginative and creative, to be an originating source of action..."*[12]

At least three more remarks can be made about human beings. They are vulnerable: susceptible to suffering and threats to their existence. They are social: they live in social and cultural settings, in relationships and communities with others, are dependent on those communities and possess an identity partly constituted by their membership of the community. Finally, they are open, open to various life options and not completely determined by their instincts—they cannot avoid making choices as to how to behave and what to do, even if it should be admitted that the options available to choose from are conveyed to them by the cultures in which they live.

As a response to their vulnerability, sociality and openness, people strive for well-being, participation and freedom respectively. In order to deal with their vulnerability they want basic *well-being*, that is, they want to be free from suffering and threats to their existence. They want to have access to the resources necessary for a decent standard of living, such as water, food, shelter and healthcare. Next, because of their sociality they want *participation*: they want to be recognized as a fellow human being, as someone who counts instead of being excluded or isolated. They want to be recognized as a member of the group they are part of, and to be involved in the organization of the society in which they live. Lastly, as a response to their openness people want *freedom*. They do not want to be forced, compelled or coerced, but to be able to live their lives as they see fit, and to do—or be—that which they have reasons to value. Or, to put it in the terms of the Human Development Report 2004, they want to have *"the capability.....to live as they would like and to have the opportunity to choose from the options they have—or can have."*[13] Well-being, participation and freedom are desired by human beings because they provide an adequate reply to their human vulnerability, sociality and openness. But humans also need them for another reason: as means to realize their various personal strivings, whatever they may be, regardless of whether such strivings are existential (being a loving father, a well-known artist or a successful scientist), or of a more specific nature (wanting to go to a football match, hold a lecture, play with their children).

These personal strivings, existential or more specific, vary from person to person. But, to realize them people need well-being, participation and freedom—for while these goods are valuable in their own right, as an answer to an individual's vulnerability, sociality and openness, they appear also to be valuable in that they are the necessary conditions for achieving any purpose whatsoever. When people lack minimal material resources, when they are excluded from their social environment and are not recognized as fellow humans, when they are prevented from living their own lives, they cannot pursue their strivings, and they cannot survive as human beings. All in all, freedom, well-being and participation are generic goods, goods that people need as human beings, as members of the human kind, the innate or fundamental goods of human life.[14]

(I would like to add here that some argue that freedom is the fundamental good people strive for, the ultimate condition. To them it can be said that it is possible to define well-being and participation in terms of freedoms. It can be said that people strive after well-being, but it is also possible to say that people want to be free from misery. It can be said that people strive after participation, but it is also possible to say that they want to be free from exclusion.)

4. A life worthy of a human being: Generic rights to freedom, participation and well-being

"Human rights express our deepest commitments to ensuring that all persons are secure in their enjoyment of the goods and freedoms that are necessary for dignified living."[15]

Humans experience themselves as beings of value, with an existence that is valuable, unique and irreplaceable. Experiencing themselves as valuable, they want freedom, well-being and participation because these are the conditions that will enable them to survive as human beings. And they do not just want to survive; they want to survive as *human beings*, to be enabled to live a live worthy of a human being. With that notion—'a life worthy of a human being'—we touch on a different aspect of human dignity, a contingent aspect to be distinguished from the inherent, intrinsic worth of human beings. Intrinsic worth does not make people's concrete lives worthy or dignified; concrete lives can be unworthy of a human being.[16] While the worth of a human *person* is inherent and intrinsic and falls equally to every human being, the worth of human *lives*, the situations in which people live their lives, may well differ from time to time and from person to person. Some people live wealthy lives, whereas others live in abject poverty. Some people have many opportunities to educate themselves or engage in meaningful work, whereas others lack any schooling or education and are jobless. Some live in peace and well-being; others are surrounded by violence and war, or even horrible crimes. And so while people who are poor, who lack schooling and work, who are surrounded by violence, may have an inherent worth, the lives they are forced to live are unworthy of a human being. As they lack freedom, well-being and participation, they desperately want these goods.

It must be pointed out, though, that people do not just *want* to enjoy freedom, well-being and participation, they will think that they *must* have them, that these goods are the necessary conditions of a life they regard themselves as worthy of living.[17] We can even go further: if they have an innate sense of having rights as a human being, or better yet, are aware that the world recognizes human rights and has instituted instruments and mechanisms in an effort to achieve them, people, indeed, will think that they have a *right* to these goods. Because having a right to these goods means something special compared to wanting these goods or saying that you must have these goods. It means that the possession of certain goods of the right-holder is guaranteed or protected by the existence of correlative duties that are owed to the right-holder. A right implies a corresponding duty to be performed by others. If people restrict themselves to saying that they simply *want* or *must have* freedom, well-being and participation, then they may very well not get them because it is nobody's responsibility to provide them. And knowing that they then run a risk of not attaining these generic goods they will, instead, use as strong an expression as possible. They will say that they have a *right* to them. Of course, they cannot say that they have a right without justification. But the justification is exactly that these goods are necessary to be enabled to live a dignified human life.

There is, however, one other question that needs answering. People as vulnerable, social, undetermined, striving beings will be of the view that *they* have rights to freedom, well-being and participation. That sounds reasonable. But why should also *other* people have the same rights? For many, the answer will be self-evident. Apparently, for many others, the answer is not self-evident, as many claim to be entitled to freedom, well-being and participation, while denying others these goods by coercing and oppressing them, by plunging them into poverty and preventing them from access to resources, by excluding them. Day in day out we witness the denial of the rights of many people to freedom, well-being and participation.

A fundamental role in the answer to this question is played by the awareness of the equal humanity of others. Others should also have these rights to freedom, well-being are participation because we are aware that they are humans too. People perceive others as humans like themselves, and one may suppose that even those who ask why others should enjoy the same rights as themselves perceive these 'others' as fellow humans. Others are beings with the same physical, psychological and mental equipment, even if they differ in the particular features of this equipment. In short, people may have different noses, legs, dreams, desires, but they all have noses, legs, dreams and desires. Human beings take part in a common humanity; or, as Ignatieff says: "... *what is pain and humiliation for you is bound to be pain and humiliation for me.*"[18]

We may combine this awareness of a common humanity with the requirement of consistency, which brings us to the following statement: if people are of the view that they have generic rights because of a humanity characterized by personality, vulnerability, sociality, and openness, and if they are aware that others have the same humanity, then they must accept that these others with the same humanity also have these rights. It is not possible to demand rights to x, y and z on the grounds of A and then argue that others, who also have A, are not entitled to x, y, and z. That would be contradictory. Unfortunately, history and today show that many apparently accept being contradictory. They exploit others, abuse them, discriminate against them, rape them or kill them. To avoid being contradictory and to justify their inhumane acts, they deny the humanity of their victims.

Recognizing that others also have generic rights to freedom, well-being and participation is not only a question of consistency, of logic, but also of morality; it is not only required by logical reasoning but also by moral feeling. This moral feeling emerges from two sources: the confrontation with others as persons and the desire of people themselves to be human. The confrontation with others forces us to recognize that they are persons, not products that turn up in our lives that we can use arbitrarily. They force us to recognize that they are not means to our goals, but ends in themselves. They have self-awareness, feelings, experiences and yearnings. As persons they make an appeal to us to treat them as fellow human beings, an appeal that results in our dismay when we are confronted with horrors—violence, war, rape, poverty and famine—that may befall others, that but for chance and circumstance, we may confront as well. This confrontation with human beings involves an appeal to treat them as persons, as human beings who are entitled to a dignified life—as we may request to be treated. We force others to recognize that we are not means to their goals, but ends in ourselves. As persons, we make appeal to them to treat us as fellow human beings.

The moral requirement to acknowledge and respect the humanity in others could also flow from people's own desire to be fellow-humans. People do not want to be isolated and excluded: they want to be one of many, to be a fellow human being. But this desire cannot be fulfilled without some commitment, a commitment that will demand effort in specific situations that cannot easily be ignored. If neglected, it implies that people do not do justice to the person they themselves want to be, to the identity they want to have. Commitment to being a specific type of person should result, therefore, in people being prepared to acknowledge moral requirements. My commitment to being a good father will result in my accepting that my children have rights and that I have duties towards them. My commitment to being a fellow-human, generated by my desire to be one, will imply an acknowledgement of the requirement to treat others with equal respect and concern.[19]

So we can conclude by saying that if people believe that they are worthy of the right to the freedom, well-being and participation that will enable them to live a life worthy of a human being, even if they fail to presently acknowledge that others also (should) have these generic rights, they likely will be vulnerable to an insistent further pursuit of the argument.[20]

5. The primary values underlying human rights

All people have generic rights to freedom, well-being and participation and correlative duties. These generic rights are general, moral, human rights. As shown above, they flow from people's worth as a human being, and at the same time they are aimed at enabling people to lead a life worthy of a human being. To guarantee these rights, there exist the more specific human rights found in moral discourse and in international legal documents. The rights to freedom of thought, to freedom of belief, to adequate housing, to healthcare and to vote are all specific rights designed to guarantee the generic rights.[21] And with regard to these specific human rights, it can also be said that human dignity is involved in two ways.

It is a *source* of these rights, and it is the *aim* of these rights, two observations that are noticeable in many documents. For instance, the Universal Declaration of Human Rights speaks about the *source* of human rights when it says: "*...whereas recognition of the inherent dignity and of the equal and inalienable rights of all members of the human family...*". The International Covenant on Economic, Social and Cultural Rights even more explicitly refers to the source of human rights when it says "*...recognizing that these rights derive from the inherent dignity of the human person...*". Human dignity as the *aim* of human rights appears in article 22 of the UDHR, which states that "*Everyone, as a member of society.... is entitled to* realization, through national effort and international co-operation.... *of the economic, social and cultural rights indispensable for his dignity and the free development of his personality.*" Article 23 also refers to the aim of human rights when it states that "...*everyone who works has the right to just and favorable remuneration ensuring for himself and his family an existence worthy of human dignity...*". To take another example: if the International Convention on the Elimination of All Forms of Racial Discrimination speaks about the "*dignity and equality inherent in all human beings*" and when it says that "*all human beings are born free and equal in dignity and rights*", it is obviously referring to human dignity as the source of human rights. When it later speaks about the necessity "... *of securing respect for the dignity of the human person*", human dignity emerges as the aim of human rights.

Freedom, well-being and participation may be called the key values of human rights.[22] They are also mentioned by Marshall as the justifying values underlying human rights.[23] Marshall, however, draws a distinction between civil, political and social rights and then argues that freedom is the key value of civil rights, participation the central value of political rights and well-being that of social rights. I am, however, of the view that all human rights, CP-rights and ESC-rights, are aimed, directly or indirectly, at the realization of freedom, well-being and participation.

The human rights idea contains other values, values that are related not to the content of human rights, but to the structure of the human rights idea. In particular, the following values can be noted: individuality, equality and secularity, values that not only underlie CP-rights but also ESC-rights.

I will now try to elaborate on these substantial and structural values underlying human rights, thereby examining to what extent they underlie ESC-rights in particular. But before doing that, I would like to make a general remark about the character of these values. The total system of values underlying human rights form the ideology of human rights. This ideology should be distinguished from a view of life, also called a conception of a good life, a life stance, a belief, or an outlook on life. A view of life tries to give an answer to the question of the meaning of life, a question that in turn contains two more specific questions: that is, the question of how life, the world and human beings are to be understood, and the question of how life is to be lived.

Correspondingly, a view of life has two dimensions. Firstly, it has an ontological dimension interpreting life, man and the world. This is an 'is'-dimension, being of a descriptive nature and describing how man, life and the world are. Secondly, it has an ethical dimension, describing how life should be lived. This is an 'ought'-dimension, having a prescriptive or normative character. These dimensions of a view of life refer to its contents. Of course, more can be said about views of life, in particular that they should have the capacity of integrating the various aspects of people's lives, and that they should be inspiring and motivating. But such characteristics refer to their function and not to their contents and I wish here to confine myself solely to their contents, to the ontological and ethical dimension.[24]

To the ontological dimension belong statements such as "although life is surprising and wonderful, it is capable of being comprehended in the long run"; "this earthly life will be followed by a life in the hereafter"; "life is a mystery and is beyond comprehension", as well as statements such as "God exists"; "God does not exist"; "it is not possible to say whether or not God exists" and statements such as "human beings are natural beings and subjected to the laws of nature" and "human beings have the capacity to reason and to choose" etc.[25] These statements belonging to the ontological dimension of a view on life are of a descriptive character. On the other hand, the idea that it is worthwhile to reflect on your actions, that it is good not to submit to dogmas nor to unconditionally subject oneself to authorities, that it is good to make your own choices, to be a responsible person and a caring, loving person or that you should obey the laws of God are all ideas about how life is to be lived and belong to the ethical dimension of a view on life; they have a normative character.

The ethical dimension of a view on life is a morality of human flourishing, a morality of the good life.[26] It states how life should be lived and how people should live to enjoy a meaningful life. This does not mean that this morality is limited to the individual sphere, holding aloof from the social sphere. It is likely that a morality of the good life will also contain guidelines with regard to interpersonal behavior and to the organization of society. For instance, one of the precepts of living a good life could be that it is worthwhile to devote oneself to social justice, or to the promotion of human rights. But these guidelines will then flow from the precepts for a good and meaningful life.

The human rights ideology has a slightly different concern. It purports to be acceptable to people with different and various views on lives and, because of that, it does not have a 'thick' ontological dimension. It is not connected with a particular ontological view, as is also said by Orwin and Pangle.[27] It does not intend to say how life, the world, or human beings should be interpreted. It concerns itself specifically with the ethical dimension, although this dimension unavoidably will have 'thin' ontological presuppositions.

This ethical dimension, this morality of the human rights ideology, is of a different nature to the ethical dimension of a view of life. It does not offer guidelines for living a good life, nor does it say how people can realize their human potentials. It only tries to give an answer to the question of *how people should behave towards one another*. Besides that, it is a *public* morality, a morality that contains generally acceptable guidelines for interpersonal relations as far as these relations can be considered to be susceptible to public regulations. So, compared with a view of life, the ideology of human rights is a 'thin' ideology in that it has no explicit ontological dimension, but only an ethical dimension, and that its ethical dimension is not a morality of the good life but a morality of a humane society.

The foregoing, however, should not be taken to mean that the ideology of human rights possesses no ontological dimension at all. Orwin and Pangle point at the presence of an implicit, if thin, ontological conception when arguing that there are some human desires and needs that people have as human beings that are part of the human constitution and that provide an objective standard for public actions and policies.[28] And Waldron argues that every political theory, including a theory in which tolerance and neutrality are the dominant elements, will be grounded in a thin view of human beings. I too have sketched such a thin view. A thin theory is, in fact, unavoidable. We need to know what characterizes human beings if we want to guarantee and promote a dignified human life.[29]

Some human rights documents even go so far as to mention explicit ontological notions. For instance article 1 of the United Declaration of Human Rights states that "*All human beings are born free and equal in dignity and rights. They are endowed with reason and conscience ...*" It looks as though these sentences hold descriptive formulations, statements about the freedom, equality and rationality of human beings. But we cannot be sure. For, despite their descriptive appearance they can be intended to be normative statements. After all, people often express normative opinions clothed in descriptive formulations. If someone says "*you're preventing me from doing my work,*" they are not only describing a factual situation, but are also saying that "*you shouldn't hinder me*". They are wrapping up a norm in a descriptive statement.

Likewise, the first sentence and the first part of the second sentence of article 1 of the UDHR could, despite their descriptive wording, mean that people *should* treat one another as free and equal fellow human beings endowed with reason. The text then continues with an explicit normative statement when the second part of the second sentence states "*... and should act towards one another in a spirit of brotherhood.*"

Whatever the character of article 1 of the UDHR, it cannot be denied that the ideology of human rights, although it does not want to express a particular ontological view, has ontological presuppositions that, while sometimes explicit, are mostly implicit. They are minimalist, in that they claim to be recognizable and acceptable to people with different, various and even incommensurable conceptions of life and it is this minimalist ontology that forms the presuppositions of the morality of human rights, a morality that—as has been stated earlier—differs from the morality of a good life.

I think it is important to keep this specific character of the morality of human rights in mind as we now attempt to elucidate its particular values.

6. Freedom or autonomy?

Jerome J. Shestack states that one common idea emerges from a variety of theories on human rights: that human rights should be directed at the value of individual freedom or autonomy.[30] Carlos Santiago Nino mentions the principle of autonomy as one of the underlying principles of human rights[31]. The word 'autonomy' is used by many writers.[32] Yet while the terms 'freedom' and 'autonomy' seem to be synonyms, differences can and should be distinguished. I would suggest to use the word 'autonomy' to refer to a value of a view of life, and the word 'freedom' to refer to a value of the ideology of human rights.

As a principle of a view of life, autonomy holds that it be considered valuable for human beings to try to be the authors of their lives. People should not uncritically subject themselves to the views of others, should not copy the behavior of others and should not attempt to live up to the ideas of others about what constitutes a meaningful life. Instead, they should try to develop their own ideas and conceptions and, in addition, be willing to reflect on those views and adjust them if necessary. An autonomous life is one opposite to an existence in which one is forced to act as one does, but it is also one in contrast to a life of making no choices, a life of drifting on without using one's capacity to choose. Interpreted this way, autonomy is an ideal of a good life that expresses a vision of people shaping their lives and determining their destiny, choosing how to live according to well-reflected beliefs and values.[33]

With regard to the idea of being the author of one's life, a distinction can be drawn between a thick and thin interpretation of such an idea. The thick interpretation holds that it is valuable that people choose how to live or act and that they try to connect their ideas and behavior to a coherent pattern— according to a particular plan or conception of a good life. The thin interpretation holds that people should reflect and make choices, regardless of whether or not they add conceptual unity to their life. In this interpretation, the importance of choosing is emphasized, whereas in the thick interpretation it is the need to give one's life a unity that is stressed.

As it is a principle of a view of life, autonomy cannot serve as a justifying principle of human rights and we cannot expect everyone to be the author of their lives. There may be persons who do not share this ideal. There may be people who do not aspire to being the author of their lives, and who do not consider it valuable to shape their own views. There may be people who consider it valuable to adhere to cultural traditions, the customs of the community or the directives of religious or secular leaders.[34] It is said that autonomy is a typically Western secular idea and that many non-Western people do not value it as much as Westerners do. Can we then take the principle of autonomy to be acceptable to those who do not care much for that principle? Rawls, who is concerned with liberalism, wonders how autonomy can be a generally acceptable value of society and at the same time a liberalist principle that is not shared by non-liberalists. He does not want to be sectarian and he wants also to avoid the idea that he is imposing liberalist values on others. His solution is to recognize that not all will adhere to autonomy in their personal lives but that, notwithstanding this, they will be prepared to accept the principle in the public domain.[35]

Will Kymlicka, in his comment on Rawls, asks why people would be willing to accept the principle of autonomy in the public domain if they do not seek such an ideal in their personal lives. For if people do not adhere to autonomy in their personal lives and instead greatly value their common group-identity and their common culture, the recognition of autonomy in the public domain could turn upon them. It could then happen that individual members of minority cultures start criticizing the practices of their cultures and that they are supported in doing so by the majority of (the wider) society, the people who do adhere to autonomy. Therefore, it is unlikely that people who do not adhere to autonomy in their personal lives will accept it as a principle of a public morality. Kymlicka therefore prefers to admit, frankly, that a liberalist advocates and *promotes* the ideal of autonomy, although he is also keen to say that he does not want to *impose* the ideal of autonomy.[36]

However, in my view, Kymlicka also has a problem. In a multicultural society, liberalists will be confronted with an unavoidable problem: either they abandon the ideal of autonomy as a principle for the organization of society or they use it as organizing principle. Using it as an organizing principle of society, while some people do not want to adhere to it, means that it will be imposed on those people.

One may, of course, wonder whether such an imposition is a bad thing. One could be an adversary of the imposition of autonomy, because it *is* imposition. But if autonomy is used as an organizing principle of society, surely this means that people will be stimulated to make choices. Is this to be avoided because it is a matter of imposition? Should we not take into account *what* is being imposed? With Kymlicka, it can be said that the fear of being sectarian on the issue of autonomy is somewhat exaggerated. A society that expects its citizens to make their own choices seems to be more acceptable than a society that expects people to be fundamentalist-religious, atheist, unconditionally obedient, or play sports, be vegetarian or eat meat every day.

Yet while this diminishes the problem, it does not remove it. The point remains that some people will not adhere to the principle of autonomy, and this makes it problematic as a guiding principle for the public domain. Here I would like to take a stand almost similar to that of Rawls, although with a slight, but important, difference. Rawls assumes that all people are prepared to accept the ideal of autonomy for the public domain, whether or not they want to use it as a guiding principle for their private lives. I, however, want to suggest that we use different words with different meanings in the different domains. I would like to use autonomy as the guiding principle for a good life, and freedom as the guiding principle for a public morality. In such a case, some people will adhere to autonomy and want to be the author of their lives, while others will not. But also the latter should be free to do as they choose.

Unlike autonomy, freedom, as I interpret it, does not demand that people should be the author of their lives. Freedom means that people should be enabled to live their lives as they think fit, whether or not they strive to be the author of their lives. Whether people live according to well-reflected ideas chosen after careful deliberation, or whether they conform to traditions and identify with cultural patterns, they should be enabled to live their own lives as they see fit.[37]

Freedom and not autonomy is the key value of the ideology of human rights.

7. Freedom, first among equals

The idea of freedom being a guiding value of human rights is generally accepted. Often it is presented as the main value. John Packer, former adviser to the OSCE High Commissioner on National Minorities, says that the fundamental goal of human rights lies in the maximization of freedom.[38]

It can be argued that freedom is the main value underlying human rights, *especially if it is taken to include well-being and participation*. And it is certainly possible to interpret it that way. Freedom means that people are enabled to live their lives as they see fit, to do or to be whatever they have reasons to value. This implies that they should not be forced by others to do or to be what they do not want to do or to be. It also implies that they should not be compelled by misery to do or to be what they do not want to do or to be, but that they be protected or remain free from misery, as well as from hunger, disease and illiteracy. Freedom can also be taken to imply that people should be free from exclusion, free to participate in the life of their community, that they be recognized as a member of the human family in general and their more specific community in particular. This broad sense of freedom is being used in a report by the OHCHR when it states that most human rights are concerned with an individual's rights to certain fundamental freedoms, including the freedoms from hunger, disease and illiteracy.[39] The Human Development Report of 2000 also uses a similarly broad interpretation of freedom when it states the following.

> Human rights and human development share a common vision and a common purpose—to secure the freedom, well-being and dignity of all people everywhere. To secure:
> Freedom from discrimination—by gender, race, ethnicity, national origin or religion.
> Freedom from want—to enjoy a decent standard of living.

Freedom to develop and realize one's human potential.
Freedom from fear—of threats to personal security, from torture, arbitrary arrest and other violent acts.
Freedom from injustice and violations of the rule of law.
Freedom of thought and speech and to participate in decision-making and form associations.
Freedom for decent work—without exploitation.[40]

I am inclined to define freedom in such a broad sense, and to regard it as the main value underlying all human rights, including ESC-rights. That freedom also underlies ESC-rights is obviously the opinion of the Human Development Report 2000, as demonstrated by the preceding quotation. The report does not leave room for doubt, when it states that *"Access to basic education, health care, shelter and employment is as critical to human freedom as political and civil rights are."*[41] And here one can take at least four different approaches to supporting the statement that freedom also underlies ESC-rights.

We can begin with Rawls, who draws a distinction between liberty and the worth of liberty.[42] He then argues that liberty is negatively affected if certain socio-economic conditions are not met. One may ask what is the use of freedom if you starve, if you are seriously ill without having access to health services, and if you do not have shelter to protect yourself from severe cold or the heat. In Rawls' view, CP-rights are aimed directly at freedom, whereas ESC-rights, giving worth to liberty, are indirectly aimed at it.

Raz appears to take a similar line. To enable people to live their own lives, he states, certain conditions are to be met, that is, appropriate mental abilities, an adequate range of options and independence.[43] If they are to be free (he himself uses the notion of autonomy) people need an adequate range of options. This does not mean that they should have as many options as possible. Rather, it means that they should be above a minimal level of material well-being, so that they are not totally preoccupied by their deprivation and not compelled by extraneous circumstances. If people fall below that level, then their choices cannot be called autonomous.

The Human Development Report 2005 also appear to share the view of Rawls when it states that *"Individual freedoms and rights matter a great deal, but people are restricted in what they can do with that freedom if they are poor, ill, illiterate, discriminated against, threatened by violent conflict or denied a political voice."*[44]

The second approach more specifically points to the usefulness of ESC-rights in fulfilling CP-rights. It stresses that the fulfillment of basic material needs enables people to exercise their CP-rights. Celina Romany, for example, observes that ESC-rights are often seen as rights designed to create the necessary conditions for the realization of CP-rights. The argument is that if people cannot provide for themselves and supply their basic needs, then they are susceptible to manipulation and incapable of exercising their CP-rights.[45] And as CP-rights, in their turn, are concerned with freedom, so ESC-rights are indirectly concerned with freedom.

The third approach wants to differentiate between negative and positive freedom, and says that freedom encompasses both positive and negative freedoms. 'Negative freedom' means the absence of coercion by others. Therefore a person is free when he or she is not coerced by others to do or to be what he or she does not want to do or to be. Yet someone can be free and not coerced by others even though, owing to miserable socio-economic circumstances, they cannot do or be what they want to do or to be. This is where the notion of positive freedom comes in.

Positive freedom is defined as the presence of enabling circumstances. The OHCHR report, "Human Rights and Poverty Reduction", takes this approach when it says that a *"a person's freedom to live a healthy life is contingent both on the requirement that no one obstructs her legitimate pursuit of good health—negative freedom—and also on the society's success in creating an enabling environment in which she can actually achieve health—positive freedom."*[46] Often it is CP-rights that are seen as rights that protect and promote negative freedom, being free from coercion by others, while ESC-rights are regarded as protecting and promoting positive freedom by trying to guarantee the presence of enabling circumstances, for example, adequate health services and housing.

The fourth approach argues that there is no need to distinguish between negative and positive freedom: socio-economic misery is a violation of freedom—period!—as it comes down to coercion by others. This approach is of the view that socio-economic situations are not natural coincidences that befall people, but are man-made: the result of human action. They have been created by man and are still being created by man, in particular by the rich and the powerful. And if socio-economic situations prevent people from leading a dignified life, it is eventually the powerful that, through socio-economic constellations, prevent the powerless from leading such a life. Socio-economic misery is not a question of the absence of enabling circumstances, but of coercion by others, that obstruct the less-advantaged in the pursuit of resources needed for a decent life. In this approach there is no need to distinguish between negative freedom being protected by CP-rights and positive freedom being protected by ESC-rights. ESC-rights that want to protect people from socio-economic misery are, like CP-rights, aimed at promoting (negative) freedom. (I will explore this fourth approach more fully in the following chapters.)

From this, it can certainly be argued that freedom is the main value, the first among equals, and that it also underlies ESC-rights. However, many people define freedom in a more limited sense, and do not accept one of the foregoing approaches. Therefore, to avoid misunderstandings, I will use well-being and participation as accompanying key values.

8. Well-being

The Human Development Report 2000 says that the purpose of human rights (like that of human development) is *"to secure the freedom, well-being and dignity of all people everywhere"*.[47] A few pages further it states that *"The promotion of human development and the fulfillment of human rights share, in many ways, a common motivation, and reflect a fundamental commitment to promoting the freedom, well-being and dignity of individuals in all societies."*[48] Well-being is mentioned as a value of human rights. But, when referring to well-being in this respect, i.e. as a value underlying human rights, we should make a conscious decision not to use the notion of well-being in too broad a sense. For instance, we should not take it to mean that people feel happy or satisfied with their lives. Human rights cannot pretend to achieve such a broad concept of well-being.

Well-being, taken in a broad sense, has a subjective component. As regards individual well-being, Raz says that *"This concept captures one crucial evaluation of a person's life: how good or successful is it from his point of view?"* [49] One cannot say that someone has achieved (individual) well-being by noting that he or she has received the Nobel-prize—or in some other way contributed to society or to the well-being of others. Well-being is actually dependent upon the achievement of the personal goals that people have set for themselves.[50]

It is the personal character of these goals that implies that others only can contribute to another's well-being in a conditional sense. That is, others cannot improve someone's well-being; they can only improve the conditions of someone's well-being. Even, if those conditions are excellent it still does not guarantee in any way that person's well-being.

Well-being, in such a broad sense, cannot be the purpose of human rights. It should be taken in a more limited sense: that is, as implying access to the resources needed for a decent standard of living. To talk of well-being is to recognize that people are vulnerable, susceptible to injury and pain and that the conditions of their very existence, let alone the conditions for their self-development, are permanently under threat. This is why the idea of well-being demands that the political structures of society be organized so as to protect people from pain and suffering and to provide them with resources they need to live a decent life for without a material base, the ground will sink from beneath people's feet.[51] People need such a base to survive and to live as true human beings. Raymond Plant argues that they need a minimum *"range of abilities and resources"* to be able to live a decent life.

One could also take the notion of security to be a leading value underlying human rights.[52] Security is often taken to refer to the possibility to stay alive physically, to one's physical life not being threatened by external factors, whether socio-economic conditions or other human beings. This security certainly is of existential importance. Larry Arnhart says that *"self-preservation is not so much the end as it is the necessary means to all of men's ends"*.[53] I regard the notion of well-being to encompass security in this sense. I prefer to use the notion of well-being as one of the underlying values of human rights, because this notion expresses that human rights not only wants to enable people to stay alive physically, but also to provide them with the possibilities to lead a *dignified* life. Guaranteeing this material base is a goal of human rights, for one cannot say that people are leading a dignified life when they live in abject poverty, are starving, suffering from illness without access to medical help, and are without shelter, food or drinking water. 'Well-being' is the absence of these deprivations, that prevent people from leading a dignified life. This is a point echoed by the Human Development Report 2004: it calls the idea of human vulnerability and the desire to alleviate—as much as possible—the suffering of every individual, the principle source of global ethics.[54]

Marshall and others see well-being as the key value of ESC-rights, because these rights are aimed at well-being.[55] I would like to add, though, that well-being is not exclusively the value of ESC-rights. In the preceding pages I have argued that freedom is not only a value underlying CP-rights but also one that underlies ESC-rights. And here, it must be said, well-being is not only the goal of ESC-rights but also of CP-rights. The ideology of human rights regards human beings as persons, as beings who are capable of leading their own lives and not just passive recipients of governmental provisions. CP-rights serve well-being by enabling people to stand up for themselves in their pursuit of it, for in striving for well-being, people must be free to organize without restriction (right of association), to meet without impediment (right of assembly), to speak up without intimidation (freedom of expression) and to follow their beliefs without hindrance (freedom of belief).

Both ESC-rights and CP-rights, therefore, are not only aimed at freedom, but also at well-being, at eliminating the deprivation that prevents people from leading a dignified life. Here, of course, it must be pointed out that it is difficult to exactly determine the level below which life can no longer be called dignified. But it is a topic being fully investigated by politicians and academics, to frame indicators that will define such a level. And, there has already been some success.[56] The Human Development Report 2000 states that statistical indicators—for example, with regard to maternal mortality, school-attendance by children in general (or of girls in particular), the number of illiterates—are important means in the fight for human rights. The *human development index*, the *gender-related development index*, and the *human poverty index* are important resources for the determination of need.[57] All three are helping to formulate the minimum conditions for a dignified life.

9. Participation

Participation, as mentioned above, is a key value of human rights and one of the principles of a just society. It accepts, as an element of a thin anthropology, that people are social beings, that they live with others, that they are one of many, and that they form societies and communities. It then, as a principle of public morality, requires that people be recognized as fellow human beings, as persons with their ideals, strivings and feelings, that they count, that they are treated with respect and are enabled to participate in the undertaking of living together. For if people are excluded, it will be nearly impossible for them to achieve their personal goals. And in addition, their self-respect will be damaged. Twine says that *"Inclusion in a society is essential to our identity and development. To socially exclude is to shrivel the social being."* Ignatieff, speaking about traditional societies, notes that *"It is not because traditional society defends practices abhorrent to Western standards that it is oppressive; but because traditional society does not accord all agents the equal right to speak and be heard. That is the universal and unconditional demand of human rights language."* A few sentences further on, he calls human rights the language of empowerment, and continues *"Its role is not in defining the content of culture but trying to enfranchise all agents so that they can freely shape that content".* [58] I heartily support Ignatieffs words but would like to add that in some traditional societies people talk and keep on talking until they all agree.

The notion of participation can be found in the UDHR, when it states that we should act towards one another in a spirit of brotherhood. (The terminology is a little unfortunate, as it looks as though sisters are excluded but the notion of brotherhood can be taken as having been meant to refer to all men and women.) Yet participation is often left out when it comes to a description of the values underlying human rights. It is striking, for example, that the Human Development Report 2000, quoted above, speaks about promoting the freedom, well-being and dignity of individuals in all societies, but says nothing about participation. However, participation is often *implied* when freedom is adduced as key principle and this is taken to imply also political freedom.[59] Nevertheless, it is worthwhile here to talk *explicitly* of participation as a value underlying human rights. People, in particular poor people, are often excluded from participation in society. They are silenced, their voices remain unheard. But they desperately want to be recognized as fellow human beings, to be heard, to be included in the making of decisions, and not always to have to receive the law handed down from above.[60]

It is the citizenship-tradition that has, in particular, attached great value to the participation of people in their society. Even as far back as Aristotle's time, he was arguing that being human meant being a citizen, that is, a full member of the *polis*, someone who is not merely governed, but who participates in governing.⁶¹ He went on to say that political power should not be exclusively vested in professional politicians, but that the citizens of a *polis* should be involved in the exercise op political power. This did not, however, mean that the idea of citizenship amounted to what is currently understood by the term 'democracy', because not every individual was regarded as a citizen. In old Athens, the term 'citizen' referred exclusively to adult men; women and slaves were not considered citizens and were, accordingly, excluded from participating in the government of the polis.[62] Yet while the political constellation in old Athens certainly cannot be called a democracy as we understand that notion today, it represented a valuable step forward in believing that free men should be able to participate in the governing of society. According to many the Athenian system also has its advantages compared to modern representative democracy as citizens voted directly on the issues concerned, rather than simply on who is to represent them, who would then (only hopefully) cast their vote in a way that the citizen would like.

Participation is mentioned by Marshall as the key value of political rights, as are the right to vote, the right to freedom of assembly and the right to freedom of association. Yet ESC-rights also have participation as a goal; they also want to protect people from being excluded. Jeremy Waldron argues that all theoreticians from the past have connected participation and people's socio-economic situation, to the extent that one need a certain level of welfare to be capable of participating as a full member of society.[63] It is extreme poverty and other forms of socio-economic deprivation that prevent people from becoming, and remaining, full members of society and that pose a threat to the general interest. Without a minimal level of welfare for all people, there is not sufficient *stability, solidarity* and *independence* and that is extremely detrimental to the public cause.

Aristotle believed that extreme inequality of welfare threatens *stability*. Those who remain very poor permanently will dispute the current distribution of resources while those who are very rich will, on the other hand, remain permanently focused on maintaining the current distribution. And because such a 'contest' of attitudes will be at the expense of the general interest it is, therefore, important to strive for the reduction of extreme inequality and for the avoidance of extreme poverty.[64]

A minimum level of welfare is also important for a sense of *solidarity*, something which is necessary if people are to be able to participate in society without distrusting one another. As long as a wide gap exists between the rich and the poor, no such solidarity will emerge or last nor will anyone be willing to dedicate themselves to the public cause. The rich will be concerned with enhancing their wealth; the poor will be concerned with surviving and will have no time for a public cause which is not theirs.

Sufficient basic welfare also contributes to citizens being *independent* and capable of forming and expressing their opinions. Rousseau argues that the arrangements of society should prevent citizens from becoming so rich that they can buy other people, and from becoming so poor that they can be bought by other people. If they are dependent, people cannot pay attention to the public cause. But independence also implies mental independence. Citizens should not be so poor that they are inclined to forego their public obligations in order to fulfill their primary needs, for people who are extremely poor cannot be expected to be devoted to public causes.[65] They will not be sufficiently motivated, and will have no 'room' to be concerned about matters of general interest, if they are totally preoccupied with their miserable socio-economic situation. They may, perhaps, be prepared to fight for their interests in the public arena and to demand that their needs be satisfied but that is *not* what is meant by participation in the tradition of republican citizenship tradition. Plato was of the view that citizenship implies trying to develop considered judgments of justice. It does not mean fighting for one's self-interest, but trying to find out what contributes to a more humane society, which of course may overlap one's own interest: it is "good citizenship" for a wealthy person to militate against poverty as being against the general interest, but also for a poor one to do so as relieving poverty is not only in the interest of the poor themselves but for the common good. The question is what is the underlying motivation: pursuing one's self-interest or contributing to a humane society. Good citizenship means a willingness to act on the basis of what contributes to a humane society. *But, if poor people try to improve their situation, not asking what would contribute to a human society, nobody can blame them for doing so. It just underlines that to have genuine citizens people should not be so poor that they are totally preoccupied by their own situation.* Poverty prevents people from engaging in the debate on such a humane society to which all participants should be able to dedicate themselves.

People must, therefore, enjoy an elementary level of economic security and welfare if they are to be able to participate. And an important part of such a level is provided by ESC-rights which means that these are, therefore, concerned not only with freedom and welfare but also with participation.[66]

We can conclude, therefore, that freedom, welfare and participation are goods that people need and have a right to if they are to live a dignified life, and that ESC-rights are concerned with promoting and guaranteeing these. They are just as important as CP-rights for the achievement of freedom, welfare and participation.

10. Individuality

As already mentioned, the idea of human rights—in addition to the substantial values described above—implies other, more structural, values. One of these is the principle of individuality. This presupposes that people are separate individuals and requires that they be treated with respect and care, and not be subordinated to the interests of the collectivity. For while it could, and no doubt will, be important to enhance the welfare of a community, this should eventually be to the benefit of individuals, although it cannot be avoided to weigh the interest of individuals the one against the other. The aim of a public policy of implementing ESC-rights will be to enable individuals, also less-advantaged individuals, to lead a dignified life, which may require forced contributions from the wealthy, or restrictions on the freedom of action that their superior economic position might otherwise permit. In the end such a public policy is not about the collectivity but about individuals.[67]

The principle of the individuality of human rights is not uncontested. Many writers from non-Western countries resist it as it appears to regard individuals as detached from cultural and societal bonds.[68] In international politics, representatives of many Asian countries, for example, Singapore, China and Indonesia, argue that Western individualism is disastrous for the social bonds in those countries and in conflict with East-Asian traditions.[69] Objections to the individualism of human rights have not only been raised by representatives of the Third World. In 18th and 19th century Europe, such objections were raised by Christians, conservatives, utilitarians and Marxists. Common to their criticisms is the rejection of the idea that human beings have an identity solely of their own, an identity that existed prior to, and independently of, their historical or cultural bonds or social commitments. They also oppose the idea that society results from contracts people have agreed to in order to advance their own individual interests. In contradistinction to that, they regard human beings as intrinsically social, as beings with an identity partly constituted by the community and whose feelings and thoughts are to a great extent determined by the community they live in, and the socio-economic relations therein.[70] Still today, some Westerners criticize the emphasis on individualism of human rights. For instance, communitarian philosophers echo 18th and 19th century thought by reproaching the human rights idea for presenting man as an unencumbered self, a person with an identity that existed prior to his or her involvement in, and commitments to, a community.[71]

These criticisms sound plausible. Human beings are, after all, not totally separated atoms but social beings. However, the individualism of human rights cannot be equated with an 'atomistic' view of man and society. It does not regard individuals as unencumbered selves that possess an identity without commitments and relationships.[72] Such 'atomism' is not reflected even in the individualism of representatives of liberal individualism such as Rawls, Scanlon or Barry. They do not presuppose that human beings live and grow outside any social and cultural context. Their individualism, and human rights individualism, is a *normative* individualism implying that individuals should not be abused for the sake of the interests of a collectivity and that everyone ought to be enabled to live a life worthy of a human being.[73] This individualism does not accept that for the sake of the safety of the collectivity individuals are deprived of the right to an appropriate defence and judgements are handed down by special tribunals whose function and composition do not respect the elementary principles of impartiality. And it equally does not accept that for the sake of economic growth individuals are deprived of adequate medical care, education, housing. The idea of normative individualism demand that individuals are taken care of, however difficult it may be to distribute that care fairly. Such a normative individualism *is* compatible with a view that regards human beings as rooted in a social and cultural context.

It is important to draw a difference between two levels at which the relationship between individuals and community is considered, to wit: a descriptive and a normative level or, to put it differently. the 'is'-level and the 'ought'-level. The untenable atomism, the view that human beings are atoms detached from their social and cultural context, is a descriptive view, purporting to describe a factual situation. It can be called an ontological individualism *"that considers abstract individuals gifted with fixed characteristics to be the sole elementary components of social life."*[74] The descriptive counterpart of atomism is the view that regards people as social beings, rooted in a community. I propose—for want of something better—calling that view 'communitism'.[75]

Whereas a descriptive view describes a factual situation, a normative view proposes what ought to be done. And at a normative level, two positions can be distinguished. Firstly one could adhere to the position that gives moral priority to collectives. The interests of collectives then rank higher than the interests of individuals and ought to be given full weight as compared to those of individuals. I will call this 'collectivism'. Such a collectivist position was taken by Nazism and Stalinism. Hitler was clear about the collectivist signature of Nazism. In his speech of January 30 1937 he said "The National Socialist program replaces the liberalistic conception of the individual by the conception of a people bound by their blood to the soil. Of all the tasks with which we are confronted, it is the grandest and most sacred task of man to preserve his race. This will not lead to an estrangement of the nations; on the contrary, it will lead for the first time to a mutual understanding".[76] All should be at the service of the Fatherland, of the Reich, of the German People.

Also Stalinism had a collectivist signature, in which all individuals should devote their lives to the goals of the State and the Party. The Pavlik-mythe breathes the spirit of this collectivism. It is said that a thirteen year old boy, Pavlik Morozov (1918 - 1932) reported his father, who was guilty of corruption, to the police. The boy was later killed by his grandparents and his nephew, but was hailed by the government as a real hero of the people. His story became a subject of books, songs, plays, a symphonie and an opera and six biographies. His life exemplified the duty of all good Soviet citizens to subordinate the well-being of individuals, or their family, to that of the People. The State was more important than family and opposing the state was selfish and reactionary. He was adopted as a patron saint by the "Young Pioneers," the Soviet equivalent to the "Boy Scouts". A Russian collective of authors have tried to mitigate the communist morality by arguing that the communist morality gives moral priority to the social interests over the individual interests, but that this is compatible with an individualist approach. *"Placing the priority of social interest over personal ones, communist morality has never juxtaposed them."*[77]

It will be clear that collectivism in this context does not refer to all kinds of collective action or provisions. Many collective arrangements, like for instance socialized medicine, are based on the desire to promote or protect the interests or needs of individuals. They are seen as public responsibility that require collective organization. But, eventually the issue at stake is not the welfare of the organization but the well-being of individuals, although it must be stressed again that it will be unavoidable that interests of various individuals will have to be weighed the one against the other.

In the second place one can adhere to a position which is called by Gewirth 'ethical individualism', but which I would like to refer to as 'normative individualism', a position in which everything, eventually, turns on the interest of individuals.[78] Here individuals take moral precedence over collectives and should not be sacrificed to promote the interest of the community. This does not imply that individuals cannot be expected to go to great pains on behalf of a community but, should this be necessary, it should only be so if the action eventually leads to the promotion of the good for the individual members of a community.

The individualism of human rights, therefore, is not atomism but a normative individualism and, as such, the opposite of collectivism. Human rights require that the fundamental interests of individuals be protected, even when this is at the expense of an abstract thing like the State, the Party, the People, or the Common Good. As said before every single item of socio-economic policy benefits some, and acts against the interests of others. A public policy of implementing ESC-rights -guaranteeing everyone access to education, adequate housing, health care- will benefit the least advantaged, but may hurt the self-interest of the rich. Public policy will have to deal with a possible collision of interests. What is stressed by the principle of individuality of human rights is that eventually everything turns on the welfare of individual people. Human rights are meaningless in collectivism, which adheres to the primacy of the collective.

Normative individualism is compatible with atomism, as long as this does not go so far as to deny that people live with one another and take account of one another. It is also compatible with communitism, as long as this does not deny the "distinctness of individuals" or the "separateness of persons".[79] I myself am of the view that human beings are social beings—rooted in a community, their ideas, needs, desires being influenced by the community—but that they take moral priority over the collective (position x).

		Normative level	
		Individualism	Collectivism
Descriptive level	Atomism		
	Communitism	x	

This normative individualism of human rights appears from the wordings of human rights. In general, it is said that "everyone has the right to.." or that the state parties recognize "the right of everyone to..." I think that 'everyone' can be taken to mean not only that individual human beings should be the beneficiaries and holders of the rights but that *every* individual should be the beneficiary and holder of those rights. I will discuss the latter aspect in the following section on equality but, as for the former aspect, that of individuality, it must be recalled that this is not content with a utilitarian position. Often, however, ESC-rights are interpreted in a utilitarian way, for instance, in the formulating of political tasks or goals that will in the end benefit people, but which do not imply genuine rights of which individual human beings can be holders. For instance, the Dutch Constitution states in article 22 that "*The authorities shall take steps to promote the health of the population...*". The Indian Constitution states in article 39 that "*...the State shall, in particular, direct its policy towards securing -.... that the health and strength of workers, men and women and the tender age of children are not abused...*" while in article 47 it states that "*The State shall regard the raising of the level of nutrition and the standard of living of its people and the improvement of public health as among its primary duties...*". Important as this may be the principle of individuality requires more than maximizing the overall good. Using this adage (of maximizing the overall good) in the political domain seems promising. After all, in personal daily life, people weigh sacrifices against benefits. Sometimes they decide to undergo suffering because its benefits will, in the end, counterbalance the sacrifices. Likewise, it could also be argued that is it justified to sacrifice the interests of an individual for the good of a community. Robert Nozick and John Rawls give an adequate response to this reasoning by saying that when an individual is weighing costs against benefits, it is the individual who is making decisions about his or her life: only one entity is involved. But when an individual is sacrificed to enhance the overall good, they argue, more entities are involved and justifying this runs against the idea of the separateness of individuals: the individual is deprived of the possibility of living a dignified life, the only life he or she has.[80]

The principle of individuality also underlies ESC-rights, in that they do not merely call for governments (and others) to try to improve the standard of living of the people or the population, but also to pursue a policy that is aimed at the promotion and protection of a dignified life for individuals. A government cannot be regarded as having addressed its ESC obligations adequately if the overall standard of living of the population has improved but the number of those who die from hunger has increased. A government has outstanding obligations to be addressed when health care has improved but still the HIV-infected die because they cannot afford medicines. A government should not regard the overall growth of the economy, particularly as measured by GDP, as an indication of its successful economic management when the income of individual people have fallen below the poverty line. As I have argued above, these rights flow from human dignity and aim to guarantee every individual a life worthy of a human being. ESC-rights are eventually not about the overall standard of living of the people, they are about the standard of living of individuals; if they were, then societies where the majority's well-being is at first world levels might escape censure for the existence within them of minorities who suffer from a third world level of impoverishment. This original inspiration still appears from article 25 of the UDHR als it says "Everyone has the right to a standard of living adequate for the health and well-being of himself and of his family, including food, clothing, housing and medical care and necessary social services, and the right to security in the event of unemployment, sickness, disability, widowhood, old age or other lack of livelihood in circumstances beyond his control." This is obviously also the view of the Committee on ESC-rights, for instance, when it states in General Comment No. 14 that *"Every human being is entitled to the enjoyment of the highest attainable standard of health conducive to living a life in dignity."*

11. Equality

Equality also is an important element of the ideology of human rights. Equality can be seen as an anthropological principle, remaining at a descriptive level and saying something about how human beings are. It then holds that people are fundamentally equal, that despite their undeniable differences, they are equal as human beings. They show similarities which make it possible to group them within one category: humankind. Stressing equality can also lead to, and has led to, the neglect of the particularities of people. Many, for instance, have argued that the emphasis placed on equality has resulted in the neglect of the particular situation of women against men, or that of cultural minorities against a majority.[81]

But that need not be the result of the principle of equality; it need not imply the denial of differences between people. Being equal does not mean being the same. One can point to the similarities between human beings while, at the same time, also having an eye for the differences between them, as was noted by Shirin Ebadi, winner of a Nobel Prize in 2003.

> People are different, and so are their cultures.
> People live in different ways, and civilizations also differ.
> People speak in a variety of languages. People are guided by different religions.
> People are born different colors and many traditions influence their live with varying colors and shades.
> People dress differently and adapt to their environment in different ways.
> People express themselves differently. Music, literature and art reflect different styles as well.
> But despite many differences, people have one single common attribute: they are all human beings, nothing more, nothing less.[82]

It is this fundamental human equality that is explicitly recognized in various human rights documents, for example, in article 1 of the UDHR, which states that "*all human beings are born free and equal in dignity and rights.*" Equality will not only be used as a descriptive principle, saying how people are, but also as a normative one, saying what should be done.

As a normative principle, equality has a distributive signature, which makes it different from the principles of freedom, of participation, and of well-being, all of which are aggregative principles. These principles require the maximization of the freedom, participation and well-being of people: the more freedom, participation and well-being, the better.[83] Yet this could, paradoxically, result in the freedom, participation and well-being of some people being maximized at the expense of others, something forbidden by the principle of equality. This holds that an individual's freedom, participation and well-being is as valuable as that of somebody else, and that every human being is to be treated with equal concern and respect. It is the expression of the idea that being a person, being free to live as one thinks fit, being given the opportunity to participate in society, being free from pain and suffering and need are all constituent elements of a dignified life that have their own intrinsic value and are regarded as valuable by everybody. It is a belief in the basic moral equality of all human beings that can be found all over the world and is part of the morality of most belief systems. "*The injunction to treat others as you would want to be treated finds explicit mention in Buddhism, Christianity, Confucianism, Hinduism, Taoism and Zoroastrianism, and is implicit in the practices of other faiths.*" [84]

The ideology of human rights holds to the old adage, already found in Aristotle, that similar cases should be treated equally, unless a relevant difference between them exists to justify different treatment. The Aristotelian principle says that when someone who suffers from a certain disease is given a particular treatment, then someone else who suffers from the same disease and who is also in the same condition should be given the same treatment. When someone is granted admission to a university, another person with the same test sores and college grades should be admitted as well.

At first sight, this Aristotelian principle is very appealing. On second thoughts however, it seems to be at odds with common sense. When a car-driver gives a lift to a hitchhiker, is she then obligated to give a lift to other hitchhikers, too? And when I give a book to a student of mine, should I then also give books to other students? Most people would, I think, answer 'No'. This could lead to a reformulation of the Aristotelian principle, for one could point to an important difference, one that distinguishes these latter examples from the earlier ones of the patient who need treatment and of the persons seeking admission to a university.

In the earlier examples, an obligation exists before the comparison is made. By this I mean that before the comparison a societal obligation already exists, i.e. to give a patient the required treatment or to allow university admission to a qualified person. Such an obligation, preceding the comparison, does not exist in the cases of the hitchhiker or the student to whom I gave a book. This is what could lead to the reformulation of the Aristotelian principle: If an obligation exists to treat someone in a particular way, also others should be treated similarly, unless relevant differences exist that justify different treatment. But, there is no obligation to give a lift to hitchhikers, or a book to my students. Therefore, I'm free to treat the one differently from the other, so it could be argued.

Yet, this is not a satisfying move. Suppose that an employer have taken several men and women into his employ and is obliged to pay them a certain salary. Suppose further the employer is doing this properly but that, at a certain moment, he decides to give the men 20% extra, while leaving the women at the old salary level. While this is not in conflict with the reformulated Aristotelian principle (as the employer is not obligated to pay a 20% rise), it is nevertheless in conflict with common sense. Let's take another example. I'm not obliged to give either of my grandchildren an ice-cream but suppose, though, that while I'm walking with them I decide to give an ice-cream to one while withholding it from the other. Again, this is not at odds with the reformulated Aristotelian principle, but it is certainly in conflict with our moral feelings. Both examples, I believe, indicate that the reformulated principle does not, when all is said and done, suffice.

Perhaps we should return to the initial Aristotelian principle. But then we are still confronted with the problem of the hitchhiker and the student. The solution could be that we have not examined properly the situations involved. Suppose that I knew that hitch-hiker A urgently has to go somewhere while hitch-hiker B is not in a hurry. Am I still free to treat the hitch-hikers the way I want, or would it not be just to take hitch-hiker A? And, if I knew that student A is very poor, whereas student B is rather rich, would I then still free to give the book to whomever I want, or would it not be just to give the book to A? While the situations of the various hitch-hikers and the cases of the various students seem to be similar on the surface, it's apparent that, on further investigation, they are not. So when confronted with the question of whether cases should be treated similarly, it is necessary to find out to what extent they are similar. We could then hold to the initial Aristotelian principle, but complement it with criteria that indicate what differences are relevant: 'need' and 'desert' (or 'merit') could be such important criteria.

If someone is in urgent *need* of something, this could offer the relevant difference that justifies treating various persons differently. A government that exerts itself to provide adequate housing for the poor, while paying less attention to the housing of the rich, treats the poor and the rich differently, but this is however justified because a relevant difference exists: need.

Desert (merit) can also create such a relevant difference. If some people have worked hard to educate themselves and to get a job to overcome their socio-economic hardship, while others have adopted an attitude of waiting while complaining about their plight, this might be a reason to treat them differently. One should, however, guard against justifying unequal socio-economic situations by appealing to desert. The view that people *deserve* their wealth because of their talents or birth should be approached with suspicion. Talents that people happen to possess and the social position they find themselves in are arbitrary from a moral point of view.[85] The notion of *desert* is related to the idea of control. If we say that someone deserves a certain punishment, the presupposition then will be that the person involved had control over what he or she had done. It cannot be said that someone deserves punishment for something which was completely beyond his or her control. Likewise, it cannot be said that someone deserves a reward on the basis of something which was completely outside her frame of control. Treating people differently on the basis of what they deserve is only justified if it can be proved that they had control over the situation involved. Therefore, it is wrong to treat people differently with an appeal to what they are supposed to deserve, if what we really mean is that they differ in intelligence, appearance or familial socio-economic advantage.

Equality is a distributive principle, one that places limits on the aggregative principles of freedom, well-being and participation. It forbids the enlargement of the total amount of freedom, well-being and participation if this results in some people being deprived of freedom, well-being and participation.[86] Everyone is entitled to these goods: all people should be recognized as human beings, enabled to live their own lives, to participate, and possess a minimum of material well-being.[87] This is also recognized by various documents that use wordings such as *"everyone has the right to .."* or "the states parties recognize *the right of everyone to...*" 'Everyone' has, as mentioned previously, an aspect of individuality and an aspect of equality, and equality is also confirmed by many documents when they speak of *"equal rights"*. For example, the UDHR, which states that *"Whereas recognition of the inherent dignity and of the equal and inalienable rights of all members of the human family..."* Equality also appears from the prohibition of discrimination that is expressed in many human rights documents, for instance in article 2 of the UDHR *"Everyone is entitled to all the rights and freedoms set forth in this Declaration, without distinction of any kind, such as race, colour, sex, language, religion, political or other opinion, national or social origin, property, birth or other status."*

The principle of equality also underlies ESC-rights. In its General Comment No.16, regarding article 3 of the ICESCR (on the equal right of men and women to the enjoyment of all economic, social and cultural rights) the Committee on ESC-rights explicitly states that *"The equal right of men and women to the enjoyment of all human rights is one of the fundamental principles recognized under international law and enshrined in the main international human rights instruments."*

12. Neutrality

Neutrality is a characterizing principle of human rights, although it is not mentioned in human rights documents. It does not mean colourlessness, void of values. Human rights express a vision of a dignified life; they are directed at clear values (as mentioned in the preceding pages) and they require a permanent commitment to these values to make them work, since their realization will never occur if people simply wait for them to appear. But, this vision is neutral, it is not a outlook on life itself.[88] It is a public morality aimed at providing people with different beliefs with principles which will enable them to live peacefully and pursue their beliefs.

One could argue that the ideology of human rights still is contentious. That cannot be denied and it cannot be avoided, for every theory of justice will always be contentious to someone and there will always be people who dislike it. And if one holds neutrality to mean that everybody will be equally pleased with the outcome, then it will be impossible to achieve that, because there will always be people who want their conception of the 'good life' to rule the arrangements of society.

What the concept of neutrality implies though is the idea that the principles of the ideology of human rights cannot reasonably be rejected by people with different beliefs or conceptions of good. It does not itself represent, or express or manifest a particular belief, and it is neutral with regard to various outlooks on life.[89]

Often the human rights ideology is called "secular". For instance, Ignatieff writes *"Fifty years after its proclamation, the Universal Declaration of Human Rights has become the sacred text of what Elie Wiesel has called a 'worldwide secular religion.'"*[1] It can be confusing to use the word secular, as sometimes secularity is taken to be opposed to religion. The secularity of Russia and China in the communist era, for example, meant that the state kept religion out of the public domain, while at the same time permitting itself to enter the domain of religion and to mould it into a form that it considered acceptable. Such secularity—one that restricts religious freedom—is not the secularity of human rights.

Neither, I would say, should it be equated with secularity in the sense of strict separation of church and state. This notion of secularity is often used with respect to states. Separation of state and church calls for mutual exclusion of the two, an idea adhered to by many countries, as is noted by the Human Development Report 2004: the state should not want religion or religious leaders to interfere with state business, just as the state itself must refrain from interfering with religious affairs. In France, for example, the principle of *laïcité* requires separation of state and church and forbids ostentatious displays of religious affiliation in the public domain, which may make it the country with the strictest interpretation ever of the separation of the two institutions.[90] But even there, religion has pervaded the public domain: holidays are Catholic holy days, most offices and shops are closed at Sundays, cities are named after saints (St. Jean de Luz, St. Marie de la Mer) and public schools are often, in fact, Catholic schools.[91]

Many countries call themselves secular but do not interpret this as strict separation of church and state but as neutrality. This, unlike strict separation, does not necessarily mean that there is no involvement by the state in religion and it accepts that relationships may exist between state and religions. But, it demands that the state will not have an established church, that it will not promote or support one religion over others, but rather accords equal respect and concern to all religions (and to non-believers).[92]

This neutrality does not forbid a state to support religious activity provided it does not favor one religion over another.[93] It may, for example, give financial support to religious schools, although such support should always be even-handed. The state may also, and again only on an impartial basis, intervene to protect human rights. Both of which points illustrate that secularity, interpreted as neutrality, does not imply necessarily strict separation of church and state. The Human Development Report 2004 notes the secular design of the Constitution of India as an example of such a neutrality, one it calls 'secularism with principled distance'. This secularism resulted in the Indian state recognizing the customary laws, codes and practices of minority religious communities because it was beneficial to their cultural integration. On the other hand, it is also prepared to intervene when human rights have been violated, for instance when 'untouchables' are prohibited from entering temples. It must be added, however, that the recent growth of communal violence in the country makes observers skeptical of the secular credentials of today's Indian politicians.[94]

Human rights may be called secular in this sense of neutrality. This claims that human rights should be acceptable to all and wants to give equal concern and respect to all, regardless of their conceptions of a good life.

13. Concluding comments

Hopefully, I have clarified a little bit the relationship between human rights and human dignity. My own personal exploration has brought me to the insight that human dignity is involved in human rights in two respects: it is the source of human rights as well as their goal. Human rights derive from the dignity of every human being and they are directed at promoting a dignified life.

I have proposed the view that freedom, well-being and participation are the necessary conditions for a dignified life, that people have generic *rights* to freedom, participation and well-being, and that the various particular human rights are intended to realize these generic rights. To that extent freedom, participation and well-being can be called the substantial values underlying human rights.[95]

Some other values (structural in character) can also be distinguished; that is individuality, equality and neutrality values that characterize both CP as well as ESC-rights. Being free from hunger, from illiteracy, having adequate food, water, shelter and access to decent healthcare is as important to freedom, well-being and participation as any of the CP-rights. And it should be remembered that ESC-rights are, finally, about *individuals*. They are about *every* individual, assume that the life of every individual counts and that every individual should be treated with equal concern and respect, regardless of their beliefs.

In short, both categories of rights are needed to enable everyone to lead a dignified life and I see no reason whatsoever to regard CP-rights as being of greater importance than ESC-rights. Both are equally vital in the pursuit of a full, rewarding life. However, many people do not enjoy the goods that are necessary for dignified living because of their miserable socio-economic situation. That certainly is sad, but is it unjust?

BIBLIOGRAPHY

Alston, Philip, & J.H.H. Weiler, 'An EU Human Rights Policy', in: Philip Alston (ed.), *The EU and Human Rights* (Oxford: Oxford University Press, 1999).

Arnhart, Larry, *Political Questions* (New York: Macmillan Publishing Company, 1987).

Brümmer, Vincent, *Wijsgerige Begripsanalyse* (Kampen: Kok, 1989).

Human Rights, Human Plights in a Global Village / Rob Buitenweg

Cassese, A., *Human Rights in a Changing World* (Cambridge: Polity Press, 1990).

Cliteur, Paul, 'Neo-Liberal Globalism and Philosophical Presuppositions', in: Nieuwenhuys, Eva (ed.) *Neo-Liberal Globalism and Social Sustainable Globalisation* (Leiden,Boston: Brill 2006)

Committee of Ministers, Council of Europe, *Recommendation No. R (2000) 3 of the Committee of Ministers to member states on the Right to the Satisfaction of Basic Material Needs of Persons in Situations of Extreme Hardship* (19 January 2000).

Cranston, Maurice, 'Human Rights, real and supposed', in: D.D. Raphaël Macmillan (red.), *Political theory and the rights of man* (London etc: Macmillan, 1967)

Donnelly, Jack, 'Human Rights and Human Dignity: An Analytic Critique of Non-Western Conceptions of Human Rights', in: *The American Political Science Review* 76 (June 1982).

Dower, Nigel, *An Introduction to Global Citizenship* (Edinburgh University Press, 2003)

Dworkin, Ronald, *Taking Rights Seriously* (London: Duckworth, 1977).

Eide, Asbjørn & B. Hagtvet (ed.), 'Introduction', in: *Human Rights in Perspective: A global assessment* (Oxford, Blackwell, 1992).

Feinberg, Joel, *Social Philosophy* (Englewood Cliffs, NJ: Prentice Hall, 1973)

Fuller, Lon L., *The Morality of Law* (New Haven and London: Yale University Press, 1969).

Genugten, W.J.M. van, *Mensenrechten in Ontwikkeling: Het 'goede doel' voorbij* (Nijmegen: Katholieke Universiteit Nijmegen, 1992).

Gewirth, Alan, *The Community of Rights* (Chigago and London: The University of Chicago Press, 1996).

Grant, Robert, *American Ethics and the virtuous citizen* (New York: the Humanist Press, 1999)

Gewirth, Alan, *Self-Fulfillment* (Princeton, New Jersey: Princeton University Press, 1998).

Houten, Douwe van, *De standaardmens voorbij, over zorg, verzorgingsstaat en burgerschap* (Maarssen: Elsevier/De Tijdstroom, 1999).

Ignatieff, Michael, *Whose Universal Values* (Amsterdam, the Hague, Praemium Erasmianum Essay, 1999).

Kymlicka, W., *Contemporary Political Philosophy* (Oxford: Clarendon Press, 1990).

Kymlicka, Will, *Multicultural Citizenship* (Oxford: Clarendon Press, 1995).

L.J. Macfarlane, *The Theory and Practice of Human Rights* (London: Maurice Temple Smith, 1985)

Manschot, Henk, 'Als wereldburger leven: Kosmopolitisme en solidariteit, een probleemstelling', in: Theo de Wit & Henk Manschot (ed.), *Solidariteit. Filosofische kritiek, ethiek en politiek* (Amsterdam: Boom, 1999).

Marshall, T.H., *Sociology at the Crossroads* (London, 1963).

Marshall, T.H., *Citizenship and Social Development* (London and Chicago: University of Chicago Press, 1977).

Nino, Carlos Santiago, *The Ethics of Human Rights* (Oxford: Oxford University Press, 1993).

Office of the High Commissioner for Human Rights, *Human Rights and Poverty Reduction*, (New York, Geneva: United Nations, 2004)

Orwin, Clifford, and Thomas Pangle, 'The Philosophical Foundation of Human Rights', in: Marc F. Plattner (ed.), *Human Rights in Our Time* (Boulder and London: Westview Press, 1984).

Packer, John, 'The Content of Minority Rights', in: Juha Raïkkä (ed.), *Do We Need Minority Rights?* (The Hague, Boston and London: Martinus Nijhoff Publishers 1996).

Plant, Raymond, *Modern Political Thought* (Oxford etc.: Basil Blackwell, 1991).

Perry, Michaël J., "The Morality of Human Rights: A Nonreligious Ground? (Emory Law Journal, Vol.54, 2005)

Pogge, Thomas, *World Poverty and Human Rights, Cosmopolitan Responsibilities and Reforms* (Cambridge: Polity Press, 2002/2003)

Rachels, James, *Can Ethics Provide Answers?* (London, Lanham and Maryland: Rowman and Littlefield Publishers, Inc. 1997).

Rawls, J., *A Theory of Justice* (Oxford: Oxford University Press, 1971/1976

Rawls, John, 'Justice as Fairness: Political, not Metaphysical', in: *Philosophy and Public Affairs* 14 (1985).

Rawls, J. *Political Liberalism* (New York: Columbia University Press, 1993).

Raz, J., *The Morality of Freedom* (Oxford: Clarendon Press, 1986).

Rorty, Richard, 'Justice as the Larger Loyalty', in: *Ethical Perspectives, Journal of the European Ethics Network* 4, nr.3 (Leuven: European Centre for Ethics, 1997).

Sandel, Michael, 'The limits of liberalism', in: Stephen Mulhall en Adam Swift (ed.), *Liberals & Communitarians* (Oxford: Blackwell Publishers, 1992).

Shestack, Jerome J., 'The Philosophical Foundations of Human Rights', in: Janusz Symonides (ed.), *Human Rights: Concept and Standards* (Aldershot, Burlington, Singapore etc.: Dartmouth Publishing, Ashgate Publishing & Unesco Publishing, 2000).

Steenbergen, Bart van, *The Condition of Citizenship* (London: Sage Publications, 1994).

Taylor, Ch., 'The sources of the liberal self', in: Stephen Mulhall en Adam Swift (ed.), *Liberals & Communitarians* (Oxford: Blackwell Publishers, 1992).

Twine, Fred, *Citizenship and Social Rights* (London: Sage Publications 1994).

United Nations Development Programme, Human Development Report 2000 (New York: Oxford University Press, 2000).

Uyl, Douglas J. Den & Douglas B. Rasmussen, 'Rights as MetaNormative Principles', in: Tibor R. Machan and Douglas B. Rasmussen (ed.), *Liberty for the Twenty-First Century* (Lanham: Rowman & Littlefield, 1995).

Vlastos, G., 'Justice and Equality', in: Jeremy Waldron (ed.) *Theories of Rights* (Oxford: Oxford University Press, 1984).

Wal, G.A. van der, 'The individualism of Human Rights=, in: *Rechtsfilosofie en Rechtstheorie* 18, nr.3 (Zwolle: Tjeenk Willink, 1989).

Waldron, Jeremy, *Liberal Rights* (Cambridge: Cambridge University Press, 1993).

Waldron, Jeremy, >The Cosmopolitan Alternative= in: Will Kymlicka (ed.), *The Rights of Minority Cultures* (Oxford: Oxford University Press, 1995).

Xiaorong, Li, *Aziatische Waarden en de Universaliteit van Mensenrechten*, in: Martha Meijer (ed.), *Grondrecht en Wisselgeld* (Utrecht: Greber Uitgever, Humanistisch Overleg Mensenrechten, 1998).

General Comment No. 14 (2000), The right to the highest attainable standard of health(article 12 of the International Covenant on Economic, Social and Cultural Rights)

Ignatieff, Michael, "Human Rights as Politics and Idolatry", edited by Amy Gutmann (ed.), Princeton: Princeton University press, 2003).

ENDNOTES

[1] HDR 2005, Chapter 5.
[2] Macfarlane 1985 p.1,3; Donnelly 1982, p.304,305; Gewirth 1996, p.6; Dower 2003, p.55.
[3] Ignatieff 1999, p.52; Cliteur 2006, p.30.
[4] Cranston 1967, p.43.
[5] Office of the High Commissioner on Human Rights 2004, p.9.
[6] Rachels 1997, p.73.
[7] Gewirth 1998, p.163.
[8] Dworkin 1977, p.198; Feinberg 1973, p.94.
[9] Perry 2005, p.102.
[10] HDR 2000, p.16; Also the UDHR in its preamble speaks of "the worth of the human person". The ICCPR and the ICESCR say inn their preamble "Recognizing that

11. these rights derive from the inherent dignity of the human person..."
    Donnelly 1982, p.305; Wal 1988, p. 98; Wal 1989, p. 202.
12. Human Dignity, Human Rights, http://www.firstthings.com/ftissues/ft9911/articles/mnovak.html, retr. October 2005.
13. HDR 2004, p.13.
14. Gewirth 1998, p.170.
15. HDR 2000, p 16.
16. Rachels 1997, p. 73.
17. Gewirth 1996, p.17.
18. Ignatieff 1999, pp.52,54.
19. Manschot 1999, p.194 ; Rorty 1997, p.9; Rachels 1997, p.105.
20. If all people have generic rights, then it can also be said that all people are bearers of *duties* flowing from these rights. For, if not all people had the correlative duties, the possession of well-being, freedom and participation would be endangered, which would be in conflict with the statement that people should have freedom, well-being and participation.
21. According to the Human Rights Committee, the committee that monitors the implementation of the International Covenant on Civil and Political Rights, "*Article 18 protects theistic, non-theistic and atheistic beliefs, as well as the right not to profess any religion or belief. The terms 'belief' and 'religion' are to be broadly construed. Article 18 is not limited in its application to traditional religions or to religions and beliefs with institutional characteristics or practices analogous to those of traditional religions...*" (General Comment nr.22)
22. Ignatieff 1999, p.52.
23. Marshall 1963, p.70; Marshall 1977, p.78.
24. Brümmer 1989, p.140.
25. As it can be seen, I include among the ontological dimension ideas with regard to human beings. In some cases, ideas about human beings are distinguished from ideas concerning the world and only the latter are taken to be ontological ideas, whereas the former are called anthropological.
26. Fuller 1969, p.5.
27. Orwin & Pangle 1984, p.3.
28. Orwin & Pangle 1984, p.3; Fuller 1969, p.5; Grant 1999, p.113; Pogge 2002/2003, p.92.
29. Waldron 1995, p.98.
30. Shestack 2000, p.43.
31. Nino 1993, p.130.
32. Rawls 1973, p.513; Kymlicka 1995, p.75; Raz 1986, p.369.
33. Kymlicka 1990, p.17, 203; Raz 1986, p.37.
34. Rawls 1985, p.241.
35. Rawls 1985, p.240.
36. Kymlicka 1995, p.162.
37. Rawls 1985, p.240.
38. Packer 1996, p.123.
39. Human Rights and Poverty Reduction, OHCHR, 2004, p. 9.
40. United Nations Development Programme, Human Development Report 2000, Overview, p.12. United Nations Development Programme, *Human Development Report 2000* (New York: Oxford University Press, 2000) p.iii.
41. Rawls, 1971/1976, p.204.
42. Raz, 1986, p.372.
43. HDR 2005, p.18.
44. Waldron, 1993, p.276.
45. Office of the High Commissioner for Human Rights 2004 p.9.
46. HDR 2000, p.1.
47. HDR 2000, p.19.
48. Raz 1986, p.289.
49. Raz 1986, pp.290, 292.
50. Vlastos 1984, p.56.

51 Dower 2003, p.57.
52 Plant 1991, p.266; Arnhart 1987, p.193.
53 HDR 2004, p.90.
54 Marshall 1977, p.78.
55 Van Genugten 1992, p.11.
56 HDR 2000, chapter 5.
57 Van Houten 1999, p.106; Twine 1994, p.105; Ignatieff 1999, p.41.
58 HDR 2004, p.21.
59 Office of the High Commissioner for Human Rights 2004, p.18.
60 Dower 2003, p.134.
61 Waldron 1993, p.283.
62 Waldron 1993, p.284, Pogge 2002/2003, p.48.
63 Waldron, 1993, p.286, Dower, 2003, p.91.
64 Waldron, 1993, p.287.
65 Twine, 1994, p.104.
66 Gewirth 1996, p. 97; Pogge 2002/2003, p.193.
67 Legesse 1980, p. 124; Van der Wal 1989, p.195; see also http://www.foreignaffairs.org/20011101faessay5777/ michael-ignatieff/the-attack-on-human-rights.html, retrieved February 2007.
68 Xiaorong 1998, p.42; Donnelly 1982, p.308.
69 Van der Wal 1989, p.96; Cassese 1990, p.52.
70 Taylor 1992, p.110; Sandel 1992, pp.49,51.
71 Raz 1986, p.308.
72 Kymlicka 1990, p.209; Eide & Hagtvet 1992, xv; Vlastos 1984, p.56; Rawls 1971/1976, p.252,560; Rawls 1985, p.238; Pogge 2002/2003, p.193.
73 Van der Wal 1989, p.199.
74 I would like to avoid words like communism, communitarianism and communalisme that already have different meanings.
75 http://www.hitler.org/speeches/01-30-37.html, retrieved June 2007.
76 Titarenko 1986, p.54.
77 Gewirth 1996, p. 97; Pogge, 2002/2003, p.193.
78 Ignatieff 1999, pp.36,37; Rawls 1976, pp.29,27.
79 Nozick 1974, p.33; Rawls 1993, p.74; Dower 2003, p.54.
80 It can be added that emphasising the equality of human beings can lead to shutting one's eyes to the similarities between human beings and many animals. It is curious that we speak about human beings and animals as different categories when there are, in fact, more similarities between human beings and apes or elephants than between elephants and ants.
81 HDR 2004, p.23.
82 Rachels 1997, pp.166,178.
83 HDR 2004, p. 90; Dower 2003, p.54.
84 Rachels 1997, p.179; Rawls 1976, p.104; Pogge 2002/2003, p.93.
85 Nino 1993, p.164; Kymlicka 1990, p.31.
86 Vlastos 1984, p.58; Nino 1993, p.149.
87 Ignatieff, 2003, p.53.
88 Grant 1999, p.113.
89 Compare with the English notion of 'lay'.
90 And it should be noted in passing that the problem with a strict interpretation of the principle of separation of state and church is that the principle then forbids the state from interfering with religions that obviously violate human rights and threaten democratic values.
91 HDR 2004, p.56.
92 HDR 2004, p.102.
93 HDR 2004, p.56.
94 I have taken well-being to include (physical) security.

CHAPTER 4

POVERTY
IS ANYONE TO BLAME?

> *"Massive poverty and obscene inequality are such terrible scourges of our times—times in which the world boasts breathtaking advances in science, technology, industry and wealth accumulation—that they have to rank alongside slavery and apartheid as social evils."*
>
> **Nelson Mandela**

1. Introduction

"*Human rights express our deepest commitments to ensuring that all persons are secure in their enjoyment of the goods and freedoms that are necessary for dignified living.*"[1] Many people do not enjoy the goods and freedoms that are necessary for dignified living. Poverty is still widespread. About half of the world's population, some 3 billion people, live below the World Bank's poverty line of $2 a day and are faced with socio-economic misery. More than 1 billion live on less than half that, that is, below the World Bank's 1$-a-day (extreme) poverty line. Poverty is not only a problem of the so-called Third World, but also within Europe and America. The Organization for Economic Cooperation and Development (OECD) reported in *Poverty Dynamics in Six OECD Countries* that poverty in Western Europe and North America is more widespread than previously thought.[2]

The report uses a method different from those generally used, ones that primarily indicate how many people are poor at a point in time. But such 'static' poverty rates do not show how many people fall into poverty during their lives or how long they stay in such a state. If, therefore, one estimates the number of people who fall temporarily below the poverty line and those who return to this position within a given time, poverty appears to be more widespread. Over the six-year period of the study by the OECD, between twelve and almost 40 percent of the population across the six nations were affected by poverty.³ And it is certain groups in particular, that are confronted with socio-economic misery. According to the World Bank, the majority of the approximately eight million Roma people in Europe are close to poverty, while eighty percent of the Roma in Bulgaria and Romania live below the 2$-poverty-line.

As regards the United States, the US Census Bureau states that the official poverty rate in 2004 was 12.7 percent, up from 12.5 percent in 2003. In 2004, 37.0 million people were in poverty. Poverty rates remained unchanged for Blacks (24.7 percent) and Hispanics (21.9 percent), but rose for non-Hispanic Whites (8.6 percent in 2004, up from 8.2 percent in 2003) and decreased for Asians (9.8 percent in 2004, down from 11.8 percent in 2003).⁴

The occurrence of poverty in Europe and the US should not conceal the fact that poverty in the Third World is more widespread and enormous, and the cause of much suffering by vast numbers of people. While these figures are important indicators of poverty, our understanding of the indicators of poverty should not be reduced to that of low income. Poverty can be described as inadequate command over economic resources, with low income being one possible source of this inadequate command.

But low income is not the only source of poverty, as was stressed by a report of the Office of the High Commissioner on Human Rights, titled *Human Rights and Poverty Reduction*. Other sources are lack of access to publicly provided or communally owned services, or lack of access to networks in command of the relevant resources.⁵ Yet although poverty is to be interpreted in this broader way, income certainly is an important factor in the ability to exert some command over economic resources and in gaining access to services. The abovementioned low-income figures are well known facts, but hardly anybody is really upset by these figures. And while some think that poverty could be eradicated, or at least greatly reduced, many others are skeptical of the possibility of overcoming global poverty.⁶ Although their remarks are well known, I will offer a brief description of some of them below.

2. Skeptics on social justice

Often skeptics say that reducing poverty will result in overpopulation, which in turn will lead to huge demands on resources and, in the end, will result in even more extreme poverty. However, this position seems to neglect the fact that alleviating poverty in general leads to a fall in birth rates, especially so when women are given access to education and work.

It is also said that world poverty is too vast a problem to be solved, that it is a Sisyphean labor and that, despite all the efforts that have been undertaken to alleviate it, it has not been overcome, nor even been substantially reduced. No matter how you level the sand, it always humps into dunes again. That may be true. But many individuals have also been saved from starvation, many individuals have been enabled to lead a humane life, many children have been protected from child labour and exploitation, and many women have been saved from forced prostitution. So while the amount of human misery may not have diminished, it should be borne in mind that every human being that is saved from misery and enabled to live a dignified life is a contribution to a more humane world.

Sometimes it is assumed that fighting poverty is too costly. In particular, questions are raised about whether Millennium Development Goals (MDGs) are affordable. But, as has been stated by the Human Development Report 2005, what is affordable is a question of political priorities. The investments needed to implement the MDGs are modest compared to the scale of wealth in rich countries. For example, to provide 2.6 billion people with access to clean water, $7 billion is needed annually over the next decade... less than Europeans spend on perfume and less than Americans spend on elective corrective surgery.[7] Investing this amount of money in improving access to clean water would save an estimated 4,000 lives each day.

Those skeptical of the possibility of overcoming world poverty also say that we have already spent millions and millions of dollars on alleviating world poverty, but that it has not substantially changed the situation, and that all we are doing is pouring money into a bottomless pit. These skeptics may well be right, but if they are, then what conclusion should we draw? That we should do nothing while millions of the world's poor starve—or maybe that we should take another road. As Thomas Pogge points out, throwing money at poverty is not the way to alleviate it.[8] And what is the use of giving money to a developing country if economically powerful countries wanting to protect their own economy prevent it from selling its products on the world market by imposing import duties or other socio-economic measures? Alleviating poverty requires a restructuring of the world economy, and indeed, concomitant to that, an understanding of how it really functions.

These concrete judgments about the impossibility of overcoming global poverty are often accompanied and supported by ethical objections to ideas of social justice itself. Often, in such instances, even were social justice to be regarded as of concern, the alleviation of poverty or other socio-economic misery—at both the national and international level—is not seen as a matter of justice, let alone as a question of genuine rights and duties. This is a view often expressed by various representatives of "strict" libertarianism, who stress freedom-rights as paramount and are averse to a politics of social justice, to a politics of implementing ESC-rights.[9] Libertarianism is by Ian Narveson described as "... *the doctrine that the only relevant consideration in political matters is individual liberty: that there is a delimitable sphere of action for each person, the person's rightful liberty, such that one may be forced to do or to refrain from what one wants to do only if what one would do or not do would violate, or at least infringe, the rightful liberty of some other person(s). No other reasons for compelling people are allowable..."*[10] This libertarianism certainly seems an attractive ideology, but strict libertarians often do not have the same watchful eye for the violation of the freedom of others as they do for people purportedly exercising their rightful liberty.

Libertarianism does stress the importance of human rights, but it focuses on CP-rights. These rights are regarded as negative rights, rights that entail negative duties, i.e. duties to *refrain* from doing something. However, libertarians have problems with economic, social and cultural rights, seeing them as entailing positive duties, duties to perform a certain action. Often governments are seen as the duty-bearers of ESC-rights. In order to fulfill their duties, they have to impose taxes on citizens who then become, in effect, the eventual duty bearers. But if these citizens have not of their own free will consented to carry out their duties, then such rights imply that they are being coerced, compelled to do one thing rather than another and prevented from doing what they please with their lives. This is, according to strict libertarians, a violation of liberty.[11]

Libertarianism underlies the free-market ideology, which holds that a global free-market will enhance overall welfare and that its beneficial effects will eventually serve as a remedy against the socio-economic misery with which many world citizens are still confronted. It was, according to Paul Hunt, the dominant ideology of the 1990s.[12] I think that it still is. Its spirit is still noticeable in the current policies of the World Bank and the International Monetary Fund, and in the ongoing rounds of free trade negotiations which pursue market liberalization to open the markets of the developing countries, even as western countries continue to shut out third world exports.

So it may be asked whether that has relieved poverty. Since the 1970s, the World Bank and the International Monetary Fund have had much influence in Africa. According to David Sogge, these institutions dominate economic politics and public sectors in this continent: local governments have at minimum to share the sovereignty of their countries with them and with other aid organizations. Yet despite, or perhaps because of, the intervention of the aforementioned institutions, poverty in Africa has only increased. Sogge mentions that researchers from the World Bank have estimated that the number of Africans living in extreme poverty—below the 1$-a-day line—almost doubled between 1981 and 2001, from 164 million to 316 million. Now 47 percent of the population live below that line, while almost 77 percent live below the 2$-a-day line. In a world in which access to healthcare, education, adequate housing and work are no longer handled by the public sector, but are turned over to the forces of the free-market, poverty only increases.[13] Libertarianism, taken to be the ideology that advocates freedom, certainly has its good side. But, as I will show in this and the following chapter, its actual practices and the results that flow from these should be taken seriously. Then it will appear that libertarianism can have a different face, different from the face presented by strict libertarians. I will first try to unmask the illusions of strict libertarianism.

3. Libertarian skepticism

Friedrich Hayek is a leading theorist of libertarianism.[14] He opposes the idea of 'social justice', and regards talk of it as an abuse of the word justice. Of course, he is aware of the widespread use of the term social justice. *"But the near-universal acceptance of a belief does not prove that it is valid or even meaningful any more than the general belief in witches or ghosts proves the validity of these concepts. What we have to deal with in the case of 'social justice' is simply a quasi-religious superstition of the kind which we should respectfully leave in peace so long as it merely makes those happy who hold it, but which we must fight when it becomes the pretext of coercing other men."*[15] When he speaks about social justice, Hayek has in mind social justice in a national context, yet I believe that his views can also be applied to the global situation.

Hayek points in particular to three phenomena that render the idea of justice or injustice inappropriate for socio-economic deprivation and for policies aimed at relieving that deprivation. He firstly points to the "limitedness" of human knowledge. He emphasizes that a politics of social justice is based on ideas held by individual politicians in power. Taking these ideas as a starting-point, these politicians try to construct a society. But the knowledge of these politicians is imperfect and incomplete and, therefore, inappropriate as a basis for general rules. Next, he proposes that ideas about social justice differ from person to person, and that such a lack of consensus on social justice implies that the ideas of some persons will be given priority over those of others. This amounts to these others being forced to comply with rules they regard as unjust. Lastly, he argues that the idea of justice presupposes the existence of responsible moral actors. But poverty, though, is like a hurricane: it is to be regretted but no one can be blamed for it, and nobody can be singled out as being responsible for correcting such an injustice. In the following pages, I will examine these arguments.

a. The "limitedness" of human knowledge

The idea of social justice, according to Hayek, originates from 'constructivistic rationalism'. This is the view that society can be arranged on the basis of particular ideas made by men. These ideas are then transformed into binding rules. A politics of social justice, being a manifestation of constructivistic rationalism, is not aimed at guaranteeing the freedom of individuals but at achieving a particular distribution of resources. This approach is *teleocratic*, that is to say, the eventual distribution is not left to spontaneous developments but is sought through a devised goal (*telos*) that is moulded into particular artificial forms.[16] Robert Nozick, a fellow leading libertarian is, apparently, of the same view, when he speaks disapprovingly of *patterned principles of social justice*.[17]

The problem of a teleocratic approach is, according to Hayek, that these man-made rules devised on the basis of a man-made idea of social justice will be grounded in imperfect knowledge. The knowledge of individual politicians is, like that of everyone, imperfect, incomplete and, to some extent, incorrect. Even experts do not know for certain what to do to achieve a better world. We should therefore, so Hayek argues, not rely on the knowledge of individual people but on human knowledge as it has developed during human history. Human knowledge, according to Hayek, is spread over many people and many cultures and individual people have only small pieces at their disposal (an idea, incidentally, also to be found in Hayek's predecessors, Locke and Mill). Hayek touches upon a real problem here. Housing and healthcare contribute to a dignified life. But what level of healthcare and housing can be called just, what duties result from it, and for whom? Work enables people to lead a dignified life. But what distribution of work and what working conditions can be called just? People without income are entitled to financial support. But what level of support can be regarded as just? How do we know that the policies we implement will have the results that we intend, or that deleterious outcomes we had not projected will not in turn crop up, with greater harm to greater numbers?

Yet however real such problems raised by libertarians may be, they cannot be taken as a conclusive reason to renounce a politics of social justice. The limitedness of human existence plays its part in everyday life without that being a reason to forego considerations of justice. Our knowledge is imperfect: we cannot know everything, we cannot always foresee the consequences of our acts, we make mistakes. That is an existential fact. The imperfectness of our knowledge will also affect everyday questions of justice we are confronted with. Parents will have to find a just way of treating their children. Professors will have to treat their students justly. Employers will have to treat their employees in a just manner. And in doing so parents, professors and employers will take decisions they think to be just even though those decisions will be based on imperfect knowledge. Later, perhaps, they will realize that their decisions were wrong and that they should have taken different ones; they may even resolve to take other decisions in the future. But if they do, those decisions too will be based on imperfect knowledge and may also turn out to be unjust.

Yet we do not conclude that we should stop being concerned about the question of what constitutes just behavior in our personal lives. Rather, we should hope that recognition of such limitedness leads us to realize that we can make mistakes and that we should always be prepared to reconsider our ideas, value-judgments and acts.

The limitedness of our knowledge has not been a reason to renounce considerations of justice in daily life. Nor has it been advanced by traditionalists as a reason to give up trying to achieve justice in the field of civil and political rights (a field in which they believe justice can still be achieved). Obviously, traditionalists think that the limitedness of our knowledge only applies to the field of ESC-rights, though that is an illusion. They presuppose that the duties flowing from ESC-rights are positive duties, duties that require the duty-bearer, mostly the government, to actively do something, for instance to provide its citizens with adequate housing. Freedom rights, on the other hand, like the right to freedom of belief, or the right to freedom of expression, are seen as rights that generate negative duties, duties to abstain from doing something, for instance to refrain from interfering with people's beliefs. These negative duties are considered to be clear and unequivocal, unlike the duties flowing from ESC-rights that are regarded as vague.

I will argue in chapter 7 that the duties arising from civil and political rights are not confined to abstinence, and that these rights also contain positive duties.[18] But apart from this, the demands of the duties of abstinence, which certainly belong to the correlative duties of civil and political rights—and possibly are the most important—are not clear at all. A duty of abstinence is most definitely not clear when the rights of more than one person are involved and these rights come into conflict with one another. Take, for instance the right to freedom of religion which is traditionally regarded as an unambiguous and clear right. Everyone has the right to follow a religion and to profess it, and others have a duty to abstain from interfering in it. But this negative duty is not as clear as is thought: it is not obvious what acts of a person are to be seen as religious acts, that can legitimately claim to be respected, nor is it clear to what extent a government should respect someone's freedom of religion. Is a religious procession a religious act? And, should the government refrain from interfering with that procession even if it is regarded by others as provocative? Has a government to accept that homosexuals are discriminated against on religious grounds? Does it have to abstain from interfering with the practice of female circumcision when this is religiously motivated? And, to take some examples of other freedom rights: should a government respect the right to property when building roads and dikes, and if it does, what does that imply? Has a government a duty to allow people to demonstrate when and where they want to? Is the right to privacy violated when people are being watched by police cameras in shopping centers, or when someone, accused of rape, is forced to undergo a DNA test? In attempting to answer such questions, the negative duty proves to be rather unclear, for the limitedness of human knowledge also exists in the field of civil and political rights, even with regard to their negative duties. Uncertainty is unavoidable, but it offers no reason to give up striving for justice.

b. A lack of consensus on social justice

The libertarian could indeed observe that the imperfectness of our knowledge plays its part not only in the field of ESC-rights, but also in everyday, personal life and in the fields of civil and political rights. But, he could also note that in the field of ESC-rights something else is involved: that is, a fundamental lack of consensus about what is just. People's knowledge may be imperfect but if all shared the same imperfect knowledge and all agreed on a particular distribution of resources being just, then their view, although imperfect, could rightfully be implemented. In the field of ESC-rights, people's knowledge is not only imperfect, but the "imperfect-ness" of their ideas vary from person to person. It is the combination of the imperfect-ness of our knowledge and the lack of consensus about what is just that causes a problem.

Hayek argues that modern societies are not characterized by common goals, accepted by everyone. To that extent, modern societies differ from smaller organizations, like tribes, small business organizations, or sport organizations. Smaller organizations are aimed at the achievement of common goals; for instance tribes can have common goals. But modern societies, however, no longer have particular goals in common. Rather, they have just one common goal, which is only a formal one: that it should be guaranteed that individuals can strive for their own conceptions of a good life or rather, that they not be prevented by others from striving for their own conceptions of a good life. This, Hayek argues, is the formal goal shared by all.

However, people will have different ideas about social justice. Some will be of the view that resources should be distributed equally, others of the opinion that these resources should be distributed according to merit, and others who will believe that they should be distributed according to need. And even among the people who share one of these criteria, there will be differences over the question of what equal distribution exactly requires, over when someone should be regarded as being in need of something, and over whether someone can be considered to deserve a particular good.

One should, so Hayek says, not underestimate the consequences of the lack of common, generally accepted, ideas on social justice.[19] When a government implements ideas of social justice that, unavoidably, will not be shared by all, a particular conception is being advanced at the expense of some of that society's individuals: the imperfect knowledge of some is given priority over the knowledge of others. This comes down to coercing one group to follow the imperfect ideas of another, which is a violation of the freedom of people and of the neutrality of the state. *"So long as the belief in 'social justice' governs political action, this process must progressively approach nearer and nearer to a totalitarian system."*[20]

A politics of social justice also undermines certainty and security. It enhances arbitrariness, as governments will—for electoral reasons—tend to give in to the wishes of pressure groups, all of whom probably have different ideas of social justice. Hayek's fellow libertarian, Nozick, also warns us against the totalitarian effects of a politics of social justice. Such politics, he states, will impose a pattern of distribution of resources defined by an idea of social justice held by some, a pattern that is not based on the free and voluntary exchanges of goods.[21]

Hayek continues by arguing that the raison d'être of law does not lie in molding society according to ideas of social justice, but in guiding a spontaneous development of rules and order. Rules can grow spontaneously out of the reiteration of human behavior and create a spontaneous order. Such an order has not been artificially designed, but is the result of human insights and experiences in the past, just as the structure of footpaths in a landscape has resulted from the efforts of travelers to find their way. Law, Hayek says, should enable these spontaneous developments to come about. It should be abstract and impartial, giving individuals the opportunity to pursue their conceptions of the good life without being hindered by others.[22]

This implies that law should not prevent the free-market from developing spontaneously, so Hayek continues. The rules of the free-market have not been designed but have grown and changed in accordance with ideas about the efficiency of economic relationships and ways of doing justice to individual freedom. These ideas have proven to be successful. The free-market, consisting of a free and voluntary exchange of goods by individuals in pursuit of their own interests, can be seen as a game, the game of *catallaxy*. We may expect every participant to this game to play fairly, but, according to Hayek, it is nonsense to expect the outcome to be equally profitable and agreeable to everyone.[23]

In arguing in favor of the free-market, Hayek criticizes the welfare state. But, he makes a caricature of it. He suggests that the advocates of social justice pretend to be able to determine justly the salaries of butchers, nurses, miners, judges, pilots, professors, dustmen, etc., and then argues that salaries cannot be defined by appealing to concepts of social justice.[24]

But it is obvious that the advocates of the welfare state do not pretend to be able to exactly derive the levels of salaries from an idea of social justice. Social justice does not offer an unequivocal yardstick for defining salaries. Different individuals will undoubtedly think differently about the levels of salaries. There will be no agreement on whether it is more just for a butcher to earn $500 while a nurse earns $400, or whether it will be more just for a nurse to earn $500 and the butcher $400. However, the statement that the butcher should earn $500 while the nurse earns only $10 because caring for live 'flesh' is a reward in itself would raise 'consensual' indignation. Furthermore, what advocates of social justice oppose as socially unjust is that a small percentage earn millions and even billions while huge numbers cannot meet their basic needs and that it is socially just to redress that situation.

Social justice is not simply a question of being able to exactly and fairly determine salaries. Rather, it is about enabling everyone to develop basic capabilities to provide themselves with necessary means of subsistence, and providing at least for basic needs where these capabilities have not yet been achieved or perhaps are unachievable. Social justice wants to correct a situation in which only some people can develop basic capabilities while others are deprived of them.

It can be admitted that social justice is, like the idea of classical justice, not always very clear. Possibly we could make it less vague, by following an interesting suggestion made by writers such as Lucas: that while it is difficult to assess what is just, it is, perhaps, much easier to assess what is unjust.[25] For example, after the Second World War, there was a definite consensus about the social injustice that had been inflicted upon many people in the Nazi concentration camps. The general abhorrence was caused not only by the fact that people had been deprived of their freedom-rights, but also that they had been deprived of the chance to provide themselves with the necessary means of subsistence, that they had been excluded and exploited, that they had had to work as slaves in atrocious conditions that their housing had been an affront to human dignity, and that they had been treated as non-humans. The statement that we should totally abolish any community support of the poor and vulnerable, and that poor and vulnerable people should find their own ways to stay alive, would also be seen as unjust; just as the idea that little children are perfectly suitable for coal mines and would, therefore, be very profitable when used fifteen hours a day would also encounter general disapproval. The statement that because the mentally handicapped do not earn their livelihood, they might as well live in holes in the forests would also generally be seen as socially unjust.

So, certainly in some cases, it is possible to reach general agreement on what can be seen as socially unjust. Such a consensus could be widened to cover less extreme cases. What is needed then is a dialogue, in which what is just and unjust is clearly formulated. Perhaps then we can, in some of the less extreme cases, achieve almost general agreement, while in other cases we achieve a very narrow agreement. True, there will never be consensus, but that is no different from the situation in the field of classical justice.

Libertarians may contend that there exists consensus on violations of freedom. They may claim that everyone believes that nobody should be prevented from expressing their opinions, or from having and practicing any religion they choose or, in more general terms, that nobody should be prevented from living their lives in accordance with their conception of the good life. But that seems too optimistic to me. It's neither their true belief nor their practice. History has proved otherwise on many occasions.

In the preceding pages, I have argued that the *limitedness of human existence* also plays its part in the field of freedom-rights, and not only in the field of social justice. I would like to add now that *a lack of consensus* can also be found in the field of freedom-rights. There is no consensus on all freedom-rights: many people do not think that everyone should be allowed to profess and practice their religion; many do not think that women, blacks or homosexuals should be treated equally. But even when people agree on an abstract freedom-right, the effort to give that abstract right a concrete form will encounter moral disagreement and dissent. For instance, when there is agreement on the right to freedom of religion, there will be disagreement on *when* people have a right to profess and practice that religion, *what* others can be expected to do and *what* the limits of that right will be. As governmental measures will more than likely reflect the ideas of the majority, these measures will then be imposed on a country's citizens, which means that also in the field of freedom-rights some will be forced to do what others consider to be just, even though they themselves may regard it as *un*just.

Giving concrete forms to abstract rights, whether it be freedom-rights or ESC-rights, will always meet disagreement. This view is supported by the immense amount of literature on the limits of the right to freedom of religion and of the right to freedom of expression. Defining what is truly just will require a dialogue hoping to reach a consensus. In most cases though, we will have to do without consensus and be satisfied with the view of the majority.

All in all, the indeterminateness of justice due to the limitedness of human knowledge and the lack of moral consensus are not phenomena restricted to the field of social justice. Nor, in these many areas, does this serve as a pretext for bringing all action to a halt. We should also realize that, if we were to abandon the idea of social justice because of its indeterminateness and lack of consensus, we will be responsible for the socio-economic misery that exists or comes about as a result of our lack of action. But that may be precisely the point: are people responsible for the socio-economic misery of others? Can we point to a moral actor who has caused the misery?

Hayek himself considers starting from the question of what is unjust an adequate method when speaking about classical justice, the justice that demands respect for the freedom of individuals and equality before the law.[26] However, he then rejects this method with respect to social justice. What he regards as possible in the field of classical justice, i.e. starting from what is obviously unjust, he thinks impossible in the field of social justice.

c. The absence of a perpetrator

Hayek then argues, we cannot discover what is socially "unjust" because in the field of social justice no moral actor exists that has committed an act of injustice.[27] Socio-economic misery is not an injustice brought about by assignable people but it is the result of forces beyond human control. This is a remarkable turn in his argument. The question was whether what is socially unjust could be defined, but he evaded that question by saying it is inadequate to speak of social justice because no one exists who has intentionally brought about a situation of injustice.

This issue of the absence of a moral actor forms the third aspect of the vagueness of ESC-rights. The limitedness of human knowledge and the lack of consensus concern the vagueness of the *contents* of ESC-rights; the issue of the absence of a moral actor refers to vagueness with regard to the *duty-bearer*. ESC-rights are aimed at preventing unjust socio-economic situations from coming about, or at redressing unjust situations. Hayek is of the view that socio-economic situations cannot be called 'just' or 'unjust'. Consequently also socio-economic deprivation—poverty—cannot be called unjust and therefore does not call for redress. The socio-economic situation of the deprived is regrettable, but it is not susceptible to considerations of justice. The results of the free-market can indeed be to the disadvantage of some and the advantage of others. This is, so Hayek argues, neither just nor unjust. Justice and injustice are notions that have to do with the intended acts of human beings and socio-economic deprivation is not caused by the intended acts of human beings.[28] This is also the view of Narveson, who regards speaking of the justness or unjustness of socio-economic deprivation as inappropriate, because it is almost as if one might ask whether it is just or unjust that someone is felled by an illness. The notion of justice only applies to situations

Hayek admits that it makes sense to speak of justice or injustice when a society is hierarchically arranged, and certain persons can give orders as to how that society should operate. In such a society, a responsible moral actor can be found, i.e. the persons in command. However, in a modern and free society, everyone is entitled to seek to pursue his or her own conception of a good life. The activities of all these individuals will bring about a certain social situation, although one that is most likely not the situation intended by the various individuals. Nozick also stresses that the eventual 'distribution' of resources in a free-market society is the collateral result of individual choices that people are entitled to make.[29]

It will be obvious that this does not mean that libertarians do not care about the misery of the poor or deprived. In fact, they consider it important that the vulnerable should be supported. But they believe that this support should not be enforced (i.e., brought about by means of social policy) and that people should help one another on a voluntary basis –even though all socio-economic situations are governed by public policy rules and laws. Also capitalist-benefiting freedoms are promoted and protected by public policy which imply an enforcement by the state of other people. The libertarian "Advocates for Self-government"say it this way: "*Replacing the income tax with voluntary methods for financing services should be our goal, and we should begin right now*".[30] Most libertarians expect that the free-market will generate economic growth, which will certainly benefit the position of the well-off, but which will, in the long run, also benefit the least advantaged. The wealth of the rich will 'trickle down' to the less-advantaged members of society.[31]

President George W. Bush appears to be an adherent of a trickle-down economics. He has introduced tax-cuts, benefiting mainly the rich, who have as a result profited financially. Bush appears to hope this will also benefit the least-advantaged, as he observed when he addressed the pork producers in Iowa with a speech that was a manifestation of his libertarian presidential agenda. *"The best way to make sure we've got a strong farm economy and to make sure our economy recovers from the recession is to let people keep their own money. I believe that when you let a person keep his own—his or her own money, they're going to spend it. And when they spend it, it increases demands for goods and services. And with an increase of demand for goods and services, somebody has got to produce that good and service. And when they produce it, it means somebody's going to find work".*[32]

According to the libertarians, we should not intervene in the free-market to achieve social justice because we cannot point at anyone who can be blamed for the socio-economic deprivation of others. Socio-economic misery is the result of spontaneous developments, to be compared with diseases or natural disasters.[33] *If* libertarians were right, if no social actor were responsible for socio-economic misery, that does not mean that the government should not address the misery to which diseases and natural disasters give rise, just because there is nobody to blame. It does not mean that citizens facing these disasters should be aided on a purely voluntary basis by those individuals who feel charitably disposed, and that governments (despite their greater capacity to marshal resources and manage logistics) should just walk away. My question at this point is not yet whether governments have a task with regard to the relief of poverty, my question is, whether it is true that poverty is just the result of spontaneous developments and that there is no moral actor responsible for it.

4. Poverty is human-made

In my view, this idea that no moral actor is responsible for socio-economic misery, and that poverty is to be compared with hurricanes, is an optical illusion. To some extent, the libertarians are right. The notion of justice is only relevant when human action is involved.[34] The coincidences of life are not susceptible to considerations of justice. We may feel inclined to use that notion when someone is struck heavily by suffering and sorrow. We may feel inclined to say that 'it isn't just!' But we will know, though, that this is only the expression of our compassion and that life cannot, in fact, be interpreted in terms of justice.

Poverty: Is Anyone to Blame?

Socio-economic situations, however, cannot be identified with the coincidences of life such as diseases, or with natural events such as hurricanes, as Hayek suggests. Socio-economic conditions have not arisen from nothing. They are the result of human actions in the past, actions of people being confronted with each other in their struggle for a (meaningful) life. And more particularly, they are reflected in political structures which advantage some and disadvantage others.

Have not human beings always exhibited some behaviors that were similar to those of other animals? Have not human beings fought one another from the beginning of human history? Have not they tried to take control over resources? Have not they sought to enhance their power? And have not they pushed aside others, or killed others to prevent them from taking what they themselves wanted to take?

Societies may have become complex and complicated, and the struggle for life has become complicated and less clear-cut but the history of humankind has shown many violent clashes and violent confrontations have continued up to the present. Even today the weaker and more vulnerable are pushed aside in the interactional processes people find themselves in when trying to make a living. Powerful social forces determine the playing field or overall socio-economic environment in which such struggles are carried out. Similar struggles occur between groups within nations, and between nations themselves.

These clashes have often been characterized as clashes between *religions*; for example, the clashes between the Catholics and the Protestants in Northern Ireland; the Catholics, Muslims and Orthodox Christians in the former Yugoslavia; the Muslims and the Christians, the Muslims and Hindus in Sri Lanka, the Muslims and Christians in Nigeria. Many clashes have been seen as of an *ethnic* nature; for example, the Dayaks and the Madorese in Indonesia; the Hutus and the Tutsis in Central Africa; the Serbs and ethnic Albanians in the former Yugoslavia; the Turks and the Kurds in Turkey. But while these clashes may have had a religious or ethnic character, they have also had a socio-economic aspect and have also been conflicts about wealth, resources, opportunities and economic power.

In societies in which open conflict does not surface but stays underground, conflicts still remain as the vulnerable and the weak are pushed aside by the powerful in the struggle for life. Less visible than violent clashes, confrontations between groups happen, and result in institutions that issue legislation, formulate trade policies, import duties and other socio-economic measures that are to the benefit of the most well-off and to the disadvantage of the powerless. Socio-economic conditions, together with poverty and deprivation, are not the same as hurricanes: they have been, and still are, the result of human action and can therefore, be called unjust when they cross perceived thresholds of disparity between those who have and those who need.

While it can be admitted that often socio-economic misery has not been caused by *intentional* actions, sometimes it has. If powerful people try to advance their own interests fully aware that this only can be achieved by harming others, the resulting socio-economic misery can be regarded as intended. Why should deprivation resulting from such intended actions of the powerful not be labeled as unjust?

For example, I tend to label the humanitarian disaster in the Democratic Republic of Congo/Zaire as unjust in that sense. The civil war in that country continues to boil (as this book is being written), despite the signing of the Lusaka peace accord in July 1999 and it has been estimated that more than a million people may have lost their lives in the last two years due to the conflict. Apart from the violence, the fighting has caused an unimaginable humanitarian crisis that has been described as one of the worst in the world, with appalling levels of hunger, disease, and death. More than two million people are internally displaced and have sought refuge with friends, family, or strangers. The United Nations Office for Co-ordination of Humanitarian Affairs (UNOCHA) estimates that about 33 percent of the population is now vulnerable and government spending on health and education have each dropped to less than one percent of government expenditure, leaving nearly a third of the children malnourished, ten percent acutely so.

If it is thought that the fighting parties are responsible for the killings, I do not see why they are not also responsible for the humanitarian disaster accompanying the killings. This socio-economic consequence is as intended as the killings. And, to take another example, is not the humanitarian disaster in Darfur the result of intended human action? In Darfur, Western Sudan, thousands of civilians have fallen victim to the fight between black Africans, who have taken up arms against the government, and Arab militias, who allegedly have been given free reign by the government to retaliate against the blacks. Many people are in a desperate humanitarian situation and, driven away from their houses, with their villages destroyed, they have been forced to seek refuge in displacement camps, where the situation is hardly better. People do not have adequate shelter and cannot protect themselves and their children from the weather, while there is a very real threat of the outbreak of diseases, owing to the water being polluted by dead animals and human waste. Yet the inhabitants hardly dare leave the displacement camps for fear of being attacked, raped or killed.[35]

It is truly impossible to separate military fightings from humanitarian disasters. Is it possible, say, for a state to bomb and destroy a city's water processing/sewage treatment infrastructure, without it knowing that this will cause an outbreak of cholera?

Yet it is also often the case though that socio-economic conditions, including socio-economic misery, will not be the result of intentional actions to harm others, so much as a desire to protect one's interests. People are not only self-centered beings who pursue their wishes by pushing others aside; they are also loving, caring beings, capable of devoting themselves to the security of others. But, third parties will often fall victim to the care people show for their loved ones and relatives. My effort to ensure the well being of my family may turn out to have negative consequences for others in my country. On the level of nations, policies aimed at protecting American or European farmers and industries prevent Third World countries from entering American or European markets and from selling their export products in the USA or Europe. Many of these and other actions are intentional as far as they are aimed at achieving a specific situation for a particular group of people, but they are not intentional as regards the social conditions that result from the whole body of actions. Employers fire employees, intending to make their corporation more effective, not intending to cause socio-economic misery for the masses of newly-unemployed. People step into a car, intending to go from A to B but they do not intend to create traffic jams and pollute the environment.

Can people be blamed for the unintentional consequences of their actions? According to Hayek they cannot. But following Raymond Plant, I think we should draw a distinction between actions which have results that are not intended, but nevertheless foreseeable, and actions whose results are not intended and not foreseeable. Can we not assume responsibility if the consequences of someone's actions are foreseeable and if there is a way to avoid these consequences by acting differently? Plant and Shue are of the view that people can be blamed for such consequences and that they commit an act of injustice if they do not take steps to relieve the misery of those they have -unintentionally but foreseeable- affected. Injustice then consists of causing unintentional but foreseeable suffering and refusing to take steps to redress the situation.[36]

I would like to take the argument another step further. Even when the unfortunate consequences of people's actions are neither intentional nor foreseeable, people may still be responsible for the result of their actions, and the situation that they have unwittingly brought about still may be called unjust, to wit if people pay no attention to the result of their actions.

Here the injustice lies in the combination of causing suffering (even if it is neither intended nor foreseen) and the refusal to take steps to redress or relieve that suffering. Someone who causes a traffic accident without being at fault, but who then does not take care of the victim, commits an act of injustice. Likewise, people may be said to have committed an injustice if their actions have resulted in socio-economic suffering (even if it is neither intended nor foreseen) yet refuse to take steps to redress or relieve the situation of the adversely affected.[37]

In my view, socio-economic conditions are the fruit of human action. They may often be unintentional, they may even often be unforeseeable, but they are the result of human action or of the arrangements people have created. We cannot lean back and be satisfied with our situation, looking at the poor and thinking their poverty to be bad luck. Instead we should be aware that they are the victims of human injustice, and that we ourselves may be among the perpetrators as supporters of a particular political and socio-economic constellation. Tibor Machan writes that *"The bulk of poverty in the world is not the result of natural disaster or disease. Rather it is political oppression, whereby people throughout many of the world's countries are not legally permitted to look out for themselves in production and trade. The famines in Africa and India, the poverty in the same countries and in Central and Latin America, as well as in China, the Soviet Union, Poland, Rumania, and so forth, are not the result of lack of charity but of oppression."*[38]

And although Machan would probably not support all of what I'm saying in this chapter, we both share the idea that poverty is caused by human action. While Machan emphasizes the influence of domestic oppressors, I also pay attention to international relationships and to the effect the policies of rich countries have on the situation of the poor. The idea that there is no moral actor and that poverty is to be compared with hurricanes is an illusion. It may be difficult to determine the responsible actor precisely, but is that not the same with abuses of civil and political rights? Is it not just as hard to determine who is responsible when people are prevented from expressing their opinions or practicing their religion by the political system of a society?

5. A duty to refrain and a duty to protect

Socio-economic deprivation is the result of human action, which means that it is not only to be seen as an act of *omission* (omitting to do a favor) but as an act of *commission* (committing an injustice).[39] This insight leads us to a fundamental shift in the view of ESC-rights because it can be seen that they not only prescribe the addressee to do good, but they also forbid the addressee to do wrong. Previously I have said that ESC-rights have not only positive but also negative aspects. Now it turns out that they can be regarded as fundamentally negative, requiring a duty to refrain, although this has to be complemented by a duty to protect and a duty to help.

Civil and political rights guarantee certain civil and political freedoms. They say that people may not be prevented by others from expressing their opinions or practicing their religion. ESC-rights guarantee certain socio-economic freedoms. They say that people may not be prevented by others from having access to, and using, means of subsistence. The rich and the powerful should not deprive the weak of food, housing, health care, which they still do by supporting or maintaining socio-economically oppressive political arrangements. They may not take all the resources and leave only some crumbs to the weak.

Shue puts it this way: "*The first type of subsistence duty is neither a duty to provide help, nor a duty to protect against harm by third parties but is the most nearly negative or passive kind of duty that is possible: a duty simply not to take actions that deprive others of a means that, but for one's own harmful actions, would have satisfied their subsistence rights or enabled them to satisfy their own subsistence rights, where the actions are not necessary to the satisfaction of one's own basic rights and where the threatened means is the only realistic one.*"[40]

The duty to refrain from damaging someone's socio-economic interests does not guarantee that no deprivation will arise because people can always fail to live up to their duties. The question then is whether third parties (C) have a duty to protect the person (A) who has fallen victim to the neglect of the duty to refrain by the duty-bearer (B). Such a duty to protect is generally accepted in many other cases; for example, if someone (A) is being physically attacked by someone else (B), it is generally accepted that third parties (C) should take action to protect the victim. This does not mean, of course, that many other considerations should not also be taken into account: options and risks involved should be weighed against one another. A weak, old person does not have a duty to fight when five persons are waylaying a victim, but he does have a duty to take some other action: for instance, phoning the police.

Or let us take another, extreme, example. If a child is thrown into the water by another child, and the latter is pushing the former underwater, obviously trying to drown it, does there not exist a duty for a passer-by to intervene? Can passers-by say that they themselves are not drowning the child and that they therefore rightly can continue on their way? Is not doing anything as morally wrong as actually drowning the child oneself? Drowning a child is wrong because the result is dreadful, horrible and causes considerable pain and suffering. But, the same can be said of the passer-by doing nothing, because it also results in a situation which is dreadful, horrible and which causes a lot of pain and suffering. Doing nothing is also an act of injustice, the injustice consisting of refusing to take action when steps can be taken to prevent something terrible from happening. People not only have a duty to refrain from causing pain; they also have a duty to protect those upon whom pain is inflicted by others.

A critic of this argument might reply that the aforementioned examples are extreme and that they have nothing to do with ESC-rights. I admit that they are extreme. But they also show that a right to life and the correlative duty to respect life loses much of its value if it is not accompanied by a duty to protect the holder of that right against someone who threatens to kill them. One's right to life is not sufficiently guaranteed by a duty to respect or to refrain; it should be complemented by a duty to protect others when people fail to live up to their duty to refrain from killing. Likewise, a duty not to damage the socio-economic interests of people should be complemented by a duty to protect them when those whose duty it is to refrain from causing damage do not live up to *their* duty. Without such a duty to protect, the socio-economic interests involved are not sufficiently guaranteed.

6. A duty to help

The aforementioned duties to refrain and to protect do not prevent socio-economic misery from arising if people neglect the performance of these duties. And it should also be admitted that natural factors can play a role in socio-economic misery. But having said that, I would like to add immediately that I do not withdraw my statement that socio-economic deprivation is not to be compared with hurricanes and that it is the result of human action. What I do want to admit, though, is that natural disasters can *contribute* to socio-economic misery arising, remaining or worsening. They can destroy crops and houses, they can bring illnesses and diseases. But this will result in real socio-economic suffering when people are already poor and less-advantaged, or when the socio-economic constellation of a country hinders them in struggling to their feet and regaining firm ground. Like is said by the United Nations Millenniumproject: *"When individuals suffer from extreme poverty and lack the meager income needed even to cover basic needs, a single episode of disease, or a drought, or a pest that destroys a harvest can be the difference between life and death."*[41]

In 2005, natural disasters in Asia and America inflicted much suffering. The tsunami that overwhelmed many countries in Asia; the earthquakes in Pakistan, India and Afghanistan, and hurricane Katrina in America caused considerable suffering and devastation. They cost the lives of thousands of people and deprived millions of their homes and other basic amenities. But it was in particular the poor and the vulnerable who were affected by these disasters. Their access to adequate food, housing, drinking water and healthcare had already been problematic; after the disasters, it practically ceased to exist.

So, the question now is: when socio-economic misery is caused by the neglect of duties *to refrain* from causing damage, or by the neglect of duties *to protect* those upon whom damage is inflicted, or when a natural disaster have befallen on people, can a duty to redress the miserable situation be said to exist? I think it can. People have a *duty to help* those in need whether or not they themselves have played a role in the coming about of the situation that causes that need. People may not be responsible for the existence of the misery, but they can certainly be held responsible for its continuation.

Suppose, to continue the example from the previous section, that someone is taking a walk along the waterfront. Suppose he sees a child in the water, obviously not capable of swimming. Does it matter how the child has come into that situation? Can the passer-by continue his way arguing that he himself did not push the child into the water, and that the parents have behaved irresponsibly by not watching the child properly? So here, just as in the previous section, it can be said that doing nothing has the same effect as actually throwing the child into the water. The child will die and doing nothing will cause a terrible injustice. Likewise, doing nothing while people suffer from socio-economic deprivation has the same effect as causing that deprivation and it can definitely be called an injustice when people do not help those in need, certainly if they could offer help without much risk to themselves.

A right to housing or to healthcare loses much of its value when it is only regarded as entailing a duty to refrain and a duty to protect. For, it is possible that duty-holders have failed to live up to their duties to refrain and to protect, that they have failed to live up to their duty not to block access of people to adequate health care or housing and to their duty to protect people from their access to housing or health care being blocked by others. The right to housing of these people then would be undermined when the duty-holders do not fulfill the requirements of these duties to refrain and to protect, and when consequently the right-holders are prevented from access to these goods and no other duty existed, in particular the duty to help, i.e. the duty to render aid to someone who is in misery even if one has not caused the misery.

Such a duty to help is embraced in the case of natural disasters. When a natural disaster, a hurricane or a flood occurs, a duty to help the victims is generally accepted by us all. In cases like the tsunami that wreak untold human havoc, the whole world sheds its tears, and aid is soon on the way. The issue seems to be miraculously clear: you just don't let people starve, or lie out exposed to the elements. But then it can be asked: why should we acknowledge a duty to help when a tsunami hits a community, but not when socio-economic misery hits a community with the force of an tsunami?[42] We certainly have a duty to help just like we have a duty to help the victims of a tsunami or a child in danger of drowning. That is beyond doubt. But, I would like to repeat what has been said in the foregoing. Poverty is not to be compared with tsunamis. Tsunamis are not human-made, but poverty is. Fellow-humans are causing poverty to the poor. And it may be us, who are the poor victims of our fellow-humans. But is may also be us, who are the fellow-humans who -to a greater or lesser extent- cause that poverty by supporting the current political and socio-economic system. Environmental issues nowadays have come to the front. And we realize that we have caused environmental problems by our way of life, and that we should stop causing environmental damage. Why do we not realize that we by our way of life may cause and often in fact are causing socio-economic damage to others? Why can't we see that rich countries prevent poor countries from developing? As an instance, subsidies that First World governments give to their own farmers allow wealthy nations to sell farm commodities on world markets below the cost of production. As a result producers from Third World countries cannot compete with the producers from rich countries: they cannot compete on the markets of the rich countries neither on their domestic markets where thanks to the subsidies goods imported from rich countries are cheaper than domestic products. Our first duty is not to help people who are poor -although it is of course a duty- but our first duty is to refrain from making or keeping them poor.

However, duties to refrain from causing damage do not sufficiently guarantee that people have access to the socio-economic goods necessary for them to lead a dignified life. Therefore these duties should be complemented by duties to protect and to help.

7. Who is the duty-bearer?

Of course, it will be difficult to determine how individuals can perform a duty to refrain from causing damage, to protect others upon whom damage is inflicted, and to help those who have fallen victim to socio-economic deprivation. It will, in fact, be impossible for people to fulfill their duties towards one another as single individuals. But people can fulfill their duties to refrain, protect and help by establishing and supporting institutions that guarantee that everyone has access to the fundamental goods that are the object of socio-economic rights.[43]

Among these institutions, the state is seen as the main, coordinating institution, at least at the national level. A central, coordinating institution is needed to see that the goods that are the objects of the rights are distributed fairly among the right-holders. Without such a central coordinating institution, some right-holders will not receive their share because the duty-bearers, motivated by prejudice, arbitrariness or self-interest, may not want to pay attention to them, or because they are just too busy fulfilling their duties towards others (their families, their stockholders, their industry). A central institution is needed not only to guarantee a fair distribution of the benefits, but also of the burdens related to the realization of the rights. This is because some people may be inclined to shirk their duties, or are unaware of the exact duties they have to perform, when no central institution sees to it that the burdens are distributed fairly. In this way a central institution can enhance the fairness, and the effectiveness, of the distribution of benefits and burdens.

In view of this coordinating task, governments are rightly seen as the direct addressees on the human rights letter, with duties to abstain, to protect and to help. Yet some people deny that states have a duty to protect and to help. I mentioned the natural disaster of the hurricane Katrina. During the days following this disaster, many people in the United States argued that the state had a duty to protect and help the victims of the hurricane. Among other things, it was said that these victims already were in miserable circumstances as a consequence of slavery and that, accordingly, the state had a duty to correct the injustices of slavery. But this was refuted by conservatives who attacked the role of government as a protector and as an instrument for correcting the wrongs of slavery.[44] They advanced the 1989 case of *DeShaney v. Winnebago County* to support their position, a case in which the majority opinion had held that while the Constitution of the United States forbids the state to inflict harm on its citizens, it does not impose an affirmative duty to protect its citizens.[45]

I do believe that states have a duty to refrain, to protect and to help. But these duties are derivative. States act as representatives of the community of individuals. Individuals count as cooperating in the activities of the state.[46] The ultimate addressees are fellow human beings. And as ultimate addressees, it is the duty of individual citizens to see that the state is adequately organized to guarantee the rights of its citizens and that governments fulfill their duties adequately.

As long as a state adequately fulfills its duties as a representative of the community, it is entitled to support from those individuals. Which makes it a very great pity that some states have degenerated and become a threat to human rights themselves, either by the oppression of their citizens or by leaving them to their fate. While it cannot fail to be noted that states always limit the freedom of people to do whatever they like to a certain extent, many states, unfortunately, limit freedom more than is necessary and oppress their citizens. Other states retreat from their obligations to society and leave their citizens to misery, hardship and the arbitrariness and whims of the powerful—actions that cannot in any way be seen as implementing human rights or performing duties on behalf of the individual. And in such a situation, if a state has itself become a threat to human rights, it has forfeited its legitimacy and its claim to the support of its citizens.

Various human rights documents cite states as the addressees of human rights. However, in this era of globalization, other political entities may arise that can be seen as a cooperation of individuals, or as a cooperation of states that in turn are cooperations of individuals, and are also mandated to look after the duties of individual members of that cooperation. (For example the European Union, the Organization of American States, the Organization for Security and Cooperation in Europe, the International Monetary Fund. These organizations cannot say that only states are the addressees of human rights and deny having themselves duties to respect human rights) The real point, is that every human being should be enabled to have access to the goods necessary for leading a dignified life. While a simple framework of interpersonal human relationships may imply that individuals are supposed to perform their relevant duties towards one another in person, within a framework of sovereign, national independent states, it will be the states that perform the duties necessary to guarantee people's access to vital socio-economic goods on behalf of their citizens. In the current globalized world, other duty-bearers will be charged with the task of guaranteeing people's access to vital goods.

The Human Development Report 2000 states that *"in today's more interdependent world, it is essential to recognize the obligations of global actors, who in the pursuit of global justice must put in place global arrangements that promote the eradication of poverty."*[47] The European Union has recognized that not only its member-states must guarantee human rights, but that the Union itself must also guarantee. What matters is that an institutional framework is set up and supported by individuals to guarantee the performance of necessary duties. And, not only political entities other than states, can be sees as duty-bearers of human rights. The institutional approach expects not only states—or a conglomeration of states—but increasingly also business corporations to comply with human rights norms and to promote them

It can be concluded, therefore, that poverty is not like natural disasters but is a human artefact. And poverty can and should be alleviated or even eradicated. People have a duty to refrain from depriving their fellow-humans of their rights just as they have a duty to protect them from being deprived by others, and just as they have a duty to help them when these fellow-humans have fallen victim to socio-economic misery no matter who caused that misery. That is why implementing ESC-rights is extremely important in the fight against poverty.

At the opening of the thirty-fifth session of the Committee on Economic, Social and Cultural Rights, 7 November 2005, the Officer-in-Charge of the Office of the High Commissioner for Human Rights, Maria Francisca Ize-Charrin, stated that one of the most important challenges facing the United Nations was the fight against poverty. She also observed that the Plan of Action that had been launched by the High Commissioner in May 2005 had identified the protection of economic, social and cultural rights as one of the priorities to be pursued by the Office over the next five years.[48]

Yet not everyone is convinced that ESC-rights should and can be used as a tool to alleviate and eradicate poverty. As discussed in this chapter strict libertarians, in particular, are reluctant to recognize ESC-rights. I will examine their objections further.

BIBLIOGRAPHY

Arambulo, Kitty, *Strengthening the Supervision of the International Covenant on Economic Social and Cultural Rights* (Antwerpen, Groningen & Oxford: Intersentia, 1999)

Bellamy, Richard, *Liberalism and Modern Society* (Cambridge: Polity Press, 1992)

Coomans, A.W. Heringa & I. Westendorp (red.), *De toenemende betekenis van Economische, Sociale en Culturele Mensenrechten* (Leiden: Stichting NJCM-Boekerij, 1994)

Donnelly, Jack, *International Human Rights*, (Boulder, San Francisco & Oxford: Westview Press, 1993)

Dworkin, Ronald, *Taking Rights Seriously* (Londen: Duckworth, 1977)

Gewirth, Alan, *The Community of Rights* (Chicago & Londen: The University of Chicago Press, 1996)

Hayek, F.A., *Law, Legislation and Liberty: A new statement of the liberal principle of justice and political economy I* (Londen: Routledge and Kegan Paul, 1973)

Hayek, F.A., 'Equality, Value and Merit', in: Michael Sandel (red.), *Liberalism and its Critics* (Oxford [UK] & Cambridge [USA]: Blackwell, 1984)

Hayek, F.A., '"Social" or distributive justice', in: Alan Ryan (red.), *Justice* (Oxford: Oxford University Press, 1993)

Hook, S., Philosophy and Public Policy (Carbondal & Edwardsville: Southern Illinois Press, 1980)

Hunt, Paul, *Reclaiming Social Rights* (Aldershot: Ashgate, 1999)

Kymlicka, W., *Contemporary Political Philosophy: an introduction* (Oxford: Clarendon Press, 1990)

Lucas, J.R., *On Justice* (Oxford: Oxford University Press, 1980)

Machan, Tibor R., 'The Nonexistence of Basic Welfare Rights', in: Tibor R. Machan & Douglas B. Rasmussen (red.), *Liberty for the twenty-first century: contemporary libertarian thought* (Lanham, Maryland etc.: Rowman & Littlefield, 1995)

Narveson, Jan, *The Libertarian idea* (Philadelphia: Temple University Press, 1988)

Nozick, Robert, *Anarchy, State and Utopia* (New York: Basic Books Inc., 1974)

OECD Economic Studies, no.30, *Poverty Dynamics in Six OECD Countries*, 2000

Office of the High Commisioner on Human Rights, *Human Rights and Poverty Reduction*, (New York and Geneva, 2004), http://www.ohchr.org/english/issues/ poverty/docs/povertyE.pdf (retr. 5 September 2004)

Pierson, Christopher, *Beyond the Welfare State?: the new political economy of welfare* (Cambridge: Polity Press, 1991)

Plant, Raymond, *Modern Political Thought* (Oxford ect.: Basil Blackwell, 1991)

Pogge, Thomas, *World Poverty and Human Rights* (Cambridge, Oxford, Malden: Polity Press, 2002/2003)

Rawls, John, *A Theory of Justice* (Oxford: Oxford University Press, 1976)

Shue, Henry, *Basic Rights* (Princeton NJ: Princeton University Press, 1980)

Sogge, David, *Hulp vergroot de armoede, tenzij* (de Volkskrant, het Betoog, p.3, 19 November, 2005)

ENDNOTES

[1] *HDR 2000*, p 16.
[2] OECD Economic Studies no. 30, 2000, p.16. The report surveyed Canada, Germany, the Netherlands, Sweden, the United Kingdom and the United States.
[3] OECD 2000, p.9.
[4] (http://www.census.gov/hhes/www/poverty/poverty.html. The Census Bureau does not use the World Bank's poverty line, but uses a set of money income thresholds that vary by family size and composition to detect who is poor. Frida Berrigan, a Senior Research Associate with the Arms Trade Resource Center of the World Policy Institute, says that the hurricane Katrina "destroyed more than homes, lives and livelihoods; it swept away the curtain hiding the poor, confronting the richest country on the globe with its inner Third World.... For too many people, the order to evacuate was an impossibility—they had no car, no money for a bus ticket and nowhere to go even if they could have left. ... In a nation where almost half the population identifies itself as middle class, easy access to

5 credit and luxury goods, second mortgages and third jobs allow many to ignore how close to poverty they are. A storm, an extended hospital stay or a lay-off could tumble them into desperation, and the social safety net is tattered beyond repair." http://www.tompaine.com/articles/2005/09/21/americas_third_world.php
5 OHCHR, 2004, p.8.
6 See Thomas Pogge, 2002/3, p.7.
7 HDR 2005, p.8. http://www.tompaine.com/articles/2005/09/21/americas_third_world.php).
8 Pogge, 2003, p.8.
9 Nigel Dower, 2003, p.39.
10 Narveson, 1988, p.7.
11 Narveson, 1988, p.60.
12 Hunt, 1999, p.9.
13 Sogge, 2005.
14 When speaking about libertarianism in the following I refer to strict libertarianism.
15 Hayek 1993, p.123.
16 Hayek 1993, p.137; 1984, p.82; Plant 1991, p.81; Pierson 1991, p.42.
17 Nozick 1974: 155; The libertarian website "Advocates for self-government" obviously shares this view: "We can't make a perfect world. We can do more for the poor by replacing inefficient government programs with effective voluntary assistance." *David Bergland; http://www.theadvocates.org/library/libertarian-faq.html#Lib.FAQ.1,* retrieved February 2007.
18 The right to life implies a negative duty on the side of the government not to kill its citizens. But it also implies a duty on the side of the government to protect its citizens from being killed by fellow citizens. In other words the government has a duty to set up a system of criminal law and a judiciary, which is a positive duty.
19 Hayek 1993, p.137.
20 Hayek 1993, p.124.
21 Nozick 1974, p.155; Plant 1991, p.83.
22 Hayek 1973, p.113.
23 Hayek 1993, p.127.
24 Hayek 1993, pp.134,135.
25 Lucas 1980, p.4.
26 Hayek 1993, p.135.
27 Hayek 1993, p.135.
28 Hayek 1993, pp.125,126.
29 Nozick 1974, p.150.
30 http://www.theadvocates.org/library/issues-taxes.html, retrieved February 2007
31 Bellamy 1992, p.222; Kymlicka 1990, p.93.
32 http://www.ftlcomm.com:16080/ensign/desantisArticles/2002_600/desantis658/agenda.html, retrieved February 2007.
33 Hayek 1993, p.125, 137; Hayek 1984, p.82; Bellamy 1992, p.222.
34 Rawls 1976, p.3, Pogge 2002/3, p.31.
35 http://www.oxfam.org/en/news/pressreleases2004/pr040714_sudan_aid_chad.htm
36 Plant 1991, pp. 92, 93.
37 Plant 1999, p.268 ; Hook 1980, p.103.
38 Machan 1995, p.216.
39 Shue 1980, pp.50,51.
40 Shue 1980, p.55.
41 http://unmillenniumproject.org/reports/why4.htm.
42 Hook 1980, p.103.
43 Pogge 2002/3, p.62.
44 http://www.ccr-ny.org/v2/print_page.asp?ObjID=D4xevrzVmn&Content=631, November 2005.
45 The question presented was whether a state's failure to protect an individual against private violence constitutes a violation of the Due Process Clause of the Fourteenth Amendment. The conclusion of the majority was that the Due Process Clause does not impose a special duty on the State to provide services to the public for protection against private actors if the State did not create those harms.

[46] "The Clause is phrased as a limitation on the State's power to act, not as a guarantee of certain minimal levels of safety and security; while it forbids the State itself to deprive individuals of life, liberty, and property without due process of law, its language cannot fairly be read to impose an affirmative obligation on the State to ensure that those interests do not come to harm through other means." http://www.oyez.org/oyez/resource/case/634/, February 2006.
[47] Shue 1980, p.56; Gewirth 1996, p.97; Pogge 2002/3, p.172
[48] HDR 2000, p.73.
http://www.unhchr.ch/huricane/huricane.nsf/0/7DB8CF5C4B903DDAC12570B200558277?opendocument, March 2006

CHAPTER 5

THE ILLUSIONS OF LIBERTARIANISM

> *"Hunger is actually the worst of all weapons of mass destruction, claiming millions of victims every year. Fighting hunger and poverty and promoting development are the truly sustainable way to achieve world peace....There will be no peace without development, and there will be neither peace nor development without social justice."*
>
> **Brazilian President Luiz Inácio Lula da Silva**[1]
>
> Will he achieve his goals now he is following a libertarian agenda?

1. Introduction

In the former chapter I dealt with the libertarian objections to the idea of social justice. The libertarian Hayek says that the belief in social justice is *a quasi-religious superstition* to be compared with a belief in witches.[2] The limitedness of human knowledge, the lack of consensus on social justice as well as the lack of a moral actor render it inappropriate to use the word 'justice'. I have argued that in other domains of justice human knowledge is also limited and that opinions differ on what is just: there is no genuine difference between social justice and classical justice. As for Hayek's idea that socio-economic deprivation is not a result of human action, I have argued that this alleged absence of a moral actor is an optical illusion. Socio-economic conditions, including poverty and deprivation, are not the same as hurricanes: they have always been and still are the result of human actions, actions of people, individuals and groups, being confronted with each other in their struggle for a (meaningful) life. The current gap between rich and poor has resulted from human actions in the past that has led to institutional arrangements that determine the socio-economic situation, including poverty. Even today, the weaker and more vulnerable are being pushed aside in the struggle for life, because of human-made institutional arrangements that produce unfavorable legislation, trade policies and other socio-economic measures which negatively impact them.

The Illusions of Libertarianism

I have admitted that often socio-economic misery has not been caused by *intentional* actions. People eat meat, not intending to throw a negative impact on the overall production of food for the world's people. People drive a car, not intending to pollute the environment. But cannot people be blamed for their actions even if the miserable situation they create is not intended? In many cases, the situation that results from people's actions may not be intended, but is nevertheless *foreseeable*. The situation that results may then be called an injustice if the actor refuses to take steps to redress the situation. And even when the unpleasant consequences of people's actions are neither intentional nor foreseeable, people may still be responsible if there is a way to redress or relieve the situation. Someone who causes a traffic accident without being at fault, but who does not care about or help the victim, commits an act of injustice. Likewise, people may be said to have committed an injustice if their actions have resulted in (unintended or foreseeable) socio-economic suffering, for which there is a solution that will redress or relieve the suffering—that they then refuse to implement. All in all, the idea that there is no responsible moral actor and that poverty should be compared with hurricanes is an illusion. It may be difficult to exactly determine the responsible actor, because in general people do not create socio-economic situations directly: they create or support institutional arrangements that in turn cause or maintain socio-economic deprivation. But, does this putting the matter at third or fourth hand relieve them from their responsibility and accountability? And is all this not the same with civil and political rights? Who is responsible when people are prevented from expressing their opinions or practicing their religion because of the political structures of a society?

I have suggested that this insight implies a shift in the approach to ESC-rights. The idea of these rights is that the vital socio-economic interests of people are guaranteed. Traditionally, this aim is seen as being served by the positive duties of others, in particular states, to provide people with the socio-economic goods mentioned in the rights. Now it appears that socio-economic rights are mainly to be seen as negative rights, rights that imply a negative duty, a duty to refrain from causing damage to others. They call upon us to be aware that our actions may cause and in fact often cause damage to others, for instance that our economic policies prevent poor countries from developing.[3]

However, such a duty does not sufficiently guarantee that these others have at their the disposal the socio-economic goods necessary for them to lead a dignified life. Therefore the duties to refrain should be complemented by duties to protect and duties to help. So, I do recognize positive duties, although I believe that they are to be seen as secondary, rather than primary, duties. Many though have considerable difficulty in recognizing the duties of ESC-rights; the idea of duties is morally unacceptable to many—strict—libertarians. As mentioned before, Hayek says *"What we have to deal with in the case of 'social justice' is simply a quasi-religious superstition of the kind which we should respectfully leave in peace so long as it merely makes those happy who hold it, but which we must fight when it becomes the pretext of coercing other men.*"[4] The idea of a duty may give cause to measures coercing rich people or rich countries to alleviate the socio-economic misery of the poor and such coercive measures are unacceptable. This does not mean that libertarians want poverty to remain and to continue but, rather, that they do not see it as a violation of human rights, that is, ESC-rights. And implementing ESC-rights is not the way to deal with poverty as these rights contravene their libertarian principle of freedom. They expect a free-market system to do the job of alleviating poverty and exclusion.

One of the famous representatives of libertarianism is Robert Nozick. According to him, the imposition of coercive measures aimed at implementing ESC-rights comes to an illegitimate violation of the right to property of the well-off, provided of course that they are the legitimate owners of that property. This Nozickian position is still very much alive, as is demonstrated by David Kelley, founder and senior fellow of the Objectivist Center in the USA. He rejects the right-status of the right to healthcare. "*If I have such a right, some other person or group has the involuntary, un-chosen obligation to provide it. I stress the word 'involuntary'. A right is an entitlement. If I have a right to medical care, then I am entitled to the time, the effort, the ability, the wealth, of whoever is going to be forced to provide that care. In other words, I own a piece of the taxpayers who subsidize me. I own a piece of the doctors who tend to me. The notion of a right to medical care goes far beyond any notion of charity. A doctor who waives his bill because I am indigent is offering a free gift; he retains his autonomy, and I owe him gratitude. But if I have a right to care, then he is merely giving me my due, and I owe him nothing. If others are forced to serve me in the name of my right to care, then they are being used regardless of their will as a means to my welfare. I am stressing this point because many people do not appreciate that the very concept of welfare rights, including the right to healthcare, is incompatible with the view of individuals as ends in themselves. .... So the first consequence of implementing a 'right' to medical care is forced transfers of wealth from taxpayers to the clientele of programs like Medicare and Medicaid..... It is also worth noting that the Supreme Court has never recognized a constitutional basis for any welfare right, including the right to medical care. The Court recognizes that the concept of rights embodied in our legal system is the concept of liberty rights.*"[5] This Nozickian view of course raises the question when do people own their property legitimately, and should their property be respected?

2. The illusion of the legitimacy of the current distribution

According to Nozick, the justice or injustice of a particular distribution of resources is dependent on the question of how that distribution has come into being. His approach is historical, focusing on the development of the distribution, with most theories of social justice being patterned, that is, structurally oriented. A patterned theory regards a distribution as just if it complies with a structural formula, for example, if resources are distributed according to the principle of 'to each according to his need' or 'to each according to merit'. Nozick rejects these structural approaches. Neither need nor desert are decisive for the question of whether a particular distribution is just or unjust, but rather the history of the distribution. How has the distribution developed? Nozick's approach is not totally strange. In daily life, we also often—and rightly—refer to what has happened in the past to justify our ownership" "*I bought it legally from him, so it's mine*" is often regarded as more convincing than "*I needed it, so it's mine*". Nozick says that people are entitled to the goods they possess if those goods were originally (in the past) acquired legitimately, if they have been legitimately transferred or, if—when they have not been transferred legitimately—measures have been taken to correct the injustice of the transfer.[6]

So, to justify ownership in a libertarian way, we must go back into history to find out whether the initial acquisition and the subsequent transfers were legitimate. What can be said about this initial acquisition? Nozick assumes that originally goods, land, fruits, animals, were un-owned, which is slightly different from the position of his predecessor John Locke, who assumed that goods were common property. If someone takes these un-owned goods into possession, this acquisition is legitimate provided that the condition of others is not worsened as a result of the acquisition. Nozick´s idea is that we own ourselves and our talents and that we are free to use those talents in any way we want: this makes us the owner of the fruits of our labor. If we mix our talents with an un-owned thing, it becomes ours. If we farm un-owned land, it is ours. If we gather un-owned strawberries, they are ours. All of which makes me think of children who come across something which is apparently un-owned—an apple on a tree, a coin in the street—and claim it as theirs by saying "*It's mine. I saw it first!*"

It sounds reasonable, but is it? We do not have historical sources to draw on when trying to describe the initial acquisition of un-owned things in the long ago. But, let us try to follow Nozick in assuming that in the long-ago things were un-owned, and try to imagine the situation when those un-owned things were taken and claimed to be the property of the taker. May be humans worked to stay alive by gathering fruits, or grabbing their share of the prey the big predators left behind and, later on, by hunting themselves. But, to whom did the meat the humans tore off the prey the predators left behind actually belong? Did it belong to them, or to the big predator, or possibly to the prey itself? And to whom did the prey humans hunted, or the fruits they gathered from the trees belong: to the first person to lay hands on them? And did the prey and the fruits belong to them even if they took more then they really needed? And what if people claimed a field to be their private hunting-field or gathering-territory, simply because they were the first to find it? Did it belong to them? Why should something be the legitimate property of someone just because that someone was first? Someone's talents are morally arbitrary. True, it is a fact that if someone runs faster than somebody else, he or she will arrive first at a wanted item and will take that item, but it is not a question of justice.

Even if it could justifiably be said that the item belonged to them, and that the initial acquisition was legitimate, we should ask what happened after this initial acquisition. Maybe there were others who, being stronger, took the meat and the fruits from the weaker, even though the weaker were the first to acquire them. And there will have been exchanges that look like free exchanges, but that were, in fact, infected by force and manipulation. For example, if I am poor and desperately need work to earn a living for myself and my family, and if someone offers me a job which is badly paid, I may be prepared to take it because I have no alternative. Often people find themselves in a position of dependence in which their decisions are heavily influenced by their needs or situation, and in which others may exploit the situation to advance *their* interests. Or people may lack in sufficient information, knowledge or expertise and cannot avoid being manipulated. Exchanges of goods may then be called 'free'—to that extent that the participants say they want the exchange to take place—but such exchanges may then be seen as materially 'un-free', owing to the fact that one of the parties is forced by circumstances to engage in the exchange.

We may assume that a lot of violence accompanied the initial acquisition and transference of goods, and that property was, and has been, acquired by the strong to the detriment of the weak and the less-talented. Historical writings confirm this as far as later transferences are concerned. Nozick and many fellow libertarians regard such violence as having been corrected or compensated for by the free market system. They argue that, in the long run, the total system of appropriation and transfer as practiced by the free market has obviously bettered the position of the less-talented and the weak, especially compared with their situation in the past. Therefore libertarians conclude that, all in all, the current property-distribution is just and should be respected.

I take this, however, to be both a hasty conclusion and an illusion. Is the violence that accompanied the acquisition and transferences of goods legitimized if you can show that the position of the least-advantaged under capitalism has been bettered compared to the situation in the past? Should not you also take other systems into consideration? Should not you consider systems that offer compensation to the vulnerable who have lost the competition to acquire goods, or systems which do not have private property, or systems that only have communal property, or egalitarian systems? As long as it has not been shown that the poor come off the best in capitalism in comparison with (all) other possible systems, it can rightly be argued that the current distributions of goods, nationally and globally, flow from violent confrontations in the past, and that because of that, the current distribution is morally questionable, a position which is not corrected by the possible increase of total welfare under capitalism.

3. Negative and positive freedom

Realizing ESC-rights, libertarians argue, will require the imposition of coercive measures. This would represent not only an illegitimate violation of the right to property of the well-off, but it would also imply a violation of freedom in general. In the preceding paragraph we met David Kelley who takes this libertarian position. Libertarians value freedom. Therefore, libertarians want governments that limit themselves solely to a few core tasks and that do not try to organize people's lives, a point of view that also implies a reluctance to accept the power of a government to compel its citizens to pay taxes to relieve the socio-economic deprivation of the least advantaged.

Libertarians interpret freedom as freedom from interference, as the precept that people should abstain from interfering with other people's lives, which implies that also governments should refrain from intervening in the personal sphere of their citizens. But this is seen by many as a thin interpretation of freedom. They would argue that sometimes people are free to the extent that nobody is interfering with their lives, but that they hardly can be called free because of the miserable socio-economic situation in which they live. This has led some people to speak of 'positive freedom' in contrast to 'freedom from interference', or what can be called 'negative freedom'. For instance, the Office of the High Commissioner on Human Rights uses freedom in a broad sense to encompass both negative and positive freedom. It says that "*a person's freedom to live a healthy life is contingent both on the requirement that no one obstructs her legitimate pursuit of good health—negative freedom—and also on the society's success in creating an enabling environment in which she can actually achieve good health—positive freedom*".[7]

The libertarian Narveson discusses the use of the concepts of positive freedom and negative freedom, and offers the following description of them as they are generally used. Negative freedom is the absence of persons preventing someone from acting as he or she wants to act. If I prevent someone from moving from A to B by chaining that person up, that other person is not free. Positive freedom, on the other hand, means the presence of circumstances that enable people to act as they want to do. "*We can identify positive liberty with the presence of those conditions, such as the means of doing x, that enable you to do something, if circumstances permit.*"[8] For example, if a person finds himself in extreme poverty, that person lacks positive freedom. In short, negative freedom is the absence of coercion by other people, while positive freedom is the presence of enabling circumstances.

Narveson regards the notion of positive freedom as inappropriate. People may find themselves in unfortunate circumstances and those circumstances may affect their capabilities, but you cannot say that they are not free. A characteristic of 'un-freedom' is the presence of coercion: poor people may be limited as regards their capabilities, but they are not coerced by others and, therefore, they cannot be considered 'un-free', so Narveson argues.

In response to this, I would like to say a few words in favor of the idea of positive freedom.

From a libertarian perspective, being free means *"... free from the coercive dictates of others ..."*.[9] Why is freedom from coercion valuable? Why is it valuable that people are free from interference? Let us listen to the libertarians themselves. John Hospers says that *"If people are free from the coercive dictates of others, they can exercise their choices in countless ways that would have been impossible before."*[10] Narveson says that *"To be free is, to begin with, to be free to do what one wants."* And, he continues *"... freedom is fundamentally the freedom to determine, namely to determine what is the case."*[11] He then goes on to say that freedom means that we can achieve our goals and realize our values, that we can have at our disposal our talents and the fruits of our talents. So, it seems to me that according to the libertarians, freedom from interference is valuable because it enables individuals to develop their capabilities to achieve their strivings, to live their lives as they think fit. In other words, behind freedom from interference lies another, more substantial, freedom: the idea that people should have the capacity and opportunity to do, or be, the things people have reasons to value. The point is that negative freedom, freedom from interference, does not guarantee this more substantial freedom. As mentioned above, people may be free to the extent that nobody is obviously interfering with them, yet due to their unfortunate socio-economic circumstances, they do not have the capacity and opportunity to do or to be the things they value. This is where the notion of positive freedom comes in.

This is—and here I follow the circumscription of Ian Narveson—not the *absence* of impeding *persons*, but the *presence* of *circumstances* that enable people to live their lives as they think fit.[12] Both negative and positive freedom serve as a means to achieve the third freedom, substantial freedom, the key upon which everything turns. Substantial freedom is the ultimate goal. In other words, substantial freedom should be made effective by negative liberty and positive liberty working together. If you want people to enjoy substantial liberty or freedom (I use the words 'freedom' and 'liberty' interchangeably) a quest for negative freedom is not enough and should be complemented by a quest for positive freedom.

The Illusions of Libertarianism

In my interpretation it is substantial freedom, not negative freedom, that is the ultimate goal of libertarianism. Moreover, I think libertarians also want *equal* substantial freedom. They do not want only philosophers, housekeepers, drivers or priests to be free. Hayek for instance, argues that a government that pursues a policy of re-distributive justice is trying to impose a particular view of social justice on all its citizens and he suggests that a government should not promote the interests of particular groups or persons.[13] This would appear to be a manifestation of the idea of equality that also can be found with Narveson.

When describing libertarianism as contrary to the idea that some people are entitled to prescribe to others how to arrange their lives, Narveson states that *"The liberal, by contrast, holds that the selection of personal goals, of ways of life, is up to each person and may not be imposed by others."*[14] What is interesting here is that Narveson seems to assert that *everyone* should be enabled to live their lives as they deem fit. So I think that it is correct to say that libertarianism strives to attain *equal* substantial freedom. I'm aware that libertarians often are regarded as advocates of freedom whereas others, for example, socialists, are seen as promoting equality, but it would be wrong to say that there is necessarily a conflict between the values of freedom and equality, just as it would also be wrong to say that libertarians strive for freedom at the expense of equality. It cannot be denied that sometimes libertarians seem to strive for freedom at the expense of equality and may be they themselves regard it as characteristic of libertarianism, but I cannot imagine that libertarians really want their ideas to be seen as concerned only with the enhancement of the freedom of a few. If they do want that I would like to know who are those happy few and whether they would be content with such a determination, if they themselves were *not* to number among those. I take it that most libertarians will be of the view that every person is the absolute owner of his own life and should be free to do whatever he wishes with his person or property *as long as he respects the liberty of others*.

If my interpretation of libertarianism is correct, then it is actually concerned with the achievement of *equal substantial freedom*. In order to enable every human being to enjoy substantial freedom, a policy of social justice should be pursued, which may require that the negative liberty of some must be weighed against the positive liberty of others; in other words, that the richer members of a community should be forced to contribute to the alleviation of the miserable conditions of the poor. The idea that people should be able to live as they think fit certainly requires that others do not prevent them from doing so, but it also requires that circumstances be arranged so as to enable them to be or to do what they want to be or to do. In other words, substantial freedom should be effected by means of negative freedom and positive freedom.

Let us assume, then, that libertarianism is indeed aimed at equal substantial freedom. One would then expect libertarians to embrace ESC-rights by virtue of the ideal of equal substantial freedom. (I certainly believe that it would be rational for libertarians to adopt such a position.) However, it is also obvious that libertarians consider the value of negative freedom as more pressing than positive freedom and do not want to weigh one against another. And they do not want to implement ESC-rights by forcing the well-off to contribute to such an implementation. But, I think that this position will result in the substantial freedom of some being promoted at the expense of the substantial freedom of others. Or, in some cases, it would result in some deprived people having no substantial freedom at all. Thus it can be seen that paying attention only to negative freedom, thinking that it will automatically enhance equal substantial freedom, turns out to be an illusion.[15]

4. Poverty is a violation of negative freedom

Up to now I have adopted a distinction between positive and negative freedom, although I have added the notion of substantial freedom. With the help of these three notions, I have argued that a politics of social justice is justified because it enhances the positive freedom and, by so doing, the substantial freedom of the poor. And I have admitted that such a policy may infringe upon the freedom of the well-off. The eventual conclusion, then, is not that we abstain from a policy of social justice, but that we should carefully weigh one against the other.

But I would like to go further. I think that even the idea that socio-economic deprivation is to be seen as a lack of positive freedom is incorrect. As I pointed out in Chapter 4, poverty or socio-economic deprivation is not a natural coincidence: it is the result of human action. It was so in the past and it is still so today. In the primitive world of the past, the ways in which people prevented each other from living their lives as they thought fit, and how they prevented each other from taking what they needed to survive were clear and straightforward. Today's world, though, while more complicated is still, in effect, the same. Using political and juridical measures and constructions, the powerful have created a socio-economic constellation which prevents others from taking what they had taken from yet others, but which the poor now need to stay alive.

This shows that poverty is not just the lack of positive freedom—the lack of enabling circumstances—it is the violation of negative freedom, it is coercion by others. The least well-off are prevented, by others, from doing what they want to do to stay alive. They are not *"free from the coercive dictates of others ..."*[16]

On the other hand, the situation of the well-off can be interpreted in terms of positive freedom. If a government imposes taxes upon the well-off, it is described by libertarians as a violation of their negative freedom. But it also can be seen as a lack of positive freedom, as the absence of enabling circumstances. And if a government refrains from imposing taxes intended to finance social arrangements, this can be defined not only as the absence of constraining others (negative freedom), but also as the presence of favorable circumstances (positive freedom). It is therefore curious that a government policy consisting of the imposition of taxes intended to promote social justice should be described as coercing others when poverty, which is equally the result of government policy, is seen as the absence of enabling circumstances.

Seen from this perspective, libertarianist ideas about freedom turn out to be even more illusory than I pointed out earlier. I wrote that it is a libertarianist illusion to think that the cause of freedom is adequately served by focusing on negative freedom, and that substantial freedom may require a policy of social justice, one in which the negative freedom of the rich is weighed against the positive freedom of the poor. Now I would say that the libertarian presumption that abstaining from a policy of social justice at least guarantees that people's lives are not interfered with, and that negative freedom is respected, is a complete illusion. Abstaining from a policy of social justice amounts, in fact, to actively doing something: it amounts to helping the rich deprive the poor of their means of subsistence. The powerful do this not with their bare hands, but with the aid of socio-economic institutions and structures that prevent the poor from providing for themselves, with the result that not only the positive freedom, but also the negative freedom of the least-advantaged, is violated.

Governments obviously cannot avoid weighing the negative freedom of the rich, who should not be prevented by others from enjoying their possessions, against the negative freedom of the poor, who should equally not be constrained by others -through a socio-economic institutional structure- from providing themselves with the resources to stay alive, and indeed, to live in dignity. What is needed, I would conclude, is a politics of social justice to serve the value of freedom. But that said, the question remains: are ESC-rights an adequate tool to bring about a politics of social justice?

BIBLIOGRAPHY

Alston, Philip, 'Denial and neglect', in: Richard Reoch (red.), *Human Rights, the new consensus* (London: Regency Press 1994).

Bellamy, Richard, *Liberalism and Modern Society* (Cambridge: Polity Press, 1992).

Buitenweg, Rob, *Recht op een Menswaardig Bestaan* (Utrecht: de Graaff, 2001).

Cliteur, Paul, Neo-Liberal Globalism and Philosophical Presuppositions, in: Nieuwenhuys, Eva (ed.) *Neo-Liberal Globalism and Social Sustainable Globalisation* (Leiden,Boston: Brill, 2006)

Craven, Matthew, *The International Covenant on Economic, Social and Cultural Rights* (Oxford: Clarendon Press 1998).

Dower, Nigel, An Introduction to Global Citizenship, Edinburgh University Press, 2003.

Eide, Asbjörn, 'Economic, Social and Cultural Rights as Human Rights', in: Asbjörn Eide, Catarina Krause and Allan Rosas (red.), *Economic, Social and Cultural Rights* (Dordrecht, Boston en Londen: Martinus Nijhoff Publishers, 1995).

Eide, Asbjörn en Allan Rosas, 'Economic, social and cultural rights, a universal challenge', in: Asbjörn Eide, Catarina Krause and Allan Rosas (red.), *Economic, Social and Cultural Rights* (Dordrecht, Boston and Londen: Martinus Nijhoff Publishers, 1995).

Eide, A., 'Obstacles and Goals to be Pursued', in: Asbjörn Eide, Catarina Krause en Allan Rosas (red.), *Economic, Social and Cultural Rights* (Dordrecht, Boston and London: Martinus Nijhoff Publishers, 1995).

Eide, A., 'The Rights to an Adequate Standard of Living Including the Right to Food', in: Asbjörn Eide, Catarina Krause en Allan Rosas (red.), *Economic, Social and Cultural Rights* (Dordrecht, Boston and London: Martinus Nijhoff Publishers, 1995).

Eide, Asbjörn , 'Economic and Social Rights', in: Janusz Symonides (red.), *Human Rights: Concept and Standards* (Aldershot, Burlinton, Singapore and Sydney: Ashgate, Dartmouth, Unesco Publishing, 2000).

Eide, Asbjörn en Bernt Hagtvet (red.), *Human rights in perspective: A global assessment* (Oxford: Blackwell, 1992).

Flinterman, Cees, 'De ondeelbaarheid van de rechten van de mens', in: A.P.M. Coomans, A.W. Heringa en I. Westendorp (red.), *De toenemende betekenis van economische, sociale en culturele rechten* (Leiden: Stichting NJCM-boekerij, 1994).

Forsythe, David P., *Human Rights in International Relations* (Cambridge: Cambridge Univesity Press, 2000).

Hayek, F.A. 'Equality, Value and Merit', in: Michael Sandel (ed.), *Liberalism and its Critics* (Oxford: Blackwell Publishers, 1984).

Hayek, F.A., "Social' or distributive justice', in: Alan Ryan (red.), *Justice* (Oxford: Oxford University Press 1993).

Hospers, John, 'What libertarianism is', in: Tibor R. Machan & Douglas B. Rasmussen (ed.) *Liberty for the Twenty-First Century* (Lanham & Maryland: Rowman & Littelfield Publishers, Inc., 1995).

Hunt, Paul, *Reclaiming Social Rights, International and Comparative Perspectives* (Aldershot: Ashgate, 1999).

Kymlicka, W., *Contemporary Political Philosophy: an introduction* (Oxford: Clarendon Press, 1990).

Narveson, Jan, *The Libertarian Idea* (Philadelphia: Temple University Press, 1988).

Robert Nozick, *Anarchy, State and Utopia* (New York: Basic Books, Inc., Publishers, 1974).

Plant, Raymond., 'Needs, agency and welfare rights', in: J.D. Moon (red.), *Responsibility, Rights and Welfare, the theory of the welfare state* (Boulder etc.: Westview Press, 1988).

Plant, Raymond, *Modern Political Thought* (Oxford etc.: Basil Blackwell, 1991).

Pogge, Thomas, World Poverty and Human Rights, Cosmopolitan Responsibilities and Reforms (Cambridge: Polity Press, 2002/2003).

Rawls, John, *A Theory of Justice* (Oxford: Oxford University Press, 1971/1976).

Shue Henry, *Basic Rights* (Princeton NJ: Princeton University press, 1980).

Shue, Henry, *Basic Rights: Subsistence, Affluence and US Foreign Policy* (Princeton NJ: Princeton University Press, 1996).

ENDNOTES

1 HDR 2005, p.74.
2 Hayek 1993, p.123.
3 http://www.commondreams.org/views03/0923-04.htm, retrieved July 2007.
4 Hayek 1993, p.123.

[5] http://www.objectivistcenter.org/ct-14-Is_There_Right_Health_Care.aspx.
[6] Nozick, 1974, p.150.
[7] OHCHR 2004, p.9.
[8] Narveson 1988, p.22.
[9] Hospers 1995, p.6.
[10] Hospers 1995, p.6.
[11] Narveson 1988, pp.18,22.
[12] Narveson 1988, p.22.
[13] Hayek 1984, p.82.
[14] Narveson 1995, p.28.
[15] Hayek 1984, p.82.
[16] Hospers 1995, p.6.

CHAPTER 6

THE SURPLUS VALUE OF A RIGHTS-BASED APPROACH

> *"Human rights are correlated with duties. Duty bearers are the actors collectively responsible for the realization of human rights. Those who bear duties with respect to a human right are account-able if the right goes unrealized. When a right has been violated or insufficiently protected, there is always someone or some institution that has failed to perform a duty."*[1]
>
> **HDR 2000**

1. Introduction

Human rights protect the fundamental interests of people, for example, their interest in not having their religion interfered with, their interest in having a fair trial, in freedom of expression, in access to healthcare, in being educated. The idea is that through the protection of these interests, certain substantial and structural values will be achieved that will, eventually contribute to a dignified life. The substantial values that human rights aim to achieve are freedom, well-being and participation. They offer people the freedom to live as they think fit, they provide them with the opportunity to participate in their communities and they guarantee them a minimal level of material well-being.[2] A rights-based approach to development recognizes that the promotion of human rights should be an important goal of development policies and that the realization of human rights is not something that automatically emerges as a reward or result of development: human rights are critical to *achieving* development. And the notion 'human rights' refers to both sets of rights: civil and political rights as well as economic, social and cultural rights. A rights-based approach to development implies the promotion of CP-rights, as it is only with civil and political freedoms that people can genuinely take advantage of economic possibilities. And a rights-based approach to development also requires the promotion of ESC-rights, that is, it demands that these rights are not regarded as mere wishes but treated as genuine human rights.[3]

We have seen, in chapters 4 and 5, that many people—for example libertarians—do not deny that freedom, well-being and participation are important goods. Yet while they are certainly willing to do so by promoting CP-rights, they oppose the notion of ESC-rights; they regard that notion as morally unacceptable. In Chapter 4, I presented Hayek as one such libertarian opposed to ESC-rights. He suggested that socio-economic deprivation and the alleviation thereof are not questions of justice that call for redress by ESC-rights. In Chapter 5, I discussed the libertarians who argue that the implementation of ESC-rights amounts to a violation of freedom, in particular of the right of property, of the well-off.[4]

In addition to these moral objections, however, there are also those who raise conceptual objections against the notion of ESC-rights. Many people call into question whether ESC-rights are even genuine rights and question their status as such. Steiner and Alston argue that the question of whether socio-economic rights are human rights has already been settled, but that seems to be too optimistic. Of course, it could be pointed out that socio-economic rights are included in various human rights documents, such as the Universal Declaration of Human Rights and the International Covenant on Economic, Social and Cultural Rights, and that their recognition as (human) rights seems irrefutable.

Yet while many writers (Cranston, Vierdag, Orwin and Pangle, Jacobs, Cliteur, and Robertson and Merrills) agree that socio-economic rights are included in human rights documents, they nevertheless assert that they are somehow not *genuine* rights; in particular, that they do not entail real duties on the part of the addressees. It is said that the word 'rights' presupposes clear duties on the side of the addressee.[5] And with social rights the duties of the addressee are that vague and unclear that it is inappropriate to use the notion of a right.[6] In this view, ESC-rights are rather to be seen as utopian aspirations or political goals of governments which do not belong to the realm of morally or legally compelling rights. Some suggest to consider scaling back the list of ESC-rights, thereby proposing to differentiate between rights that could remain as universal rights, like basic nutrition and education, and others that could be viewed as universal high-priority *goals*.[7] Robertson and Merrills say that the Covenant on Economic, Social and Cultural Rights should be seen as a *"promotional convention"... "that is to say it does not set out rights which the parties are required to implement immediately, but rather lists standards which they undertake to promote and which they pledge themselves to secure progressively, to the greatest extent possible, having regard to their resources."*[8] And it should also be noted that politicians—and even those activists who specifically label themselves as "human rights" activists—often rank civil and political rights higher than socio-economic rights and regard the latter, unlike the former, not as genuine rights.

I am concerned in this chapter with the objections to socio-economic rights as actual *rights*. It should be clear, however, that I am not referring to the view that international law cannot be seen as real law. I believe that a distinction should be drawn between two questions: "Are socio-economic rights real *rights*?" and "Are socio-economic rights as part of international law, real *law*?" This distinction should be borne in mind when objections to socio-economic rights are being discussed.

Many people criticize what they see as the pretensions of international law and deny that it is even *real* law. They emphasize that, unlike national laws, the rules of international law cannot be enforced, a fact which enervates the pretensions of international law.[9] Others take a less extreme stand. They admit that the rules of international law cannot be enforced but acknowledge, nevertheless, that international law displays the essential characteristics of law.[10] For instance, in international law, judicial or quasi-judicial organs exist, and act like real judges and they issue formal decisions that are often complied with. In the field of both civil and political rights as well as in that of socio-economic rights, committees working under international covenants monitor the compliance by states with the rights in question. This leads many people to state that there are abundant justifications for regarding international law as real. This is confirmed by the actual behavior of states: whether it be the United States, France, China, Israel or Palestine, all refer to the rules of international law to justify their acts or to condemn the acts of others. Academics may dispute on the question of whether international law is real law, in practice the juridical character of international law is generally accepted.[11]

While it would be beyond the scope of this book to elaborate on the juridical character of international law, I do hope that it is clear that this question is different from that of whether socio-economic rights are real rights. The recognition of international law as real law and of socio-economic rights as part of it need not imply that these rights are real rights. It could instead mean that socio-economic rights can be seen as aspirations or goals included in international law. For after all, national laws may also contain aspirations or goals that cannot be considered rights, but which indisputably belong to domestic law. ESC-rights are, in fact, often included in national constitutions, and are recognized by that inclusion as part of the law of a country, even though their status as rights is disputed. Look for instance at the Dutch Constitution. Its article 22 says that "*The authorities shall take steps to promote the health of the population*". Or take a look at article 47 from Part IV, the '*Directive Principle of State Policy*' of the Indian Constitution. This article, ('Duty of the State to raise the level of nutrition and the standard of living and to improve public health') states that "*The State shall regard the raising of the level of nutrition and the standard of living of its people and the improvement of public health as among its primary duties and, in particular, the State shall endeavor to bring about prohibition of the consumption except for medicinal purpose of intoxicating drinks and of drugs which are injurious to health.*" These articles undoubtedly belong to domestic law, but it can be questioned whether they are real rights. Often these rights cannot be invoked before a court, which according to many undermines the rights-character of these rights.[12]

On the other hand, the recognition of socio-economic rights as real rights need not mean that they are real law; they could also be regarded as moral rights, for rights can be legal or moral. Locke and others, who advocated human rights, realized that while these were not yet law they should definitely be seen as real (moral) rights that ought to be transformed into law. And when the Universal Declaration of Human Rights was framed and adopted, it was generally felt that moral rights were laid down within the text, even though it was not yet a document with juridically binding rights.[13]

My concern in this chapter will be with the question of whether ESC-rights are genuine rights. Answering that question also demands that I provide an answer to what a real right is supposed to be. This is not a new question. Indeed, it is one that Rex Martin says has engendered debate for centuries and one to which, he adds, the answers given are very diverse.[14] It would be an illusion to think that, by the end of this chapter, I will have found a definite answer to it. Far too many efforts have already been undertaken to justify such a pretension. Yet it is the very lack of unanimity that demands that I make clear what position I take with respect to the question what a right is.

My search will proceed in three steps. First, I will consider the relationship between rights and duties. According to many writers, the duties of socio-economic rights are flawed. This need not imply that socio-economic rights are not real rights, because a classical theory exists that argues that some rights do not have duties.[15] In fact, it is argued that some rights can be rights without entailing corresponding duties. I will briefly examine that theory, its division of rights into claim-rights, liberties, immunities and powers and its belief that only claim-rights have corresponding duties while liberties, immunities and powers have none. I will try to determine whether socio-economic rights belong to one of the categories of rights with no corresponding duties because, if it is plausible so to do, it can be maintained that socio-economic rights are rights, while the view of the critics that socio-economic rights imply no duties can also be upheld.

After examining the relationship between rights and duties, I will then—in Chapter 7—consider the statement that ESC-rights are vague and try to determine to what extent they have genuine duties as their correlatives. The third step, in which I ask in Chapter 8 what more can be said about rights, will lead me to a definition of the characteristics of socio-economic rights and to my overall conclusion that there is no reason to withhold from them the qualification of rights. But I have a long way to go before reaching that conclusion, so let me get started on the first step.

2. Interests

If the rights to healthcare or housing are considered, it will be generally accepted that people want these goods. However, people's wanting something is no reason to assert that they have a right to them. People sometimes wrap their wishes into rights. It has even become common practice to do so. We hear people say that they have a right to children, a right to die, to a care-free youth, to an unconcerned old age, to in-vitro fertilization, to entertainment, to listen to music, to bear arms, to use marijuana, to sunlight, to use contraception, even to holidays without rain. Undoubtedly people want these goods. But do they have a right to them? People do not necessarily have a right to what they want.

If the domain of rights lies beyond the realm of what people want, then what about interests? Do people have a right to what is in their interest? It's certainly a notion that could be more appropriate than that of wants or desires, for it sounds more objective than the notion of want, which has a more subjective ring.[16] After all, it is possible to say what is in someone's interest without consulting that person, for example, as regards healthcare or adequate housing, or (in the field of civil and political rights) with regard to freedom of religion and speech. People certainly have an interest in these goods, but is that *all* that is meant by the statement that people have a right to those goods?

'Interest' refers to the relationship between an interested person and an object. (A has an interest in X). But others have not yet appeared on the scene. Saying that someone has an interest in something does not say yet whether others should take that interest into consideration.[17] Can we expect others to respect and honor that interest? Or taking a more moderate stand, can we expect them to show that they have taken that interest into consideration, even if their decision eventually turns out not to be to the benefit of that person?

My answer would be no: we cannot. Some acts are not susceptible to accountability. It may be against someone's interest that his love is not returned by the beloved, but it would be unjust to expect the beloved person to account for her (or his) lack of love. And while it might also be at odds with someone's interest to loose a game of chess, it would be unjust or inappropriate to expect the winner to justify his or her winning the game. Other acts can also be seen as susceptible to accountability, while still remaining within someone's discretion. For example, the decision to go by plane may be to the detriment of the railway company, but it is up to the travelers themselves to act on their discretion. And other acts are beyond accountability because accountability would undermine their effectiveness: the decisions of military commanders can definitely go against the interests of an individual soldier, yet requiring the commanders to account for their decisions would render military command ineffective, which in turn would undermine the goals of the military to serve the greater good of the majority.[18]

It is difficult to determine in advance when people can be expected to take other's interests into consideration, or to account for their acts if these run against the interests of another. Here, the notion of a right may be helpful, in that it clarifies the position of others with regard to someone's interest by suggesting that someone's interests deserve protection, and that guarantees are offered—or should be offered—that the interests concerned will, in fact, be protected.

It should be clear that the idea of certain interests of people being protected does not mean that people do not have or are not allowed to have other legitimate interests. Anthony de Jasay describes 'rightsism' as recognizing that people have rights to do certain things or to certain things not being done to them. But, so he argues, "rights" turn out to be the exceptions to a tacitly understood general rule that everything else is forbidden. *"For if such were not the case, announcing rights to engage freely in certain acts would be redundant and pointless."*[19] I disagree with him. If you have a right to a particular medical treatment, it does not imply that it is forbidden for you to decide not to take that treatment. Granting rights only means that certain interests are protected.

3. Normative guideline or duty?

Gewirth puts it this way: *"To have a right is to have an interest that ought to be protected and promoted."* A right, so he continues, has two aspects. Firstly, others should take that interest into consideration. Secondly, the protection of an interest is an act owed to someone else.[20] I will return to this second aspect in Chapter 8 but, as regards the first aspect, I want to point out that it will not always be obvious *who* the 'others' expected to take someone's interests into consideration are, just as it will not always be clear *how far* people should take the interests of someone else into consideration.

Sometimes, it will be completely unproblematic. When A has bought a car from B, A has a right to that car and B has a right to payment. B has to reckon with A's interest in getting that car while A has to take B's interest in being paid into consideration and cannot say that it doesn't concern him. At other times, it can be less clear. If we say that someone has a right to food, this means that that someone has an interest that ought to be protected, even though it can be extremely difficult to ascertain who, and in what manner, has to reckon with that interest. What we cannot say is that nobody has to care. If the notion of a right is used with respect to someone's interests, there must by implication be someone else who must be concerned about that interest. A right to food that nobody has to bother about, and which says nothing about other people's behavior, is a mirage. It is a right that doesn't exist. For rights not only say something about the relationship between the right-holder and the object of the right, they also say something about the relationship between the right-holder and other people. Rights contain directives for other people's acts. But can we say that rights imply duties?

According to Nino, a distinction should be drawn between the notion of 'ought' and 'a duty'.[21] If we follow this distinction, then people who deny that ESC-rights imply duties could say that these rights imply 'oughts' instead of 'duties'. Nino describes two differences. Firstly, 'duties' are individualized, but an 'ought' need not be. This means that *duties* cannot exist without specific people being charged with them. On the other hand, what *ought* to be done does not depend on the presence of specific people charged with doing it. Secondly, when a particular act is impossible to perform, it cannot be the object of a 'duty', but it can be the object of an 'ought'.

Yet it seems to me that Nino overstates the difference between the two. As for the first point, Nino rightly says that an 'ought' need not be individualized, but we should bear in mind that the word 'ought' can be, and often is, used in relation to specific people charged with a specific task. For instance, it is quite appropriate to say that the government ought to guarantee its citizens' right to adequate housing, or that parents ought to take care of their children. But it can also be admitted that the notion of 'ought' can be, and often is, used without explicit reference to specific people. So it makes sense to say that the hungry ought to be given food or, to put it less directly, that the hungry ought to have food. But can this be stated sincerely and honestly if there are no consequences whatsoever for specific individuals?

Nino argues that "*... what ought to be done does not depend on the existence of specific people charged with the task of performing it. Even when there is no such person, to say that an action ought to be done would imply, for instance, that acts which would impede its being done may be justifiably prevented.*"[22] So, does the statement that the hungry ought to have food mean only that acts that impede people from getting food may be prevented? Surely it means more. Does it not mean that specific individuals—or even all of us—should refrain from acts that impede others from access to food? Is the statement that the hungry ought to have food compatible with the assumption that no one is responsible for making sure that they have it (even though routinely this occurs)? I believe Nino is right when he says that the word 'ought' can be used without explicitly referring to specific people. But I also believe that this does *not* mean that no reference to specific people is made whatsoever. In my view, it makes no sense to use the word 'ought' when there is no possibility of the desired situation being achieved by human efforts. While the word can, and often will, be used to indicate that at this very moment it is unclear who should do what ought to be done, it presupposes that—eventually—some people are responsible for achieving the desired situation. The sentence 'The poor ought to have food' inevitably raises the question of who (or what agency) has to make this 'ought' a reality. Which means, in turn, that an 'ought' amounts—eventually—to a 'duty'.

Then we come to Nino's second point—with which I agree—that someone cannot have a duty to do the impossible. But does not that also hold for 'ought'? As will have become clear from the foregoing, the word 'ought' can be used in combination with an explicit reference to specific people; for instance, when saying that the government ought to provide its citizens with adequate housing. In such cases one cannot say that someone ought to do something if it is impossible to do it. That is what is meant by the adage *'ought implies can'*. If it is totally impossible for a government to immediately provide all its citizens with adequate food or adequate housing, it does not makes sense to say that the government ought to do it.[23] But that does not imply that a government need not do anything at all and that inaction is justified. For, it could make sense to say that a government ought to provide most or some of its citizens with adequate housing or food and to investigate ways to do more, if it is possible for a government to do that.

In this context it is worth noting more 'oughts' or duties can contend for the mastery. The person who *ought* to do what *ought* to be done is often confronted with more 'oughts', and the result may be that one particular 'ought' is chosen at the expense of another. But that does not remove the 'ought'; it only means that the person involved has to weigh one *prima facie* 'ought' against another.

What is the situation when something ought to be done without any reference being made to specific people? I have already argued that in the background of such a situation, the idea will lurk that specific people will have been charged with the task of doing what ought to be done. So using the word 'ought' while thinking that the desired situation will be totally impossible to achieve makes no sense. Yet sometimes it is used that way, for example, when we say that children 'ought not to die'. The desired situation is impossible, because children sometimes *will* die. That said, though, I think this is a rather peculiar use of the notion of 'ought'. The speaker knows that the word is basically inappropriate, but they still want to use it to express a strong desire.[24] In my view, however, the word 'ought' only can be used meaningfully when there is a possibility of achieving the desired situation by human action.

So the differences between the notion of 'ought' and 'duty' are not as severe as Nino thinks they are. While the word 'duty' sounds perhaps more rigid and stringent than the word 'ought' both express demands on the behavior of other people which they cannot ignore and justifies saying that rights imply duties. The existence of a right always supposes other people to have a duty. Rights without duties are castles in the air.

4. Duties, disabilities, liabilities, no-rights

The concluding statement of the last section is, however, not shared by everybody. The American philosopher of law, Wesley Hohfeld, has developed a famous theory on the relationship between right-holders and other individuals.[25] He draws a distinction between four categories of rights, all of which are characterized by different relationships between right-holder and others, and only in one category do others have duties. In the other three categories, their situation is not adequately characterized by saying that they have a duty. Hohfeld's distinctions have been used in the writings of many authors, for instance Carlos Santiago Nino, Judith Jarvis Thomson, Peter Jones, Maurice Cranston.[26] Although Hohfeld developed his theory for legal rights, his distinction certainly has relevance for moral rights as well. In addition I would like to note that Hohfeld presented his distinction almost a century ago, but that it is still very much alive.[27] Hohfeld distinguishes between *liberties, claim-rights, powers* and *immunities*. I will briefly present these notions and will then elaborate on these notions, asking in particular whether ESC-rights can be seen as liberties, claim-rights, powers and immunities.

1. Sometimes the notion of a right is used to indicate that someone has a liberty or privilege. Saying that A has a right to do X, meaning that she has a liberty to X, holds that A does not have a duty not to do X. Saying that A has a right, meaning a liberty, to walk in the forest then implies that the right-holder does not have a duty *not* to walk in the forest nor, could be added, a duty to walk in the forest.[28] This concerns the right-holder. What can be said about others. According to Hohfeld, others do not have corresponding duties. The correlative of liberties is other people's *no-right*.[29] This means that others do not have a right to interfere in the activities of the right-holder. They have neither a duty *not* to interfere, any more than they have a duty to assist. If two people are walking in the street, and both see a coin lying on the ground with no clue whatsoever as to its ownership, both have the right (meaning liberty) to pick it up. Neither has a duty to refrain from picking it up, nor a duty to assist the other in picking it up.[30]

It appears to be a strange phenomenon, this right that signifies a liberty. Nevertheless, it occurs, and quite often, especially when it is disputed. For instance, if someone says to someone else "Should you go to the cinema? You've already been twice this week," it would not be strange if the reply were "I have a right to go to the cinema as often as I want."[31]

2. The word 'right' is also used to say that someone has a claim-

The Surplus Value of a Rights-Based Approach

right against some other person. This other person then has a duty. In opposition to the right of A is a duty of B. The formula of a claim-right is: A has a right to X against B, who has a duty towards A with respect to X. This meaning of a right will be the dominant one in the domain of contracts. If A has agreed with B that the latter should deliver her X, B has a duty to provide A with X.[32] Having a claim-right means that others, or some others, have duties. It need not mean that the right-holder is in a position to legally effectuate her claim. If you promised me that you would prepare me a dinner, then I have a claim-right to that dinner and you have a duty to keep your promise, although it is likely that I would never be able to realize my claim in court.[33]

3. The notion of a right also can refer to a power. This means that the right-holder is in a position to determine the relationship between her and others and, by so doing, the status of others. The right of a police officer to take someone into custody can be seen as a power. So can the right of someone to leave her money to B. There is, so Hohfeld argues, no duty of B that corresponds to A's right. The correlative of A's right is B's liability: B, the addressee, is liable to the power of the right-holder, to the extent that the right-holder determines their legal relationship.

4. The term 'right' is not only used to refer to indicate that someone has the power to determine the legal relationship of others, but also to refer to the opposite: to indicate that someone is immune from changes in his or her legal situation. 'Right' then means 'immunity'. If A has a right-immunity to X, A is immune from the efforts of others to change his or her situation with regard to X. For instance, someone may have diplomatic immunity, which implies an immunity to being taken into custody. When a police officer who, normally speaking, has a right-as-power to arrest people, is confronted with this right-as-immunity, he is not able to exercise his power: the correlative of a right-immunity is *disability*. The addressee is unable to change the legal position of the right-holder.

TYPE OF RIGHT	CORRELATIVE	OPPOSITE
Claim-right	Duty	No-right
Liberty	No-right	Duty
Power	Liability	Disability
Immunity	Disability	Liability

In the preceding paragraphs, I have said that rights contain directives or guidelines for others, even duties. But according to Hohfeld I am completely wrong: his distinctions show that only claim-rights have duties as their correlatives and that the other categories do not imply corresponding duties. This does not mean, by the way, that Hohfeld himself is in favor of using the word 'right' in these various meanings. On the contrary, he prefers using the word only when it concerns claim-rights. But he observes that, in legal practice, it is a word also used in the other meanings.

Hohfeld's distinction is interesting and may help to illuminate the status of ESC-rights, given that they are often seen as rights that do not imply real duties and are not regarded as claim-rights. If so, then the question can be raised as to whether they belong to one of the other categories. That would explain their supposed lack of real duties. Apart from that, it can reasonably be asked whether Hohfeld's distinctions makes sense and whether he is right in assuming that rights as immunities, powers and liberties do not imply duties. I will try to give a brief answer to both questions in the following section.

5 Rights as immunities and ESC-rights

I will start with rights as immunities. The Human Development Report 2000 is clearly of the view that human rights have the characteristics of immunities when it says that "*In normative discussions human rights are often championed as entitlements, powers or immunities that benefit all who have them*"[34] But the question is, what is meant by immunities and what is its correlative?

If it is said that A has a right/immunity, then it is often implied that A is immune from efforts by others to change his or her legal situation. If A has a right/immunity from being arrested, a police officer is unable to legally arrest A. The officer can put him in jail, but that would amount to an unlawful detention. In this case it concerns a legal right/immunity and not a moral one. And, indeed, it will often be the legal system that grants such a right/immunity. But, moral rights/immunities are also conceivable and may indeed be granted by the morality of a community as was shown, for example, by the prohibition on slavery. Although the right not to be held in slavery is today a legally recognized right, the prohibition of slavery can also be seen as a moral principle, and, human history had known periods in which slavery had been morally denounced yet not expressly forbidden by law.

The morality of a community could, and can, contain the idea that nobody may hold the status of a slave, irrespective of what is said by the law. If so, then from a moral point of view, A is not B's slave, even if B asserts that A is his slave and can demonstrate that he has legally bought A. A is immune from others wanting to change her moral status as a free person. Rights/

immunities are also conceivable in a critical morality, the moral conviction of a minority or even an individual, that nevertheless pretends to be acceptable to all. For instance, in a society in which slavery is accepted and defended by the law *and* by the morality of that society, it is still possible to argue that human beings have a right not to be held in slavery, irrespective of what is said by the law or morality of the society. In the United States at the beginning of the 19th century, slavery was legally allowed and morally accepted. Then individuals came to the fore who regarded it as morally suspect, people whose critical morality contained a right/immunity not only that no one should be held in slavery but that they should not hold the status of a slave, even if they are treated as such. (Also in many other countries slavery was legally and morally accepted in former centuries. Many of the slaves in America were brought there by the Portuguese, Dutch and British, who were very much involved in the slave trade between the Africa and the Americas. Slavery was not a phenomenon of the modern time. The slave trade flourished in the early Middle Ages in particular between Arabs and African kings who were prepared to sell their own people. It was also very common under the Roman Empire.)

As said before, the correlative of a right/immunity is, according to Hohfeld, not a duty but a disability: nobody can change the legal or moral status of the right-holder. But, is not there also a duty lurking behind the disability? In the preceding pages I have argued that the idea of a right is that it guarantees that an individual's interest is protected. So it can be said, taking Hohfeld's view, that in the case of rights/immunities, the guarantee is provided by a disability inflicted on others to change the legal or moral status of the right-holder.[35] However, if we look at A's right/immunity not to be arrested, we can say that his interest in not being arrested is only partially realized by the disability of B, for the disability suffered by B does not prevent B from putting A in jail. This may not change A's *legal* position, but it is nevertheless unpleasant. That is why, in my opinion, the disability is accompanied by a duty.[36] B cannot arrest A but, also, he should not do so. He has a duty not to do so.

Let me take the example of the right/immunity not to be held in slavery. If A has that right, it is not impossible that she may nevertheless find herself taken as a slave, a situation in which many people still find themselves today for, unfortunately, slavery is still very much alive, despite legal prohibition by international and domestic law. It has taken a modern and contemporary form, including such practices as forced labor, servile marriage, debt bondage, child labor, and forced prostitution.

The website of 'Slavery Today' offers many smarting examples of contemporary slavery.[37] Anti-Slavery International (ASI), the world's oldest human-rights organization, states that there are at least 27 million people in bondage who are forced to carry out labor under the threat of violence. Though today's slaves do not wear shackles and are no longer sold at public auction, they are often no better off than their more familiar predecessors. For example, many children in India's carpet-industry work from 4:00 in the morning to 11:00 at night, every day, without breaks and without being given a single rupee for their labor. According to the Bonded Labour Liberation Front, between 200,000 and 300,000 children are involved in India's handmade carpet industry, while approximately 500,000 and 200,000 are similarly employed in Pakistan and Nepal respectively. Which means that the number of Asian child slaves in the carpet industry may reach one million. And all over Southeast Asia, many other children have been taken from their homes by traffickers under the pretence of being given a job, only to find themselves sold to brothels to service the lusts not just of locals but (chiefly) those of Western and Japanese men.

But slavery is not only an Asian problem; it's also still alive in various parts of Africa. For instance, according to the website of BBC World Service, black people in the south of Sudan are captured in militia raids on their villages and given as slaves to people in the north who then treat them as animals. They must endure regular beatings, eat rotten food and sleep next to the farm animals. In Mauritania, a small West African country just north of Senegal, chattel slavery has existed for centuries and a ruling class of Arabo-Berber tribes holds black African slaves as inheritable property.[38]

The BBC reported from Mali that thousands of children are being kidnapped, shipped to the Ivory Coast and sold as slaves to cocoa farms. The going price is about US$30.

These children earn no money for their work, do not get sufficient food and are beaten if they try to escape. Nearly 50% of the world's chocolate production starts in the Ivory Coast.[39]

Slavery also exists in South-America. 'Slavery Today' tells the story of the Rocha family, living in Brazil, who had been recruited to work in a distant part of the country and who accepted, hoping for a better life. After a difficult and heavy journey they arrived at the work camp, only to be informed by the recruiter—at gunpoint—that they would be charged for travel, tools, food, and shelter. The website continues the tale. "*The family suddenly found itself trapped in forced labor, working 18-hour days to pay off an ever-accruing debt. While at the batteria, Marta Rocha, eight years old, inhaled smoke on a regular basis. She began to cough blood and now can no longer work. The Rochas are underfed and their debt continues to amass with no end in sight. Marta's medical needs further increase the debt, and without her work, the debt climbs even higher. Hundreds of miles from their native village, the Rochas are isolated and enslaved in their own country.*" [40] Today many live as the Rochas. They are lured to remote regions and forced to work without payment. It is impossible to leave the work camps, either because of armed guards or the impossibility of surviving in the wilderness that surrounds the camp.

In North America, human trafficking takes many people from Mexico into the US. In Europe, the traffic in women flows from East to West with thousands of women lured or abducted into involuntary servitude and forced to work in brothels or as domestics.

More examples could easily be given, but a conclusion can already be drawn: contemporary slavery exists and, in many cases, the lives of those contemporary slaves are as harsh, brutal and hazardous as the lives of their predecessors.

So, if someone has a right/immunity not to be held in slavery, based on our law or morality, does this then only place a disability on others? Does this right only imply that someone cannot be a slave? Recognizing only a disability may be of little help to those who really are being forced to work as slaves and it is the reason why I believe that the right/immunity not only implies a disability but also a duty: that others ought not to treat people as slaves. To put it differently, people have a duty to refrain from factually treating other people as slaves and, should people be taken as slaves, other people have a duty to correct that situation.

As said before, the notion of a right holds that someone's interest is protected. But there are a number of interests at work here. A has an interest in not having her legal or moral situation changed; that is, in not being legally arrested and in not having the status of a slave. That interest is protected by a disability: she cannot legally be put in jail, and she cannot have the status of a slave. But, as said above, despite these legal or moral disabilities, she can factually be put in jail and she can be treated as a slave. So, she also has an interest in not actually being put in jail or actually being treated as a slave. And this interest is protected by a legal or moral duty on the part of others. It could, perhaps, be argued that a difference exists between the notion of an *immunity* and the notion of a *right*/immunity. If it is only the word 'immunity' that is used, the correlative is simply a disability. Yet surely, if the word 'right' is used to refer to an immunity, the correlative of that right is not only a disability but also a duty. It is not only said that a legal or moral situation is incapable of being changed, it is also said that others have a duty to ensure that that situation remains unchanged, or that a factual situation that is in conflict with the legal or moral situation is brought into agreement with it. If, despite the legal or moral disability, someone is put in jail or treated as a slave, a duty exists to correct that and to bring it in accordance with the legal or moral situation.

The question, of course, is who are those others who have a duty? In the first place it will be those who are directly addressed, i.e. those upon whom the disability is inflicted. If A has a right/immunity not be made a slave, the woman-trader B is incapable of changing the moral status of A as a free human being. And he has a duty not to do so. In the second place, also others (other people and governments) have a duty. They have a duty to realize that, even if A has been factually forced into slavery, she is still not a slave. And such people then have a duty, as far as it is possible for them, to bring the factual situation (of A being treated as a slave) into line with the moral one (that she always is a free person and not a slave).

All in all, the correlative of a right/immunity is a disability accompanied by a duty. The question then is whether this is relevant to ESC-rights. The statement that rights/immunities also imply duties may be interesting in general insofar as it supports the idea that all rights imply duties, but is it also relevant to ESC-rights? In other words, are ESC-rights rights/immunities?

In general, the answer is 'no': these rights, like the right to adequate housing or the right to healthcare, will not be regarded as rights/immunities, even though they do possess some aspects of rights/immunities. For example, there is the aforementioned right not to be held in slavery. In general, it is not seen as an ESC-right, probably because it isn't mentioned in the International Covenant on Economic, Social and Cultural Rights, but is only included in article 8 of the International Covenant on Civil and Political Rights. However, it could definitely be argued that this right should be regarded as an ESC-right, for slavery clearly has socio-economic aspects. Eide treats the right not to be held in slavery as an aspect of the right to work and states that people should be free from slavery and compulsory labor.[41] The right to form trade unions or the right to fair and healthy working conditions can also be seen as being partly right/immunities, implying as they do that *"you cannot treat employees as machines, they have a status as free person and are immune from your efforts to reduce them to production factors."* In addition, other ESC-rights such as the right to adequate housing and healthcare can be regarded as having some aspects of a right/immunity insofar as they are inspired by the principle that people have a unassailable status as free persons endowed with dignity and are immune from attempts to deny that status.

It follows, therefore, that, so far as ESC-rights are considered rights/immunities, they imply not only disabilities but also duties. But it must also be admitted that, in general, they can only be considered rights/immunities to a certain extent. Let us see whether it might perhaps be more sensible to regard them as showing aspects of powers.

6 Rights meaning powers

"...to be poor is still to be powerless and vulnerable. Life remains a torment for children in the teeming barrio of a developing country city, for refugees caught up in a con-flict, for women in a society that still denies them equality and freedom..."[42]

Rights are a means to empower people who are powerless. It is generally said that securing both CP-rights and ESC-rights in law can contribute to empowering people, in particular the vulnerable in their fight to escape poverty.[43]

But, does that make rights similar to the Hohfeldian powers? Having a (Hohfeldian) right/power means that the right-holder is in a position to determine the relationship between her and others and, by extension, the status of others. According to Hohfeld, the correlative of a right/power is a liability: the addressee is liable to the power of the right-holder, to that extent that he must submit to the right-holder. The addressee cannot ignore their power and must reckon with it.

Rights/powers are sometimes related to particular offices or functions. For instance, a registrar or a magistrate has the right/power to solemnize a marriage, a judge has the right/power to pass a sentence, and a police officer has a right/power to arrest people who are supposed to be guilty of a crime. Other persons, for instance, someone arrested by the police officer, are liable to the power of the right-holder; he cannot deny being arrested. A right to conclude contracts, a right to vote and a right to leave money to others after one's death are other frequently mentioned examples of legal rights/powers, situations in which the law has given the right-holder certain powers that others have to accept.

While rights/powers will occur in particular in the legal sphere, they can also occur in the sphere of morality, for example, in the right of parents to exercise authority over their children, an authority that is, in general, granted them by the morality of the community.

The word 'duty' does indeed not seem to be appropriate as a correlative of a right/power; that honor should more correctly go to 'liability'. But it is possible to ask whether this means that no duty whatsoever exists. In my view, the direct addressees are not only faced with a liability, but also with a duty to act in conformity with the power of the right-holder. If Q has been arrested by police-officer P, he is not only liable to his arrest to that extent that he cannot deny his being arrested, but he also has a duty to behave in conformity with the legal situation. Other individuals are also expected to behave in a certain way. For instance, the authority that has provided the police officer with the right/power involved has a duty to respect that power and cannot withdraw it arbitrarily, while people watching the arrest have a duty not to hinder the police officer. And if A has a right/power to conclude contracts or to vote, others are not only faced with a liability, to that extent that they cannot ignore the power, but they also have a duty to take that right/power into account and to behave in accordance with its requirements.

It's worth noting that the interest being protected here also shows two aspects. The right-holder has an interest in having a power to determine the situation, but he also has an interest in the situation being factually accepted by others. The first aspect is guaranteed by a liability, the second by a duty. And, parallel to what has been said with regard to immunities, also here a distinction can be drawn between the notion of a power pure and the notion of a right/power; the correlative of a power pure could then be called a liability. But if the term 'right' is used to refer to the power, the idea will be that a normative guideline accompanies the liability.

As I have written before, such a normative guideline may be silent on specific people, but it certainly requires elaboration into the duties of specific people. What sense does it make to say that the police officer has a right/power to arrest a suspected criminal if the latter does not have a duty to behave as an arrested person? What sense does it make when a registrar has a right/power to solemnize marriages if other persons do not have a duty to recognize that power and to act accordingly?

Let us look more particularly at ESC-rights. Are ESC-rights powers, or can they at least be seen as having aspects of powers? Of some ESC-rights, it can be said that they have aspects of rights/powers; for instance, the right of trade unions to establish national federations (art. 8.1.b ICESCR) or the right to bargain collectively (art.6 ESC). Others cannot but acknowledge that a federation has been established or that trade unions come forward as a collectivity that represents laborers. These others are liable to what the right-holder has done; they cannot ignore that. The question then, of course, is who can be considered the addressees faced with a liability. Surely employers belong to the addressees: they have to accept that employees organize themselves and that trade unions function as legitimate interlocutors. In addition, fellow employees are addressees who must accept the power of trade unions to bargain collectively and affect their situation even when they themselves are not a member of the union. But there is also, apart from the liability, a normative guideline present. Employers and employees—as well as many other people—ought to accept the existence of trade unions and their powers, and such acceptance will eventually result in duties.

The aspect of a power is clearly visible in the rights mentioned above. It is less visible, but nevertheless present, in other ESC-rights, when it is interpreted as the right/power to act as free persons, with the correlative that others are liable to that power and must accept that as a fact. This power manifests itself as a partner of an immunity, both expressing the 'personhood' of human beings and the view that human beings are free persons, endowed with dignity. The idea of immunity stresses that human beings are immune from efforts to deny their status as free persons, while the idea of power emphasizes that human beings have been authorized to be or do something. Interpreted in this sense—somewhat weaker than the original Hohfeldian sense—all rights have an aspect of power. It is included in the language of rights.[44] Human beings are authorized to use this language. Rights recognize people as persons. By saying that someone has a right to housing or healthcare, it is emphasized that he or she has the power to act as a free person, a status which cannot be denied or ignored, either legally or morally. Granting people ESC-rights to housing or health care means more than giving people houses or health care. It lifts them from the world of objects of charity into the world of self-acting, autonomous and responsible human beings.[45]

The Surplus Value of a Rights-Based Approach

However, the status of person is, in fact, often ignored and denied to many people. This demonstrates the necessity of correlative duties in addition to liabilities. Saying that addressees are liable to the power of people to act as free persons without holding these addressees to a duty to respect that power and to behave accordingly, makes the power a phantom.

7. Rights/liberties

ESC-rights show some aspects of rights/immunities and of rights/powers. And as far as they show the characteristics of these categories, they not only imply disabilities and liabilities as special correlatives of immunities and powers, but also duties as general correlatives of rights. But what about liberties? Can ESC-rights be regarded as rights meaning liberties? And, do rights/liberties imply duties?

A characteristic of rights/liberties is that, according to Hohfeld, the right-holder has neither a duty to do X, nor a duty *not* to do x. If A has a right/liberty to pick up a coin lying on the ground, she does not have a duty *not* to pick up the coin, neither does she have a duty to pick it up. The opposite to this right is no duty of others: the correlative of A's right is not a duty to support A, nor a duty to refrain from interfering. Nino draws here a distinction between two categories of rights/liberties: he speaks of "*rights as the absence of prohibitions*" and of "*rights as direct permissions*".[46] 'Rights as the absence of prohibitions' would seem to fall under the heading of rights/liberties, while 'rights as direct permissions' cannot be considered a sub-category of the Hohfeldian rights/liberties for, in general, permissions will imply duties. If someone has a permission, he may expect others to reckon with that permission; or to put it differently, if someone has a permission then others have a duty to respect that permission. Because of this, direct permissions do not belong to the rights/liberties. In the Hohfeldian rights/liberties, others remain behind the horizon. To use Nino's words: "... *from the sole fact that someone has a right to (do) something in this minimal sense nothing is inferred about how the rest should react in the face of his action.*"[47]

Although the term would suggest that rights/liberties will occur in particular in the category of civil and political rights (among which are many so-called freedom-rights) rights/liberties are quite conceivably outside this category. Recently, as a result of international developments, the question has come to the fore as to whether the violation of human rights can provide a justification for other countries to intervene with military force. For instance, in 1999, the European Union and NATO were of the view that Serbia was guilty of serious violations of human rights in Kosovo, and decided to intervene. International law enables the international community to intervene when the United Nations Security Council has accepted a resolution to that effect. However, such a resolution was lacking with regard to the Kosovo situation.

The question was then asked in Europe whether the international community is obliged to stand aside and watch people suffer, or whether they (the international community) have a *right* to armed humanitarian intervention.[48]

Yet how is this right to be understood? Those who use the term do not always clarify its meaning. But, it could be intended as a right/liberty. Then it means that 'Europe' or the international community did not have a duty to intervene, but neither a duty *not* to intervene; just as others did not have a duty to support the intervention, nor to refrain from interfering.

The same occurred with regard to Iraq. In 2003 the US invaded Iraq. Did then the US have a right to invade, and if so, what is meant by the notion of a right? Could it have been a right/liberty? That is, could it have meant that the US did not have a duty to invade Iraq, nor had it a duty *not* to invade it, and in addition that others did not have a duty to support the American actions, nor a duty to prevent the US from acting as it did? Maybe it was meant to be such a Hohfeldian right/liberty. Whether or not that was the case, both examples show that this Hohfeldian category can be used outside the domain of traditional civil and political rights.

ESC-rights can also easily be constructed as rights. The right to healthcare, for instance could, as a right/liberty, mean the following: people have the freedom to provide themselves with necessary healthcare provisions; they do not have a duty to do so, nor a duty *not* to procure themselves healthcare provisions; others do not have a duty to support them in providing themselves with those provisions, nor do they have a duty to refrain from hindering the right-holder in trying to obtain the necessary healthcare treatment. Seen from this perspective, the right to work could then mean that people have neither a duty to work, nor a duty not to work; they simply have the freedom to work. Equally, others have no duty to support them, nor do they have a duty to refrain from throwing up impediments to their finding work.

It is a strange thing, this right/liberty of Hohfeld. Is it possible to have a right/liberty without a claim to be supported or, at the very least, not to be thwarted? For if the right-holder had a claim, then the issue at stake would be a claim-right, and not a right/liberty. While Judith Jarvis Thomson is of the opinion that such a thing is both conceivable and useful she does, however, prefer the term 'privilege' to 'liberty' because 'liberty', according to her, suggests the existence of a correlative duty. And it is the very characteristic of rights/liberties that no duties exist. Although I use the terms 'liberty' and 'privilege' interchangeably, I will briefly sketch her line of thought, using the right to work as an example.

Suppose that a seventy-year old woman wants to have a job. Suppose too that she is considered to have a right to work, the notion of 'right' signifying a liberty. This right/liberty would imply that A is at liberty to get herself a job, but that she has no duty to do so, nor that she has a duty not to do so; just as others do not have a duty to support her in finding herself a job, nor do they have a duty to refrain from hindering her in getting herself a job (Thomson 1990: 51). Does such a thing make sense? It does, according to Judith Jarvis Thomson, and it is correct to use the term 'right' in this situation.[49] For suppose that A does not have a right/liberty, and suppose she gets herself a job: she can then be accused of an illegitimate action, for it can be said that she has done something wrong. If she has a right/liberty, though, she ought not to be faced with legal or moral sanctions when she succeeds in getting a job.

But in my view, this demonstrates that a right/liberty does indeed imply a duty; that is, the duty of others to refrain from confronting A with moral or legal sanctions if she has succeeded in finding herself a job. And as in the preceding paragraphs, there are two interests of A at stake. With regard to A's interest in getting a job, no duty of others is involved when the notion of a liberty is used. A's interest in not being charged with moral or legal accusations when she succeeds in getting a job, however, is protected by a duty. The right/liberty to work then has two dimensions. The first dimension is the—mere—liberty or privilege to get a job, an action which does not imply duties; although it is precisely because no duties are involved, in my view, that the term 'right' is still not relevant. It is the second dimension that justifies using the term 'right' because it does imply a duty: the duty of others not to charge A with the consequences of getting herself a job.

It may be interesting here to pay attention to a distinction drawn by Ronald Dworkin when he says that *"There is a clear difference between saying that someone has a right to do something in this sense and saying that it is the 'right' thing for him to do, or that he does no 'wrong' in doing it."*[50] If one want to say that A does no wrong in getting herself a job, the term 'liberty' or 'privilege' appears to be adequate. If the seventy-year old woman is capable, why should she not seek employment? But I consider that the term 'right' is inappropriate, for if the word 'right' is used, it not only implies that A does no wrong in getting herself a job, but also that others have a duty not to reproach her for doing so. (It is though questionable whether this is all that people want to say when they say that the woman has a right to work. I assume that most people want to say more when using that expression, although it is possible for them to use the word right, only implying a duty for others not to reproach the woman for getting herself a job)

Let me take another example. The right to healthcare could, as a Thomsonian right/privilege, imply that the right-holder is at liberty to get himself medical treatment, that he does not have a duty to do so, nor that he has a duty not to do so; just as others do not have a duty to support him in getting medical treatment, nor do they have a duty to refrain from hindering him in getting medical treatment. For instance, it could be argued that people over eighty only have a right to healthcare in this sense: nobody is then supposed to be under a duty to help an eighty year old when he is seriously ill and doctors are allowed to refuse treatment by arguing, for instance, that medical treatment is pointless and that too many young people are waiting for the same treatment. Neither do others have a duty to refrain from hindering the eighty year old in getting medical treatment. But, if A succeeds in finding a doctor who is prepared to treat him, then nobody can reproach him for having himself treated, even though many young people are waiting for similar treatment. This last element justifies, according to Thomson, calling such a privilege a 'right'. But in my view, that is precisely because it implies a duty, a duty of others not to accuse the right-holder of illegitimate behavior. (Also here the question arises whether this is all what people mean when referring to "a right to health care" although it is possible to use that expression for such a right/privilege only implying a duty not to reproach someone for having himself treated.)

Jones, too, regards the concept of rights/liberties as meaningful. He interprets them as implicit permissions. Rights/liberties for him "...*concern what the right-holder is himself entitled to do or not to do.*" [51] He goes on to say that "...*liberties are most appropriately spoken of as rights in contexts where there is an understanding that, in the absence of a duty not to do something, one is entitled to do it.*"[52] But here also, it seems to me that precisely because there is an understanding that the right-holder is entitled to *do* X, he or she cannot be blamed for doing it. And this in turn implies a duty on the part of others not to reproach the right-holder.

So, it turns out that a Hohfeldian right/liberty has a duty as its correlative, next to its specific correlative, that is, a no-right. And it has also become apparent that ESC-rights can be conceived as rights/liberties: they can be interpreted as indicating that the right-holder does no wrong in finding himself or herself with work, or healthcare or housing, without implying that others are expected to support them or to refrain from hindering them. As it is not wrong for the right-holder to do X, then they should not be blamed for what they do.[53] This is one way of interpreting ESC-rights. But is it appropriate to interpret them in this way?

8. Claim-rights

If ESC-rights can, with respect to certain aspects, be interpreted as rights/immunities, rights/powers and rights/liberties and so entail duties in addition to other more specific correlatives, can they also be seen as claim-rights?

With claim-rights, no doubts arise as regards the existence of duties. The concept of a claim-right presupposes a right-holder, an object and an addressee who is the bearer of a duty. I would like to add here that the existence of a duty does not imply that the right-holder has at his disposal the means to enforce the fulfilling of that duty. The only thing the existence of a duty implies is that the duty-bearer should act in a certain way, and that he or she can be *expected* to act in that way. Often, though, the right-holder will have the means to enforce the fulfilling of a duty, either by such legal means as a lawsuit, or moral ones such as laying blame and engaging in a general outcry.

The question then becomes: are human rights claim-rights? Jeremy Waldron argues that, in general, it is assumed that Hohfeld's claim-right applies to the concept of human rights.[54] Human rights not only say something about the relationship between a right-holder and an object (for instance that someone has an interest in health-care), but also about the right-holder and other individuals. They not only intend to emphasize that certain goods are of existential importance for people, but that the availability of these goods should be guaranteed by imposing duties on others, in particular, on governments.

Some raise objections to calling human rights claim-rights. As for civil and political rights, one could take them to be Hohfeldian liberties. After all, civil and political rights are often called freedom-rights or, at any rate, many of them can be regarded as freedom-rights. Accepting this could give rise to the idea that freedom rights are Hohfeldian liberties, the more so as freedom-rights are interpreted, for example by Reinders, as rights that create a sphere within which people do not have to take into account the interests of others and in which they do not have to answer to others for their behavior. This interpretation of freedom-rights show similarities with the Hohfeldian liberties that state that a right-holder has the freedom to do X, but not a duty either to do X or not to do X. Or, as Jones points out, that liberties "concern what the right-holder is himself entitled to do or not to do."[55]

Freedom-rights undoubtedly have aspects of Hohfeldian liberties, but they cannot be reduced solely to those liberties. Someone who has the right to freedom of religion surely does not have a *duty* to be religious, just as he or she has no duty *not* to be religious. But, freedom-rights in addition and in particular want to emphasize that others should not interfere with the religion of the right-holder: they give them a duty. This leads us to conclude that freedom-rights turn out to be claim-rights, even though the duties they imply are considered to of a negative nature, one implying that the duty-bearer has a duty of forbearance.

What about ESC-rights? Does the general assumption, noted by Waldron, also cover ESC-rights? Are they generally regarded as claim-rights? It was the starting point of this chapter that many doubt whether ESC-rights are real rights; in particular it is said that these rights lack real duties as correlatives. I raised the possibility that they belong to one of the Hohfeldian categories of rights supposed not to have duties as their correlatives. I examined this possibility. More specifically, I raised two questions: firstly, whether Hohfeld's implication that some categories of rights do not involve duties was correct; and secondly, to which category ESC-rights *do* belong.

As for the first question, my considerations have shown that rights/

liberties, rights/powers and rights/immunities all entail duties in addition to their more specific correlatives. It may be possible that the words 'liberties', 'immunities' and 'powers' can be used without referring to something so precise as a duty, but when the word 'right' is used to mean a liberty, power or immunity, one wants to stress that the power, immunity or liberty is guaranteed by holding others to a duty. Some, of course, may tend to use other words than 'duties', for example, 'normative guidelines'; they may prefer to say that someone *ought* to do something. But such words cannot, and do not conceal that someone has a duty, either to act or to avoid acting. In their own words, many authors, including Narveson, Cranston, Shue, Golding, Hart and Raz stress that rights entail duties.[56] That rights imply duties does not mean that rights cannot have the character of liberties, powers, and immunities. But what is essential is the presence of a duty; without a duty, a right is a mirage. Yet, in addition, a right could involve the absence of a duty on the part of the right-holder who is at liberty to do as he or she likes, or it could involve the presence of a power to do something to which others are susceptible, or the presence of a immunity because of which others are incapable of doing something else. These additional characteristics can be seen as the specifications of the normativity of a right.

    So, to the extent that ESC-rights belong to rights/liberties, rights/immunities or rights/powers, they too entail specific correlatives, in addition to duties as general correlatives. However, I think most people will not consider them mainly as rights/powers, rights/immunities or rights/liberties. ESC-rights are usually seen as claim-rights, but as claim-rights with defects; as positive rights with a structure similar to that of other positive rights. For example, when one has bought and paid for a car, one has a right to have that car delivered. And when one has done the work one was hired to do, one has a right to be paid the agreed salary. ESC-rights have a structure that is similar to that of normal positive rights, and the right to adequate housing or the right to healthcare could be interpreted as a right to be provided with adequate housing or the required healthcare, i.e. to be given a house or medical treatment. But, it is generally accepted that these rights should not be interpreted that way. One cannot claim to be given a house or treatment in the way someone can claim to be paid the agreed salary if one has done the work that one was hired to do or to have delivered the car one has bought. The contents and the corresponding duties of ESC-rights are less clear. A right to housing or a right to healthcare requires the government to do something, but it is not clear what a government has to do as regards housing or healthcare to comply with the relevant rights. That is why many see ESC-rights as political aspirations rather then as real rights.[57] Orwin and Pangle speak of "*letters to Santa Claus*" believing that ESC-rights express what people regard as important to have, but which do not impose duties on others.[58] Others, for example Bossuyt, are prepared to speak of duties, but emphasize that these duties cannot be equated with the duties of normal positive rights. The duties flowing from ESC-rights should be seen as duties to do one's best rather than as duties to achieve something.[59]

So let us try to find out whether ESR-rights, and in particular their corresponding duties, are really as vague as is said by critics of ESC-rights. But, before doing that, a final remark should be made.

We have, in this chapter, spoken about the duties other people have toward the right-holder. But it should not be forgotten that the right-holder also has duties. The world cannot be divided in people who are right-holders in all respects and others who are in all respect duty-bearers. We are *all* both right-holders and duty-bearers: I have a right to freedom expression towards other people who have a duty towards me, but I also have a duty to respect and promote the right to freedom of expression of other people. I have a right to healthcare and other people have a duty to contribute to the realization of that right, but other people also have a right to healthcare towards me, which implies that I have a duty towards them. People are embedded in a network of rights and duties and one should not recklessly claim rights while forgetting that one also has duties.

BIBLIOGRAPHY

Arend, Anthony Clark, 'Toward an understanding of International Legal Rules', in: Robert J. Beck, Anthony Clark Arend en Robert D. Vander Lugt (ed.), *International Rules: Approaches from international law and international rules* (New York en Oxford: Oxford University Press, 1996).

Bossuyt, M, 'International Human Rights Systems: Strength and Weaknesses', in: K.E. and P. Mahoney (ed.), *Human Rights in the Twentieth Century* (Dordrecht, Londen en Boston: Martinus Nijhoff, 1993) p.52.

Cliteur, Paul, 'Neo-Liberal Globalism and Philosophical Presuppositions', in: Nieuwenhuys, Eva (ed.) *Neo-Liberal Globalism and Social Sustainable Globalisation* (Leiden,Boston: Brill, 2006)

Cranston, Maurice, *What are human rights?* (London, Sydney & Toronto: The Bodley Head, 1973).

Del Bó, Corrado, 'Assisted Suicide and Euthanasia: Arguing for a Distinction', Etica & Politica / Ethics & Politics, 2004, 2, http://www.units.it/etica/2004_2/DELBO.htm

Dower, Nigel, *An Introduction to Global Citizenship* (Edinburgh University Press, 2003)

Dundes Renteln, Alison, *International Human Rights: Universalism versus Relativism* (Newbury Park : Sage, 1990).

Dworkin, R., *Taking Rights Seriously* (London: Duckworth, 1977).

Eide, Asbjörn, 'Economic and Social Rights', in: Janusz Symonides (red.), *Human Rights: Concept and Standards* (Aldershot etc.: Unesco Publishing, 2000).

Falk, Richard, 'Human Rights and Global Civil Society', in: Paul Gready (ed.) *Fighting for Human Rights* (London, New York: Routledge 2004)

Freeden, M., *Rights* (Buckingham: Open University Press, 1991)

Galenkamp, M., *Individualism versus Collectivism* (Rotterdam: Rotterdamse filosofische studies, 1993)

Gewirth, A., 'Are There Any Absolute Rights?', in: Jeremy Waldron, *Theories of Rights* (Oxford: Oxford University Press, 1984).

Gewirth, Alan, *Self-Fulfillment* (Princeton, New Jersey: Princeton University Press, 1998).

Golding, M.P., 'The Primacy of Welfare Rights', in: *Social Philosophy & Policy* 1, nr.2 (1984).

Hart, H.L.A., 'Are there any natural rights?', in: Anthony Quinton (ed.), *Political Philosophy* (Oxford: Oxford University Press, 1967)

Hart, H.L.A., *Essays on Bentham* (Oxford: Clarendon Press, 1982)

Hohfeld, W.N., *Fundamental Legal Conceptions: as applied in judicial reasoning* (New Haven: Yale University Press, 1919)

Hohfeld, W.N., *Fundamental Legal Conceptions: as applied in judicial reasoning* (Westport, Conn.: Greenwood Press, 1978)

G.J.H. van Hoof, 'The Legal Nature of Economic, Social and Cultural Rights: a Rebuttal of Some Traditional Views', in: *The Right to Food: From Soft to Hard Law* (Utrecht: Netherlands Institute of Human Rights, 1984)

Jasay De, Anthony, 'liberalism, Loose or Strict, in: *The Independent Review*, Volume IX, Winter 2005, 427 – 432.

Jones, P., *Rights* (London: Macmillan Press, 1994)

Kelsen, Hans, 'The nature of international law', in: Robert J. Beck, Anthony Clark Arend en Robert D. Vander Lugt (ed.), *International Rules: Approaches from international law and international rules* (New York en Oxford: Oxford University Press, 1996)

Lucas, J.R., *On Justice* (Oxford: Oxford University Press, 1980)

Martin, Rex, *A System of Rights* (Oxford: Clarendon Press, 1997)

Narveson, Jan, *The Libertarian Idea* (Philadelphia: Temple University Press, 1988)

Nino, Carlos Santiago, *The Ethics of Human Rights* (Oxford: Oxford University Press, 1993)

Pogge, Thomas, *World Poverty and Human Rights* (Cambridge, Oxford, Malden: Polity Press, 2002/2003)

Raz, J., *The Morality of Freedom* (Oxford: Clarendon Press, 1986)

Robertson, A.H., & J.G. Merills, *Human Rights in the World: an introduction to the study of the international protection of human rights* (Manchester, New York: Manchester University Press, 1992)

Shue, Henry, *Basic Rights* (Princeton, New Yersey: Princeton University Press, 1980)

Steiner, H. *An Essay on Rights* (Blackwell, Oxford UK en Cambridge USA, 1994)

Steiner, Henry J. and Philip Alston, *International Human Rights in Context, Law, Politics, Morals* (Oxford: Clarendon Press, 1996)

Thomson, Judith Jarves, *The Realm of Rights* (Cambridge, Mass. etc.: Harvard University Press, 1990)

Vierdag, E., 'The Nature of the Rights Granted by the International Covenant on Economic, Social and Cultural Rights', in: *Netherlands Yearbook of International Law* 9 (1978)

Waldron, Jeremy, 'Introduction' in: J. Waldron, *Theories of Rights* (Oxford: Oxford University Press, 1985)

ENDNOTES

[1] Human Development Report, 2000, p.16.
[2] In addition to these substantial values, human rights are also directed at actualising certain structural values, in particular individuality, equality, and secularity. 'Individuality' means that the ultimate goal of human rights is the good of the individual rather than that of the nation or of the community, and that individuals should, therefore, not be sacrificed to benefit the community as has, unfortunately, sometimes occurred in collectivist political systems. 'Equality' implies that everyone is entitled to the generic goods and that it is not acceptable that some have these at

their disposition, while others do not have even a minimum quantity and quality of freedom, participation and well-being. 'Secularity' stresses the importance of a dignified life—today, regardless of whether people believe that some other, even better life, may follow after death. This life here and now is important and should be respected. 'Secularity' also implies that the idea of human rights is neutral with regard to various outlooks on life.

[3] Human Development Report 2000, p.iii.
[4] http://en.wikipedia.org/wiki/Libertarianism, retrieved February 2007.
[5] Steiner & Alston 1996, p.268; Cranston 1973, p.67.
[6] Plant 1988, p.62.
[7] Cliteur 2006, p.35.
[8] Cranston 1973, p.68; Robertson and Merrills 1992, p.230.
[9] Kelsen 1996, p.61; Arend 1996, p.291.
[10] Vierdag 1978, pp.80,93.
[11] Arend 1996, p.291, Hoof 1984, p.35.
[12] In any case the Indian Constitution's article 37 of Part IV, 'Directive Principle of State Policy,' states that "The provisions contained in this Part shall not be enforceable by any court, but the principles therein laid down are nevertheless fundamental in the governance of the country and it shall be the duty of the State to apply these principles in making laws."
[13] Falk 2004, p.37; Dower 2003, p.39; see also HDR 2000, p.25: "The Universal Declaration demands protection from unjust laws and practices on the grounds that no matter what the laws may be, individuals have cer-tain rights by virtue of their humanity, not on the basis of their citizenship or contingent facts about the legal reality of the country of which they are citizens."
[14] Martin 1997, p.25; Dundes Renteln 1990, p.515.
[15] Hohfeld 1978, Cliteur 2006, p.36.
[16] Lucas 1980, p.8.
[17] Lucas 1980, p.21.
[18] Lucas 1980, p.22.
[19] de Jasay, 2005, p.430.
[20] Gewirth 1998, p.95.
[21] Nino 1993, p.33.
[22] Nino 1993, p.33.
[23] It can, however, still make sense to say that others, for instance other countries, ought to assist the government involved to enable it to provide its citizens with adequate housing.
[24] I am assuming that the person who says that children ought not die is not referring to children dying as a result of human action such as war or poverty. In such cases, the word 'ought' could more appropriately be used.
[25] Hohfeld 1978.
[26] Nino 1993, p.25.
[27] See for instance: Corrado del Bó 2004, 2; also Wikipedia, http://en.wikipedia.org/wiki/Civil_rights#Hohfeld. 27s_ concept_of_right, retrieved February 2007; Human Development Report 2000, p.26.
[28] Freeden 1991, p.4.
[29] Hohfeld 1978, p.39.
[30] Hart 1967, p.57.
[31] Hohfeld 1978, p.42.
[32] Gewirth 1984, p.92; Freeden 1991, p.77; Galenkamp 1993, p.63.
[33] Nino 1993, p.27.
[34] Human Development Report 2000, p.26.
[35] Steiner says that 'disability' means that the scope of an individual's behaviour is limited, and that this is sufficient reason to speak of a right (Steiner 1994, p.61). This is also the view of Rex Martin, who regards the disability as a normative guideline which, according to him, is to be distinguished from a duty. This allows him to conclude that although the correlative of a right/immunity is not a duty, it nevertheless is a normative guideline, one that provides protection for someone's

interests (Martin 1997, p.31).What kind of normative guideline is the disability supposed to be? If it is not a duty, it could be an instrumental normative guideline (Martin 1997, p.30). Such a guideline states that in order to achieve a certain result, you should act in a particular way. For example, if you want your eggs to be hardboiled you should boil them for more than 4 minutes. You could regard the correlative of a right/immunity as such an instrumental norm. If so, it then means that if you want to perform a legal arrest, you should not arrest a person who has a right/immunity from being arrested. But, there is then still a difference with the eggs. You are allowed to boil your eggs for less than 4 minutes. In fact, you are morally and legally permitted to boil your eggs for only one minute. However, if you want them to be hard-boiled you won't be acting sensibly if you boil them for only one minute and you won't end up with hard-boiled eggs. In the case of a legal or moral right/immunity, though, things are different: then the disability means not only that you cannot do something, but that you are not *allowed* to do it. The correlative of a right/immunity, therefore, is obviously more than just a instrumental normative guideline: it also is a legal or moral duty.

36. A real (not only instrumental) legal norm.
37. http://www.iabolish.com/slavery_today/index.html. Visited in March, 2006.
38. http://www.bbc.co.uk/worldservice/specials/1357_slavery_today/
39. BBC News, 12-04-2001, http://news.bbc.co.uk/1/hi/world/africa/1272522.stm; http://www.radicalthought.org/
40. http://www.iabolish.org/slavery_today/country_reports/br.html, July 2007.
41. Eide 2000, p.144.
42. Human Development Report 2000, p iii.
43. Building on mutually reinforcing rights — to free expres-sion, assembly, participation, food, housing, healthcare and many others — is essential to empowering poor people to lift themselves from poverty. Human Development Report 2000 p.88
44. "*Since the process of human development often involves great struggle, the empowerment involved in the language of claims can be of great practical importance*". Human Development Report 2000, p.22.
45. Human Development Report 2000 p.88.
46. Nino 1993, p.26.
47. Nino 1993, p.26.
48. The term 'right' was used, among others, by a Dutch organisation of human rights jurists.
49. Thomson 1990, p.52.
50. Dworkin 1977, p.188.
51. Jones 1994, p.21.
52. Jones 1994, p.22.
53. Freeden 1991, p.78.
54. Waldron 1985, p.8.
55. Hohfeld 1978, p.42; Jones 1994, p.21.
56. Narveson 1988, p.44; Golding 1984, p.130; Cranston 1973, p.67; Hart 1982, p.173; Raz 1986, p.167; Shue 1980, p.37.
57. Robertson and Merills 1992, p.232.
58. Orwin and Pangle 1984, p.15.
59. Bossuyt 1993, p.52.

CHAPTER 7

THE VAGUENESS OF ECONOMIC, SOCIAL AND CULTURAL RIGHTS

> *"Access to safe water is a fundamental human need and a basic human right. Many people take water for granted: they turn on the tap and the water flows. Or they go to the supermarket, where they can pick from among dozens of brands of bottled water. But for more than a billion people on our planet, clean water is out of reach. And some 2.6 billion people have no access to proper sanitation. The conse-quences are devastating. Nearly 2 million children die every year of illnesses related to unclean water and poor sanitation—far more than the number killed as a result of violent conflict. Meanwhile, all over the world pollution, overconsumption and poor water manage-ment are decreasing the quality and quantity of water."*
>
> **Kofi A. Annan**
> **Secretary General United Nations**[1]

1. Introduction

In the preceding chapters, I discussed the idea that ESC-rights are generally regarded as lacking the characteristics of genuine rights because they do not entail real duties. ESC-rights show characteristics of claim-rights, but they are generally seen as claim-rights with defects. Claim-rights typically entail duties as their correlatives, but this is precisely where a defect arises. For while it is true that the word 'duty' is often used in reference to the tasks and goals that the addressee of an ESC-right, often a government, is supposed to undertake as a consequence of such a right, traditionalists argue that it would be more appropriate to use other words, such as 'tasks' or 'goals'.[2] Therefore, after examining the notion of a right in the foregoing chapter, and having concluded that rights imply duties, I will in this chapter take a closer look at the nature of the duties flowing from ESC-rights.

Rights can be taken to have this formula: A has a right to X towards B, by virtue of Y.[3] A is the bearer of the right, with a legal or moral justification for limiting the freedom of B, who is the addressee of the right, or the norm-receiver, and who has a duty towards the right-bearer.[4] Rights constitute duties in others. Human rights documents, though, do not show much concern for the formula of a right, and most are not very explicit in determining the right-bearer and the addressee of the right. However, it is widely accepted that individuals are the bearers of civil and political rights and of ESC-rights, whereas, in general, states or governments are considered by scholars and politicians to be the main addressees of both CP-rights and ESC-rights.[5] (In previous chapters I have spoken about fellow-citizens or fellow human beings as addressees of freedom rights and ESC-rights, but hopefully I have made clear that they are to be considered the ultimate addressees and that states or governments as representatives of their citizens are the direct addressees of these rights.)

As regards ESC-rights, governments may well be the addressees, but they are not considered bearers of genuine duties. The duties of civil and political rights are of quite a different nature than the 'duties' of ESC-rights.[6] I have already dealt with the different nature of both categories of rights in Chapter 2, so I will only offer a brief summary of those remarks here. The duties of the addressees of rights can be either positive or negative: the addressees of positive rights have a duty to act in a certain manner, whereas the addressees of negative rights have a duty *not* to perform an action. Traditionally, CP-rights are regarded as negative rights held by individuals towards their government. The government is considered to be under a duty to refrain from interfering within the defined aspects of the private realm. ESC-rights on the other hand are looked upon as positive rights held by individuals towards their government. It is held that government is under a duty to do its utmost to provide its citizens with the goods mentioned in those rights.[7] To put it differently, CP-rights imply duties of non-interference while ESC-rights imply duties of active assistance.

Another point has been put forward in connection with this difference in the nature of both categories of rights. As the realization of civil and political rights only requires forbearance on the part of the government, it is supposed to be without cost. This implies that the correlative duty of freedom-rights can always be discharged and that CP-rights can be respected immediately, totally and guaranteed to everyone. On the other hand, the realization of economic, social and cultural rights requires financial efforts and investments on the part of the State. Due to the scarcity of resources, it will be impossible to meet the demands expressed by economic, social and cultural rights for everyone, to the same extent, and at the same time. This implies that economic, social and cultural rights can only be realized progressively and partially, and that they must be implemented selectively once it has been determined what rights, to what resources and on behalf of whom will be realized.[8] Cranston argues that *"The Government of India, for example, simply cannot command the resources that would guarantee each one of over 500 million inhabitants of India 'a standard of living adequate for the health and well being of himself and his family' let alone holidays with pay."* [9] This characteristic of ESC-rights has brought many people to speak of 'manifesto rights'.[10]

In addition, it has also been argued that the duties arising from negative CP-rights are obvious and beyond doubt, whereas the correlative duties of ESC-rights are vague and equivocal. For instance, the duty-bearer of the right to freedom of religion has to do nothing more than refrain from interfering with the religious life of the right-holder.[11] On the other hand, it is not obvious what duties are constituted by economic, social and cultural rights. What healthcare arrangements are people entitled to and what must the government subsequently provide? And what kind of housing do people have a right to and what must the government guarantee them? There are as yet no generally recognized objective needs which enable us to clearly formulate the contents of economic, social and cultural rights and the duty of the addressee.[12]

Consequently, so traditionalists argue, as the duties arising from CP-rights are clear, it is also clear when someone has violated these rights, namely when that person has done what he or she was forbidden to do. Hence that person can be held responsible for the injustice that has been caused by their acts. With regard to ESC-rights, so the traditionalists continue, it is difficult to speak of the violation of those rights. Poverty, homelessness, famine, illiteracy are regrettable, but they are not the result of intended human action.[13] It could, perhaps, be said that the addressee—for instance, the government—has omitted to confer a benefit on another person, or that the addressee has not succeeded in performing the task adequately. But it is, according to the traditionalists, not appropriate to say that the addressee has violated a right.[14]

This aforementioned presumed character of ESC-rights, when compared to civil and political rights, has brought some scholars and politicians to the conclusion that they are not to be looked upon as genuine rights.[15] For rights presuppose duties on the side of the addressee. And with economic, social and cultural rights there is a lack of clarity and vagueness about the duties of the addressee, which is at odds with the idea of a right.[16] It is argued that it is not appropriate to expect governments to comply with such unclear and vague duties. In many developing countries the addressee cannot be held responsible because the realization of ESC-rights is too costly and, therefore, almost or totally impossible. For this reason, ESC-rights, so traditionalists conclude, are to be seen as utopian aspirations which do not belong to the realm of morally or legally compelling rights.[17]

2. The dynamics of human rights

Although one may discern certain distinctions between CP-rights and ESC-rights, the differences presented above are far too rigid and outmoded. They ignore the fundamentally dynamic nature of human rights and overlook historical developments. Human rights are not to be looked upon as rights that are unchangeable, rooted in an immutable and universal human nature, for history has shown that it is virtually impossible to realize such an immutable nature. Human rights are to be regarded as the criteria for a life worthy of a human being in a particular historical situation—although their content may vary in different contexts, and depend upon the specific circumstances which arise at a given time and are felt to be a threat to human dignity.[18]

In 17th and 18th century Europe, it was considered important to guarantee human freedom from interference by the state. The relationship between the individual and the state was seen as a relationship in which the individual stands opposite the state, with the state felt to be a threat to human freedom. In that historical context, human rights were, as a matter of course, formulated in terms of freedom-rights, which were interpreted as the negative rights of an individual against the state. The state was under a duty *to respect* the private realm of its citizens, which was interpreted as a duty not to interfere with this private realm. This approach to human rights also played an important role during the adoption of the Universal Declaration of Human Rights, based on the awareness that totalitarian states had failed to respect the private realm of their citizens and the idea that a 'dam' should be erected against the destructive force of such states. But, we should realize that civil and political rights need not possess only this character of negative rights against the state: they also imply other duties that have to do with their horizontal and structural dimension.

Currently, civil and political rights are considered not only to be vertically addressed to the state, but increasingly to take horizontal effect. Fellow citizens are also supposed to be under a duty not to interfere within the realms protected by such rights: for example, to respect the right to life or the right to freedom of speech. As a consequence, the correlative duty of the state has changed: it now not only itself has to abstain from interfering and to *respect* the rights, but it also has to prevent other citizens from interfering within the private spheres of each individual. In other words, the state now also has to *protect* the right.[19]

The Vagueness of Economic, Social and Cultural Rights

Actually, this function of the state had already been noted by the philosopher John Locke, who envisioned an important role for the state in protecting human freedom. He believed that people in the original situation, '*the state of nature*', had rights and obligations towards one another. They had natural rights, such as the rights to life, liberty and estate. Unfortunately, due to human limitedness, as well as to human failings and difficult circumstances, such rights were not always respected. Therefore the state was established by social contract in order to protect people from violations of their rights by others. And the reason for people to engage in a contract by which they would give up their almost absolute freedom and constitute a state was *"the mutual preservation of their lives, liberties and estates, which I call by the general name—property. The great and chief end, therefore, of men uniting into commonwealth, and putting themselves under government, is the preservation of their property; to which in the state of nature there are many things wanting."*[20] In Locke's view, the state was to some extent a protector of human freedom. But, he added, the state itself should, of course, also respect the natural rights of people. Increasingly, however, in real life, the state was seen less as a protector than a threat to human freedom itself, which resulted in emphasizing the duty of the state not to interfere with the private sphere of its citizens.[21]

Today, like Locke, many writers emphasize the role of the state in protecting freedom, with the duty to protect seen as a positive duty. It can, of course, be argued that such a duty is basically negative by nature, as it is eventually aimed at achieving a situation in which the freedom of the right-holder is not interfered with by his fellow citizens.[22] But such an argument does not undo the positive character of the duty of the state to protect freedom.

CP-rights have other positive duties than the duty to protect. I'm referring to the duties which flow from the structural dimension that freedom-rights are increasingly supposed to have attained. For example, freedom of speech is worthless without the existence of a plurality of free press, broadcasting corporations, and so on. Freedom of speech, therefore, may imply a duty for the state to *provide* for a structure that enables right-holders to enjoy their right to freedom of speech, and to prevent the exercise of monopoly control of media, as an instance. That also holds for other freedom-rights: guaranteeing freedoms requires the state to be under a positive duty *to provide* for enabling structures. For that matter, many rights, in the category of civil and political rights, have always had positive aspects due to their structural dimension. For instance, the right to a fair trial and the right to vote have always required extensive activities on the part of the government.

So, as regards civil and political rights, the state appears to have an obligation to respect, to protect, and to provide and these rights clearly have both negative and positive aspects. This has been recognized by jurisprudence. The UN Human Rights Committee, the committee charged with the task of monitoring the International Convention on Civil and Political Rights has, with regard to the rights of minority cultures, said that the state should not only respect those rights, but also that positive measures should be taken by the state to guarantee them.[23] The European Court of Human Rights is also of the opinion that some of the Convention's rights do indeed imply both positive and negative duties. For instance, the right to life, article 2 of the ECHR, involves a duty for the state to refrain from illegally taking someone's life. Yet at the same time, the state also has a duty to protect people from threats to their lives by others. Therefore the state should bring about and maintain a system of penal law and criminal justice that enables people to enjoy their right to life. This even implies a duty to take preventive measures to protect an individual who runs a risk of losing his life because of the criminal actions of others.[24] According to the European Court of Human Rights, the right to respect of family life, mentioned in article 8 ECHR, sometimes requires positive action by the state. For instance, it implies that in the case of adoption, the natural parents should be involved in the decision. If they are not consulted, then the right to respect of family life has been violated. Further, the Court has explicitly acknowledged that this article and article 11, the right to freedom of association, sometimes require structural measures to be taken. In addition, the right not to be discriminated against not only demands that the state does not discriminate against its citizens, it also demands that the state creates a structure in which people are not discriminated against and which ensures that handicapped people are treated equally, even in the private sphere.

3. Obligations flowing from ESC-rights

Economic, social and cultural rights can be seen as efforts to respond to the menace to human dignity that was constituted in 19th and 20th century Europe by economic and social powers. The state was considered to be under a duty to ensure its citizens a dignified life by helping them to acquire certain goods that would enable them to live such a life. Often these rights and their correlative duties to *help* are interpreted as requiring that the government actually *provide* its citizens with a house, medical treatment, or a job. In some cases, that could indeed be the contents of these rights, in particular when the right-holder is totally incapable of taking care of himself or herself. But the holders of ESC-rights are not to be seen as passive consumers of governmental provisions. Rights aim to ensure that people can lead a human life. That, among other things, means the life of a responsible, autonomous actor. Subsequently, duties to help, arising from ESC-rights, have not always taken—and do not always take—the form of duties to provide, but of duties to *assist*. These duties will require that the government promotes an appropriate socio-economic structure and creates a system of arrangements that enables people to care for themselves and their relatives,

The Vagueness of Economic, Social and Cultural Rights

as well as protect themselves against the overwhelming economic powers of others.[25] The HDR 2000 also says that "*these rights do not mean an entitlement to a handout. They are claims to a set of social arrangements—norms, institutions, laws, an enabling economic environment—that can best secure the enjoyment of these rights. It is thus the obligation of governments and others to implement policies to put these arrangements in place.*"[26] Duties to assist may range from duties to set up vocational training and information programs, to duties to pursue a particular financial and economic policy that promotes the interests of the vulnerable members of society.

So, ESC-rights may imply a *duty to help*, one that can take the form of a duty to provide or a duty to assist. They may, furthermore, include a duty *to protect*. For instance, as regards the right to food, the state has a duty to protect people from others who prevent them from providing themselves with the means of subsistence.[27] Suppose, to refer to a similar example by Shue, that a particular family in a village owns all the land and grows beans. Suppose also that fellow villagers have worked for many years on the land and that beans are the staple food of the villagers. Suppose then that the current owner is offered a contract to grow tulips, together with equipment, which means that he will be independent of laborers. The contract means a great deal for the landowner.[28] If the landowner accepts the contract, it will ruin his fellow villagers. They will no longer have any beans and, as the new equipment will put them out of work, they will not have any money to buy beans elsewhere. In such a situation, the interests of the villagers would be protected if the government were to stop the landowner: the right to food can be seen as implying a duty to protect people from landowners who want to produce export products at the expense of the production of goods for local consumption.

Other ESC-rights may also imply duties to protect. For instance, the right to adequate housing may generate a duty for the state not to allow a real estate company that owns the dwellings of the poor to tear down those huts and replace them with luxury houses which the poor cannot afford unless compensating measures are taken. Fried van Hoof argues that a government that does not protect people against such actions by real estate companies violates the right to adequate housing. And the right to healthcare may contain a duty for governments to protect children from those who want to dump food declared unfit for consumption on local markets.[29]

Eide summarizes the duty to protect that can arise from ESC-rights by saying that such a duty requires a state to take measures against *"Usurious money-lenders, bonded labour relations, discrimination based on caste, colour, race or gender; encroachment of their unprotected land by treasure hunters and gold-diggers, exploitation of labour due to weakness or non-existence of trade unions. The agenda for protection is vast and constitutes the most important area in the realization of social, economic and cultural rights."*[30] Of course, saying that states have a duty to protect does not answer the question of what that duty precisely implies; that should be determined in a dialogue participated in by judges, politicians, scientists and stakeholders. That dialogue has already started. Increasingly it is accepted that ESC-rights not only imply duties to help, but also duties to protect.[31]

The insight has recently emerged that ESC-rights not only entail these duties to help and protect, but that they also involve elements of *forbearance*. Shue speaks of duties to avoid depriving others, duties that demand that no acts be committed that deprive others of their means of subsistence, and that are not necessary to maintain one's own basic rights. Nigel Dower acknowledges that ESC-rights are not only positive rights for receiving support or benefits, but also negative rights to safeguard against the undermining of people's well-being.[32] Many examples of negative duties can be put forward here. For instance, the right to food may imply a duty on the part of the state not to expropriate land from people who need access to that land to satisfy their food needs. Or it may require the state to abstain from development programs that encourage the production of cash crops for export at the expense of the production of traditional food for local consumption. It could also be argued that the right to food entails the duty of the state to refrain from forbidding people to beg, or to gather food from public refuse bins in the street.[33]

The right to healthcare can also be seen as entailing negative duties. Article 11 of the European Social Charter—among others—prescribes that governments take measures *"to prevent as far as possible epidemic, endemic and other diseases, as well as accidents"*. This could be regarded as a duty to protect and be seen as implying the prescription to fight diseases. But it could also be considered a duty of governments to abstain from actions that might lead to emergence of disease. The right to adequate housing also offers examples of the multiple dimensions of ESC-rights. As argued above, it entails a duty of the government to provide adequate housing, or to assist people in acquiring adequate housing. It also entails a duty to protect poor hut dwellers against the owners of the huts who want to remove the huts and replace them with luxury houses that the poor cannot afford; in addition it entails a duty on the part of the government to abstain from evicting people from their houses. Such a duty of abstinence, generated by the right to adequate housing, has been explicitly acknowledged by the UN Committee on Economic, Social and Cultural Rights in a general comment. The Committee has ruled that the Dominican Republic and Panama have violated the right to adequate housing by "*the massive expulsion of 1,000 families in the course of five years...*"[34]

I will end this presentation of examples that show that ESC-rights also imply elements of forbearance by referring to a Press Release of 26th November 2002 of the Committee on Economic, Social and Cultural Rights in which it announces that the Committee has adopted a General Comment on the right to water. It then says that the right to water contains both *"reedom and entitlements; the freedoms include the right to maintain access to existing water supplies necessary for the right to water; and the right to be free from interference, such as the right to be free from arbitrary disconnections or contamination of water supplies"*.....Further, the General Comment notes that *"States parties have a constant and continuing duty, in accordance with the obligation of progressive realization, to move expeditiously and effectively towards the full realization to the right to water. Realization of the right should be feasible and practicable, since all States parties exercise control over a broad range of resources, including water, technology, financial resources and international assistance, as with all other rights in the Covenant."*[35]

All in all, ESC-rights prescribe that the state help people in acquiring the basic goods which they need to lead a life worthy of a human being. They prescribe that the state perform the role of protector, that it should try to prevent society from becoming a battlefield in which the stronger *"enjoy the freedom to twist the arm of the weaker"*.[36] They also prescribe that the state forbear from interfering, when that is appropriate, to guarantee a dignified life.

In the foregoing I have spoken about the duties of governments. I should note, though, that governments are not the only addressees of human rights. Also other organizations can be regarded as addressees of human rights, as will be clarified in chapter 10. In its preamble the Universal Declaration of Human Rights says that every individual and every organ of society shall strive by teaching and education to promote respect for these rights and freedoms and to secure their universal and effective recognition and observance. The phrase, "every organ of society", includes non-state actors, such as companies, public and private. In August 2003, the Sub-Commission for the Protection and Promotion of Human Rights agreed to the text of Norms on Responsibilities of Transnational Corporations and Other Business Enterprises with Regard to Human Rights, the first set of comprehensive international human rights norms specifically applying to companies.

4. What do various authors say?

Many authors draw distinctions between various duties, and I will have a look at their distinctions. Henri Shue puts forward the attractive view that, for every kind of basic subsistence right, three kinds of duties can be distinguished. He speaks of *"duties to avoid depriving, duties to protect from deprivation, duties to aid the deprived."* [37] But it is interesting that he deviates from the traditional view of ESC-rights, the view that sees ESC-rights mainly as positive rights implying duties to help, although, as is mentioned, this view increasingly also accepts negative duties. Shue starts from the other side. His first category of duties involves negative duties: no acts should be committed that deprive others of their means of subsistence, and which are not necessary to the maintenance of one's own basic rights. This, according to Shue, is the primary obligation that—in principle—renders redundant the other obligations—but only if people comply with the primary obligation. This is, unfortunately, not the case.

We then arrive at the second category: the duties to protect from deprivation. These are needed because people do not fulfill their primary duty to avoid depriving others. They imply that those who do not fulfill their primary duty voluntarily, be forced to conform to that duty by third parties, and that institutions and arrangements should be designed to suppress the possible inclination of people to neglect their primary duty. But even this cannot guarantee that people will never find themselves in socio-economic misery. We need, therefore, a third category of duties: those that aid the deprived.

This third category prescribes that help be given to those for whom one has a special responsibility, to those who have fallen victim to the neglect of the duties of the first or second category, and to those who have been the victim of natural disasters.[38]

As I said earlier, it is striking that Shue does not depart from a positive obligation, but from a negative obligation, the obligation to avoid deprivation, which is similar to the position I took in Chapter 4. It is also striking that he does not explicitly mention the state as the addressee of socio-economic rights, a viewpoint also different from traditional views on these rights, which consider the state to be the most appropriate addressee of socio-economic rights. For Shue, the addressees are 'the others' and he defines basic rights as *"everyone's minimum reasonable demands upon the rest of humanity."* In addition, he constantly refers to 'others' when speaking of the addressees of socio-economic rights.[39] (His view—that other people are, eventually, the addressees of socio-economic rights—is one that I share and one that is also held by Gewirth and Plant.) But it should be pointed out that these 'others' have transferred their obligations to the state, which makes it correct to regard the state or the government as the addressee of socio-economic rights. The state or government acts, rather, as a representative of its citizens, while for the individual citizen, a duty remains to support the government in fulfilling the duty it has been given, or otherwise to support an institutional structure that guarantees socio-economic rights.[40]

Eide also draws a distinction between three categories of duties. The first category is formed by the obligations to respect; that is, the obligation to avoid damaging the means of subsistence of the right-holder. The second category consists of duties to protect; that is, to protect right-holders when their means of subsistence are damaged by others, or when they are prevented by others from using their means of subsistence. The third category contains, as he argues in 'Economic, Social and Cultural Rights as Human Rights', the duties to assist and to fulfill, duties that amount to taking measures designed not only to improve production, but also to provide concrete goods: for example, food.[41] Elsewhere, Eide even distinguishes four categories. In addition to the abovementioned three, he also mentions the duty to be the provider.[42] Later, he changed the third category into a duty to facilitate, while the fourth category talked of obligations to fulfill or to be the provider.[43]

Although he may seem to be somewhat inconsistent in naming and differentiating between the third and fourth categories, in my view Eide's differences amount to the difference between duties to assist and duties to provide for goods or arrangements, a subtle but important point. Also important is that, to Eide, the duties to respect form the first level even though, traditionally, the duty to support, to help or to provide has been seen as the most prominent and essential duty flowing from ESC-rights. As he says, "... *the first level of state obligations is, wherever possible, to respect the freedom and the resources of those at risk, in order for them to find solutions to their own problem wherever they can.*"[44]

In these distinctions (noted by Eide, but also by other writers) Shue's duty to avoid depriving has been replaced by an obligation to respect, while his duty to aid the deprived has been replaced by duties with different names. Kitty Arambulo notes that Shue does not object to his duty to avoid depriving being replaced by the duty to respect. In fact, she says that Shue regards it as more problematic that the duty to aid the deprived has been replaced by obligations to ensure, to fulfill or to promote (or similar categories by other authors). His fundamental objection is that this replacement obscures the fact that the third category results from the lack of compliance with the duties of the first and second categories. People in distress are often the victims of other people's failure to perform their primary and secondary duties. Using the term 'duty to aid the deprived' places the emphasis, so Shue argues, more on the conscience of the addressee than on using the abovementioned replacements of that term.[45] Arambulo, however, does not see why Shue objects to replacing the duty to aid by such categories as duties to fulfill and to promote and she wonders whether the state will be motivated by a moral appeal to make up for its supposed wrongdoings. I think, however, that in doing so Arambulo is overlooking the fact that, in Shue's view, the state is not the ultimate addressee but other people, people who may be susceptible to moral appeals. They may realize that they have made a mistake and that they have a duty to repair it. They may realize that they have a duty to aid the deprived, even though they will delegate this duty to the state. In such a situation the state has then become the direct addressee and the citizens have remained the ultimate addressees.

5. Some more categories

Other distinctions are drawn by other authors. It may seem unnecessary and redundant, even boring, to go further into these distinctions but, examining these distinctions is, in my view, important. It helps us in determining to what extent the duties of ESC-rights are genuine, maybe even justiciable duties. And I believe that not recognizing the various (aspects of the) duties could result in people maintaining that ESC-rights contain no more than intentions and programs.

Van Hoof differentiates between "*... an obligation to respect, an obligation to protect, an obligation to ensure, and an obligation to promote*".[46] While the meaning of the first and second category is the same as that of other authors, the question may arise as to what the meaning is of the third and fourth categories, the obligations to ensure and promote. Van Hoof himself argues that the obligation to ensure "*requires more far-reaching measures on the part of the government in that it has to actively create conditions aimed at the achievement of a certain result in the form of a (more) effective realization of recognized rights and freedoms*". He follows this by saying that the obligation to promote is "*also designed to achieve a certain result, but in this case it concerns more or less vaguely formulated goals, which can only be achieved progressively or in the long term.*" Is Van Hoof referring to the well-known difference between 'obligations of result' and 'obligations of effort or conduct'?[47]

By 'obligation of result', I mean the obligation to realize a certain result, while I take an 'obligation of conduct' to be an obligation to undertake activities that are supposed to generate a particular result. The latter obligation also can be described as one of effort, meaning an obligation to do one's best to achieve a certain result. Doctors generally do not have an obligation of result but an obligation to do their utmost to cure a patient and may be considered to have fulfilled their duties of conduct adequately even if the patient dies. To use the words of the International Law Commission: obligations of conduct are 'best-effort obligations', while obligations of result are 'tantamount to guarantees of outcome'.[48]

This distinction is also recognized by the Maastricht Guidelines, guidelines drafted at an expert meeting in Maastricht, 1997. "*The obligations to respect, protect and fulfill each contain elements of obligation of conduct and obligation of result. The obligation of conduct requires action reasonably calculated to realize the enjoyment of a particular right. In the case of the right to health, for example, the obligation of conduct could involve the adoption and implementation of a plan of action to reduce maternal mortality. The obligation of result requires States to achieve specific targets to satisfy a detailed substantive standard. With respect to the right to health, for example, the obligation of result requires the reduction of maternal mortality to levels agreed at the 1994 Cairo International Conference on Population and Development and the 1995 Beijing Fourth World Conference on Women.*"[49] This example can, of course, be extended to other ESC-rights. Applied to the right to food, for example, the obligation of conduct will require the development and implementation of a plan aimed at eliminating malnutrition. The obligation

The Vagueness of Economic, Social and Cultural Rights

of result would require that malnutrition levels be reduced to a particular and agreed level.[50] It may make sense here to mention distinctions between perfect and imperfect duties, as is drawn by the Human Development Report 2000, which defines those duties as follows. *"Perfect duties specify both how the duty is to be performed and to whom it is owed. Imperfect duties, by contrast, leave open both how the duty can be performed and how forceful the duty is that must be carried out."*[51] It may be left open both how the duty can be performed and how forceful the duty is, but doing nothing cannot be an option.[52] So I return to the question of whether Van Hoof refers to this distinction between obligations of result and of conduct when presenting his third and fourth categories, the obligations to ensure and promote. Although he does not explicitly mention the terms 'obligations of result' and 'obligations of conduct', the question then remains whether he is implicitly referring to that distinction. The answer to that question can, in my view, go both ways because he uses the word 'result' in both his definitions of the obligations to ensure and promote which could well lead to the conclusion that both obligations are obligations of result. On the other hand, he continues by saying that these two obligations together encompass what traditionally are called programmatic obligations. So, it can be said that both the obligations to ensure and to promote have the character of obligations of conduct; that is, obligations to pursue a program, which hopefully, but not surely, will result in a particular situation being achieved.

Why am I trying to determine whether the obligations to ensure and to promote run parallel to the obligations of result and of conduct? I do so because I think it important to be aware that, apart from the first and second category of obligations (to respect and to protect, which are undisputed and similar for various authors) a third category of duties exists, duties that—contrary to what is often assumed—are not only to be seen as obligations of conduct. Take, for instance, Coomans. Coomans speaks of three levels of duties: obligations to respect, obligations to protect and obligations to fulfill. The first and second levels correspond with the first and second of Van Hoof's categories. As for Coomans' obligations to fulfill, he explicitly calls these obligations of effort because they are aimed at an effective realization of rights through a long-term process that intends to achieve—at an increasingly higher level—a gradual realization of these rights.[53] I, however, would like to stress that obligations to fulfill—or whatever they are called and however many categories in addition to the first and second categories may be distinguished—cannot only be obligations of conduct, but can also be obligations of result. And, to be complete, the obligations of the first and second categories can also be obligations of result or obligations of conduct. This is an important distinction, because obligations of result are in general more susceptible to judicial monitoring than obligations of conduct.

There is yet another distinction arising from that of Van Hoof's between

195

obligations to ensure and to promote, one that would seem to fall in with the distinction between short and long term obligations. While it's important, and should be taken into consideration, it should be noted that this distinction is different from that between obligations of result and obligations of conduct. Obligations of result and conduct can be either short or long term obligations. For example, the obligation to realize basic education for all people within two years is a short term obligation of result while the obligation to realize it within fifty years is a long term one. The obligation to do the utmost to realize basic education within five years is a short-term obligation of conduct whereas the obligation to do the utmost to realize basic education within fifty years is a long-term obligation of conduct. And, to be complete, all obligations can be either long or short term.

I have almost finished my task of examining what obligations flow from ESC-rights. There remains only one more, the obligation to promote and I use the word 'promote' differently to Van Hoof. By obligation to promote, I want to refer to the obligation of a government to promote a human rights attitude in people in general and, in particular, to promote an awareness of the human rights character of the right involved. For instance, the right to healthcare implies an obligation to promote an awareness that healthcare is not simply something people appreciate, but something they are entitled to by virtue of their humanity. And the right to water implies an obligation to promote the idea that people as human beings are entitled to access to water. "*And water and sanitation are at the heart of our quest to enable all the world's people, not just a fortunate few, to live in dignity, prosperity and peace.*"[54] This, of course, leaves open the question of what particular arrangements people are entitled to.

The promotion of human rights, or a particular human right, is important, for when people have a human rights attitude they will support governmental policy that is aimed at realizing human rights: they will know that the government is not just trying to fulfill people's wishes, but that it is enabling everyone to lead a dignified life. Such an obligation to promote can be found in the United Nations' Human Development Report 2000 when it states that "*Community leaders, religious leaders, business leaders, parents, teachers—all have a role in building norms and upholding the values of respect for human dignity, freedom and equality. ... The state also has to promote awareness.*"[55]

6. The result of the search: a scheme of obligations

On the basis of the foregoing, the obligations flowing from ESC-rights can be summarized as follows.

1. An ESC-right entails a duty of forbearance, a duty to respect. This implies that addressees should not deprive the right-holder of their means

The Vagueness of Economic, Social and Cultural Rights

of subsistence, means to stay alive; that is, they should not cause damage to the right-holder's means of subsistence, nor should they block access to those means of subsistence. And causing poverty means depriving people of the means to stay alive that will kill them in the face of hunger, disease, and environmental hazards.

2. An ESC-right implies a duty to protect. Addressees should protect right holders against others depriving them of their means of subsistence. This duty to protect can consist of a duty to force those who do not fulfill their primary duty (the duty not to cause damage to the right-holder's means of subsistence) to desist from causing damage to the right-holder's means of subsistence, and it can also consist of a duty to develop institutions that keep down a possible inclination of people to neglect their primary duty.

3. An ESC-right entails a duty to help, and this can consist of a duty to assist or provide. A duty to assist implies helping the right-holder to provide themselves with the necessary means of subsistence. A duty to provide entails providing right-holders with the goods they need to lead a dignified life when they cannot provide those goods for themselves.

4. An ESC-right entails a duty to promote. This means promoting not only the idea that people need certain goods to lead a dignified life, but also that everyone is *entitled* to lead a dignified life and, therefore, also entitled to those goods.

It should be added that almost all of the foregoing obligations can have the character of obligations of result or of conduct, as well as of both short or long term obligations.

	obligation of result		obligation of effort	
	short term	long term	short term	long term
duty to respect				
duty to protect				
duty to help (duty to assist / duty to provide)	....	....	....	....
duty to promote				

The distinction between types or levels of obligations is also recognized by the Committee on ESC-rights. As mentioned before, the Committee has issued various 'General Comments' on substantive issues that may arise in the implementation of the International Covenant on ESC-rights. It refers, for example, to this distinction in the General Comments on the right to food, the right to education, the right to health and the right to water. It will be shown in the General Comments that the Committee distinguishes between the duty to respect, to protect and to fulfill.[56] I prefer to speak of a duty to help instead of a duty to fulfill, because the notion of "fulfilling a duty" also can used with regard to a duty to respect or a duty to protect. It makes sense to say that the government fulfilled its duty to respect the rights of X, or its duty to protect the rights of Y.

> *General Comment no. 12, on the right to adequate food*,
> (1999) paragraph 15.
> The right to adequate food, like any other human right, imposes three types or levels of obligations on States parties: the obligations to respect, to protect and to fulfill. In turn, the obligation to fulfill incorporates both an obligation to facilitate and an obligation to provide. The obligation to respect existing access to adequate food requires States parties not to take any measures that result in preventing such access. The obligation to protect requires measures by the State to ensure that enterprises or individuals do not deprive individuals of their access to adequate food. The obligation to fulfill (facilitate) means the State must pro-actively engage in activities intended to strengthen people's access to and utilization of resources and means to ensure their livelihood, including food security. Finally, whenever an individual or group is unable, for reasons beyond their control, to enjoy the right to adequate food by the means at their disposal, States have the obligation to fulfill (provide) that right directly. This obligation also applies for persons who are victims of natural or other disasters.

> *General Comment no. 13, on the right to education*,
> (1999) paragraph 46 and 47.
> 46.The right to education, like all human rights, imposes three types or levels of obligations on States parties: the obligations to respect, protect and fulfill. In turn, the obligation to fulfill incorporates both an obligation to facilitate and an obligation to provide.
>
> 47.The obligation to respect requires States parties to avoid measures that hinder or prevent the enjoyment of the right to education. The obligation to protect requires States parties

to take measures that prevent third parties from interfering with the enjoyment of the right to education. The obligation to fulfill (facilitate) requires States to take positive measures that enable and assist individuals and communities to enjoy the right to education. Finally, States parties have an obligation to fulfill (provide) the right to education. As a general rule, States parties are obliged to fulfill (provide) a specific right in the Covenant when an individual or group is unable, for reasons beyond their control, to realize the right themselves by the means at their disposal. However, the extent of this obligation is always subject to the text of the Covenant.

General Comment no. 14 , on the right to health,
(2000) paragraph 33
33. The right to health, like all human rights, imposes three types or levels of obligations on States parties: the obligations to respect, protect and fulfill. In turn, the obligation to fulfill contains obligations to facilitate, provide and promote. The obligation to respect requires States to refrain from interfering directly or indirectly with the enjoyment of the right to health. The obligation to protect requires States to take measures that prevent third parties from interfering with article 12 guarantees. Finally, the obligation to fulfill requires States to adopt appropriate legislative, administrative, budgetary, judicial, promotional and other measures towards the full realization of the right to health.

General comment no. 15, on the right to water (2002)
The right to water, like any human right, imposes three types of obligations on States parties: obligations to respect, obligations to protect and obligations to fulfill.

(a) Obligations to respect
The obligation to respect requires that States parties refrain from interfering directly or indirectly with the enjoyment of the right to water. The obligation includes, inter alia, refraining from engaging in any practice or activity that denies or limits equal access to adequate water; arbitrarily interfering with customary or traditional arrangements for water allocation; unlawfully diminishing or polluting water, for example through waste from State-owned facilities or through use and testing of weapons; and limiting access to, or destroying, water

services and infrastructure as a punitive measure, for example, during armed conflicts in violation of international humanitarian law.

The Committee notes that during armed conflicts, emergency situations and natural disasters, the right to water embraces those obligations by which States parties are bound under international humanitarian law. This includes protection of objects indispensable for survival of the civilian population, including drinking water installations and supplies and irrigation works, protection of the natural environment against widespread, long-term and severe damage and ensuring that civilians, internees and prisoners have access to adequate water.

(b) Obligations to protect

The obligation to protect requires State parties to prevent third parties from interfering in any way with the enjoyment of the right to water. Third parties include individuals, groups, corporations and other entities as well as agents acting under their authority. The obligation includes, inter alia, adopting the necessary and effective legislative and other measures to restrain, for example, third parties from denying equal access to adequate water; and polluting and inequitably extracting from water resources, including natural sources, wells and other water distribution systems.

Where water services (such as piped water networks, water tankers, access to rivers and wells) are operated or controlled by third parties, States parties must prevent them from compromising equal, affordable, and physical access to sufficient, safe and acceptable water. To prevent such abuses an effective regulatory system must be established, in conformity with the Covenant and this General Comment, which includes independent monitoring, genuine public participation and imposition of penalties for non-compliance.

(c) Obligations to fulfill

The obligation to fulfill can be disaggregated into the obligations to facilitate, promote and provide. The obligation to facilitate requires the State to take positive measures to assist individuals and communities to enjoy the right. The obligation to promote obliges the State party to take steps to ensure that there is appropriate education concerning the hygienic use of water, protection of water sources and methods to minimize water wastage. States parties are also obliged to fulfill (provide) the right when individuals or a group are unable, for reasons beyond their control, to realize that right themselves by the means at their disposal.

The obligation to fulfill requires States parties to adopt the necessary measures directed towards the full realization of the right to water. The obligation includes, inter alia, according sufficient recognition of this right within the national political and legal systems, preferably by way of legislative implementation; adopting a national water strategy and plan of action to realize this right; ensuring that water is affordable for everyone; and facilitating improved and sustainable access to water, particularly in rural and deprived urban areas.

To ensure that water is affordable, States parties must adopt the necessary measures that may include, inter alia: (a) use of a range of appropriate low-cost techniques and technologies; (b) appropriate pricing policies such as free or low-cost water; and (c) income supplements. Any payment for water services has to be based on the principle of equity, ensuring that these services, whether privately or publicly provided, are affordable for all, including socially disadvantaged groups. Equity demands that poorer households should not be disproportionately burdened with water expenses as compared to richer households.

States parties should adopt comprehensive and integrated strategies and programmes to ensure that there is sufficient and safe water for present and future generations. Such strategies and programmes may include: (a) reducing depletion of water resources through unsustainable extraction, diversion and damming; (b) reducing and eliminating contamination of watersheds and water-related eco-systems by substances such as radiation, harmful chemicals and human excreta; (c) monitoring water reserves; (d) ensuring that proposed developments do not interfere with access to adequate water; (e) assessing the impacts of actions that may impinge upon water availability and natural-ecosystems watersheds, such as climate changes, desertification and increased soil salinity, deforestation and loss of biodiversity; (f) increasing the efficient use of water by end-users; (g) reducing water wastage in its distribution; (h) response mechanisms for emergency situations; (i) and

establishing competent institutions and appropriate institutional arrangements to carry out the strategies and programmes.
Ensuring that everyone has access to adequate sanitation is not only fundamental for human dignity and privacy, but is one of the principal mechanisms for protecting the quality of drinking water supplies and resources. In accordance with the rights to health and adequate housing (see General Comments No. 4 (1991) and 14 (2000)) States parties have an obligation to progressively extend safe sanitation services, particularly to rural and deprived urban areas, taking into account the needs of women and children.

In earlier comments, the Committee did not explicitly draw the abovementioned distinction, although it did, implicitly, recognize various levels of obligations. For instance, in its General Comments on the right to housing (1991, 1997) the Committee, contrary to general opinion, argues that the right to housing entails a negative obligation; that is, the obligation to refrain from forced evictions. It should be noted that the distinction between various levels of obligations flowing from ESC-rights is today accepted by many human rights bodies and by many academics.

Having made these distinctions, I should also make clear why it is useful to draw them in the first place. We may conclude that the proposition that civil and political rights require the forbearance of others while ESC-rights require active support will not, or not any longer suffice.[57] As both CP-rights and ESC-rights imply various duties, negative as well as positive, the foregoing pages have shown the untenability of the view that the implementation of CP-rights is costless, whereas the realization of ESC-rights requires financial effort. Guaranteeing the right to protection against torture (which is traditionally viewed as a negative right), or the right to a fair trial, require extensive governmental programs and measures involving the training of the police and judiciary, and the maintenance of implementing and monitoring institutions. To give another example, the right to non-discrimination will also require extensive state action, especially when a policy of affirmative action is carried out. And, as has been shown, the guaranteeing and promoting of the right to freedom of speech requires great financial effort. Obviously, civil and political rights are not just costless negative rights, but also positive rights that require financial effort. This implies that, contrary to what has often been assumed, such rights cannot always be realized immediately, totally and with regard to everyone.

In addition, we may conclude that the distinctions I have made also undermine the traditional view that ESC-rights, unlike CP-rights, are not susceptible to monitoring. If negative duties are easy to monitor, there is no reason to assume that the negative duties flowing from ESC-rights cannot be monitored. And if positive duties are difficult to monitor, there is no reason to say that the positive duties flowing from CP-rights can be monitored just because they concern CP-rights. That positive duties are difficult to monitor means just that, i.e. that they are difficult to monitor, not that that difficulty precludes monitoring.

7. Justiciable duties?

Among the duties will be 'justiciable' duties. By this I mean duties the fulfilling of which can be submitted to monitoring organs. ESC-rights have negative duties, which to a large extent are justiciable. The Committee on Economic, Social and Cultural Rights has listed a number of the rights from the International Covenant on Economic, Social and Cultural Rights that contain elements of abstinence and non-interference and that are *"capable of immediate application by judicial and other organs in many legal systems."* ESC-rights aimed at the equal treatment of men and women are also regarded by the Committee as justiciable.[58]

It is not only the negative duties of ESC-rights, but also some positive ones, that can be justiciable. As mentioned above, duties can be obligations of conduct and obligations of result. Obligations of result require the duty-bearer to bring about a particular situation, while obligations of conduct require the duty-bearer to do their utmost to achieve a particular result, but without putting the duty-bearer under an obligation to actually achieve that result. Obligations of result are in principle justiciable. And the (positive) duties to protect and to help can indeed be obligations of result, which are then in principle justiciable.

In its General Comment 3, regarding states parties' obligations, the Committee on ESC-rights recognized that the full realization of ESC-rights will be achieved progressively. It has added, though, that states parties have a duty to immediately take steps, with a view to achieving progressively the full realization of the rights recognized. This is an obligation of result: steps should be taken. The term 'progressive realization', however, should not be misinterpreted. It constitutes a recognition of the fact that the full realization of all economic, social and cultural rights will generally not be achievable in a short period of time. *"Nevertheless"* it states, *"the fact that realization over time, or in other words progressively, is foreseen under the Covenant should not be misinterpreted as depriving the obligation of all meaningful content."* The term reflects the realities of the real world and recognizes the difficulties involved for any country in ensuring full realization of economic, social and cultural rights. But it imposes a clear obligation on states to do something now; that is, to take steps.[59]

A more specific example of a positive obligation to protect with the character of an obligation of result is the duty of a state, mentioned in article 4 of the International Convention on the Elimination of All Forms of Racial Discrimination. It says that the state:

> (a) Shall declare an offence punishable by law all dissemination of ideas based on racial superiority or hatred, incitement to racial discrimination, as well as all acts of violence or incitement to such acts against any race or group of persons of another colour or ethnic origin, and also the provision of any assistance to racist activities, including the financing thereof;
> (b) Shall declare illegal and prohibit organizations, and also organized and all other propaganda activities, which promote and incite racial discrimination, and shall recognize participation in such organizations or activities as an offence punishable by law...

A judicial body can determine whether the state has issued these declarations and whether is has fulfilled its duty. And even when discrimination has not disappeared, it can be that the state is considered to have fulfilled the duty mentioned in article 4. Of course, this does not mean that this is the end of state obligations. My point only is that positive obligations to protect with the character of an obligation of result are not by definition unjusticiable. But, it may be that the state must fulfill other obligations to wipe out discrimination.

But what about positive duties (to protect or to help) that are to be regarded as obligations of conduct. Are they justiciable? In article 12 the International Covenant on Economic, Social and Cultural Rights says that:

> 1. The States Parties to the present Covenant recognize the right of everyone to the enjoyment of the highest attainable standard of physical and mental health.
> 2. The steps to be taken by the States Parties to the present Covenant to achieve the full realization of this right shall include those necessary for:
> (a) The provision for the reduction of the stillbirth-rate and of infant mortality and for the healthy development of the child;
> (b) The improvement of all aspects of environmental and industrial hygiene;
> (c) The prevention, treatment and control of epidemic, endemic, occupational and other diseases;

(d) The creation of conditions which would assure to all medical service and medical attention in the event of sickness.

I take many of the duties flowing from this article to be duties of conduct. Such duties of conduct are difficult to monitor but this does not mean, however, that states are free to postpone their efforts ad infinitum. On the contrary, they should try to achieve a progressive realization of ESC-rights, and judicial or quasi-judicial bodies can determine whether or not they have taken that duty seriously; for example, in determining whether or not a plan has been developed and is being implemented. And to determine whether any such progress has been made, monitoring bodies can use statistical indicators.[60] Such bodies can also determine whether retrogressive measures have been taken. If so this would require particular justification, which then is capable of being monitored by judicial or quasi-judicial bodies. This does mean that, to some extent, also positive obligations of conduct can also be considered justiciable.

All in all, I think it can safely be concluded that ESC-rights entail genuine duties, and that many of the duties are justiciable. In closing, I would like to mention an indirect strategy for monitoring the implementation of ESC-rights, that is used in a country such as India, which does not recognize justiciable ESC-rights in its constitution. It has a so-called 'directive principle', but housing is not mentioned in it and even if it were mentioned, it still would not be justiciable because article 37 declares that the provisions contained in the section on directive principles shall not be enforced by any court. However, as reported by the Human Development Report 2000, the courts of India have now established housing as a necessary means to the constitutionally guaranteed right to life, thus giving people protection from forced evictions in cases where no alternative housing has been arranged.[61]

In short, ESC-rights imply duties, genuine duties, even justiciable duties. But, can more be said about rights in general and ESC-rights in particular?

BIBLIOGRAPHY

Arambulo, Kitty, *Strengthening the Supervision of the International Covenant on Economic Social and Cultural Rights* (Antwerpen, Groningen & Oxford: Intersentia, 1999)

Betten, L., 'De internationale bescherming van economische en sociale rechten', in: Petrus van Dijk (ed.), *Rechten van de Mens in Mundiaal en Europees perspectief* (Nijmegen: Ars Aequi Libri, 1991)

Cliteur, Paul, Neo-Liberal Globalism and Philosophical Presuppositions, in: Nieuwenhuys, Eva (ed.) Neo-Liberal Globalism and Social Sustainable Globalisation (Leiden,Boston: Brill 2006)

Coomans, Fons, 'Schending van economische, sociale en culturele rechten', in:

A.P.M. Coomans, A.W. Heringa & I. Westendorp (red.), *De toenemende betekenis van Economische, Sociale en Culturele Mensenrechten* (Leiden: Stichting NJCM-Boekerij, 1994)

Cranston, Maurice, *What are Human Rights?* (Londen, Sydney & Toronto: The Bodley Head, 1973)

Craven, Matthew, *The International Covenant on Economic, Social and Cultural Rights* (Oxford: Clarendon press, 1998)

Donnelly, Jack, 'Human Rights and Human Dignity: An Analytic Critique of Non-Western Conceptions of Human Rights', in: *The American Political Science Review* 76 (June 1982)

Donnelly, J., 'The interdependence and Indivisibility of Human Rights', in: J. Donnelly, *Universal Human Rights in Theory & Practice* (Ithaca & Londen: Cornell University Press, 1989)

Donnelly, J., 'Conceptual Issues in Monitoring Human Rights Violations', in: A.P. Schmid & A.J. Jongman (ed.), *Monitoring Human Rights Violations* (Leiden: Centre for the Study of Social Conflicts, 1992)

Donnelly, Jack, *International Human Rights*, (Boulder, San Francisco & Oxford: Westview Press, 1993)

Dower, Nigel, *World Ethics, The New Agenda* (Edinburg: Edinburg University Press, 1998)

Dower, Nigel, An Introduction to Global Citizenship, Edinburgh University Press, 2003.

Eide, Asbjørn & Bernt Hagtvet (ed.), *Human Rights in perspective: A global assessment* (Oxford: Blackwell, 1992)

Eide, Asbjörn and Allan Rosas, 'Economic, social and cultural rights, a universal challen-ge', in: Asbjörn Eide, Catarina Krause and Allan Rosas (red.), *Economic, Social and Cultural Rights* (Dordrecht, Boston and Londen: Martinus Nijhoff Publishers 1995) - (1995a)

Eide, A. 'Economic, Social and Cultural Rights as Human Rights', in: Asbjörn Eide, Catarina Krause and Allan Rosas (ed.), *Economic, Social and Cultural Rights* (Dordrecht, Boston and Londen: Martinus Nijhoff Publishers 1995) - (1995b)

Eide, A., 'The Rights to an Adequate Standard of Living Including the Right to Food', in: Asbjörn Eide, Catarina Krause and Allan Rosas (ed.), *Economic, Social and Cultural Rights* (Dordrecht, Boston and London: Martinus Nijhoff Publishers 1995) - (1995c)

Eide, A, 'Cultural Rights as Individual Human Rights', in: Asbjörn Eide, Catarina Krause and Allan Rosas (ed.), *Economic, Social and Cultural Rights* (Dordrecht, Boston and London: Martinus Nijhoff Publishers 1995) - (1995d)

Eide, A., 'Obstacles and Goals to be Pursued', in: Asbjørn Eide, Catarina Krause en Allan Rosas (ed.), *Economic, Social and Cultural Rights* (Dordrecht, Boston and Londen: Martinus Nijhoff Publishers 1995) - (1995e)

Eide, Asjbørn, 'Economic, Social and Cultural rights', in: Janusz Symonides (ed.), *Human Rights: Concept and Standards* (Aldershot, Burlinton, Singapore & Sydney: Ashgate, Dartmouth, Unesco Publishing, 2000)

Freeden, Michael, *Rights* (Buckingham: Open University Press, 1991)

Fried, C., *Right and Wrong* (Cambridge Mass: Harvard University Press, 1978)

Galenkamp, M., *Individualism versus Collectivism: the concept of collective rights* (Rotterdam: Rotterdamse filosofische studies, 1993)

Galtung, J., 'The Universality of Human Rights Revisited: Some Less Applaudable Consequences of the Human Rights Tradition', in: Asbjørn Eide & Bernt Hagtvet (red.), *Human Rights in perspective: A global assessment* (Oxford: Blackwell, 1992)

Gerwirth, A., 'Are There Any Absolute Rights', in: J. Waldron (ed.), *Theories of rights* (Oxford University Press, 1984)

Gewirth, Alan, *The Community of Rights* (Chicago & Londen: The University of Chicago Press, 1996)

Grant, Robert, *American Ethics and the Virtuous Citizen, basic principles* (Washington DC: Humanist Press 1999)

Grant, Robert, *American Ethics and the Virtuous Citizen, the right to life*

(Washington DC: Humanist Press 2003)

Gray, J., 'Classical Liberalism, Positional Goods and the Politicization of Poverty', in: A. Ellis & K. Kumar (ed.), *Dilemmas of Liberal Democracies: Studies in Fred Hirsch's Social Limits to growth* (Londen: Tavistock Publications, 1983)

Hoof, G.J.H. van, 'The Legal Nature of Economic, Social and Cultural Rights: a Rebuttal of Some Traditional Views', in: P. Alston & K. Tomasevski (ed.), *The Right to Food: From Soft to Hard Law* (Utrecht: Netherlands Institute of Human Rights, 1984)

Hunt, Paul, *Reclaiming Social Rights: International and Comparative Perspectives* (Aldershot: Dartmouth, 1996)

Keane, J., *Democracy and Civil Society: On the predicaments of European socialism, the prospects for democracy and the problem of controlling social and political power* (Londen etc.: Verso, 1988)

Koch, Ida Elisabeth, "The Justiciability of Indivisible Rights", in: *Nordic Journal of International Law*, (Brill Academic Publishers, Volume 72, Number 1 / February, 2003), p.3-39

Locke, John, *The Second Treatise on Civil Government* (New York: Prometheus Books, 1986)

Plant, R., 'Needs, agency and welfare rights', in: J.D. Moon (ed.), *Responsibility, Rights and Welfare, the theory of the welfare state* (Boulder ect.: Westview Press, 1988)

Plant, Raymond, *Modern Political Thought* (Oxford ect.: Basil Blackwell, 1991)

Pogge, Thomas, *World Poverty and Human Rights, Cosmopolitan Responsibilities and Reforms* (Cambridge: Polity Press, 2002/2003)

Raz, J., *The Morality of Freedom* (Oxford: Clarendon Press, 1986)

Robertson, A.H. & J.G. Merrills, *Human Rights in the World: an introduction to the study of the international protection of human rights* (Manchester, New York: Manchester University Press, 1992)

Schreuder-Vlasblom, M., 'In Gemeenschap met Anderen', in: *Filosofie & Praktijk* 14, nr.3 (landsmeer: Daedalus, 1993)

Sengupta, Arjun (and Asbjörn Eide, Stephen P. Marks, and Bärd A. Andreassen) *The Right to Development and Human Rights in Development: A Background Paper, Prepared for the Nobel Symposium in Oslo from 13 - 15 October 2003* http://www.humanrights.uio.no/forskning/publ/rn/2004/0704.pdf (Oslo: Norwegian for Human Rights 2004)

Shue, Henry, *Basic Rights* (Princeton NJ: Princeton University Press, 1980)

Williams, Maurice, 'Human centred development', in: Richard Reoch (red.), *Human Rights, the new consensus* (New York & Londen: Regency Press, 1994)

Maastricht Guidelines on Violations of Economic, Social and Cultural Rights, Maastricht, January 22-26, 1997. http://www1.umn.edu/humanrts/instree/Maastrichtguidelines_.html

ENDNOTES

[1] HDR 2006, p.78.
[2] Betten 1991, p.134; Robertson and Merrills 1992, p.230; Williams 1994, p.122; Craven 1998, p.9.
[3] Moon 1988, p.35.
[4] Hart 1967, p.56,60; Raz 1986, p.167; Galenkamp 1993, p.63; Galtung 1992, p.153; Gewirth 1984, p.92.
[5] Eide 1992, p.5, Galtung 1992, p.153.
[6] See also: Pogge 2002/2003, p.68,69; Dower 2003, p.61; Cliteur 2006, p.30.
[7] Donnelly 1989, p.32; Plant 1991, p.268.
[8] Plant 1991, p.270; Hoof van 1984, p.23.
[9] Williams 1994, p.122; Cranston 1973, p.67.
[10] Pogge 2002/2003, pp.67,68.
[11] Fried 1978, p.120.

12 Gray 1983, p.182.
13 Plant 1991, p.270; Hoof van 1984, p.23; Williams 1994, p.122.
14 Plant 1991, p.279.
15 Cranston 1973, p.67.
16 Plant 1988, p.62.
17 Robertson and Merrills 1992, p.230; Cranston 1973, p.68.
18 Donnelly 1992, p.86.
19 Donnelly 1992, p.86.
20 Locke 1986, p.70.
21 Locke 1986, p.72; Schreuder-Vlasblom 1993, p.123; Grant 1999, p.23,24; Grant 2003, p.3.
22 Gewirth 1996, pp.35,36.
23 Human Rights Committee 1994; Hunt 1996, p.33; this position is reiterated by the Committee at various occasions, for instance in its 'Concluding Observations' on the Human Rights situation in the UK, 07-11-2002, see: http://www.unhchr.ch/tbs/doc.nsf/c12563e7005d936d4125611e00445ea9/ac3028880 f9343ddc1256ce20036db7a/$FILE/G0246211.pdf
24 NJCM Bulletin 24 1999, p.515.
25 Hunt 1996, p.31.
26 HDR 2000, p.73.
27 Donnelly 1993, p.27; 1989, p.33.
28 Shue 1980, p.42.
29 Hoof van 1984, pp.97,107.
30 Eide 1995e, pp.386, 387.
31 Amnesty International, Human Rights and Privatisation, 17-03-2005, http://web.amnesty.org/library/ index/engpol340032005, retrieved February 2007.
32 Dower 1998, pp.80, 81.
33 Hoof van 1984, p.26; Donnelly 1989, p.33; 1993, p.27.
34 UN Doc. E/C.12/1990/8, 64.
35 http://www.unhchr.ch/huricane/huricane.nsf/0/271A763E727C481FC1256C7E002B1201?opendocument.
36 Keane 1988, p.22.
37 Shue 1980, p.52; Koch 2003, pp.3-39.
38 Shue 1980, p.55.
39 Shue 1980, p.19.
40 Plant 1991, p.285; Gewirth 1996, p.39.
41 Eide 1995b, pp.37, 38.
42 Eide 1995c, p.104.
43 Eide 2000, pp.138,139,140.
44 Eide 1995, p.386.
45 Arambulo 1999, p.122.
46 Hoof, van 1984, p.25 .
47 Hoof, van 1984, p.25; Coomans 1994, pp.59, 60, 71.
48 http://www.minorityrights.org/Legal/development/rtd_pt2_process.pdf, retrieved December 2006.
49 http://www1.umn.edu/humanrts/instree/Maastrichtguidelines_.html, retrieved December 2006.
50 It should be noted that Eide uses this terminology but that his interpretation is quite different. Eide suggests that the provisions of the International Covenant on Economic, Social and Cultural Rights are to be taken more in terms of obligations of result than in obligations of conduct (Eide 1995b, p.39). Because of this, I interpret Eide's obligation of conduct to be a prescription of how people should act and his obligation of result to refer to the eventual aim of the obligation. Eide's obligation of conduct then becomes equal to my obligation of result. He stresses that a particular act should be performed, while I stress that a particular situation should be achieved. Eide's obligation of result is different from my obligation of result and comes down to my obligation of conduct. I take it that Eide wants, with that term, to point to a desired goal, the outcome of the obligations. I, on the other hand,

The Vagueness of Economic, Social and Cultural Rights

emphasize the efforts that should be undertaken here and now to - eventually - achieve the desired goal. Whatever interpretation of the difference between obligations of result and conduct held by Eide, I think the abovementioned interpretation of the distinction is an important one, since it helps us to determine the duties of duty-bearers. I will elaborate on this point later; for now, it suffices to stress the importance of the distinction. (See also: Coomans 1994, p.59,60,71)

[51] Human Development Report 2000, p.16.

[52] I think, however, that it goes too far to accept the distinction that is drawn by Immanuel Kant, at least when we are speaking of 'rights'. According to Kant "Perfect duties are proscriptions of specific kinds of actions, and violating them is morally blameworthy; imperfect duties are prescriptions of general ends, and fulfilling them by means of performing appropriate particular actions is praiseworthy." (Routledge Ecyclopedia of Philosophy, http://rep.routledge.com/article/DB047SECT10, retr. 04-06-2006). When it comes to duties flowing from rights, I think that also not fulfilling imperfect duties is morally blameworthy.

[53] Coomans 1994, p.71.
[54] Kofi A. Annan, HDR 2006, p.78.
[55] HDR 2000, p.7.
[56] See also: Sengupta 2004, p.115.
[57] Donnelly 1993, p.26.
[58] UN Doc.E/1991/23, Annex III.
[59]. http://www.unhchr.ch/tbs/doc.nsf/(symbol)/ CESCR+General+comment+3.En?OpenDocument, retrieved Februari 2007.
[60] Coomans 1994:, p.72; Arambulo 1999, p.124.
[61] HDR 2000, p.76.

CHAPTER 8

A RIGHT IS A PRECIOUS THING

"Some commentators see the application of rights language to water and other social and economic entitlements as an example of rhetorical "loose talk". That assessment is mistaken. Declaring water a human right clearly does not mean that the water crisis will be resolved in short order. Nor does a rights framework provide automatic answers to difficult policy questions about pricing, investment and ser-vice delivery. However, human rights represent a powerful moral claim. They can also act as a source of empowerment and mobilization, creating expectations and enabling poor people to expand their entitlements through legal and political channels—and through claims on the resources of national governments and the international community."

HDR 2006

1. Introduction

Can ESC-rights genuinely be called human rights, or is it just loose talk? That is the central question of this book, a question that has arisen from the assumption that ESC-rights, when treated as genuine rights, can contribute to the alleviation of socio-economic misery. Many say that ESC-rights, although they are called rights, only imply political aspirations or tasks of government, and that they do not entail duties. But there are no compelling reasons to make such a statement, as I have argued in the previous chapters. If article 25 of the UDHR states that *"Everyone has the right to a standard of living adequate for the health and well-being of himself and of his family...."* it implies that others, generally governments, have duties. And if Article 11 of the International Covenant on Economic, Social and Cultural Rights says that *"The States Parties to the present Covenant recognize the right of everyone to an adequate standard of living for himself and his family, including*

A Right Is a Precious Thing

adequate food, clothing and housing, and to the continuous improvement of living conditions..." I take this to imply duties. And as we have seen in chapter 7, while they may be duties of forbearance, duties to protect or to help, duties of result or conduct, even long or short term duties, they will always be duties.

Also national documents use the term 'right' when dealing with ESC-rights. For instance, article 49 of the Ukrainian Constitution states that "*Everyone has the right to health protection, medical care and medical insurance....*". To me this implies that the Ukrainian government has a duty, whatever the nature of that duty. To take another example, the Constitution of South Africa states in article 26, that "*Everyone has the right to have access to adequate housing...*" while article 27 states that "*Everyone has the right to have access to healthcare services, including reproductive healthcare; sufficient food and water; and social security, including, if they are unable to support themselves and their dependants, appropriate social assistance...*" Once again, I take this to mean that both articles are implying that the state has a duty, because mentioning rights implies duties. It is only an illusion to speak of rights without duties: for 'rights' imply duties in others.[1]

But, does mentioning duties imply the existence of rights? Are rights the automatic reverse of duties? Some documents do not even use the term 'right' and prefer to speak of duties. Take, for instance, the Indian Constitution. It does not treat ESC-rights on the same footing as CP-rights. In fact, Part III of that Constitution, titled '*Fundamental Rights*' lists only CP-rights. But while it even includes the rights of minorities, that could be called cultural rights, social and cultural rights are not included in this Part III. Part IV, however, under the heading '*Directive Principles of State Policy*' contains provisions that may be seen as referring to ESC-rights.

For instance, article 45, titled '*Provision for free and compulsory education for children*' states that "*The State shall endeavour to provide, within a period of ten years from the commencement of this Constitution, for free and compulsory education for all children until they complete the age of fourteen years.*" This would suggest that the article wants to refer to a duty of the state. But, does the Constitution mean to refer to *rights*? Article 47 of the Constitution, "*Duty of the State to raise the level of nutrition and the standard of living and to improve public health*' states that "*The State shall regard the raising of the level of nutrition and the standard of living of its people and the improvement of public health as among its primary duties...*", which is a clear reference to duties of the state. But does it mean to refer to *rights*?

And let us look at the constitution of the Netherlands, a country that is one of the so-called welfare-states—states that regard themselves as responsible for the socio-economic well-being of their citizens. Article 19 [Work] of its constitution states that "*It shall be the concern of the authorities to promote the provision of sufficient employment*" while article 22 [Health] states that "*The authorities shall take steps to promote the health of the* population." Although neither article uses the word 'duty' it can, I think, be successfully argued that both are referring to duties of the state. But, again, do they want to refer to specific *rights*, in this case, to a right to work and a right to health?[2]

One could argue that of course the Dutch Constitution refers to rights; there is, after all, a two-sided correlativity of rights and duties: rights imply duties, and duties imply rights. This would appear to be the view of Rodolfo Stavenhagen when discussing article 29 of the African Charter on Human and Peoples' Rights, which specifically mentions the duty of individuals to preserve and strengthen positive African values. Stavenhagen then goes on to say that "*if to preserve and strengthen positive African cultural values is spelled out as a duty, it may be assumed that there is a countervailing right to African cultural values*".[3] In our day-to-day life, many of us tend to assume that where there is a duty, there is a right. (I think that pleas for animal rights are based on this assumption. Many people today recognize that they have a duty to treat animals well and, from this thought, then conclude that animals have rights. What is interesting is that only a few decades ago, hardly anybody spoke of animal rights, even though many people recognized a duty to treat animals well.)

But, is the presence of a duty enough to conclude that there is a right? When driving a car, we have a duty not to exceed a certain maximum speed, but is it appropriate to speak of a right and, if it is, who then has that right? We have a duty not to park our car where it is forbidden, but is it appropriate to speak of a corresponding right and, if so, who has it? Many officials have a duty to comply with certain rules when fulfilling their duty, but is it appropriate to speak of a right?

I would like to submit that rights are not simply the automatic reverse of duties but something special. By saying that people have a right to healthcare, to adequate housing or food, we do not only say that others—governments or fellow human beings—have a duty to protect or guarantee the health, adequate housing or food of the right-holder. If that was all we wanted to say, we could just as easily have confined ourselves to a Universal Declaration of Human Duties. Yet we *do* use the word 'right'. Obviously we not only want to say that others have a duty, we also want to say something about the right-holders themselves.[4] But, what do we want to say?

Peter Jones observes that it's possible to distinguish various ideas about the notion of a right, but that they should be grouped into two approaches to the specific characteristics of rights; that is, the *benefit*- or *interest*-theory, and the *choice*- or *choice-approach*.[5] This distinction is similar to that of Carlos Santiago Nino, who also speaks of two approaches to rights, one equating rights to expressions of will, the other equating them with interests.[6] In the following section, I will offer a short introduction to both these views.

2 Duty + interest = right: a minimalist view

Jeremy Bentham is a representative of the benefit or interest approach. He argues that a right is not just the reverse of a duty. While it is true that the presence of a duty-holder is a central element of the notion of a right, it is not sufficient to speak of a right. There must be someone else but, more importantly, this person should be a beneficiary of the duty of the duty-holder. In addition to the person with a duty, there should be someone who *benefits* from the fulfillment of that duty.[7] The necessary presence of a duty-holder *and* a beneficiary may seem to be a matter of course, but I think, nevertheless, that it may be interesting to pay some more attention to this statement.

When the law imposes a duty on the hangman to hang a condemned criminal, a direct relationship exists between the hangman and the criminal. However, it does not seem appropriate to speak of a right of the criminal to be hanged, as is said by Nino, because the convicted is not a beneficiary of the duty concerned.[8] Society in general can, perhaps, be seen as benefiting from the duty of the hangman, as it is in the interests of society that criminals are punished for their crimes. And society has also, perhaps, a right to expect that the hangman performs his duty adequately. But in this we are discussing the relationship between the hangman and society; we are not talking about the relationship between the hangman and the criminal. In the latter relationship, the criminal appears not to benefit from the duty of the hangman and, accordingly, does not have a *right* to be hanged. It must be added, however, that it is possible that the convicted may have a right towards the executioner to be hanged; for example, when the law gives a convicted the right to chose between being hanged and being quartered. Then the convicted also becomes a beneficiary with an interest; that is, an interest in being allowed to choose between two methods of execution. It is said that in the past a peer had the right to be hanged by a silken rope, should he be condemned to hanging.[9] Also then the peer is supposed to have an interest in being hanged by a silken rope. Apart from that, it may also possible that the criminal has other rights with regard to the hangman, not related to the duty of the hangman to execute the criminal. For instance, the hangman has a duty to treat the criminal with respect and the criminal benefits from that duty. On the basis thereof, the criminal may have a right not to be mocked or sneered at by the hangman. This right, however, has nothing to do with the duty of the hangman to execute the criminal; it concerns only his duty to treat the convicted with respect.

So, in addition to a duty-holder, the presence of a beneficiary is—according to this Benthamite approach—a necessary element of the notion of a right. But Bentham stresses that the duty-holder and the beneficiary must be different people. If they are the same person, the term right cannot be used.[10] And in saying this, Bentham is able to refute the criticism that H.L.A. Hart levels against the 'interest' view. Hart criticizes the adherents of the view that having a right means that one is the beneficiary of a duty. Hart says that these adherents have insufficiently realized the consequences of their view, because a consequence would be that people would have rights towards themselves. After all, we have a duty to keep ourselves alive and, at the same time, we are the beneficiaries of that duty. Do we then have a right towards ourselves to keep ourselves alive? Hart regards this as rather odd.[11] Bentham avoids this problem by stressing that duty-holder and beneficiary should be different. In his view, people have a right to life towards other people and these other people have a duty to respect the lives of the right-holders but people do *not* have a right to life towards themselves.

The aforementioned approach can be called minimalist, because it contains only two elements: a duty and an interest. Beauchamp is of the view that having a right does not always mean having an interest. For instance, he believes that people may have a right to apply for positions that are less attractive than their current position even when they have no interest in doing so.[12] But, I would like to suggest, does it make sense to use the word 'right' for situations in which people do not have an interest in X and do not want this X to be protected or guaranteed? Of course it may be that A is not interested in X, although others are. Then it still may make sense to use the word 'right' as it is assumed that people in general do have an interest in A. But if it is thought that nobody has an interest in A does it make sense then to use the word 'right'? What then is the meaning of the notion of 'a right'? I think that it can make sense to say that people have a right to apply for positions that are less attractive than their current position. But then, it will be thought that those people will—for whatever reason—have an interest in doing so or, at the very least, that they will be of the view that they have such an interest.

According to this minimalist approach, the presence of only two elements is sufficient to speak of a right, an interest and a duty or, to put it in terms of human beings, an interest-holder and a duty-holder. The question then arises whether ESC-rights are rights in this minimalist sense. Well, many legal documents obviously refer to a duty-holder and a beneficiary. For instance, article 11 of the International Covenant on Economic, Social and Cultural Rights (ICESCR) states that "*The States Parties to the present Covenant recognize the right of everyone to an adequate standard of living for himself and his family, including adequate food, clothing and housing, and to the continuous improvement of living conditions. The States Parties will take appropriate steps to ensure the realization of this right, recognizing to this effect the essential importance of international co-operation based on free consent.*" Article 12 reads "*1. The States Parties to the present Covenant recognize the right of everyone to the enjoyment of the highest attainable standard of physical and mental health. 2. The steps to be taken by the*

States Parties to the present Covenant to achieve the full realization of this right shall include those necessary for: (a) The provision for the reduction of the stillbirth-rate and of infant mortality and for the healthy development of the child; (b) The improvement of all aspects of environmental and industrial hygiene; (c) The prevention, treatment and control of epidemic, endemic, occupational and other diseases; (d) The creation of conditions which would assure to all medical service and medical attention in the event of sickness."

I assume we have a duty-holder here: the state. (In the preceding chapter, I put forward that many people doubt whether real duties exist with respect to the rights of the ICESCR. For example, Robertson and Merills think that the ICESCR defines ESC-rights more in terms of the undertakings of the state than in terms of actual rights: *"... we find an undertaking or a recognition by states rather than the affirmation of a right inherent in the individual as such."*[13] Therefore, if it is thought that ESC-rights only entail the tasks of a government, rather than duties, then basically you cannot speak of a right. But let us assume that we can speak of real duties. They may be duties to respect, protect, help or to promote, they may be long-term or short-term duties, they may be duties of effort or duties of result, but in all cases they are duties.) Apart from the duty-holder, we have in the ICESCR beneficiaries (that is 'everyone'). So, as we have at least these two elements we can, from a minimalist view, speak of real rights.

I also would like to consider here the Indian Constitution, and the previously discussed article 47 from Part IV, the '*Directive Principle of State Policy*'. This article, ('Duty of the State to raise the level of nutrition and the standard of living and to improve public health') states that "*The State shall regard the raising of the level of nutrition and the standard of living of its people and the improvement of public health as among its primary duties and, in particular, the State shall endeavor to bring about prohibition of the consumption except for medicinal purpose.*" It appears to me that also here both a duty-holder (the state) and beneficiaries (its people) are mentioned. So, although the word 'right' is not used we may, from a Benthamite perspective, conclude that this directive principle of art. 47 *is* a right. The same can be said of article 22 [Health] of the Dutch Constitution that states that "*The authorities shall take steps to promote the health of the population*" and which mentions a duty-holder (authorities) and a beneficiary (the population). One may, however, doubt whether article 19 [Work] of the Dutch Constitution contains a right. When it states that "*It shall be the concern of the authorities to promote the provision of sufficient employment*", it is referring to a duty-holder. But then where, and who, is the beneficiary? There is no mentioning of a beneficiary. Can we assume that the population of the Netherlands is the beneficiary and yet speak of a right in a Benthamite sense as there then is a duty-holder and a beneficiary?

But, apart from that, are ESC-rights only rights in this minimalist sense? In my opinion, ESC-rights not only show more dimensions than those of interest-holder and a duty-holder, they *should* have more dimensions: for if they only contain these two dimensions, they cannot be called human rights.

3. Intentionality

To have a right means, in the minimalist approach, to be the beneficiary of the duties of somebody else.[14] Sometimes people indeed are the beneficiaries of somebody else's duties, in instances where it seems inappropriate to speak of a right. For example, people have a duty to drive on the right-hand or left-hand side of the street, to pay taxes, to respect the traffic-lights, to do military service (in some countries). And while other people undoubtedly have an interest in these duties being fulfilled, is it really appropriate to speak of their rights? The government has a duty to preserve public order, to establish and maintain a system of transport, to organize an army. Citizens undoubtedly benefit from the fulfillment of these duties but, in such circumstances, is it appropriate to speak of the *rights* of the country's citizens?

In these cases, it is hardly possible to point at certain determinate individuals in whose interests such duties exist. Therefore we cannot speak of a right, as can be, and is, argued. David Lyons says that someone (only) can be seen as having a right when that person is the *direct* and *intended* interest-holder of the duty of someone else.[15] Being simply the beneficiary of the duty of someone else is not sufficient to regard that person as a right-holder. Speaking of a right requires that the duty-holder is obliged to do, or to refrain from doing, something with a view to promoting the interests of the beneficiary.[16] Also other writers who subscribe to the interest-theory are of the view that duties only give rise to rights when the duties are "individualizable", i.e. when they are aimed at promoting the interests of individuals severally. Duties to pay taxes or to observe traffic laws are designed to benefit people, but they are not directed towards assignable individuals. Right-holders are not just anonymous beneficiaries of the duties of the duty-holder: they are the intended beneficiaries.[17] Jones emphasizes that a duty may be a duty towards all members of a society and still give rise to a right. The point is whether the duty is directed at benefiting people as members of an undifferentiated collectivity (in which case it does not give rise to a right; for instance the duty to pay taxes or the duty of a government to build roads) or whether it is directed at benefiting individuals severally (in which case it does; for instance the duty not to assault others or the duty of a government to respect people's freedom of expression).[18]

The question now is whether ESC-rights can be seen as rights in this intentionalist sense, or whether they only can be seen as rights in a minimalist sense. The answer, I believe, depends on how the beneficiaries of the duties of governments are defined or seen. Various documents use various and different wordings.[19] The Universal Declaration on Human Rights explicitly mentions 'everyone' as the beneficiaries. It states that *"Everyone, as a member of society, has the right to social security... Everyone has the right to work... to free choice of employment, to just and favourable conditions of work and to protection against unemployment... Everyone has the right to rest and leisure... Everyone has the right to a standard of living adequate for the health and well-being of himself and of his family, including food, clothing, housing and medical care... Everyone has the right to education... Everyone has the right freely to participate in the cultural life of the community, to enjoy the arts and to share in scientific advancement and its benefits."* The use of the word 'everyone' implies, in my view, that the duties of the duty-holders are individualizable, duties of which everyone is a direct and intended beneficiary. Therefore the ESC-rights of the UNDHR can be seen as rights in an intentionalist sense.

The International Covenant on Economic, Social and Cultural Rights does not hesitate to use the word right either, although it is less fierce than the UDHR. It states that *"the States Parties to the present Covenant recognize the right to work... The States Parties to the present Covenant recognize the right of everyone to social security, including social insurance... The States Parties to the present Covenant recognize the right of everyone to an adequate standard of living for himself and his family, including adequate food, clothing and housing, and to the continuous improvement of living conditions... The States Parties to the present Covenant, recognizing the fundamental right of everyone to be free from hunger... The States Parties to the present Covenant recognize the right of everyone to the enjoyment of the highest attainable standard of physical and mental health... The States Parties to the present Covenant recognize the right of everyone to education."* And here it can also be assumed that the rights refer to intended and direct beneficiaries and that, as a consequence, the rights of the ICESCR are rights in an intentionalist sense. The government does not have duties the fulfillment of which benefit people in general, but it does have duties with a view to the interests of every individual citizen.

If I look at some constitutions, though, I must say that I doubt whether the beneficiaries mentioned in them can be interpreted as direct and intended beneficiaries. I already have mentioned some doubts—with regard to article 19 of the Dutch Constitution—as to whether it refers to a right in a minimalist sense, because it does not mention a beneficiary. I was prepared to regard article 22 of the same constitution, as well as article 47 of the Indian Constitution, as mentioning a right in a minimalist sense. But I am reluctant to consider them as referring to rights in an intentionalist sense. If article 22 of the Dutch Constitution states that *"The authorities shall take steps to promote the health of the population"*, can we then speak of an intended or direct beneficiary? And, if article 47 of Part IV of the Indian Constitution states that "*The State shall regard the raising of the level of nutrition and the standard of living of its people and the improvement of public health as among its primary duties...*", do there exist intended beneficiaries? In other words, are there individuals who can come forward as intended beneficiaries of the duties and demand that the state fulfills its duties towards them? And, should the government be bothered about that or can the government shrug its shoulders and say that it has raised the level of nutrition, the standard of living of its people and public health and has nothing to do with individual problems?

To take another example from the same constitution, article 38 (1) states that "*The State shall strive to promote the welfare of the people by securing and protecting as effectively as it may a social order in which justice, social, economic and political, shall inform all the institutions of the national life.*" If we assume, therefore, that states can be seen as having duties pursuant to this article then undoubtedly people are the beneficiaries of these tasks. But, again, can we point to intended beneficiaries? The wording of the article does not mention such beneficiaries.

The answer to the question of whether a constitution contains genuine ESC-rights depends on the view of the notion of a right that one has. Let us stick to Part IV of the Indian Constitution. If one takes a minimalist position, then the answer of whether that constitution contains genuine ESC-rights could be in the affirmative. If one takes an intentionalist view, then it could be argued that most directive principles of the constitution cannot be called rights because there is a duty-holder, there are beneficiaries, but there are no intended beneficiaries.

The element of intentionality is, in my view, by definition an element of human rights. It may be confusing that all human beings are right-holders of human rights. That could give the impression that it only concerns the undifferentiated members of a group. But that is not the case. Every single human being is a beneficiary with a view to whose interest the government has a duty: every individual is the intended and direct beneficiary. That is the ratio of the notion of human rights.[20] In the preceding chapter I argued that if you take ESC-rights to imply only tasks or aspirations of governments and not genuine duties, then it is inappropriate to speak of rights. I would now like to submit that, if you take the beneficiaries of the duties of governments to be nothing but undifferentiated anonymous beneficiaries, then it is again inappropriate to speak of (human) rights. You cannot use the terms '(human) right to healthcare' or '(human) right to housing', without wanting to say that everyone is the intended and direct beneficiary of the duty generated by these rights. Saying that everyone has a right and then stating that this only implies that a government has duty to promote the well-being of people in general—in other words using the term right in a minimalist sense only—does not make sense in the case of human rights. It is at the very least a *contradictio in terminis.*

4. Personhood

It could be suggested that, in the minimalist and intentionalist approach, the right-holder is presented more as an object of care and less as a human person. And, so it can be added, one cannot speak of rights if right-holders are not presented as persons. The personhood of right-holders is emphasized by Agnes Heller who makes clear that having a right means more than being the (intended) beneficiary of a duty, an approach which I will call the 'personalist approach'.[21] She shows that the notion of a right refers to a special relationship between the right-holder and duty-holder. There have been cultures that have had law and morality, that have formulated duties and obligations, but which have never been familiar with the notion of a right. One can say, for example, that people have a duty to take care of their relatives without once referring to the notion of a right. One can say that governments have duties to provide their citizens with adequate housing, healthcare or education, again without referring to the notion of a right. And, as has been said in the preceding paragraphs, many national constitutions—the Indian and the Dutch, for example—do formulate duties regarding housing, healthcare and education without speaking in terms of rights. The notion of a right refers to something special.

From a minimalist position, it could be argued that rights exist when the duties are accompanied by the presence of beneficiaries. From an intentionalist approach duties can only be interpreted in terms of rights when the duties are directed at intended beneficiaries. But, even when benefiting people could be regarded as the intended and direct beneficiaries, there is still—from a personalist approach—insufficient reason to speak of rights. What is added by speaking in terms of rights is the fact that some duty is owed to the right-holder and that the duty involved is grounded in the person of the right-holder. This approach can be found in many authors and is one which I would like to share.[22] For these writers a right-holder is a person who has a special moral status as a human being and who calls upon others to protect his or her interest, and these others cannot ignore such a call.

The central idea of the personalist approach becomes clear with the help of an example presented by Agnes Heller, who describes a situation in which a woman is ill-treated by her husband. Let us assume that we are in a world without rights. We may assume that in such a world, the husband will have a duty not to mishandle his wife and the woman will have an interest in not being ill-treated. We may even say that the woman is the intended and direct beneficiary of that duty. If the man mistreats his wife, he neglects her interests, acts badly, violates his duty and, in effect, commits a crime. He may even infringe the law. But one cannot say that he has done an injustice to his wife or that he has wronged her, for in a world without rights the duty one has is not owed to the beneficiaries, but to a religious or secular authority.[23] For instance in a biblical world the duties people have are owed to God. The Ten Commandments formulate what God expects of people.[24] They are a list of imperatives which, according to religious tradition, were written by God and given to Moses on Mount Sinai in the form of two stone tablets. It is God to whom the duties are owed.

In a world without rights every legal or moral relationship become a three-party relationship, one consisting of the beneficiary, the duty-holder and the religious or secular authority: "*It takes three to make a marriage.*" (If one wishes one could use the notion of a right for this authority, but not for the wife. The authority could be seen as a monopolist right-holder.)[25] Such a world without rights may have been a historical reality until modernity showed the emergence of the notion of a right. Beauchamp observes that "*...in the sweep of human history the language of rights is a distinctly modern phenomenon. Until the seventeenth century, problems of political ethics were rarely discussed in terms of rights.*"[26] This emergence of the notion of a right has changed the relationship between the duty-holder and the beneficiary, for in a world of rights, such a relationship is unmediated. The beneficiary is no longer the object of a duty owed to a religious or secular authority. Duties flowing from rights are not owed to these authorities but to the beneficiary themselves, who can, therefore, be called right-holders, while the religious or secular authority may confirm and sanction the existence of a right and even punish violators of rights.

But the authority is not the source, the basis, of the rights. Pogge, speaking about the coming about of natural rights, says it this way: "*By violating a natural right one wrongs the subject whose right it is. These subjects of natural rights are viewed as sources of moral claims and thereby recognized as having a certain moral standing and value. The natural law idiom contains no such idea: it need not involve demands on one's conduct towards other subjects at all and, even if it does, need not involve the idea that by violating such demands one has wronged these subjects—one may rather have wronged God, for example, or have disturbed the harmonious order of the cosmos*".[27] Saying that a wife has a right not to be ill-treated by her husband means that the basis of the duty of the man lies in the interests of his wife, a person, to whom he is expected to fulfill his duty. If the man mishandles his wife, he not only commits a crime, neglects her interests, forsake his duty and infringes the law, but he also does injustice to her. He wrongs her. (I have mentioned this difference between natural law and natural rights in chapter 1)

5. Discretion

Characteristic of the personalist approach is the idea that human beings are presented as persons. This empowers people. Using the rights language implies that people are treated as subjects of moral value. That is elaborated on in a particular way by Heller, but it need not be done in that way. The right-holder as a person can be also be found in the 'choice approach', for instance, in the theory of H.L.A. Hart, who criticizes the 'interest approach' by arguing that beneficiaries are not always right-holders and right-holders are not always beneficiaries.[28]

He takes an example from the domain of morality. Suppose that A promises to B that he will take care of the mother of B. This makes the mother, C, the beneficiary of the duty of A. One may even say that C is the intended beneficiary. But, while B is not the beneficiary he is, nevertheless, the right-holder and has a right towards A. Obviously, one cannot say that having a right means being the intended beneficiary of the duty of somebody else. It is more appropriate, according to Hart, to say that the right-holder is the one who runs the show, the one who is in charge of the relationship between the right-holder and the duty-holder. "...*the precise figure is not that of two persons bound by a chain, but of one person bound, the other end of the chain lying in the hands of another to use if he chooses.*"[29]

The example is from the moral domain but it holds equally for the legal domain. Moral and legal rights have similar elements.[30] If A and B conclude a contract implying that A will give a monthly financial contribution to C, then C is the beneficiary of the duty of A. But it is B to whom A has a duty, it is B who can require the fulfillment of the duty, it is B who can relieve A of his duty, and it is B who can sue A for damages of breach of promise. In short it is B who is in a position to determine the relationship and who can limit A's options for action. That, and not being a beneficiary, makes B a right-holder, for characteristic of a right is the fact that the holder of the right is in control of the relationship.[31] The relationship is at his discretion.

Such discretion presents two aspects. Firstly, it may relate to the very existence of a right and the corresponding duty: the right-holder can insist upon having her right or she can waive her right, and by that determine whether the duty-holder remains bound by the duty or whether he or she will be relieved of the duty. Secondly, the discretion may relate to the execution of the right and corresponding duty. The right-bearer can determine whether legal or moral pressure will be exerted on the duty-holder if the latter does not fulfill his duty. For example, in the case of legal rights, the right-holder can determine whether she will sue the duty-holder if the latter does not fulfill his duty. As regards moral rights, the right-holder can, for example, decide whether a campaign of shaming will be launched. In addition, the right-holder can determine whether she will hold the duty-bearer to his obligation to pay damages or to fulfill a compensating task, if he is bound to do so because of his neglect of his duty.[32]

Hart's approach is an example of an approach in which human beings appear as free persons, as persons who determine their fate and decide who they want to be in relation to others.[33] This emphasis on freedom may lead one to think that there exists a similarity between Hart's approach and the 'rights-as-liberties' of Hohfeld, mentioned in the chapter 6. But, as you may recall, Hohfeld—wrongly—assumes that rights-as-liberties do not have duties as their correlatives. That is not Hart's point: in his approach duties *do* exist. His point is that the duty-holders are meant to be subjected to the control of the right-holder.

The emphasis on freedom in the choice-approach versus the emphasis on interest in the minimalist and intentionalist approach may lead to another misunderstanding. One might think that the former approach is relevant for civil and political rights, often called freedom-rights, whereas economic, social and cultural rights are to be interpreted in terms of the latter. One could find support for this impression in Western history, a history that shows that, to a certain extent, the development of the interpretation of the notion of a right runs parallel with the development of the categories of rights (CP-rights and ESC-rights). When the idea of rights emerged, they were defined in terms of choice and will, as 'option-rights' and emphasis was laid on the freedom and autonomy of the right-holder. According to Golding, the 18th century author Blackstone interpreted a right as "*a power of acting as one thinks fit, without any restraint or control, unless by the law of nature.*"[34] At the time of the emergence of the notion of a right, it was freedom-rights in particular that existed. Only later were rights interpreted in terms of interest when, at the end of the 19th century, Rudolf von Ihering described a right as a legally protected interest. That was also the time that economic, social and cultural rights appeared on the scene.[35]

In view of these coincidences, it may be tempting to define freedom-rights in terms of choice-rights, and ESC-rights in terms of interest-rights but I would advise against doing that, for freedom-rights can also be described in terms of interests: people, after all, have an interest in freedom of belief, of expression, etc. And, as we have seen in Chapter 3 and 5, ESC-rights can be described in terms of freedom: they are aimed at enhancing freedom.

6. Discretion and human rights

In this context, I would like to spend a few more words on demonstrating that the freedom of the choice-approach is different from the freedom of the civil and political rights. The freedom of the choice-approach implies that the right-holder is in control of the relationship, both with regard to the existence of the right and the corresponding duty and the execution of the rights and the corresponding duty. She can waive her right, determine whether a duty (still) exists, she can insist upon the performance of the duty or she can relieve the duty-holder of his duty.

But is discretion a characteristic of CP-rights? Can, for example, right-holders of freedom-rights waive their rights? To answer this question, we can make use of the distinction drawn by Freeden. He distinguishes between *"a right that it is not wrong for someone to realize and a right that is necessary for human flourishing."* [36] I think that right-holders can waive a right which is not wrong for someone to realize. For example, if someone owes me $100, I can relieve the duty-holder from his duty to pay me $100 and, by that action, waive my right. But this is different with respect to human rights, rights that are necessary for human flourishing: one cannot waive a human right, whether it be a civil and political right or an ESC-right. One can, of course, decide not to make use of a human right at a specific moment, for example, by not claiming a right to freedom of expression or to adequate housing. But one cannot relieve the duty-holders from their duty to respect one's human rights, and one cannot say that one does not have a human right any more.

Many international documents—such as the UDHR, the ICESCR and the ICCPR—speak about inalienable rights. To quote the UDHR: *"Whereas recognition of the inherent dignity and of the equal and inalienable rights of all members of the human family is the foundation of freedom, justice and peace in the world..."*

The freedom of freedom-rights does not refer to a characteristic of the right-holder, discretion, for the freedom of freedom-rights is not about discretion. The freedom of freedom-rights concerns the object of those rights. It says what people are entitled to: freedom of belief or of association.

I raised the question of whether the choice-approach is relevant in particular for freedom- rights. It now appears as though this approach is totally inappropriate with regard to freedom-rights, indeed to human rights in general. If one is a proponent of the choice-approach and regards freedom of choice as an essential element of a right, one then obviously cannot regard freedom-rights as rights. To avoid this conclusion, one could modify the choice-approach by drawing a distinction between discretion with regard to the *existence* of a right, and discretion with regard to the *execution* of the right. One could then continue by saying that for something to be a right, it is not necessary that the *existence* of the right be at discretion of the rightholder, but that it is enough for the rightholder to be able to control the *execution* of the right. Such a modified version of the choice-approach seems to be compatible with the inalienability of human rights. One could then recognize that human rights are inalienable—meaning that they cannot be waived—but insist that the right-holder should be in control of the execution, to the extent that she can determine whether (legal or moral) measures should be taken to guarantee the realization of the right.

Consider, for example, the European Convention on Human Rights. It offers those whose rights are violated the opportunity to lodge a complaint with the European Court of Human Rights in Strassbourg. Now, the adherent of a modified version of the choice-approach could say that this demonstrates that the right-holder is in control of the execution of the rights mentioned in the European Convention and that this proves that those rights, seen from a modified choice-approach, are real rights. In addition, the rights of the International Covenant on Civil and Political Rights can be seen as real rights from a modified choice-approach, given that this covenant has an Optional Protocol, one that enables individuals whose rights are violated to submit written communications to the Committee set up by the ICCPR.

A modified choice-approach can be used to describe the rights-character of civil and political rights. But is this approach also usable for ESC-rights, or is only an interest-approach appropriate for these rights? Hart himself was of the opinion that, in principle, a choice-approach is applicable to domestic social rights. If a country has a national law, one that provides social security arrangements and gives its citizens rights to social security benefits, then a citizen can determine whether he or she will make use of those arrangements. And that citizen can decide whether he or she will sue the national or local government if it wrongly refuses to give them that benefit. But, my question would then be, can a choice-approach can be used with regard to economic, social and cultural *human* rights?

It will be clear that an unqualified version of a choice-approach is as inapplicable with regard to ESC-rights as it is with regard to civil and political rights. Human rights are inalienable, civil and political rights as well as economic, social and cultural rights. One can choose not to use one's right to adequate housing or access to healthcare, but one cannot waive one's human right to them in the first place. If one insists upon an unqualified version of a choice-theory and considers discretion with regard to the *existence* of a right and the corresponding duty a necessary characteristic of a right, then ESC-rights cannot be considered rights. But here, also, someone could advocate a modified choice-approach and say that it is sufficient for something to be considered a right if the right-holder is in control of the *execution* of the rights and the duty of someone else. Then, however, we have a problem, for unlike civil and political rights, ESC-rights do not provide individuals whose rights are violated with an opportunity to go to court or to lodge complaints with a monitoring body.

Some politicians and academics argue in favor of recognizing such an opportunity and a draft Optional Protocol to the ICESCR has been formulated, but currently the execution of the ESC-rights and the duties flowing from these rights is still not at the discretion of right-holders.[37] Seen from a modified version of the choice theory, ESC-rights lack the necessary characteristic of a right, that is, the discretion of the right-holder as regards the execution of the duty correlative to the right.

The foregoing need not, however, be the end of the pretensions of ESC-rights to be rights. The question is whether discretion—either with regard to the existence, or continuation of the existence, of a right and the corresponding duty; or with regard to the execution of a right and the corresponding duty—is a necessary element of a right. I think that discretion is often an element of rights in general, but I don't think that it is a necessary element of a right. It is even absent in an important part of law; that is, criminal law. For, in general, the law commands us to respect one another's property and demands that we not rob our fellow human beings: it grants people the right not to be robbed. When, however, someone is robbed by someone else, it is, in general, not up to the former to decide whether or not the latter should be brought to justice or whether the violation of the right concerned should be submitted to the judiciary: that is up to the public prosecutor to decide. So it is certainly problematic to regard discretion as a necessary element of a right. Yet the choice theory points at a characteristic which is, in my view, indeed a characteristic of a right: personhood.

Many authors underline this characteristic. Some find themselves even in the camp of the choice-theory, but many others do not take that consequence and show views that are akin to those of Agnes Heller. Wellman, for example, connects rights with the allocation of a sphere of freedom and control for the right-holder, a sphere in which it is up to the right-holder to determine which decisions within that sphere will count. Donnelly, looking for a description of a right, argues that the right-holder is not only placed in an advantageous position towards the duty-holder, but that he is placed in charge of the relationship insofar as it is based on his right. Beauchamp believes that having a right means that one is in a position to determine what others are supposed to do, while Ronald Dworkin describes rights as trumps that enable the holders to play them to stop the political measures that threaten to violate their protected sphere. Anthony de Jasay says that a right concerns a relation between two persons and an act, the right-holder and the duty-bearer. It signifies that the right-holder has the option to require the duty-bearer to perform the act (or to forbear from performing it). Charles Taylor argues that recognizing rights implies that individuals or groups are given the power to limit the scope of other people's actions: the right-holder is given a *margin of liberty*.[38] Al these authors will agree, so I presume, that the notion of a right refers to the special moral status people have as human beings.

7. Societal recognition of rights

To summarize the preceding paragraphs: a minimalist approach regards the presence of a duty-holder and a beneficiary of that duty as necessary elements of a right. I believe that is correct, but more elements are needed before we are able to speak of a right. The intentionalist approach adds that to be a right-holder, one should be the direct and intended beneficiary. I think that is also correct. What is also necessary, to my mind, for something to be a right is the idea of personhood, the idea that a right-holder is a person to whom a duty is owed.

And when considering ESC-rights, I tend to believe that they not only contain the elements of duty, interest, and intentionality, but also that of personhood. Every individual human being has a right to food, to adequate housing, to education; other people owe them that. And every human being is not only the intended beneficiary of a duty, but the duty to guarantee food, adequate housing and education is also *owed* to every human being. As will have become clear from the foregoing I do not regard discretion as a necessary element of a right, as is done by the choice-theory, that stresses that being a right-holder means that one is in control of the relationship. While I agree that a right-holder is often in control of the relationship, I don't believe that this is a necessary element of a right.

More elements of a right can be distinguished. The statement that someone has a right needs justification for, if justified, and only if justified, the interest referred to in the right should be protected.[39] In daily life today we are witnessing a huge increase in claims that certain rights exist and that, accordingly, certain interests should be protected. We could even speak of a proliferation of 'rights talk'.[40] We hear people saying that they have a right to children, a right to die, to a care-free youth, to an unconcerned old age, to in-vitro fertilization, to entertainment, to listen to music, to bear arms, to use marijuana, to sunlight, to be loved, to use contraception, even to holidays without rain.... And the people presenting these 'rights' may even dare to say that duties exist in others, that they are intended beneficiaries and that such duties are owed to them. But the question is whether these claims are, indeed, justified and whether, indeed, such rights exist. A right does not exist just because someone wants it to exist.

If a law gives me a right to an old-age pension, then my claim that a right exists and that my interest in such a pension is protected, is self-evident: it is justified by a rule of national law, a rule that I can advance to justify my claim. And if a right to food is mentioned in a document of international law, it means that the claim of a poor person that a right exists and that his interest in food should be protected is also justified by international law. In both cases, one can say that the claim is justified by a form of societal recognition. But, can someone justifiably claim protection of his or her interests if no (national or international) legal provision gives that person the right involved? Can someone claim to have his or her interest in having children protected if no legal provision gives that person a right to children? Can someone who wants children refer to a right to obtain in-vitro fertilization if no such right exists in national or international documents?

If no legal recognition was granted, someone could still justify a claim that a right exists, albeit a moral right. People then could refer to the ethics of the society in which they live to justify their claim that a certain right exists. Not national or international law but social ethics would then provide the necessary societal recognition and ethics could then be seen as the basis of a moral right. Let us take, for instance the right to food, a right now recognized by international human rights law and by many national law documents. Yet in the period before 1966 (the year of the adoption of the ICCPR and ICESCR), the right to food was not included in legally binding documents. It was mentioned (since 1948) in the UDHR, yes, but that was no more than a declaration at the time, not a legally binding document, and one that had not yet even achieved the status of customary law.

Nevertheless, it clearly stated that human beings have a right to food and this was regarded by most people at the time as a correct moral statement. The claim that people had such a right and that their interest in food had to be protected was seen as justified, not by reference to legal documents, but by the ethics of society.

But if no legal documents exist, and if the morality of a society or the international community does not recognize a right to X, can one still justifiably speak of a right to X? Consider the example of a "right to die". It is often claimed that people have a right to die with dignity, that a person with a terminal illness should be allowed to commit suicide before death would otherwise occur. But in most countries today, people do *not* have the right to die[41]. So can someone speak of a right to die if it is not included in legal documents and if the moral beliefs of a community remain silent? I think they can, but if a person cannot refer to legal documents or social ethics as a basis for her argument, she cannot use the notion of a right as and when she pleases. She needs to be able to offer a *justification* of her assertion that a right to die exists.

She cannot, as a justification, refer to a criterion that is acceptable only to herself. For instance, she cannot say that she thinks that living without a partner is a reason to stop living. She must offer a reason that she thinks will be acceptable to others, a reason she believes to be socially recognizable. The reason may not be generally accepted or recognized, but it should at least, in her view, be acceptable or recognizable by others. She could, for example, say that living in certain conditions of unbearable suffering is undermining her human dignity, and that dying with dignity is preferable to such a life. That is indeed in fact offered as a justification of the right to die. Such justification refers to a value that is considered generally acceptable and, by that, calls upon societal recognition.

There are even some people who give the impression that they are arguing for a general right to euthenasia. The website www.antipsychiatry.org mentions the psychiatrist Herbert Hendin, M.D. who, in his book *Suicide in*

America, published in 1982, wrote "*Partly as a response to the failure of suicide prevention, partly in reaction to commitment abuses, and perhaps mainly in the spirit of accepting anything that does not physically harm anyone else, we see suicide increasingly advocated as a fundamental human right.*"[42] The right to suicide is not mentioned in international law, nor has it been included in the US constitution and, as far as I know, is not generally accepted by the ethics of today's US society. Yet it cannot be denied that it is, and has been, advocated by some people. So is it arguable to speak of a right? I think it is. However, if such advocates cannot refer to legal documents or social ethics, they should still be able to justify their assertion that a right to suicide exist in another way, in particular by showing that such a right flows from values that are generally acceptable; for instance, from the value of autonomy or freedom.

And, if it is said that "Children of Divorce have a moral right to grandparents", or that people have a moral right to abortion (in countries where a legal right does not exist and also the morality of the country does not allow abortions), the assertion that a right exist should be capable of being justified by referring to generally acceptable values.[43] In my view, a form of social recognition, however vague it may be, is indeed an element of the notion of a right.

8. Effective societal support: justiciability, enforceability, social control

The notion of a right presupposes that an interest is guaranteed by the holding of others to a duty. But such a guarantee is minimal in the extreme if it merely states that others have a duty without introducing procedures to substantiate such a guarantee. In such a case, one can only speak then of a right in a nominal sense. For a right to be substantial, the societal recognition should be effective and should result in real support. And that support can take various forms.

If a right is recognized by law, such support can be given by granting the possibility of invoking the right before an independent judiciary body: it then becomes justiciable, which is another possible element of rights apart from those already mentioned. Elisabeth Meehan uses the notion of 'judicialization' as an element of rights that distinguishes them from entitlements and she draws a distinction between 'entitlement' and 'rights'. Entitlements become rights if the decisions of an organ charged with the allocation of goods—for example, food, healthcare or education—can be checked by another organ. To put it another way, entitlements become, according to Meehan, rights through judicialization.[44]

I will use the notion of justiciability—taking it to be similar to Meehan's judicialization—to refer to the possibility of submitting the existence or realization of a right to the judgment of an independent body. For instance, if a question arises as to whether and to what extent someone's right to freedom of expression or belief is violated, and if that question can be submitted to a judiciary body, for instance to a national court, or to the European Court of Human Rights, then that right is justiciable. However, unlike Meehan, I do not believe that justiciability marks the borderline between entitlements and rights, but between legal and moral rights. Without justiciability a right can exist—to the extent that it has the dimensions that are dealt with in the preceding paragraphs—but it is then 'only' a moral right. It only evolves into a legal right by becoming justiciable.

To prevent misunderstandings, justiciability should be distinguished from the discretion advocated by Hart as a necessary element of a right. 'Discretion' implies that the right-holder can choose whether a right and a corresponding duty still exist, and whether and to what extent that duty should be fulfilled. 'Justiciability', on the contrary, is about the possibility of an independent body offering a judgment on the existence and realization of a right; and it leaves undecided whether this possibility is used by the right-holder, or some other person or body. It is generally accepted that people have a right not to be robbed. But when, however, one person is robbed by another, it is not up to the former to decide whether or not the latter should be brought to justice, or whether the violation of the right concerned should be submitted to the judiciary: that is up to the public prosecutor. The right then is justiciable, but there is no question of discretion of the right-holder. (Though sometimes the violated person has the possibility of civil proceedings).

If a right is justiciable, it will often result in it also being enforceable, which is again another possible element of a right. For example, if A and B formally agree that B will give a particular good to A, A has a right to that good from B. The right will be justiciable, so that if B does not fulfill his contractual obligations, the judge will command that B will do as agreed. And if B does not voluntarily obey the judicial command, he will then, in one way or another, be forced to do so. Such societal support is not limited only to justiciability but also appears in the form of 'enforceability', another possible element of a right.

While enforceability is often seen as the most elementary characteristic of legal rights, it must be noted that it is an element not always present: many rights have an uncontested status as rights even though they are not enforceable. For instance, the rights of the European Convention for the Protection of Human Rights and Fundamental Freedoms are widely regarded as genuine rights. They are even justiciable, owing to the fact that a judicial body, the European Court of Human Rights, is entitled to deal with complaints about them. Despite that, however, the rulings of the Court cannot be enforced as can the rulings of domestic judges. If a country, for example, is convicted by the European Court of Human Rights for having violated an ECHR right, and it chooses not to comply with the sentence of the court, it cannot be forced to do so. (This applies even more to the rights of the international human rights documents, that in general do not have courts but only monitoring committees.)

Effective societal support will also be present in moral rights, although it will take neither the form of justiciability or enforceability, but of social control. I should add here that, to some extent, moral rights do contain the elements of justiciability and enforceability: justiciability and enforceability will be seen as desirable. Stating that someone has a moral right will be backed up by the idea that it would be desirable if the right involved could be submitted to a judicial body and then enforced. In expectation of the right becoming justiciable and enforceable, it will now be supported by social control. Social expectations to respect a (moral) right, as well as social indignation when a (moral) right has been violated can provide effective support. If it is said that someone has a moral right (a right recognized by the moral beliefs of a community) but no impetus whatsoever exists to respect that right and no sanction—be it indignation, or 'shaming and blaming'—accompanies such a violation, it can be doubted whether a moral right exists.[45]

Yet what about a situation in which a right is recognized neither by law nor by the moral beliefs of a community, but by someone *pretending* that it exists: such as when the psychiatrist Herbert Hendin pretends that people have a right to suicide? Here the element of effective societal support will be present as a desire. The person who pretends that a right exists will probably admit that it is not, in fact, recognized by law, or by the moral beliefs of the community. He will also probably admit that it cannot be invoked before a court and cannot be enforced, but will, nevertheless, argue that it is desirable for it to be recognized, and that it be supported by social control or justiciability and enforceability.

9. Elements of a right: the notion of a right versus a concrete right

The central question of this chapter is: are ESC-rights genuine rights? In order to answer this, we first need to answer two preliminary questions. One, what is meant by genuine rights? Two, what are the contents of the right involved?

As to the first question, I have distinguished many factors that can be considered the necessary elements of a right: the presence of a duty-holder, the presence of a beneficiary of the duty, intentionality, discretion, personhood, societal recognition, effective support in the form of social control or justiciability and enforceability. Various persons may have different ideas about the necessary elements of a right and, therefore, different views on the notion of a right. Some may regard every element as necessary for something to be a right, while others may regard only a few dimensions as necessary.

elements of a right		legal right	moral right
duty		x	x
interest/beneficiary		x	x
intentionality		x	x
personhood		x	x
discretion			
societal recognition		x	x
societal support	justiciability	x	
	enforceability		
	social control		x

Personally, I regard the presence of a duty(-bearer), the presence of a beneficiary, intentionality, personhood, societal recognition, and a form of effective support as the necessary dimensions of a right. Discretion is, in my view, not a necessary element, certainly not of human rights. As demonstrated earlier, human rights are inalienable and the implementation or realization of such a right is often not at the discretion of the right-holder. With respect to effective support, justiciability is a necessary element of a legal right and social control a necessary element of a moral rights. Enforceability is, in my view, not a necessary element of a legal right and certainly not of a moral right. And while others may have a different view on the necessary dimensions of a right, I think that many would support my view. So let us call that a 'medium size' view and take it as a starting-point for the following considerations.

When it is clear what is meant by *a right*—that is, what the notion of a right implies—the next issue is to determine the supposed content of a particular right, for example the right to food, or the right to housing of article 11 of the ICESCR (*"The States Parties to the present Covenant recognize the right of everyone to an adequate standard of living for himself and his family, including adequate food, clothing and housing, and to the continuous improvement of living conditions"*). Determining the content of the right comes down to its interpretation. In particular, it must be determined whether the elements regarded as necessary elements of *a* right are, in fact, present in the right involved. Someone who takes a medium-size view on rights will ask the following questions: What is the interest that is being protected? By what kind of duty is it protected and who is the duty-holder? Is the beneficiary an intended and direct beneficiary? Are beneficiaries regarded as persons to whom the duty is owed? Is the right recognized? Is it effectively supported? And a person who, as Hart, is an adherent of the choice-approach of rights and regards discretion as a necessary element of a right, will ask in addition whether indeed the right-holder of the right in question is in charge of the relationship. In considering these questions, various people may well have different ideas and interpretations of the contents of the right in question. Some may interpret it as presenting duty-holders, intended beneficiaries, sovereign persons, societal recognition, effective support, while others may interpret it as having only some of those elements.

As regards civil and political rights, I take it that most people will agree on the presence of the various elements of the notion of a right (medium-size) in the contents of the concrete CP-rights. Let us consider as an example the right to be free from torture. Article 7 of the ICCPR, containing the right to be free from torture, states that *"No one shall be subjected to torture or to cruel, inhuman or degrading treatment or punishment. In particular, no one shall be subjected without his free consent to medical or scientific experimentation."* Is this right to freedom from torture a genuine right? Most people would regard that as a redundant and somewhat ridiculous question. All the elements of a right (medium-size) are present in the concrete right. Hardly anybody will have problems in demonstrating that the right to be free from torture meets the requirements of a right: they will have few problems in indicating the duty-holder and the intended beneficiary, or in proving that the beneficiary is a person to whom a duty is owed. They will also have few problems in pointing out societal recognition and effective societal support.

So it is, therefore, a right. And, when article 18 of the ICCPR states that *"Everyone shall have the right to freedom of thought, conscience and religion..."* most people would accept that the necessary elements of a right are, in fact, present in this concrete right. And I doubt that article 19, stating that *"Everyone shall have the right to hold opinions without interference,"* would cause few problems either.

But what about ESC-rights? One could forego a uniform model that uses one conception of a right for all rights and move to a flexible approach that uses different conceptions of a right with respect to different rights. Such an approach would proceed as follows. Some ESC-rights do not meet the requirements of a 'medium-size' right, but they *do* meet the requirements of a 'thinner-sized' right. As for article 11 of the ICESCR[46] for example someone could argue that it contains all the elements of a medium-size right except for the element of justiciability. One might however be prepared to call it a right by downplaying one's conception of a right for ESC-rights and state that for ESC-rights to be a right the element of justiciability is not necessary. And with regard to some other ESC-rights one might be prepared to downplay one's conception of a right even further. The first paragraph of article 10 of the ICESCR states that *"The widest possible protection and assistance should be accorded to the family, which is the natural and fundamental group unit of society..."* It seems to me that this "right" lacks many elements of a right (medium-size). Nevertheless someone may be prepared to call it a right by using a very thin conception of a right. Moving to a thin conception of a right for the rights mentioned in the previously discussed article 47 from Part IV of the Indian Constitution and article 22 of the Dutch Constitution might also allow one to call these "rights" rights, although they, so it seems to me, do not have all the necessary elements of a right (medium-size).

But why should one take such a flexible approach? Why, when it comes to ESC-rights, should we not stick to a 'medium-sized' conception of a right? It could be argued, of course, that a particular legal or moral right may be stronger than another, that it demonstrates more elements of a right than others. But why should we, when confronted with an ESC-right, assume that it has less elements of a right than a civil and political right? And, why should we then use a 'thin' view of rights to enable us to continue to speak of a right? The answer might be that we should look reality in the face and that we cannot deny the difference between CP-rights and ESC-rights, in particular with respect to the element of justiciability. If we stick to a medium-sized conception of a right also with regard to ESC-rights and insist that these rights, in order to be genuine rights, should have all the elements of a medium-size right, justiciability included, then hardly any ESC-right can qualify as a right, because none of them are justiciable. Is this presupposition correct? Are ESC-rights un-justiciable?

10. Justiciability again

I have described justiciability as the possibility that an independent and competent body issues a judgment on the realization of a right and the fulfillment of a duty flowing from that right. Following on from Paul Hunt, I would like to distinguish two aspects of justiciability.[47]

Firstly, justiciability can refer to the character or nature of the right. A right then can be seen as justiciable if the possibility of an independent and competent body issuing a judgment on the realization of the right is not blocked by the nature of the right. Saying that ESC-rights are not justiciable in this sense means that they are, by their very nature, incapable of being judged, in particular because they are too vague and because it is difficult to define their corresponding duties.

Secondly, it can refer to the presence of a competent judicial or quasi-judicial body. A right then can be seen as justiciable if the possibility of an independent and competent body issuing a judgment on the realization of the right is not blocked by the absence of such a body. Therefore, if it is said that ESC-rights are not justiciable in this sense it means that no judicial or quasi-judicial bodies exist that are entitled—and competent—to judge whether or not certain measures of the government (or other duty-holders) are just. This 'un-justiciability' is defended by the argument that allowing independent judicial or quasi-judicial bodies to pass judgments on governmental policy is a violation of the idea of separation of powers: that judgments on governmental policy should be left to political bodies.[48]

Civil and political rights are considered to be justiciable in both aspects. Their very nature does not prevent the possibility of submitting their realization to the judgment of judicial bodies. Unlike ESC-rights, so it is generally thought, they are clear and lucid. Because of that they are justiciable in the first sense. Besides, both at the national and international level, independent and competent bodies exist that are entitled to pass judgments on the realization of the rights, which implies that they are justiciable in the second sense.

National courts are often entitled to judge the realization of civil and political rights incorporated in a national constitution. The Indian Constitution, for instance, states in article 32 of Part III, *'Fundamental Rights'*, that *"the right to move the Supreme Court by appropriate proceedings for the enforcement of the rights conferred by this Part is guaranteed."* Some constitutions also give national courts the authority to judge the realization of international civil and political rights. For instance, the national judge in the Netherlands is competent to deal with violations of the rights of the European Convention for the Protection of Fundamental Rights and Freedoms.

In addition to national judiciary bodies that are competent to judge the realization of national or international civil and political rights, international judicial or quasi-judicial bodies exist that are entitled to judge the realization of CP-rights. The European Convention has set up a European Court of Human Rights, at which complaints about violations of the convention can be launched. But while it is beyond dispute that the rights of the ECHR are justiciable, they are not formally enforceable. However, in practice, almost all countries comply with the rulings of the European Court and, if they show any inclination not to comply, political pressure by other European countries usually moves them in the right direction.[49]

The UN counterpart of the ECHR, the ICCPR, does not have a genuine court. However, it does have a monitoring body, the Human Rights Committee, to which states are expected to submit reports on their human rights record. The committee then gives its verdict on the realization of the rights of the ICCPR. In addition, there is an Optional Protocol to the ICCPR, which provides for an individual complaints procedure, so that citizens of countries that have ratified the protocol are entitled to submit complaints to the Committee. So, all in all, it can be said that civil and political rights are justiciable.

Unlike CP-rights, however, ESC-rights are seen as lacking justiciability, in both aspects. It is often thought that they are too vague and that it's difficult to assess precisely what they contain. It's also thought that they belong to the political domain and that judges should stay aloof from this area. Some documents even go so far as to state that ESC-rights are not justiciable. The Indian Constitution's article 37 of Part IV, *'Directive Principle of State Policy,'* states that *"The provisions contained in this Part shall not be enforceable by any court, but the principles therein laid down are nevertheless fundamental in the governance of the country and it shall be the duty of the State to apply these principles in making laws.*" The principle of Part IV essentially offer guidelines for the state. They do not create any justiciable rights in favor of the individuals.[50]

11. Aspects and elements

When we try to determine whether ESC-rights are genuine rights we must, as I have said, compare what we consider to be the necessary elements of a right with the elements of the concrete ESC-rights. But it is less simple than that. The point is that ESC-rights—like other rights—have many sub-rights, a fact which is extremely relevant to the question of what elements a particular ESC-right contains. These sub-rights may have their own elements, and ones which are different from the elements of another sub-right belonging to the same main right.

The Committee on Economic, Social and Cultural Rights has made clear that the right to adequate housing refers to various interests: the interest of having shelter, the interest of not being evicted, the interest of having a safe location, the interest of being with your family, the interest of having an adequate governmental policy on housing. In 1988, the General Assembly of the United Nations adopted the *UN Global Shelter Strategy to the Year 2000*. This states that adequate housing means not just adequate room, but also adequate privacy, lighting, ventilation and sewerage systems. The right to work can also be considered to protect various interests and, as a result, possess various aspects. It can be concerned with the protection of the right to be allowed to work, protection from being prevented from working, the protection of being free from arbitrary dismissal, of safe working conditions and of good governmental policy on work, etc. The same can be said for all ESC-rights (and CP-rights, too). Rights are complex and, being intended to protect the various interests, therefore possess various aspects.

If it is clear what interest or sub-interest is being protected, the next question is through what duty or duties that interest is protected. I call to mind the distinctions I made in the preceding chapter: the distinction between a duty of forbearance, a duty to protect, a duty to help or a duty to promote; the distinction between a duty of conduct and a duty of result, the distinction between a long term duty or a short term duty. For example, when speaking about the right to housing, are we speaking about an interest of people not to be expelled from their houses, protected by a long term duty for the government not to expel people from their houses? Are we speaking about a short term obligation of result to provide people immediately with adequate housing? Or maybe to a long term obligation of conduct for the government to develop a policy on housing? In addition it should be determined whether the interest-holder mentioned by the right is an intended beneficiary, whether the beneficiary is attributed some personhood, whether societal recognition and effective support is being given. It will be clear from this that an ESC-right can contain various aspects, i.e. sub-rights and that each sub-right will have its own elements (protected interest, beneficiary, intentionality, personhood, duty) that can differ from the elements of another sub-right. Only when it is clear what exactly we are talking about, can we say whether or not we are dealing with a genuine right.

Eide says that the right to healthcare entails two aspects: a right of individuals to access to healthcare arrangements, and a right to a public healthcare system in which epidemic diseases are fought. The former, so Eide argues, can be transposed into an individual, subjective right. But the latter is more difficult to translate into an individual, subjective right that can be invoked by individuals before tribunals or courts, even though it is nevertheless an essential part of the normative human rights system. Eide continues "*It can be made use of both nationally and internationally by non-governmental organizations (NGOs) and concerned groups, calling upon monitoring bodies at the international level to request the state to adopt more effective measures, and at the national level to demand changes in policies. The neglect of such obligations can have more serious consequences for individuals than the violation of rights which have been transformed into individual, justiciable rights.*"[51] Obviously, for Eide, the right to health contains both a justiciable and a non-justiciable right, although one could reasonably ask whether the second aspect of the right is indeed unjusticiable. In my view, it could well be said that while it is not enforceable, it can be dealt with by a monitoring body and that a monitoring body can pass judgments on its realization. I would prefer not to elaborate on that but, rather, to emphasize that the right to health and other ESC-rights have various aspects and that at least some of those aspects are justiciable.

12. Genuine, justiciable rights

I would like, finally, to advance an example that expresses the view that (many aspects of) ESC-rights are justiciable. The Constitution of South-Africa has a Chapter 2, '*Bill of Rights.*' It contains both CP-rights and ESC-rights and the rights share a similar formulation: "*Everyone has a right to...*" For instance, it states not only that everyone has a right to freedom of expression and freedom of movement but also that "*Everyone has the right to have access to adequate housing*" (article 26) and "*Everyone has the right to have access to a)- healthcare services, including reproductive healthcare; b) sufficient food and water; and c) social security, including, if they are unable to support themselves and their dependants, appropriate social assistance.*" (article 27). Article 38 then states that "*Anyone listed in this section has the* right to approach a competent court, alleging that a right in the Bill of Rights has been infringed or threatened, and the court may grant appropriate relief, including a declaration of rights. The persons who may approach a court are ..." The Constitution does not differentiate between categories of rights and obviously, therefore, sees both CP-rights and ESC-rights as equally justiciable.

The Constitution of South Africa has inspired the drafters of a new constitution for Kenya. The proposed new constitution (2005), that only remained a proposal, contained a Bill of Rights (Chapter 6) that encompassed both CP and ESC-rights. The draft Constitution presented the rights to social security, to health, to education, to housing, food, water and to sanitation as genuine, even justiciable, rights. Unlike, for instance, the Indian and Dutch constitutions, but similar to the Universal Declaration of Human Rights and the Constitution of South Africa, the rights declared used the following formula: "*Every person has the right to...*" For instance, article 63 provided that "*every person has the right to affordable and adequate housing*"; article 64 stated that "*every person has the right to be free from hunger and to adequate food of acceptable quality*"; article 65 stated that "*every person has the right to water in adequate quantities and in of reasonable quality*"; article 66 stated that "*every person has the right to a reasonable standard of sanitation.*" These rights were justiciable as CP-rights. Article 32 of the proposed constitution also stated that "*A person referred to in clause 2 has the right to complain to the Commission on Human Rights and Administrative Justice and to institute court proceeding alleging that a right in the Bill of Rights has been denied, violated, infringed or threatened.*" This effectively covered ESC-rights. A constitutional referendum was held on 21 November 2005, with the result that the proposed new constitution was voted down by a 58% majority of Kenya's voters.

As for international ESC-rights, the ICESCR does not provide a court and it does not yet have an Optional Protocol, although many argue in favor of such a protocol and one has, indeed, already been drafted. However, the ICESCR *does* have a monitoring committee and a reporting procedure and contracting parties must submit reports on the implementation of ESC-rights. The committee, set up by the Economic and Social Council of the UN in 1985, as the successor to a working-group that did not function very well, has acquired an independent and esteemed position. As noted in Chapter 2, the committee presents *concluding observations* as a result of a constructive dialogue on the reports submitted by countries.

In addition, it issues *General Comments*, that is, general considerations on specific subjects. These activities differ from judicial activities but, nevertheless, it can be said that an independent body determines whether an ESC-right is being realized. International ESC-rights cannot be considered justiciable if this is taken to mean that individuals can launch complaints about violations of these rights before a court or an monitoring body. They can be called, however, justiciable if this is taken to mean that an independent body is entitled to pass judgments on the realization of these rights.

All in all, we can conclude that there is no reason to withhold from ESC-rights the status of genuine rights in advance. Many people have a thin view on a right when it comes to ESC-rights, as opposed to a thick view where civil and political rights are concerned. Many others are prepared to use a thick view for both civil and political and ESC-rights, but then choose not to call the ESC-rights genuine rights because they lack the necessary elements. Personally, I take all the elements mentioned in this chapter, except for discretion, to be necessary dimensions of a right, with justiciability a necessary element of legal rights and social control a necessary element of moral rights. I would like to use this conception of a right (which I have called a 'medium-sized' conception) both for civil and political rights and for ESC-rights. Why should we use a different conception of a right when it comes to ESC-rights? Of course, a particular legal or moral right may be stronger than another; it may even have more elements of a right than another. But why should we, when confronted with an ESC-right, assume in advance that it has fewer dimensions of a right than a civil and political right? Why should we not accept the consequences of our calling ESC-rights rights? After all, it is not for nothing that a right is called a 'right' and that the international community has decided to call ESC-rights rights. Calling something a right means that you want it to have the elements of a right. The international community has expressed certain intentions and ideas by calling ESC-rights 'rights' and not, for instance, 'directive principles'. It wanted, and wants, ESC-rights to have the necessary dimensions of a right. Therefore we should take as a starting-point the fact that they are genuine rights and not a pale shadow of a right with only a few elements. We should then engage in a dialogue in which the complexity of an ESC-right is unraveled and in which the various interests and duties are distinguished. And such dialogue will then make clear that some aspects of ESC-rights have the character of 'directive principles' or aspirations, but that many other aspects of ESC-rights can be considered genuine, justiciable, rights.[52]

BIBLIOGRAPHY

Arambulo, Kitty, *Strengthening the Supervision of the International Covenant on Economic, Social and Cultural Rights* (Antwerpen: Intersentia, 1999)

Beauchamp, Tom L., *Philosophical ethics: an introduction to moral philosophy* (New York: MacGraw-Hill Inc., 1991)

Beauchamp, Tom L., *Philosophical Ethics* (Boston: MacGraw-Hill, 2001).

Cliteur, P.B., 'Waardoor worden de rechten van de mens het meest bedreigd: door utopisme of cynisme?', in: K. Groenveld (red.), *Proliferatie van mensenrechten* ('s

Gravenhage: Prof. Mr. B.M. Teldersstichting, 1996)

Cliteur, Paul, Neo-Liberal Globalism and Philosophical Presuppositions, in: Nieuwenhuys, Eva (ed.) Neo-Liberal Globalism and Social Sustainable Globalisation (Leiden,Boston: Brill 2006)

Donnelly, Jack, 'Human Rights and Human Dignity: An Analytic Critique of Non-Western Conceptions of Human Rights', in: *The American Political Science Review* 76 (1982)

Dworkin, Ronald, *Taking rights seriously,* (London: Duckworth, 1977)

Eide, Asbjörn, 'Economic and Social Rights', in: Janusz Symonides (red.), *Human Rights: Concept and Standards* (Aldershot: Unesco Publishing, 2000)

Feinberg J., 'The Nature and Values of Rights', in: E. Bandman en B. Bandman, *Bioethics and Human Rights* (Boston, Mass.: Little, Brown and Company, 1978)

Freeden, M., *Rights* (Buckingham: Open University Press, 1991)

Genugten, van W.J.M., 'Is het begrip "mensenrechten" aan inflatie onderhevig?', in: *NJCM-Bulletin, Nederlands Tijdschrift voor de Mensenrechten* 23, nr.3 (1998)

Gewirth, Alan, *The Community of Rights* (Chicago & London: The University of Chicago Press, 1996)

Golding, Martin P., 'The Concept of Rights: A Historical Sketch', in: Elise L. Bandman & Bertram Bandman (ed.), Bioethics and Human Rights (Boston: Little, Brown, 1978)

Golding, Martin P.,'The primacy of welfare rights', in: *Social Philosophy & Policy* I (Oxford: Bowling Green State University, Issue 2, 1983)

Green, Leslie, 'Internal Minorities and their Rights', in: Will Kymlicka (ed.), *The Rights of Minority Cultures* (Oxford: Oxford University Press, 1995)

Hart, H.L.A., 'Bentham on Legal Rights', in: A.W.B. Simpson (ed.), *Oxford Essays in Jurisprudence* (Oxford 1973)

Hart, H.L.A., 'Are There Any Natural Rights?', in: A.Quinton (ed.), *Political Philosophy* (Oxford: Oxford University Press, 1978)

Hart, H.L.A., *Essays on Bentham* (Oxford: Clarendon Press, 1982)

Heller, Agnes, *Beyond Justice* (Oxford en Cambridge: Basil Blackwell, 1989)

Herman Burgers, J.,'The Function of Human Rights as Individual and Collective Rights', in: J. Berting et al. (ed.), *Human Rights in a Pluralist World: Individuals and Collectivities* (Westport, Conn. etc.: Meckler; The Hague: Netherlands Commission for UNESCO; Middelburg: Roosevelt Study Center 1990)

Jasay, De Anthony: *Permission, Prohibition, Presumption: Three Ps in Political Philosophy*, dejasay.org 2004 - 2007

Martin, Rex, *A system of rights* (Oxford: Clarendon Press, 1997)

Meehan, Elizabeth, *Citizenship and the European Community* (London: Sage, 1993)

Narveson, Jan, *The Libertarian Idea* (Philadelphia: Temple University Press, 1988)

Pogge, Thomas, *World Poverty and Human Rights, Cosmopolitan Responsibilities and Reforms* (Cambridge: Polity Press, 2002/2003)

Nino, Carlos Santiago, *The Ethics of Human Rights* (Oxford: Oxford University Press, 1993)

Robertson A.H. and J.G. Merills, *Human Rights in the World* (Manchester en New York: Manchester University Press, 1992)

Shue, Henry, *Basic Rights* (Princeton en New Yersey: Princeton University Press, 1980)

Raz, J., *Ethics in the Public Domain: essays in the morality of law and politics* (Oxford: Clarendon press 1994)

Raz, J., *The Morality of Freedom* (Oxford: Clarendon Press, 1986)

Stavenhagen, Rodolfo,'Cultural Rights and Universal Human Rights', in: Asbjörn Eide, Catarina Krause, Allan Rosas (ed.), *Economic, Social and Cultural Rights* (Dordrecht, Boston and London: Martinus Nijhoff publishers, 1995)

Taylor, Charles, 'Human Rights: The legal culture', in: Henry J. Steiner and Philip Alston (ed.), *International Human Rights in context* (Oxford: Clarendon Press, 1996)

Wellman, C., *Morals and Ethics* (Glenview, Illinois: Scott, Foresman, 1975)

ENDNOTES

1. It should be kept in mind, though, that right-holders themselves also have duties, because people are embedded in a network of rights and duties within a community. I may have a right towards somebody else who has a duty towards me, but at the same time I will be a duty-bearer towards somebody else, who has a right towards me. If we do not recognise that we are members of this community of people, with both rights and duties towards one another, we are not entitled to claim a right towards that community.
2. These articles can be found in Chapter I of the Dutch Constitution, *'Fundamental Rights*. While this could indicate that these articles want to refer to rights their formulations are, nevertheless, far from the well-known formulation "everyone has a right to...", that can be found in the CP-rights of the Dutch Constitution. For instance, article 6 [Religion, Belief] states that "Everyone shall have the right to manifest freely his religion or belief..."
3. Stavenhagen 1995, p.70.
4. Pogge 2002/2003, p.56.
5. Jones 1994, p.26.
6. Nino 1993, p.31.
7. Bentham, Burns and Hart 1970, p.206; Bentham, Laurence, Lafleur, 1948, p.224,225; Lyons 1969, p.173.
8. Nino 1993, p.27.
9. http://www.emilyhendrickson.com/regency.html, retrieved February 2007
10. Bentham 1970, pp.206, 207.
11. Hart 1978, p.57.
12. Beauchamp 1991, p.306.
13. Robertson and Merills 1992, p.232.
14. Lyons 1969, p 173.
15. Jones 1994, p.28.
16. Lyons 1969, p.176.
17. Dworkin 1977, p.91; Martin 1997, p.29; MacCormick 1977, p.204.
18. Jones, 1994, p.28.
19. The Universal Declaration on Human Rights is not reluctant to use the word 'right'. However, as we have seen in the previous chapters, using that word may lead to the question of whether these rights really imply duties on the part of the government. But that is not at issue here. Here we are not interested in the question of whether rights imply duties, but in what the characteristics of the rightholder are.
20. Pogge 2002/2003, p.57.
21. Heller 1989, p.20; Golding 1984, p.23.
22. Feinberg 1978, p.20; Raz 1994, p.243; Raz 1986, p.166, 182; Green 1995, p.258; Herman Burgers 1990, p.69; Narveson 1988, p.46, Pogge 2002/2003, p.57.
23. Heller, 1989, p.21.
24. http://www.christiananswers.net/q-eden/commandments.html, retrieved 17-07-2006.
25. Feinberg 1978, p.24.
26. Beauchamp 1991, p 305; Pogge 2002/2003, p.54.
27. Pogge 2002/2003, p.55.
28. Hart 1978, p.57,58; MacCormick 1977, p.208.
29. Hart 1979, p.58.
30. Hart 1978, p.55.
31. Hart 1978, pp.58, 59, 60.
32. Hart 1979, p.58, Hart 1982, p184.
33. Hart 1978, pp.56, 60; Hart 1973, p.197; Golding, 1978, p.47.

34 Golding 1978, p.48; Golding, 1983, p.123.
35 Golding 1978, p.49.
36 Freeden 1971, p.47.
37 Arambulo 199, p. 173; Gewirth 1996, p.38; Cliteur 2006, p.34.
38 Wellman 1975, p.252; Donnelly 1982, p.305; Beauchamp 1991, p.305; Taylor 1996, p.74; De Jasay, http://www.dejasay.org/bib_journals_detail.asp?id=21, retrieved January 2007.
39 Shue 1980, p.13.
40 Cliteur 1996, p.17.
41 http://en.wikipedia.org/wiki/Right_to_die, January 2007.
42 http://www.antipsychiatry.org/suicide.htm, Nov.2005.
43 http://www.cyberparent.com/gran/divorce.htm, January 2007.
44 Meehan 1993, pp.125,126.
45 Martin 1997, p.38.
46 "The States Parties to the present Covenant recognize the right of everyone to an adequate standard of living for himself and his family, including adequate food, clothing and housing, and to the continuous improvement of living conditions"
47 Hunt 1996, p.25.
48 Cliteur 2006, p.33.
49 In 2006 a Turque court decided that there will not be a new court-case against the PKK-leader Öcalan despite a ruling by the European Court of Human Rights that the previous trial against Öcalan had not been fair.
50 See also: Cliteur 2006, p.36.
51 Eide 2000, pp.123,124.
52 Hunt 1996, p.30.

CHAPTER 9

GLOBAL NORMS FOR A GLOBAL VILLAGE

"How can universal human rights be legitimized in radically different societies without succumbing to either homogenizing universalism or the paralysis of cultural relativism?"[1]

Rebecca Cook

1. Introduction

The universality of human rights is often disputed. Many philosophers and anthropologists propose that it is impossible to draw a list of substantial, universally accepted, human rights, that at best some minimal, vague and hardly substantial rights can be considered universal. Most rights only have validity within a particular culture.[2] The development of international human rights has been accompanied by cultural-relativistic criticisms of the universality of human rights. Already in 1947, before the adoption of the *Universal Declaration of Human Rights (UDHR)* in 1948, a *Statement on Human Rights* was issued by the *American Anthropological Association*, which queried the suggested universality of the UDHR.

According to Raghunandan Swarup Pathak cultural relativism means that morality varies from culture to culture, that the variety of morality only can be understood by locating it in the cultural context and that moral claims are dependent on the cultural context which is itself the source of the validity of the claims. He says that, in the opinion of the cultural relativist, a universal morality does not exist and that the history of the world is a history of a plurality of cultures. Efforts to introduce universal values amount to imperialism, because values of one particular culture are imposed on people of other cultures.[3] The circumscription of Pathak holds three elements which also can be found in many other writers. Cultural relativism asserts that different cultures have different moral codes, that a universal standard to assess the various codes does not exist which makes it impossible to determine which code is best, and that people should refrain from judging the cultural values and practices of other cultures.[4] In Pathak's circumscription these three elements are integrated. Cultural relativism undoubtedly shows these three elements. But, they do not necessarily presuppose the existence of one another, and can and in fact do occur separately. It is possible to accept one element while rejecting the other, as hopefully will become clear in the following sections.[5]

Basically, cultural relativism covers a wider area than that of human rights. It disputes the universality of moral codes in general. Human rights can be seen as part of these codes, and many cultural relativists especially level their criticisms at human rights. The claimed universality of human rights in general is subject to the cultural relativist's fire. Besides, it is particularly the universality of ESC-rights that is doubted. Some are willing to accept the universality of civil and political rights but reject the universality of ESC-rights. Formally the universality of ESC-rights is, like that of civil and political rights, beyond question. Many declarations stress the universality of all human rights. The declarations of the world conferences in Vienna (1993) and Beijing (1996), for instance, state that (1993) "*all human rights are universal, indivisible and interdependent and interrelated*".

Despite these formal assurances, ESC-rights are not always and by all regarded as universal human rights. The criticism by Maurice Cranston is well-known. Already in the seventies of the former century, he refuted that ESC-rights are universal, in contradistinction with civil and political rights.[6] But, the universality of ESC-rights was not only disputed in that time. Also today many have their doubts about this claimed universality.[7] It must be recognized that it is often western authors and politicians, who, while setting themselves up as defenders of the universality of human rights, oppose the universality of ESC-rights.

In what follows I will investigate the three forms of cultural relativism that are leveled against human rights in general and the criticism by Cranston and others that in particular dispute the universality of ESC-rights. This undertaking will lead me to discern and distinguish six aspects of universality. I regard it as important to tell them apart, since universality in one sense does not automatically and necessarily imply universality in another aspect. Not recognizing the various aspects may result in spasmodic positions. Someone could vigorously defend the universality, not having an eye for possible relativist aspects. Someone else might cling to the relativity of human rights, not being able or willing to see that they are universal in some respects.

The six aspects of universality appear in the following sentence, to which I will refer in the course of this chapter: *"All people support human rights and are of the opinion that generally accepted or acceptable reasons can be advanced to assert that all (others) should accept the rights of all to the same goods towards all others."* The content of this sentence could still be unclear, but I hope the mist will lift as we go along. In this chapter I will deal with the first three *"alls"*. *All* support human rights, and/or are of the opinion that *generally* accepted or acceptable reasons can be advanced to assert that *all* (others) should accept human rights. In the next chapter I will deal with the norm itself, being that everyone has a right to the same good towards everyone else, or to put it differently that all should respect the rights of all to the same goods.

2. Historical relativity vs. historical universality

The first *all* says that all support human rights. This can be called descriptive universalism, describing a factual situation of all people supporting human rights. With respect to descriptive universalism two perspectives can be distinguished, a historical and a contemporary perspective. From a historical perspective descriptive universalism says that in the course of history *all* people have always supported human rights. And from a contemporary perspective descriptive universalism says that at this moment *all* support human rights. It is disputed by descriptive cultural relativism. This too limits itself to a description of a factual situation. It queries whether all people share similar values. It says that moral codes differ from culture to culture and that the differences are related to the cultural context in which these codes can be found.[8] Also human rights norms cannot be regarded as being shared by all. With respect to descriptive relativism also a historical and contemporary perspective can be distinguished. Seen from a historical perspective descriptive relativism dismisses the idea that all people have always adhered to the idea and contents of human rights. It adds that human rights are not eternal but have developed within a particular historic context. Seen from a contemporary perspective, it asserts that currently various moral codes can be found and that these codes are connected with various cultural contexts.

Obviously a historical, descriptive universalism cannot be sustained. The aforementioned *Statement on Human Rights*, issued by the *American Anthropological Association*, showed a historical, descriptive relativism, when it argued that the *UDHR* had to be seen as the fruit of Western liberalism. Also many later criticisms of the UDHR assert that it has originated from the West. Pathak among others, says that the UDHR *"is the product of a period when the United Nations was dominated by the West, and not unnaturally the Declaration presented a Western conception of human rights."*[9] Charles Leben brings forward that it is not difficult to show that the invention of human rights that has led to the UDHR and its subsequent documents, is related to the religious, philosophical and political history of Europe.[10] Jack Donnelly is quite clear when he says: *"As a matter of historical fact, the concept of human rights is an artifact of modern Western civilization."*[11] Also Ignatieff has to acknowledge the Western signature of human rights although he is keen to stress that countries from various traditions participated in the process of drafting the UDHR.[12]

The Western origin of human rights can hardly be denied. Seen from a historical perspective human rights are relative. They are not universal in a naturalistic respect: eternal rights rooted in an unchangeable universal human nature do not exist.[13] Some people though gives the impression that they believe in natural and eternal rights rooted in a universal human nature. The historical survey of chapter 1 makes clear that in the long ago human rights did not exist. It can easily be demonstrated that numerous rights that currently are regarded as fundamental human rights were unknown in past ages. (Slavery and torture were accepted practices in the past.) Human rights should not be seen as eternal rights rooted in a universal, unchangeable human nature, but as standards for a dignified life that arise in a particular time and a particular culture. If human dignity is threatened people will try to safeguard and protect that dignity. The manner and means used will be dependent on particular historical and cultural contexts. The modern world has employed individual rights. It is not unimaginable that in different times and in different cultures other means were and are used to avert threats to human dignity. Not only the idea of individual rights but also the contents of the rights are incumbent on the historical and cultural context in which the threats to human dignity are experienced. In seventeenth and eighteenth century Europe human dignity was considered to be in danger because of the possible and actual violations of human freedom by the state. This resulted in the proclamation of freedom rights aimed at providing a bulwark against violations of freedom. The nineteenth century showed that human dignity was threatened by societal powers that exploited economically weak people. As a result socio-economic rights were proclaimed to protect human dignity of the least advantaged against the powerful well-off. Today human dignity is threatened in another respect, according to many human rights activists, scholars and politicians. It is said that the cultural identity of minority groups and indigenous peoples is being violated. This results in arguments for the recognition of rights of cultural groups to have their identity preserved. Also human dignity is said to be threatened by environmental pollution and by armed conflicts. This has lead to arguments for the right to a clean environment and the right to peace.

In a historical, descriptive sense human rights are not universal, but the historical product of Western modernity. However, I would like to add that this statement does not imply that they are purely Western. Nasr Abu Zayd has argued that Western modernity has been built upon modernities that existed previously and somewhere else. Western modernity and its product human rights are the heritage of *"the history of human struggle, since Spartacus in Rome till Nelson Mandela in South Africa, against all kinds of human injustice."*[14] This should be borne in mind when it is said that human rights are the product of Western modernity.

3. Contemporary relativity or universality

The historical relativity of human rights does not mean that they could not subsequently have become universally accepted. Historical relativism of human rights does not exclude that at a particular moment of human history a phase is reached in which all subscribe to these rights.[15] To avoid misunderstandings I would like to call to mind that subscribing to rights need not be the same as respecting them.[16] We are still dealing with the first "all" in *"All people support human rights and/or are of the opinion that generally accepted or acceptable reasons can be advanced to assert that all should accept the statement that all have to respect the rights of all to the same good towards all others."* The question now is: Have we, despite the historical relativity of human rights, in fact arrived at a moment that human rights are generally endorsed? Are human rights in a contemporary sense universal?[17]

Since the adoption of the UDHR other cultures have manifested themselves in the human rights field and have become active. It is mainly due to the efforts and endeavors of non-Western countries that socio-economic rights have been making up arrears with respect to civil and political rights. Most of these countries may have been absent when the UDHR was adopted, but now they are playing their part. There have been world conferences on human rights (in Teheran 1968, in Vienna 1993, and also the Women's Conference in Beijing, 1995) where also the newly emerged states endorsed the human rights of the UDHR and of subsequent documents. Moreover, most countries have formally signed and ratified most human rights documents.

This may induce people to say that human rights are currently generally endorsed and in that sense universal.[18] The drafters of the final declaration of the World Conference on Human Rights in Vienna obviously thought so. The declaration says that the universality of human rights is beyond question.

It should be noted though that the formal endorsement of human rights shows some defects. There is no formal consensus in all its particulars. No human rights document has been subscribed to by all nations and many documents have been approved with sometimes very substantial reservations.[19] Besides, the formal endorsement is partly to be seen merely as lip-service to human rights. It cannot be denied that at least some people or countries do not whole-heartedly subscribe to human rights. This looks to support the view of Samuel Huntington. His ideas have often been quoted, in particular after the eleventh of September 2001. He argues that the world currently can be divided up into nine civilizations, i.e. the Western, Latin American, African, Islamic, Chinese, Hindu, Orthodox, Buddhist and Japanese civilization. These civilizations have their own particular ideas about the meaning of life, family relations, honor, friendship, interpersonal relations, the relationships between the individual and the community, and the arrangement of society. Human rights are a Western invention. They are alien to non-Western civilizations. The more Western countries press non-Western countries to consent to so-called universal human rights the more the latter will resist the human rights idea and resort to their own traditional ideas.[20] It must be admitted that many Third World countries harbor a suspicion against human rights. They consider human rights to be a Western product. And as they have suffered and still suffer from the imperial and colonial exploitation of their resources, they regard human rights as an instrument used by the West to advance its economic interests.

Some countries obviously look askance at human rights in general. Apart from objections against human rights in general many countries have trouble with particular human rights or categories of rights. As said before, many Western countries are reluctant to recognize ESC-rights, in contrast with other countries that rank these rights higher than civil and political rights.[21] For instance, the United States of America has signed the International Covenant on ESC-rights, but has not ratified it. China, on the other hand, did sign the International Covenant on CP-rights but did not ratify that covenant. Undeniably different cultures emphasize different rights. This can be conceded to cultural relativism.[22] However, watchfulness is needed. The differences should not be neglected, but on the other hand they should not be overestimated. Often it is argued that the Asian view of human rights has important differences from the Western view. But, what is meant by Western and Asian? Do we by Asian mean Japan, Israel, Singapore, China, Saudi Arabia, Iran, Kazakhstan or Tadjikistan? And what is Western? Is it Finland, the United States, Chile, Italy or Belgium? Asian and Western cultures have subcultures, that in turn have subcultures. All will have different interpretations and accents with respect to human rights. We should also be apprehensive of not equating the leaders of a country or its dominant elites with its population. During a regional meeting in Bangkok, preceding the 1993 conference in Vienna, the leaders of Asian countries stated that human rights are universal but that cultural particularities should be borne in mind. However, non-governmental organizations, also preparing for the Vienna conference, changed the word-order, which resulted in an importantly different position. They said that although cultural particularities should be borne in mind these should not infringe upon the universality of human rights. The views of leaders do not always run parallel to those of citizens, and also the views of citizens of a country will vary. For instance, the view of men often will resound louder in the political arena than the opinion of women. It cannot be taken for granted that the view on the position of women or of non-dominant minorities held by leaders of many countries is shared by the women or minorities themselves of those countries.

There is another reason for being careful about assuming differences. Similarity may lie behind seeming differences. Herodotus relates the well-known story of King Darius, who had within his kingdom peoples who buried their deceased relatives and other peoples who ate them. Both abhorred the idea that they would be forced to follow the practices of the other. For Herodotus this was an illustration of the descriptive relativity of cultural practices. The practices involved can also be regarded differently. The seeming difference between those cultural practices can be considered to conceal a common value of both peoples, i.e. respect for their relatives, which induces one party to entrust their relatives to the earth and the other to ingest them and to incorporate them into their own existence.

Lee Kuan Yew, prime minister of Singapore from 1959 to 1990, speaks about differences between Asian and Western cultural values. He emphasizes that in East Asia, the community is highly valued and that human beings are seen less as separate individuals than as members of a family. He mentions that Western thinking is individualistic, whereas in Eastern Asia individuals come to self-realization in and through a community. Lee may be right in assuming differences between Asian and Western values. But, his words bring to mind both conservative Western *family values* and ideas of Western communitarianism, a political philosophy that criticizes political liberalism. This shows that seeming differences often conceal fundamental similarities.[23] It cannot, however, be denied that differences do exist. It appears that these differences are neglected when it is complacently brought forward that *"the universality of human rights is beyond question"*.

Until now I have restricted myself to the descriptive aspect of universality or relativity. Within that aspect I have distinguished between a historical and a contemporary perspective. It then can be concluded that from a historical, descriptive perspective human rights are relative. Seen from a contemporary, descriptive perspective human rights can be regarded as universal if we look at formal documents, for instance the final declarations of world conferences. On second and informal thought, however, it must be admitted that some countries do not subscribe to human rights from the heart and that different and varied interpretations and accents are held by different countries. On the basis hereof it can be said, still remaining within a contemporary, descriptive position, that human rights are relative.

Human rights	descriptive level	
	historical	contemporary
relative	x	x
universal	x	

4. Normative relativity or universality

Cultural relativists in general will adhere to a descriptive relativism. But, stressing the variety of cultural codes will raise the question how the various codes relate to each other. Which code is better? This brings us to the second element of cultural relativism, which I call justificatory relativism. It says that people only have their own cultural values when they try to justify cultural norms or practices. It is not possible to resort to a value neutral position from which to compare moral codes and to assess them.[24] MacIntyre says that rationality is linked to a particular historical tradition. Not only the moral codes or practices differ from culture to culture, rationality is also interwoven with a particular historical tradition. Standards that are adduced to justify codes and practices are themselves culturally biased.[25] Also this justificatory relativism has a universalist counterpart. Justificatory universalism asserts that certain common and generally accepted criteria to judge the various codes and practices do exist. I will let the question of the justificatory relativity or universality of human rights rest for this moment and return to it in subsection 6. I will first pay attention to the normative level, at which the third aspect of relativism and of universalism can be found.

Starting from a descriptive relativity of human rights and passing the justificatory relativity of human rights, the cultural relativist will go on to a normative level. This does not describe what *was, has been* or *is*, it says what *should* be the case.[26] Normative relativism argues that one should not confront members of other cultures with claims of universality of one's own values. One instead has to respect other cultures and regard other cultures as equally valuable.[27] The aforementioned *Statement on Human Rights* of 1947 apparently not only wants to describe the variety of cultures, but also takes a normative position: it requires respect for cultures. I take this normative relativism to be the most important characteristic of a cultural relativist. What makes people cultural relativists is not just their saying that various cultural codes exist, nor their saying that we lack generally accepted standards to judge the various moral codes. What makes them cultural relativists is their adding that other cultures should be respected and that we should not judge norms and practices of other cultures by our own standards.

Opposite to normative relativism stands normative universalism which says that it is desirable that all people endorse a certain norm, i.e. a human right. The norm is thought to be of value for all, even for those who themselves do not yet endorse it. Normative universality of human rights can be expressed in weak terms or can be put strongly. It can be said that it is desirable that people endorse a human right or that people should endorse the right. The term "it is desirable .." sounds friendlier. But it does not conceal that a judgment on others' attitudes or actions is expressed, which is characteristic of normative universalism.

It should be pointed out that normative universality is different from descriptive universality. For only a few people can be of the opinion that all should endorse a norm, i.e. that all should endorse that people have a human right. When slavery was common practice, it will have been only some people who thought that slavery was unjust. It is likely, though, that they will have thought that others also had to endorse that norm. The 2003 Nobel Prize winner, Shirin Ebadi, argues that cultural relativity never should be used as a pretext to violate human rights, since these rights embody the most fundamental values of human civilization. She then says that the UDHR is needed universally, applicable to both West and East and compatible with every faith and religion. She hereby does not say that human rights in fact are generally endorsed but that they *should* be endorsed, accepted and respected, worldwide.[28]

Normative universalism has encountered widespread opposition. Many politicians and scholars argue that human rights are a Western invention and that they cannot be regarded as valid for non-Westerners. From within the West criticisms have been launched against the claimed universal validity of human rights. For instance post-modernist thinkers challenge what they view as the pretensions of the Enlightenment, in particular the idea of norms that are universally valid. This idea is seen as a way for the West to impose its will on other cultures.[29]

It is said that there are some points of tension between universal human rights and Islam. For instance Michaël Ignatieff argues that the separation of state and religion, and the freedoms of the articles 18 and 19 of the UDHR do not fit in with the religiously oriented society of Islam.[30] The universal validity of human rights or the claim that human rights have absolute priority is indeed disputed by the Cairo Declaration on Human Rights in Islam, which was adopted on August 5, 1990 by 45 foreign ministers of the Organization of the Islamic Conference. The Declaration recognizes only those human rights that are in accordance with Sharia, subordinating universal human rights to Sharia law. But the Declaration also is indicative of the interest of the Muslim world in human rights.

There are also different voices within the Islamic world. Nasr Abu Zaid, an Egyptian philologist, currently living in the Netherlands, says that one should not equate Islam with the views and practices of some Muslim states.[31] Although, undeniably, some of the political manifestations of Islam are in conflict with human rights and its underlying values, it cannot be said that the Qur'an and the authentic tradition of the Prophet or Islamic thought are inimical to human rights and their underlying values. Abu Zayd endorses many of the values of human rights, which he refers to as principles of humanity. He declares that the basic and essential teaching of Islam is equality of all humans regardless of race, color, religion or gender. This view is shared by An-na'im who argues that the justifying principles of human rights can be found in different religious traditions, including Islam. Riffat Hassan even calls the Qur'an the Magna Carta of human rights.[32]

Rejection of the universality of human rights is not always detached from considerations of power. Often the importance of cultural particularities and the need to protect cultural practices against universalizing forces is stressed in order to justify violations of human rights. Human Rights Watch mentions that cultural preferences, often wrapped in a religious veneer, are cited to justify restrictions on human rights, in particular the rights of women. To respond to these supposed sentiments, some governments press for international human rights standards that vary with local cultural desires.[33] The Special Rapporteur on Violence against Women has strongly rejected any appeal to culture to justify restrictions of the rights of women. "*States cannot invoke any cultural discourses, including notions of custom, tradition or religion, to justify or condone any act of violence. This also means that they may not deny, trivialize or otherwise play down the harm caused by such violence by referring to these notions.*"[34] Feminists have pointed out that that relativist arguments are used to justify suppression of women. Hilary Charlesworth mentions that it is seen as important to investigate the gender of the 'cultures' that relativism privileges. "*Relativism is typically concerned with dominant cultures in particular regions and these are, among other things, usually constructed from male histories, traditions and experiences.*"[35] (Speaking about women's rights we should be aware that these rights not only are violated in non-western countries as sometimes is thought. For instance, women are worldwide victims of the slavery-like practice of trafficking in persons. Even in countries that are regarded as fierce defenders of human rights, women are being trafficked. Many of the prostitutes in the Netherlands and Belgium have been trafficked from Eastern European countries, but also from Nigeria. In its Concluding Comments on the Report of the Netherlands the Committee on the Elimination of Discrimination against Women has said that is "is concerned about the number of women and minor girls who are victims of trafficking."[36]

Rebecca Cook thinks it is our task to find an answer to the question "*How can universal human rights be legitimized in radically different societies without succumbing to either homogenizing universalism or the paralysis of cultural relativism?*"[37]

Not only relativist arguments are invoked to justify political interests. Also the universality of human rights is adduced for political purposes. Some states only pay lip-service to universal human rights and use these as an instrument in foreign policy. They demand that others comply with human rights and are prepared to enforce compliance with universal human rights with interventions, whereas these interventions are carried out to advance their own interests. The British political theorist, Peter Jones, says that it is difficult not to be cynical about the way human rights are sometimes used in contemporary foreign policy. The invocation of human rights by governments is often "too convenient and too selective to carry conviction."[38] Similar opinions are held by others, for instance by Nasr Abu Zayd. He says that human rights have become an instrument in foreign policy, and admits that sometimes this may be to the advantage of people who suffer from violations of human rights. However, he continues to say that human rights are often being politically manipulated by the powers of the North as a means of exercising domination over the Third World countries.

When participating in the universalism-relativism debate it is important to keep in mind that the notion of culture is very difficult to determine and itself endlessly mutable.[39] Culture is not something homogeneous, it is dynamic, it is constructed, deconstructed, reconstructed. It is itself multicultural and consists of elements of other cultures. Also people are multicultural, having a variety of cultural bonds with various cultural communities, and borrowing from more and different cultures. Having said this, even if people are multicultural, even if their identity is complex and permanently changing, and even if cultures are complex and multicultural, this does not remove the existential importance of cultures as an anchoring ground of identities.

It is also important to mind the words of Coomaraswamy who warns that we should not fall into the "Orientalist trap" of dividing the world into two separate subworlds. Those in the West must guard against the idea that the West is superior as regards human rights and that the East is inferior and backward. Those in the East must equally be cautious not to accept the East-West dichotomy and must guard against the idea that the East is superior as it is communal and less self-centered with no place for this adversarial concept of rights.[40]

Human rights embody the fundamental values of human civilizations

People are different, and so are their cultures. People live in different ways, and civilizations also differ. People speak in a variety of languages. People are guided by different religions. People are born different colors, and many traditions influence their lives with varying colors and shades. People dress differently and adapt to their environment in different ways. People express themselves differently. Music, literature and art reflect different styles as well. But despite these differences, all people have one single common attribute: they are all human beings—nothing more, nothing less. And however different they may be, all cultures embrace certain common principles: No culture tolerates the exploitation of human beings. No religion allows the killing of the innocent. No civilization accepts violence or terror. Torture is abhorrent to the human conscience. Brutality and cruelty are appalling in every tradition. In short, these common principles, which are shared by all civilizations, reflect our fundamental human rights. These rights are treasured and cherished by everyone, everywhere. So cultural relativity should never be used as a pretext to violate human rights, since these rights embody the most fundamental values of human civilizations. The Universal Declaration of Human Rights is needed universally, applicable to both East and West. It is compatible with every faith and religion. Failing to respect our human rights only undermines our humanity. Let us not destroy this fundamental truth; if we do, the weak will have nowhere to turn.

Shirin Ebadi 2003 Nobel Peace Prize winner[41]

5. Unacceptability and inconsistency of cultural relativism

Cultural relativism argues in favor of respect and tolerance. This argument can be applauded. However, cultural relativism shows certain well-known defects, which I will mention briefly. These defects do not lie in the descriptively-relativist position that there are a variety of moral codes. That position is quite acceptable. Also reasons can be advanced to assume that we do not have a generally accepted standard to judge cultural codes and to determine which one is the best. But, why should this lead to a normative relativist position that we should refrain from judging codes of other cultures? Cultural relativism derives a normative statement from a factual position, which is a risky undertaking. From the fact that people of various cultures have different moral codes and that generally accepted standards to assess these codes are not available, it does not follow that nobody is right. That people disagreed about the question whether the earth turns around the sun or the sun around the earth, did not mean that neither position was correct.[42] Besides, if no generally accepted criteria exist why should we not stick to our own culturally defined criteria? What reasons then could be advanced to forego our own moral criteria?

This points at another criticism of cultural relativism, in particular its normative element. Normative relativism, which implies that people should not judge practices of a different culture by their own norms, is in fact a normative universalism—because it wants all people to subscribe to the norm of respect for cultures. Normative relativism reproaches normative universalism for impressing its norms upon persons who do not in fact accept these norms. But the pot calls the kettle black. The conclusion of cultural relativism is that cultures should be respected and that this norm of tolerance has universal validity. It holds a universal norm which itself cannot be based on a universal fact. In order to be able to promote tolerance cultural relativism should—if it wants to be consistent—base promoting tolerance on the fact that people already practice tolerance. But, it is far from sure that that happens. It is likely that cultures exist which themselves do not adhere to tolerance or the idea of respect for other cultures. This raises the question why a general norm which is not based on a general fact, should be followed.

This shows that cultural relativism is inconsistent.[43] A further inconsistency of cultural relativism regards the cultural-relativist claim that the practices of cultural communities should be regarded as equally valuable. The notion of value presupposes difference in value. If all practices are equally valuable the notion of value ceases to exist. If all soldiers are generals, ranks no longer exist.[44]

Next, it has to be stressed that cultural relativism is not only inconsistent but that it is also unacceptable. Normative relativism deprives us from the possibility of judging practices of other cultures that are in conflict with our fundamental values. Cultures could oppress individual freedom, they could practice slavery or torture, but we should, according to cultural relativism, abstain from judgments. Beauchamp says: "*The idea that practices as sexual exploitation, terrorism, slavery and genocide cannot be evaluated across cultures by some common standard seems patently unacceptable. It is only one thing to suggest that these practices might be excused, still another to suggest that they are correct or right, as this theory does*".[45] The impossibility for people to take a critical stand does not remain limited to practices of other cultures, but extends to the judging of subcultures within one's own culture. Also with respect to practices of subcultures people will have to keep silent. A next step can be taken: Cultural relativism can be put in a historical perspective. It then negatively affects the possibility and acceptability of judging past or future practices of one's own culture. If slavery was common and generally accepted practice within our culture somewhere in the past, can we then criticize it by means of our norms of today? The relativist idea can be moved to the individual level. One may then wonder whether relativism admits people to judge acts of other individuals and acts performed by themselves in the past. To quote Beauchamp again: "*When a former terrorist shudders in horror at the thought of what he or she believed last year, is it correct to say* that what the terrorist did last year was right at the time, but wrong now?"[46] Or can the terrorist say that what he believed previously was wrong, even if he then believed it to be right?

Cultural relativism is often defended by referring to the value of cultural diversity. I would like to say though, following the Human Development Report 2004, that cultural diversity is not a value in itself. It is only valuable as it offers people the freedom to live their lives as they think fit. Cultural diversity is valuable if, and to the extent as, it promotes freedom. Invoking the value of cultural diversity in defense of practices that in fact violate this freedom is unacceptable. Defending for instance discrimination against women by referring to the value of cultural diversity would be manifestly perverse, since the freedom of the women involved is violated, not promoted.[47] (It will be clear that prohibition of discrimination does not rule out difference in treatment between men and women. Discrimination is more than distinction or differentiation; it is action based on prejudice resulting in unfair treatment of other people. Different treatment may be justified if it is based on relevant considerations)

The cultural-relativist claim that it offers a basis for tolerance is an illusion. It has to be admitted that cultural relativists are right in saying that a dogmatic position, in which people are not open to reason and argument, is a barrier to tolerance. Cultural relativists can be given credit for that. In a dogmatic position people are not motivated to search for truth or justice, because they already (think they) have them. But, cultural relativism is not an adequate response to a dogmatic position, in that it does not necessarily lead to tolerance. It no more than dogmatism motivates people to search for truth and justice. What reason could there be for such a search if objective truth or justice do not exist, as is the opinion of the cultural relativist? If each culture has its own norms and practices, and if every effort to judge norms and practices of other cultures will run aground because we do not have at our disposal objective criteria to assess them, it is meaningless to search for truth and justice. If any tolerance is offered by cultural relativism, it will be a very thin one. It will consist of just being indifferent towards other cultural norms and practices. It will suffice with keeping peace and avoiding conflicts.

6. Normative universalism and justificatory universalism

This criticism of cultural relativism seems to have paved the way for normative universalism, the position that argues that all should accept a norm, or to put it more kindly that it is desirable that all accept a norm, in this case a human right. It will be clear that descriptive universality and normative universality need not go hand in hand. For only *a few* people, for instance twenty percent of the world population, or just one person, can be of the opinion that *all* should recognize human rights. It should also be clear that both descriptive universality and normative universality do not say anything about who should *respect* human rights. This is again a different aspect of universality, with which I will deal later and which I will call universality of the addressee. If it is said that *all* people accept human rights and think that *all* should endorse that *all* have to respect human rights, we are faced with three universalities. But, every "all" can be replaced by "some" without the sentence losing sense. For instance, it can be said that *some men* think (descriptively not universal) that *all* should accept (normatively universal) that *women* (not universal as regards the addressees) dedicate themselves exclusively to children's care. For this moment I will let the matter of the universality of the addressees rest and return to normative universality.

Normative universalism argues that a norm, in this case a human right, is a good norm, not only for the person who in fact poses or accepts the norm, but for all. It has value for everyone. Can such a position be justified? Here we touch on the second element of the definition of cultural relativism by Pathak, already mentioned in the foregoing. This element does not regard the descriptive level, nor the normative level, but the justificatory level. Pathak says that according to cultural relativism the source of the validity of norms is the cultural context. The justification of norms will remain within that cultural context. In trying to justify a norm people only have their own culturally defined criteria. It is impossible to resort to objective, supra-cultural criteria to resolve conflicts between competing norms from different cultures. As said before, MacIntyre argues that rationality is interwoven with a particular, historical tradition. Not only practices or norms vary and differ from culture to culture, but even the criteria, the underlying values that are adduced to justify norms and practices.[48] This justificatory relativism fiercely undermines normative universalism. If indeed no generally accepted criteria exist, the normative universalist claim that human rights are valuable for all, cannot be sustained. However, it remains to be seen whether no generally accepted criteria exist. The previously mentioned example of differing funeral practices of various cultures showed that generally accepted values lie behind seemingly different practices. It was respect for ancestors that motivated both cultures, although to different practices. Possibly also generally accepted criteria can be adduced to justify human rights. In chapter three I have elaborated on these criteria. I will summarize my argument here.

Human rights want to enable people to lead a dignified life. It is unavoidable that an idea of a dignified life underlies human rights. That idea of course should not coincide with a particular view of life, be it a religion or a non-religious view of life. After all, human rights claim to be generally acceptable. Therefore, also the underlying view should not identify itself with a particular view of life. But that does not mean that that underlying view does not contain a morality and an anthropology. The most important element of this anthropology is the idea that the true identity of human beings lies in their being a person. Human beings are subjects, beings who have self-awareness, feelings of joy, sorrow, distress, pride, beings who intend to have something or to be somebody, and who, endowed with moral and mental capacities, try to realize their goals.[49] These persons are vulnerable, susceptible to suffering and confronted with threats to their existence. They are social beings, humans among humans. They are open, i.e. not totally determined by their instincts and accordingly obliged to make choices and to take their own course. As vulnerable persons people want to have a certain level of material well-being to be free from suffering and to cope with threats to their physical survival. As social beings, they want to participate, to be recognized as human beings, as persons who count and are entitled to speak and to be heard. As open beings, people need freedom, i.e. be enabled to live their lives as they think fit. Well-being, participation and freedom are not only desired by people as an answer to their vulnerability, sociality and openness. They are also desired because they enable people to achieve their goals and to fulfill their aspirations. If people do not have at their disposal some minimal means of subsistence, if they are not somehow recognized or do not count within their community, if they do not have any possibility to live their lives as they think appropriate, they cannot realize their goals and aspirations and live a life as a human person.[50]

Freedom, well-being and participation may be called the key values of human rights. They form the justification of the specific human rights. Apart from these substantial values, the human rights idea contains other values, that do not relate to the content of human rights, but to the structure of the human rights idea. These structural values are individuality, equality and secularity. I have dealt with these values in chapter 3.

7. A dialogue

The question now arises whether these values (well-being, participation, freedom, individuality, equality, secularity) can be considered as generally accepted criteria to justify the particular human rights norms. I tend to think that they are generally accepted. Perhaps, not all people subscribe to the current human rights, but I think that all people support the values that underlie human rights. These values need not necessarily lead to the current human rights. Some people may share the aforementioned values, but they can be of the view that these values should be realized by other means than the current human rights. It may even be that they do not walk the road of the idea of human rights, but that they take another approach to achieve the same values. After all, not all cultures have or did have human rights. This does not mean that people do not pursue or did not pursue the values of freedom, well-being and participation. Also Shirin Ebadi, Nobel Prize winner 2003, appears to think that generally accepted principles exist. As shown above, she mentions that people have many differences. But, so she continues, "...despite these differences, all people have one common attribute: they are all human beings - nothing more, nothing less. And however different they may be, all cultures embrace certain common principles.... In short, these common principles, which are shared by all civilizations, reflect our fundamental human rights..." I think it can be defended that these principles have much in common with the values that I have mentioned above. But, apart from that, it is interesting that Ebadi says that the principles he mentions are shared by all civilizations. I hope they are. I hope the values I have argued for are accepted by all.

But, Ebadi's hope can be idle. My hope can be idle. Perhaps there are some who do not accept these values underlying human rights. Does that mean that I should abandon a normative universalist position with respect to human rights, for lack of generally accepted criteria to justify that position? Should I move to a cultural relativist position that, as shown, turns out to be inconsistent and unacceptable? In other words, does it mean that I should refrain from saying that human rights are valuable for all and that all should accept that people have human rights? Not necessarily so.

My solution could be to withdraw to a more modest position. I could abandon a belief in a real, justificatory universality of human rights, and admit that it is impossible to sustain the normative universality of human rights by criteria that are *in fact* generally accepted, i.e. accepted by all. But I can argue that the aforementioned criteria are regarded by myself as criteria that are generally accept*able* to every reasonable person, i.e. that in my view every reasonable person can see their importance for a dignified life, even if not all actually accept these criteria.[51] By "reasonable person" I mean someone who is prepared to search for agreement with others on the organization of society, on the basis of argument and communication without violence. By "acceptable" I mean that the values are susceptible to acceptance, in other words that according to the speaker the importance of the values concerned can be recognized by every reasonable person and that such a person will see that these values contribute to a dignified life, although they will be aware that in concrete circumstances the values should be weighed the one against the other and the outcome of this process will vary from person to person. The source of these criteria may be subjective, the applicability, however, is objective. I will call this position potential, justificatory universality.

I admit, I would have preferred a position in which I could justify my normative universalist claim on values that are in fact generally accepted. If these appear to be lacking, the solution cannot be to resort to cultural relativism, because then we would be faced with the inconsistencies and unacceptability of it. The remaining option is a modest normative universalism, in which the statement that human rights are valuable for all and should be supported by all, is justified by values that are regarded by the speaker as generally acceptable.

It is precisely this position that gives rise to tolerance, as I have suggested before. People who, like me, take this position may be expected to engage in a dialogue aimed at enhancing the acceptability of the values that are used to justify the position that all should support human rights. A cultural relativism makes such a dialogue redundant since it acquiesces in the variety and differences of cultural norms. A dogmatic universalism also makes a dialogue superfluous since the dogmatic universalist already knows for certain what is best for everyone.

The dialogue implies the willingness to mutually accept one another as equal partners and the willingness to accept that the common values agreed upon will be different from one's initial position.[52] In the dialogue arguments can be raised to show that one's own view is valuable also for others, as is theirs for us. People, including ourselves, may also be expected to reflect critically on their own ideas and to wonder whether their own ideas really are valuable. They can be expected to approach others' norms and practices with a presumption of value, i.e. to be prepared to see the value of these norms and practices.

The willingness to engage in a dialogue does not mean that the arranging of international society has to wait for consensus to be reached or that people in the meantime should refrain from expressing their views on particular norms or practices. We cannot start from nowhere. We should not fall into the trap of endlessly delaying our value-judgments. We should be prepared to engage in a real dialogue aimed at bringing into line human rights and the underlying values. But, at the same time we should strongly make a stand for human dignity as we now see it. After all, human dignity is at stake.

To conclude this chapter: universality can be found at three levels, at a descriptive, justificatory and normative level. The three forms of universality are present in the following sentence: *All* support human rights and are of the view that *generally* accepted or acceptable criteria allow (or even require) to say that *all* should accept human rights. As for the descriptive level, we can conclude that human rights are relative if we take a historical perspective; if we look at the current situation, we can argue that human rights are universal, but it is also defensible to say that they are relative. As for the justificatory level, we can conclude that human rights are universal if one thinks that generally accepted criteria do exist, but relative if it is thought that generally accepted criteria do not exist; they are universal if we confine ourselves to criteria the speaker regards as generally accept*able* and objective. As for the normative level, human rights are regarded as universal by proponents of human rights, and as relative by cultural-relativists. (The x's in the figure reflect my position.)

Human rights	descriptive level		justificatory level		normative level
	historical	contemporary	real	potential	
relative	X	X	X		
universal		X	X	X	X

BIBLIOGRAPHY

Abu-Zayd, Nasr, 'The Concept of Human Rights, the Process of Modernization and the Politics of Western Domination', *International Politics and Society* 4/1998, http://www.fes.de/ipg/ipg4_98/debabuzayd.html

Alston, Ph., 'The United nations and the Elliptical Notion of the Universality of Human Rights', in: *Is Universality in Jeopardy: report of a symposium organized by the United Nations in connection with the commemoration of the fortieth anniversary of the Organization, Geneva, 16-17 December 1985* (New York: United Nations, 1987)

Baehr, Peter R., *De rechten van de mens: Universaliteit in de praktijk* (Amsterdam: Boom, 1998)

Barry, Brian, *Justice as Impartiality* (Oxford: Oxfort University Press, 1995)

Beauchamp, Tom L., *Philosophical Ethics* (Boston: MacGraw Hill, 2001)

Cliteur, P.B., 'Cultuurrelativisme versus universalisme', in: *Civis Mundi: maandblad voor Nederland en België* 33/3 (1994)

Cliteur, P.B., *De filosofie van Mensenrechten* (Nijmegen: Ars Aequi Libri, 1997)

Cranston, M., *What are Human Rights?* (Londen, Sydney and Toronto: The Bodley Head, 1973).

Cook, Rebecca J. "Women's International Human Rights Law: The Way Forward," in Cook, Rebecca J., Human Rights of Women: National and International Perspectives. University of Pennsylvania Press, 1994.

Coomaraswamy, Radhika, 'Women, Ethnicity and the Discourse of Rights', in: Cook, Rebecca J., Human Rights of Women: National and International Perspectives. University of Pennsylvania Press, 1994.

Donnelly, Jack, 'Human Rights and Human Dignity: An Analytic Critique of Non-Western Conceptions of Human Rights', in: *The American Political Science Review* 76 (1982)

Falk, Richard, 'Cultural foundations of the international protection of Human Rights', in: Abdullahi Ahmed An-Na'im (ed.), *Human rights in cross-cultural perspectives: a quest for consensus* (Pennsylvania; University of Pennsylvania Press 1992)

Falk, Richard, 'Human rights and global civil society: on the law of unintended effects', in: Gready, Paul, *Fighting for Human Rights* (London, New York: Routledge 2004)

Forsythe, David P., *Human Rights in International Relations* (Cambridge: Cambridge Univesity Press, 2000)

Gert Bernard, The Definition of Morality, Stanford Encyclopedia of Philosophy 2005, http://plato.stanford.edu/entries/morality-definition)

Huntington, Samuel P., 'The Clash of Civilizations?', in: Foreign Affairs, *Summer 1993 Vol 72, Number 3*

Ignatieff, Michael, *Whose Universal Values?* (Amsterdam, The Hague: Praemium Erasmianum Essay, 1999)

Jacobs, F.C.L.M., 'Humanisme en mensenrechten', in: Paul Cliteur and Douwe van Houten (ed.), *Humanisme, theorie en praktijk* (Utrecht: de Tijdstroom, 1993)

Jones, Peter, *Rights* (London: Macmillan Press, 1994)

König, Matthias, *Menschenrechte* (Frankfurt, New York: Campus Verlag, 2005)

Leben, Charles, 'A European Approach to Human Rights?', in: Philip Alston (ed.), *The EU and Human Rights* (Oxford: Oxford University Press, 1999)

MacIntyre, Alasdair, *Whose Justice? Whose Rationality?* (Notre Dame: University of Notre Dame Press, 1988)

Maris, C.W., 'Culturele minderheden in een liberale samenleving', in: A.W. Musschenga, F.C.L.M. Jacobs (ed.), *De liberale moraal en haar grenzen* (Kampen: Kok, 1992).

Mayer, Ann Elizabeth, 'Cultural Particularism as a Bar to Women's Rights: Reflections on the Middle Eastern Experience', in: Julie Peters en Andrea Wolper (ed.), *Women's Rights, Human Rights: international feminist perspectives* (New York and London: Routledge, 1995)

Pathak, Raghunandan Swarup, 'Introductory report', in: *Universality of human rights in a pluralistic world* (Straatsburg: Council of Europe, N.P. Engel, 1990)

Rachels, James, *Can Ethics Provide Answers?* (Lanham enz: Rowman & Littlefield Publishers, 1997)

ENDNOTES

1. Cook, Rebecca J. "Women's International Human Rights Law: The Way Forward," in Cook, Rebecca J., Human Rights of Women: National and International Perspectives. University of Pennsylvania Press, 1994, p.7.
2. Alston 1987, p.54.
3. Pathak 1990, p.7, n.1;The interpretation of cultural relativism by Pathak is shared by many: For instance the Philosophy o f Religion says: "Cultural relativism is the form of moral relativism that holds that all ethical truth is relative to a specified culture. According to cultural relativism, it is never true to say simply that a certain kind of behaviour is right or wrong; rather, it can only ever be true that a certain kind a behaviour is right or wrong relative to a specified society." Tim Holt 2003 - 2006, http://www.philosophyofreligion.info/culturalrelativism.html.
4. Mayer 1995, p.176; Cliteur 1997, p.41; Pathak 1990, p.7.
5. Maris 1992, p.191; see also Gert, 2005, http://plato.stanford.edu/entries/morality-definition.
6. Cranston 1973, p.69, König 2005, p.115.
7. Forsythe 2000, p.29, 46,47; Jones 1994, p.146; Jacobs 1993, p.406; Cliteur 2006, p.38.
8. Jacobs, 1993, pp.405,406; see also Dower 2003, p.124.
9. Pathak 1990, p.7.
10. Leben 1999, p.73.
11. Donnelly 1982, p.303.
12. Ignatieff 1999, p.34.
13. Falk 1992, p.44; Leben 1999, p.82.
14. Abu-Zayd 1998b, par.5.
15. Cliteur 1994, p.63.
16. Pathak 1990, p.10.
17. Baehr 1998, p.27;.Cliteur 1994, p.63.
18. Sengupta 2004, p.2.
19. McKay 1979, p.67; See for example the reservations to the ICCPR and ICESCR on the website of the Office of the High Commissioner for Human Rights (http://www.ohchr.org/english/countries/ratification/3.htm#ratifications, February 2007
20. Huntington 2001, p.197.
21. Forsythe 2000, p.46.
22. Dower 2003, p.124.
23. Dower 2003, p.123,124.
24. Maris 1992, p.191; Dower 2003, pp.124,125.
25. MacIntyre 1988, p.7.
26. Dower 2003, p.125.
27. Beauchamp 2001, p.32.

28   HDR 2004, p.23.
29   Ignatieff 1999, p.32.
30   Ignatieff 1999, p.30.
31   Abu Zayd, N. (1998a), "Islam and Human Rights. Legal Resource and Research Center for Human Rights, 1998-2001" Cairo, Egypt. Retrieved November 5, 2001 from: http://www.geocities.com/~Irrc/Zaid/zaidhr.htm
32   Hassan, R. (1995), 'Are Human Rights Compatible with Islam? The Issue of the Rights of Women in Muslim Communities'. In: (1995) Human Rights in China and Islam. Retrieved October 26 2001, from: http://www.religiousconsultation.org/hassan2.htm#intro.
Hassan, R. (1996), AA Muslim's Reflections on 'New Global Ethics and Cultural Diversity'. In: A new Global ethics. Conference: 'The power of culture', November 8, 1996. Amsterdam. Retrieved November 5 2001, from: http://kvc.minbuza.nl/kvcframe.html?/verslag_hassan.html.
An-Na'im, A. (2000), 'Human Rights, Religion and Secularism: Does it have to be a Choice?' [full text]. In: (2000) The Butler University Seminar on Religion and World Civilization. September 19. Retrieved October 26 2001, from: http://www.butler.edu/philrel/an_naim.html.
An-Na'im, A. (2001), "Islam and Human Rights: Beyond the Universality Debate. Religion and the universality of human rights". In: Centrum voor Islam in Europa (CIE) (2001). Retrieved October 29 2001, from: http://allserv.rug.ac.be/~hdeley/CIE/an-naim1.htm.
33   http://www.hrw.org/reports/1994/WR94/Intro-03.htm, retrieved July 2007
34   http://www.crin.org/docs/SRVAW_07.pdf, retrieved July 2007
35   Hilary Charlesworth, http://www.austlii.edu.au/au/other/HRLRes/2001/9/, retrieved July 2007.
36   http://www.unhchr.ch/tbs/doc.nsf/(Symbol)/6c1554063d4c10f5c12572a4003cb6dc?Opendocument, retrieved July 2007
37   Cook, 1994, p.7.
38   Jones, 1994, p. 2.
39   Cook, 1994, p.7.
40   Coomaraswamy, 1994, p.40.
41   HDR 2004, p.23.
42   Rachels, 1997, p. 22.
43   Dower, 2003, pp.125,126. Beauchamp, 2001, p.33.
44   Rachels, 1997, p.22.
45   Beauchamp, 2001, p.33.
46   Beauchamp, 2001, p.33.
47   HDR 2004, p.24.
48   Maris, 1992, p. 191; MacIntyre, 1988, p. 7; Dower, 2003, p. 125.
49   Van der Wal, 1989, p. 202; Donnelly, 1982, p.303; Dower, 2003, p. 56, 57.
50   Van der Wal, 1988, p. 98; Dower, 2003, pp. 56, 57.

CHAPTER 10

IN DEFENSE OF UNIVERSALISM: WORLD CITIZENSHIP

> *"A central feature of a rights-based approach is that it is premised on the principles of equality, universality and freedom from discrimination...*
>
> *One of the features of a human right is universality. National governments bear primary duty for delivering on the obligation to provide water for all—but there are also global responsibilities. The 2002 General Comment recognized a special responsibility of the developed states to support poorer countries through "the provision of financial and technical assistance and necessary aid."* [1]
>
> **HDR 2006**

1. Cultural relativism vs. universalism

The preceding chapter has shown that universality and relativity can be found at three levels: descriptive, justificatory and normative. It may also have become clear that it is possible to be a relativist at one level and a universalist at another. For instance, people who themselves accept human rights can agree that norms vary from culture to culture, and even recognize that some cultures do not accept human rights. At the same time they can be of the view that human rights should be accepted by all, even by those who as yet do not accept them. Although such people are relativist at a descriptive level, they are obviously universalist at the normative level.

The universalist-relativist debate concerns norms in general and is linked to the question of who supports them, or should support them. As for human rights, some other, more particular issues come to the fore. If all people take the position that generally accepted criteria exist to say that everyone should accept that only men may have property, that only men are entitled to work and education, that only men may determine whom they will marry, such a position can be called universalist, thereby pointing to the meanings of universality dealt with in the preceding chapter: all people support the norm, and are of the view that all should support it on the basis of criteria accepted by all. Notwithstanding that, many defenders of human rights will argue that such a position contrasts with the universality of human rights. Apparently, another universality is referred to than the one covered by descriptive, justificatory and normative universalism.

The universality referred to by these defenders of human rights is not related to the supporters of the human rights norms, but it does concern the contents of the norm and is specific to human rights norms. Human rights can have three forms of universality peculiar to their specific character. A human rights norm takes the following structure: '*Everyone* has a right to the *same* good against *everyone*.' If we add this sentence to the foregoing, we get: '*All people* support human rights and it is thought that *generally* accepted or acceptable criteria exist that justify stating that *all people* should support the statement that *everyone* has a right to the *same* good against *everyone*.'

This sentence illustrates that the universality of human rights can have six meanings. And it is important to be aware of the specific meaning of it when speaking about universality. I have dealt with the first three meanings of universality in the previous chapter. I will now consider the three remaining meanings, all of which have to do with the specific character of the norm involved, that is, human rights norms.

2. The universality of the right-holder

Maurice Cranston argues that human rights are universal in two respects.[2] If a right is to be a human right, then it first has to be a right held by everyone. This universality of the right-holder also can be found in the writings of Ann Elizabeth Mayer, who describes universalism as the position that all members of the human family have the same unalienable rights.

Also the UDHR in its preamble speaks of the rights of "all members of the human family", an expression that is reiterated in many other documents.[3] Secondly, Cranston argues, a human right has to be a right against everyone. As is well-known, a right implies a duty. In the case of human rights, therefore, everyone is seen as the bearer of the duty that originates from the right. Here we encounter the universality of the duty bearer. Both this universality and that of the right holder are present in Shue, who speaks about "*everyone's minimum reasonable demands upon the rest of humanity.*"[4]

Cranston regards civil and political rights as universal in these two respects. Everyone is the right holder of the rights to freedom of religion, freedom of expression and freedom of association. Everyone is also the bearer of the duty and must respect these rights. But, Cranston opens fire on socio-economic rights, asserting that socio-economic rights do not comply with his twofold universality requirement. Let us in this paragraph confine ourselves to the claimed and disputed universality of the right-holder. We can notice that still many people share Cranston's view that ESC-rights are not universal as, according to them, not everyone is the holder of these rights.[5] It must be said though that many others take a different position. For instance, the HDR 2005 speaks, as mentioned previously, about the commitment of the Millennium Development Goals (MDGs) to basic human rights. It states that *"these rights—to education, to gender equality, to survival in childhood and to a decent standard of living—are universal in nature. That is why progress towards the MDGs should be for all people, regardless of their household income, their gender or their location..."* It gives the impression that the notion 'universal' refers to the universality of the right-holder. And if the Human Development Report 2005 speaks about universal primary education as one of the targets of the Millennium Development Goals to be reached before 2015, it also obviously refers to the universality of the right-holder.[6] To take another example, when the HDR 2005 says that the United States is the only wealthy country with no universal health insurance system and that its mix of employer-based private insurance and public coverage has never reached all Americans, it is obviously using the word 'universal' to refer to the idea of the universality of the right-holder.[7] Therefore, at least the HDR 2005 believes in the universality of the right-holder, even when it comes to ESC-rights. But, let us now have a look at the objections of Cranston.

Cranston suggests that many socio-economic rights exist of which not everyone is a holder. For instance, the right to just and favorable conditions of work, article 23 of the Universal Declaration of Human Rights, is not a right of everyone, but only of workers. The right to periodic holidays with pay, article 24 of the Universal Declaration of Human Rights, is also a right of workers. *"... the so-called human right to holidays with pay ... For it is a right that is necessarily limited to persons who are paid in any case, that is to say, to the employee class. Since not everyone belongs to this class, the right cannot be a universal right, a right which, in the terminology of the Universal Declaration, 'everyone' has."*[8] Other socio-economic rights are also not universal; that is, are not rights of which everyone is the holder, but the rights of particular persons or groups of persons. For example, only people who are ill and need health care, have a right to healthcare. People only have a right to social security when they are unemployed or otherwise in need.

This cannot be denied. But it can be refuted that, to this extent, socio-economic rights do not differ from civil and political rights. People only have a right to a fair trial when a trial is impending for them. People only have a right to vote when they have reached a certain age. I must admit, that this reply, stating that also right-holders of civil and political rights belong to a limited category, is rather weak in defending the universality of the socio-economic rights-holders. I would do better to argue that the all people are right-holders of ESC-rights and that everyone is, indeed, entitled to the goods provided for by the socio-economic rights.

The universality of the right-holder does not mean that people exercise their right permanently. What is important is that everyone can make use of the right when they come into a situation in which they need the protection it provides. Gewirth states that *"The universality of a positive right is not a matter of everyone's actually having the related need ... It is, rather, a matter of everyone's always having, as a matter of principle, the right to be treated in the appropriate way when he has the need ... Even if the rights are not always universally exercised, they are always universally had."*[9] These sentences are taken from his defense of positive socio-economic rights, the rights that require the duty-bearer to take action in order to provide the right-holder with the object of the right (for example, healthcare). But his position can be extended to cover negative rights as well, the rights that require the duty-bearer to refrain from doing something, for example, from preventing someone from expressing his opinion. It can also, with regard to these negative rights, be said that the right-holder is not always actually exercising his right. Am I exercising my right to freedom of opinion when asleep? And does that mean that I do not have that right during such a time? Am I, when teaching my students or cooking my meals, exercising my right to be prevented from torture? Most human rights are *not* always being exercised, it is true, but that fact does not encroach upon the universality of the right-holder.

I take it that we can assume that everyone is the holder of human rights. But is not the universality of the right-holder linked with the universality of the object of the right? Can the universality of the right-holder be proclaimed by saying that everyone has a right to X (to healthcare, to adequate housing, to work), without saying something about the quantity and quality of that X? If everyone has a right to healthcare, but people in country A are entitled to more and better healthcare than people in country B, is it then appropriate to use the notion of the universality of the right-holder? It could be argued that human rights should not only be universal in that everyone is the right-holder, but also in that the object of the right is the same: everyone would then have a right to the same quantity and quality of a particular good.

Critics of socio-economic rights assume that the problem of the universality of the object of a right will not arise with regard to civil and political rights. They take the line that everyone is entitled to the same quantity and quality of freedom of religion, or of freedom of expression, but they also take the universality of the object of a right to be problematic with regard to socio-economic rights.

3. The universality of the object of the right

Cranston touches upon the requirement of the universality of the object of a human right, although he does not explicitly present it as a requirement for universality. But he argues that human rights, apart from complying with his twofold universality requirement, should meet the test of 'practicability'. *"A right is like a duty in that it must pass the test of practicability. It is not my duty to do what it is physically impossible for me to do ... What is true of duties is equally true of rights. If it is impossible for a thing to be done, it is absurd to claim it as a right".* The duties generated by a right have to be practicable. If a country has very few resources at its disposal, it cannot fulfill its duty to provide its citizens with adequate housing or healthcare. *"For millions of people who live in those parts of Asia, Africa, and South America where industrialisation has hardly begun, such claims are vain and idle."*[10] It must be said that this is not an outdated opinion of someone living long ago, Cranston's ideas are still very much alive, like it said by König.[11] And Pogge shows that also nowadays many people regard the eradication of poverty as unpractical. Not only are many poor countries not capable of ending poverty themselves, they contend, but the rich countries are not capable of giving enough assistance to end poverty, certainly not within a reasonable period of time. Many think that ending global poverty would *"sap our arts and culture and our capacity to achieve social justice at home"*.[12]

I think Cranston is right in saying that it is not just to expect people to do something which they cannot do: people cannot be considered to have a duty when it is impossible for them to perform their duties. It is also an undeniable fact that the resources of various countries vary importantly. Given this fact, should we then conclude that the duties of the various countries vary and that the objects of social rights will differ from country to country? To put it differently, must we conclude that ESC-rights are not universal as far as the object of the right is concerned?

ESC-rights are aimed at fulfilling fundamental human needs, that offer people a level of freedom, participation and well-being that in turn will enable them to live a truly 'human' life.[13] Such fundamental human needs are universal. People in Italy have a need for healthcare, just as do people in Nepal. People in Chile have a need for food, just like their counterparts in Ukraine.

But, even if needs are fundamental, to the extent that they can be found in all people, their concrete manifestation is dependent upon the circumstances in which they live. They are dependent upon *natural* circumstances that surround them. People in Alaska or Greenland have a need for housing, just like the people in Zaire or Indonesia. Their concrete need, however, will be different because it is based on different natural circumstances. While some people have a need to be protected from cold, others have a need to be protected from heat. The dependency of needs on natural conditions may lead to different concrete needs and a human rights system that guarantees different quantities or qualities of a good, based on different natural circumstances, need not contradict the idea of the universality of the object of a right. What is crucial is whether the guaranteed protection is, in view of the particular natural circumstances, adequate.

People's needs are not only naturally relative, but also relative in a *social* respect: they cannot be detached from the social conditions people live in.[14] Needs of people are determined by what must be available for them to function adequately as a member of their community. And that is incumbent upon the particular arrangement of the society concerned. In a society in which no postal services exist and all communication is effected through phones and computers, people will have a greater need for phones than in a society whose inhabitants write letters to one another. In a society in which elderly people live with their children, there will be less need for governmental elderly care than in a society in which parents and (adult) children live separately.

Moreover, needs are not only socially defined by the factual social context, for instance, the ways of communication or the particular relationships between parents and children. An important point is that the needs of people also are constructed and deconstructed in a process of interaction: the extent to which people need a particular good is dependent on what others have and what others obviously want. This is shown by René Girard, who stresses the phenomenon of imitating desires.[15]

People desire an object if someone else has it. We are all familiar with the well-known example of somebody wanting a new car because their neighbor has one. But, what is more interesting is that people also want something if others obviously *want* it: our desires are generated by the desires of others. If someone becomes aware that his neighbor who as yet does not have a car, wants to have a car, he also may develop a desire to get a car, realizing that a car is a desirable thing. If a boy, who as yet has not yet been touched by the charms of a girl, becomes aware that she is desired by many other boys, he will very often develop a desire for her too. The fact that she is desired makes her a desirable person. This phenomenon of imitating desires can be transplanted to the neighboring world of needs: it is not unlikely that people's needs will be generated not only by what others *have* but to some extent also by what others obviously *need*.

Although needs can be fundamental in that they are owned by all, their concrete manifestations will be naturally and socially relative and the provisions for fulfilling those needs will, accordingly, differ from country to country. It must be add that differences may decrease. Globalization has created an environment in which many problems have become global problems, in which production and consumption no longer take place within a single society, in which knowledge becomes accessible all over the world and in which channels of communication cover the whole globe. This can affect the emergence and spread of needs. People in developing countries see what people in rich countries obviously have or need, which can result in an imitation of needs.

Notwithstanding this globalization process needs will, at least to some extent, vary from country to country, as will the possibility of fulfilling needs. This does not have to contradict the idea of the universality of the object, provided that everyone has an adequate quantity and quality of that object, given their particular, natural and social circumstances. The ideal would be that all human beings in their society, with its particular circumstances, possess sufficient freedom, participation and well-being to live a dignified life. If, however, many people in that society do not have access to these fundamental goods and, therefore, lack the necessary freedom, participation and well-being to live a dignified life, the idea of the universality of the object is undermined. However this should not necessarily lead to the conclusion that the universality of the object is absent. For, it is also possible that this miserable situation is due to the fact that the duty-bearers do not fulfill their duty, or are unable or prevented from doing so, which means that other duty-bearers are not fulfilling their duties. (For instance, IMF forcing states to comply with spending conditions)

4. The universality of the addressees of human rights

People do not necessarily have a right to the same quantity and quality of the objects of human rights, since the circumstances in which they live are naturally, and socially, different. However, they *are* entitled to the fulfillment of the necessary conditions for a dignified life. It could be that in some countries, even these necessary conditions cannot be fulfilled. It is generally understood that it cannot be demanded of a very poor country that it enables access to basic necessities beyond its capacities. It can only be demanded that the country provide access to basic necessities as far as is reasonably possible.[16] This leads Cranston to doubt whether socio-economic rights are universal human rights, because the adage that '*ought implies can*' cannot be complied with. "*The government of India, for example, simply cannot command the resources that would guarantee each one of over 500 million inhabitants of India 'a standard of living adequate for the health and well-being of himself and his family'...*"[17] As I have said before, Cranston is right: for if it is impossible for duty-bearers to do what is claimed to be their duty, they do not have that duty. But in the case of India, two questions can be raised. First, is it really impossible for India to fulfill its duty? Second, is India the only duty-bearer of the socio-economic rights of the Indian people?

An answer to the first question requires a political and economic analysis which falls outside the scope of this booklet, so I shall, instead, concentrate on an answer to the second question, the question of who the duty-bearer of socio-economic rights is.

Many regard governments as the addressees of socio-economic rights: the bearers of the duties flowing from these rights. Socio-economic rights are rights of people against their own government.[18] That makes such rights differ from real human rights, since they are rights against everyone else. I, however, prefer the company of others, for instance Nigel Dower, Alan Gewirth, Paul Hunt and Shue. They are of the view that the duties flowing from ESC-rights rest on everyone.[19] Sengupta and others say: *"A widespread misunderstanding has been that all economic, social and cultural rights must be provided by the state ... This view is the result of a very narrow understanding of the nature of these rights ..."*[20]

People have duties to one another, an argument which I advanced in Chapter 3 and which I summarize here: people are not isolated atoms, but members of a larger entity. They are members of familial groups, of cultural and national groups, and of the human family. They are beings with the same physical, psychological and mental equipment, even though they will differ in the particular features of this equipment: they may have different noses, legs, dreams, desires, but they will all *have* noses, legs, dreams and desires. They take part in a common humanity, as Ignatieff notes when he writes that *"... what is pain and humiliation for you is bound to be pain and humiliation for me."*[21] This universal human identity is our primary identity and more fundamental than any special identity.

Such an insight into a common humanity will raise a willingness to treat others as fellow human beings if people want to be consistent. People want to have freedom, well-being and participation in order to be able to live as a human being. If they claim to be entitled to these goods by virtue of their humanity, consistency will require that the same goods are accorded to others who share in that humanity. To assert otherwise would be contradictory.

But the reason for treating others as fellow human beings does not only lie in rationally argued consistency. Such an argument may be complemented by a moral willingness not only to perceive and note the humanity in others, but also to acknowledge and respect that humanity. This willingness will have two sources: the appearance of others as a person and the desire of people themselves to be human. Other people are not 'things' that turn up in our life and which we can use arbitrarily. They are not the means to our goals, but ends in themselves: their existence makes an appeal to us to treat them as fellow human beings. And that appeal results in our dismay when confronted with the horrors that may befall people, such as violence, war, rape, poverty and famine.

The moral willingness to acknowledge and respect the humanity in others could also flow from the desire of people to be fellow-humans themselves. People do not want to be isolated and excluded: they want to be one of many. But this desire cannot be fulfilled without some commitment, just like all the other desires we have with regard to being a certain person. People may want to be a nice neighbor, a good father, a loving spouse, a reliable colleague. Such desires make an appeal to them in concrete situations that cannot easily be ignored, for ignoring such an appeal implies that the people doing so are not doing justice to the person they themselves want to be, to the identity they want to possess. To a certain extent, they are even betraying that identity by ignoring the appeal, for they will not be the person they want to be, if they only do as they please without taking into consideration the requirements of their ideal.

It is commitment to being a particular person that will result in a preparedness to acknowledge rights and duties. My commitment to being a good father will result in my accepting that my children have rights and that I have duties towards them. My commitment to being a fellow-human, generated by my desire to be so, will imply an acknowledgement of the right of everyone to be treated with equal respect and concern and the correlative duty to treat others with equal respect and concern.[22]

People have duties to one another to guarantee the generic goods of freedom, well-being and participation, as well as the more specific human rights. However, in a modern society, people cannot themselves provide others with adequate housing, food or healthcare and it is impossible for them to carry out all duties towards all others personally. It is, therefore, far more efficient to agree on an allocation of tasks such as, to begin with, agreeing that the honoring of duties flowing from socio-economic rights should take place country by country. This would, by limiting them to one's own country, make such duties more convenient. Next, it could be agreed that the government of each country act as the representative of its citizens and perform, on behalf of its citizens, the duties of those citizens towards their fellow citizens.

Such an allocation of tasks can be justified by considerations of affectivity and of morality. Individuals cannot honor the ESC-rights of every other individual; it is far more *effective* when this is undertaken by countries and, in particular, by the governments of those countries.

In addition, ESC-rights can be honored more *fairly* if this is undertaken by countries and governments, because if the *distribution of the goods* necessary for a dignified life is left to individuals, arbitrariness or personal preferences may play an unfair role: people may, for example, only honor the rights of those they like or those who belong to their religious or cultural group.

Furthermore, the *distribution of duties* should be fair, for example, through a system of taxation that is intended to distribute duties fairly; that is, according to ability. For again, if the fulfillment of duties is left to individuals, some may be inclined to benefit from the efforts of others, without fulfilling *their* duties and giving anything back in return. Thus equal universal rights can be honored more effectively and morally if the duties flowing from these rights are fulfilled by countries and their governments. But this does not completely exempt individuals from their obligations. Governments are the direct addressees, but their constituents remain the ultimate respondents.[23] For it is upon them that the obligations to support this system of the allocation of tasks rests. It is they who should stimulate their government to ensure that worldwide everyone enjoys their socio-economic rights, and it is they who should enable their government morally and financially to fulfill its duties. Governments are responsible for honoring the ESC-rights of their citizens but they also are global actors, who represent their citizens who, as members of a global moral community are the ultimate addressees of ESC-rights of all human beings, and have a duty to fulfill the duties flowing from ESC-rights of their fellow human beings in the rest of the world. Individual human beings are expected, as the ultimate addressees, to direct their government to respect its local and global honoring of ESC-rights, even though, dependent on the situation, more can be expected of them than mere support. It may be, for example, that governments do not fulfill their task adequately: people can then be expected to find ways to bring their governments to the right path, or to find other, complementary ways to fulfill their tasks as fellow human beings, for instance, by giving support to NGOs in the field of development co-operation. Like Pogge says: *"Each member of society, according to his or her means, is to help bring about and sustain a social and economic order within which all have secure access to basic necessities."*[24]

4. Global citizenship

It should be noted that this picture of states being the direct addressees of ESC-rights, while individuals remain the ultimate addressees, is changing. In addition to states, other actors are entering the international field. Consider, for example, a political entity such as the European Union (a mixture of a supra-national organization and an intergovernmental organization); various international or intergovernmental organizations such as the Council of Europe, the World Trade Union, and the World Bank; pro-profit organizations such as multinational businesses; non-profit organizations such as churches, trade unions; and nongovernmental organizations such as Amnesty International and GreenPeace. All these organizations have become global actors in recent years and are all going to play their part in the realization of human rights. Also the HDR 2000 is of the opinion that it is not only states, but also other global actors who can be seen as the duty-holders of ESC-rights when it observes that *"As the world becomes increasingly* interdependent, both states—in their policies that affect other state—and other global actors have greater obligations to create a better enabling environment for the realization of economic and social rights".[25] All these global actors will have to be prepared to act as the representatives of individual duty-bearers, who remain the ultimate addressees, and to fulfill the duties flowing from ESC-rights.[26]

One could point to an important difference between CP-rights and ESC-rights. ESC-rights see individuals as the *ultimate* addressees and states as the *direct* addressees. CP-rights, so it is argued, see fellow citizens as the direct addressees too. The issue of *'ought implies can'* does not throw up a dam against the idea of individuals being the direct addressees: everyone can fulfill their duties flowing from CP-rights, because these duties are only duties of abstinence and are not costly. Everyone can and should, this argument runs, fulfill their duties flowing from CP-rights.

However, it is an argument that can be refuted. Firstly, it can be pointed out that ESC-rights, like CP-rights, entail negative duties in addition to positive ones. And if it is thought that negative duties can be fulfilled for everyone, this also holds good for the negative duties of ESC-rights. Besides, if it is thought that positive duties cannot be fulfilled for everyone, it also applies to the positive duties of CP-rights. A poor society may not have adequate resources to fulfill the ESC-rights of all its citizens; it then is likely that neither it will have adequate resources to protect the bodily integrity of all its citizens.[27] Apart from that, it does not seem correct to say that a negative right can be claimed towards everyone and that, therefore, CP-rights can be seen as complying with the requirement of the universality of the right-holder.

Is it correct, and does it make sense to say that Juan Valdez in Colombia can claim a right to freedom of opinion towards me, living in the Netherlands—that I have a duty not to hinder Juan Valdez from expressing his opinion, and that I respect his right because I do not prevent him from expressing his opinion? Is it correct to say, and does it make sense to say that Katomba Rozan in Liberia has a right to life towards me and that I respect his right because I do not kill him and obviously fulfill my duty towards him simply by—living far away from him in the Netherlands—doing nothing? And does Aisha Bagmatiar in Afghanistan have a right to physical integrity towards me and do I fulfill my duty by not assaulting her?

I think it is carrying things too far to answer these questions in the affirmative because I am not in a position to do otherwise. Given the physical distance between us, I am not in a position to violate the rights of Juan Valdez, Katomba Rozan and Aisha Bagmatiar. I do not even know these people, which means that I am as incapable of not-fulfilling my duty as I am of not attacking Mars. 'Ought implies can', yes, but 'ought' also implies being capable of violating the norm. Only when I am in a position to infringe someone's right does it makes sense to speak of a duty of abstinence. As long as I am not capable of not fulfilling my duty of abstinence it may make sense to speak of a potential duty.

It appears that also with respect to negative CP-rights, a distinction can be drawn between direct addressees and ultimate, potential, addressees. Juan Valdez, Katomba Rozan and Aisha Bagmatiar all possess the rights mentioned above. Their rights should be guaranteed. Their national governments and fellow citizens are the direct addressees and have a clear duty towards them. Of course it is possible that some fellow-citizens are not in a position in which they can neglect their duties. They are not-directly-addressed fellow-citizens. These not-directly-addressed fellow-citizens and all other human beings are the potential, ultimate, addressees whose duty is activated *when they come in contact* with the right-holders. Only *then* will it truly become clear whether or not they respect the rights of these right-holders.

The direct addressees—the national government and (most) fellow citizens—not only have a real duty of abstinence with regard to the CP-rights of citizens, but also positive obligations to protect and to help. Ultimate addressees also have positive *potential* duties in addition to the negative potential duties of abstinence, but which need not be activated at the same moment. Their positive duties may even be real, even when no contact has taken place between them and the right-holder, for instance they may have a positive real duty to bring about and to sustain a political order that guarantees the enjoyment of CP-rights.

It is odd to say that I have a (negative) duty to respect the rights of freedom of expression, to life or to physical integrity of all other people, including Juan Valdez, Katomba Rozan and Aisha Bagmatiar. But it is less odd to say that I have a (positive) duty to protect or to support these rights of all other people on the planet, even when I am not in a position to meet them. Right now, at this moment, I do not have a duty to abstain from hindering someone in Kabul from expressing his opinion. But I may well have a duty to contribute to the protection of that person's right to freedom of expression, particularly when their national government is an oppressive one, frustrating the right to freedom of expression of its citizens. I can fulfill this positive duty, inter alia, by supporting an organization such as Amnesty International or any other human rights organization.

Therefore, from all this, it *can* be argued that the universality of the negative aspects of CP-rights is far more problematic that that of the positive aspects. Cranston is right in saying that human rights presuppose the universality of the addressee. But, both with regard to CP- rights and ESC-rights, that universality will be vested in the ultimate addressees, who have potential duties which will be activated when they find themselves in a position to perform those duties. There is no reason to state, like Cranston and others do, that ESC-rights do not comply with the requirement of universality of the addressee.

All in all, it cannot be denied that differences exist between various rights. It can even be admitted that most ESC-rights show some characteristics that many CP-rights only have to a lesser degree. But, there is no reason to withhold them the status of human rights: the preceding chapters have shown that ESC-rights are important for a dignified life, that they imply real duties, that they are genuine rights and that they are universal. Ultimately we all are members of a global moral community, having rights that enable us to lead a dignified life and duties that enable others to have such a life as well. Up to now, many die without ever having had the possibility to live a life in dignity.

BIBLIOGRAPHY

Cranston, Maurice, *What are Human Rights?* (London, Sydney & Toronto: The Bodley Head, 1973)

Dower, Nigel, *World Ethics, The New Agenda* (Edinburgh: Edinburgh University Press, 1998)

Dower, Nigel, An Introduction to Global Citizenship (Edinburgh University Press, 2003)

Gewirth, Alan, *The Community of Rights* (Chicago: The University of Chicago Press, 1996)

Goodin, Robert E., 'Relative Needs', in: Alan Ware en Robert E. Goodin (ed.), *Needs and Welfare* (London: Sage Publications, 1990)

Heimbach-Steins, Marianne, 'Menschenrechte der Frauen, Universaler Anspruch und kontextbezogene Konkretisierung', in: *Herder Korrespondenz*, 2006/8, 546 - 561

Hunt, 2000 verdere gegevens ontbreken, of bedoel je 1999?.

Ignatieff, Michael, *Whose Universal Values?* (The Hague: Praemium Erasmianum Essay 1999).

Ignatieff, Michael (Amy Gutmann, ed.). Human Rights as Politics and Idolatry (Princeton, NJ: Princeton University Press, 2003)

Ignatieff, Michael, ed. American Exceptionalism and Human Rights (Princeton, NJ: Princeton University Press, 2005).

Jacobs, F.C.L.M., Humanisme en Mensenrechten in: P.B. Cliteur & D.J. van Houten (ed.), *Humanisme, Theorie en Praktijk* (Utrecht: De Tijdstroom, 1993).

König, Matthias, *Menschenrechte* (Frankfurt, New York: Campus Verlag, 2005)

Luijf, Reginald, Die vreemde Abelard toch; over mimetische begeerte en gelijkheid, in: Wouter van Beek (ed.), *Mimese en Geweld, beschouwingen over het werk van René Girard* Kampern: Kok Agora, 1988).

Manschot, Henk, Als wereldburger leven: Kosmopolitisme en solidariteit, een probleemstelling, in: Theo de Wit & Henk Manschot (ed.), *Solidariteit*. Filosofische kritiek, ethiek en politiek (Amsterdam: Boom 1999).

Mayer, Ann Elizabeth, 'Cultural Particularism as a Bar to Women's Rights: Reflections on the Middle Eastern Experience', in: Julie Peters & Andrea Wolper (ed.) *Women's rights, Human* Rights: international feminist perspectives (New York, Lodon: Routledge, 1995.

Perry, Michaël J., "The Morality of Human Rights: A Nonreligious Ground? (Emory Law Journal, Vol.54, 2005)

Pogge, Thomas, World Poverty and Human Rights, Cosmopolitan Responsibilities and Reforms (Cambridge: Polity Press, 2002/2003)

Rachels, James, *Can Ethics Provide Answers?* (London, Lanham & Maryland:

Rowman & Littlefield Publishers, Inc., 1997).

    Rorty, Richard, 'Justice as the Larger Loyalty', in: *Ethical Perspectives, Journal of the European Ethics Network* 4, nr.3 (Leuven: European Centre for Ethics, 1997).

    Sengupta, Arjun (and Asbjörn Eide, Stephen P. Marks, and Bärd A. Andreassen) *The Right to Development and Human Rights in Development: A Background Paper, Prepared for the Nobel Symposium in Oslo from 13 - 15 October 2003* http://www.humanrights.uio.no/forskning/publ/rn/2004/0704.pdf (Oslo: Norwegian for Human Rights 2004)

    Shue, Henri, *Basic Rights: Subsistence, Affluence and US Foreign Policy* (Princeton NJ: Princeton University Press, 1996)

    Twine, Fred, *Citizenship and Social Rights* (London: Sage Publications, 1994).

ENDNOTES

[1] HDR 2006, p.60.
[2] Cranston presented his ideas a few decades ago, but he has been very influential and serves as an example for those who have doubts about the universality of ESC-rights.
[3] Mayer 1995,, p.176; Heimbach 2005, p.546; Perry 2005, p.102.
[4] Shue 1996, p.52.
[5] König 2005, p.115.
[6] HDR 2005, p.5.
[7] HDR 2005, p.58.
[8] Cranston 1973, p.67.
[9] Gewirth 1996, pp.63,64.
[10] Cranston 1973, p.66.
[11] König 2005, p.115.
[12] Pogge 2002/2003, p.7.
[13] Twine 1994, p.19.
[14] Goodin 1990, p.14.
[15] Luijf 1988, pp.129,133.
[16] Pogge 2002/2003, p.68.
[17] Cranston 1973, p.67.
[18] Cranston 1973, p.69; Jacobs 1993, p.406; Pogge 2002/2003, p.68.
[19] Dower 1998, p.81; Gewirth 1996, p.55; Dower 2003, p.140.
[20] Sengupta 2004, p.15.
[21] Ignatieff 1999, pp.52, 54.
[22] Manschot 1999, p.194.; Rorty 1997, p.139; Rachels 1997, p.105; Dower 2003, p.145.
[23] Gewirth 1996, p.55; Dower 2003, p.145.
[24] Pogge 2002/2003, p.69.
[25] HDR 2000, p.82.
[26] Gewirth 1996, p.7.
[27] Pogge 2002/2003, p.68.